UNDERSTANDING REVOLUTIONS: OPENING ACTS IN TUNISIA

'In 1916, when I discovered the Arabic version of Dr Azmi Bechara's work on the Tunisian revolution, I was struck by the relevance of his points of view, in particular the fact that he inscribed the Tunisian revolution in a long-term perspective, that of a process of "going out in defense of the rights". His work inspired me to write my own book on the Tunisian revolution. Ten years later, the author revisits his inaugural work written in 2012 in an English edition and from a multidisciplinary perspective that takes into account both new developments in the Arab world, in particular in the light of the revolts and revolutions that have taken place since 2018, and the author's most recent research on democratization. This update was necessary. This gives the book even more brightness. I fully share the author's point of view on the future prospects and like him "I believe that a new stage has been set and that we are now witnessing its opening acts. The Arab world will never again be as it was before 2011". For that, I have the great pleasure to present it to its old and new readers.'

Yadh Ben Achour

'Through this exhaustive study of the Tunisian case, Azmi Bishara has grasped the novelty of the "Arab spring" and its far reaching consequences for all Middle Eastern societies, whatever the political ups and downs of the subsequent years. He convincingly shows how the Arab Spring is a real revolution, rooted in deep social and cultural changes that make impossible any return to the past. A must read book.'

Olivier Roy, Professor, Robert Schuman Centre for
Advanced Studies, European University Institute, Italy

'This updated translation of Bishara's outstanding study of Tunisia's transition to democracy could not be more timely or more relevant. Whether Tunisia's fragile democracy will survive is uncertain. Yet this volume gives us an incisive and sophisticated analysis of the extraordinary moments in 2011 when Tunisians took their political future into their own hands and initiated a democratic experiment that was and remains unapparelled in the Arab world. Whatever Tunisia's path might hold, this volume is essential reading for those wishing to understand the origins of this experiment and why it succeeded.'

Steven Heydemann, Ketcham Chair in
Middle East Studies, Smith College, USA

UNDERSTANDING REVOLUTIONS: OPENING ACTS IN TUNISIA

Azmi Bishara

I.B. TAURIS
LONDON • NEW YORK • OXFORD • NEW DELHI • SYDNEY

I.B. TAURIS
Bloomsbury Publishing Plc
50 Bedford Square, London, WC1B 3DP, UK
1385 Broadway, New York, NY 10018, USA
29 Earlsfort Terrace, Dublin 2, Ireland

BLOOMSBURY, I.B. TAURIS and the I.B. Tauris logo are trademarks of Bloomsbury Publishing Plc

First published in Great Britain 2021
Paperback edition published 2023

A catalogue record for this book is available from the British Library.

A catalog record for this book is available from the Library of Congress.

ISBN: HB: 978-1-7845-3222-2
PB: 978-0-7556-4486-5
ePDF: 978-0-7556-4472-8
eBook: 978-0-7556-4473-5

Early and Medieval Islamic World

Typeset by Deanta Global Publishing Services, Chennai, India

CONTENTS

ILLUSTRATIONS

Figures

Maps

Tables

ABBREVIATIONS

Abbreviation	French	English	Arabic	Arabic Transliteration
ANC	Assemblée nationale constituante	National Constituent Assembly	المجلس الوطني التأسيسي	al-Majlis al-Waṭanī at-Ta'sīsī
ATCE	Agence Tunisienne de Communication Extérieure	Tunisian Agency for External Communication	الوكالة التونسية للاتصال الخارجي	al-Wakāla at-Tūnisīa lil-ittiṣāl al-Khārijī
ATFD	L'Association tunisienne des femmes démocrates	Tunisian Association of Democratic Women	الجمعية التونسية للنساء الديمقراطيات	al-Jam'īa at-Tūnisīa lil-Nisā' ad-Dimoqrāṭyāt
ATI	Agence tunisienne d'Internet	Tunisian Internet Agency	الوكالة التونسية للأنترنات	al-Wakāla at-Tūnisīa lil-'Antarnāt
BAT	La Brigade Anti Terrorism	Anti-terrorism Brigade	فرقة مجابهة الإرهاب	Firqat Mujabahat al-'Irhāb
BNIR	Brigade Nationale d'Intervention Rapide	National Brigade for Rapid Response	الفوج الوطني للتدخل السريع	al-Fawj al-Waṭanī lil-Tadakhul as-Sarī'
CNLT	Le Conseil national pour les libertés en Tunisie	National Council for Liberties in Tunisia	المجلس الوطني للحريات بتونس	al-Majlis al-Waṭanī lil- Ḥurriyyāt bi-Tūnis
CPR	Congrès pour la République	Congress for the Republic	المؤتمر من أجل الجمهورية	al-Mo'tamar min 'ajl al-Jomhūriyya
CPS	Code du Statut Personnel	Code of Personal Status	مجلة الأحوال الشخصية	Majalat al-'Aḥwāl al-Shakhṣīa
FIS	Front Islamique du Salut	Islamic Salvation Front	الجبهة الإسلامية للإنقاذ	al-Jabha al-Islāmiyya lil-Inqādh
FLN	Front de Libération Nationale	National Liberation Front	جبهة التحرير الوطني	Jabhat at-Taḥrīr al-Waṭanī
FDTL	Forum démocratique pour le travail et les libertés	The Democratic Forum for Labour and Liberties (Ettakatol)	التكتل الديمقراطي من أجل العمل والحريات	at-Takattul ad-Dīmuqrāṭī min ajl il-'Amal wal-Ḥurriyyāt
HIROR	Haute instance pour la réalisation des objectifs de la révolution, de la réforme politique et de la transition démocratique	Higher Authority for Realization of the Objectives of the Revolution, Political Reform and Democratic Transition	الهيئة العليا لتحقيق أهداف الثورة والإصلاح السياسي والانتقال الديمقراطي	al-Hay'ah al-'Ulyā li-Taḥqīq 'Ahdāf ath-Thawrah wal-'Iṣlāḥ as-Siyāsī wal-Intiqāl ad-Dimuqrāṭī

Abbreviation	French	English	Arabic	Arabic Transliteration
LPR	Ligue de protection de la revolution	League for the Protection of the Revolution	الرابطة الوطنية لحماية الثورة	ar-Rabiṭa al-Waṭanīa li-Ḥimayat ath-Thawrah
LTDH	Ligue tunisienne des droits de l'homme	Tunisian Human Rights League	الرابطة التونسية للدفاع عن حقوق الإنسان	ar-Rabita at-Tūnisīa liddifa'a 'an Huquq al-Insan
MDS	Mouvement des démocrates socialistes	Movement of Socialist Democrats	حركة الديمقراطيين الاشتراكيين	Ḥarakat ed-Dimoqrāṭiyīn el-Ishtirākiyīn
MTI	Mouvement de la Tendance Islamique	Movement of Islamic Tendency	حركة الاتجاه الإسلامي	Ḥarakat al-Ittijāh al-'Islāmī
MUP	Mouvement d'Unité Populaire	Popular Unity Movement	حركة الوحدة الشعبية	Ḥarakat al-Wiḥda ash-Sha'biyya
ONAT	Ordre National des Avocats de Tunisie	Tunisian Order of Lawyers	الهيئة الوطنية للمحامين بتونس	al-Hay'a al-Waṭaniyya lil-Muḥamīn at-Tūnisiyīn
PCOT	Parti Communiste des Ouvriers de Tunisie	Tunisian Communist Workers' Party	حزب العمال الشيوعي التونسي	Ḥizb al-'Ummāl ash-Shuyū'ī at-Tūnsī
PCT	Parti Communiste Tunisien	Tunisian Communist Party	الحزب الشيوعي التونسي	al-Ḥizb ash-Shuyū'ī at-Tūnisī
PDS	Parti Démocrate Progressiste	Progressive Democratic Party	الحزب الديمقراطي التقدمي	al-Ḥizb ad-Dimuqrāṭī at-Taqadumī
PSD	Parti socialiste destourien	Socialist Destourian Party	الحزب الاشتراكي الدستوري	al-Ḥizb al-Ishtirākī ad-Dustūrī
PSP	Parti Social du Progrès	Social Progress Party	حزب التقدم	Ḥizb at-Taqaddum
PUP	Parti de l'Unité Populaire	Popular Unity Party	حزب الوحدة الشعبية	Ḥizb al-Wiḥda ash-Sha'biyya
RCD	Rassemblement Constitutionnel Démocratique	Democratic Constitutional Rally	التجمع الدستوري الديمقراطي	at-Tajammu' ad-Dustūrī ad-Dimuqrāṭī
RSP	Rassemblement Socialiste Progressiste	Progressive Socialist Rally	التجمع الاشتراكي التقدمي	at-Tajammu' al-ishtirākī at-Taqaddumī
SNJT	Syndicat National des Journalistes Tunisiens	National Union/ Syndicate for Tunisian Journalists	النقابة الوطنية للصحفيين التونسيين	an-Niqābah al-Waṭanīyyah lil-Ṣiḥafiyīn at-Tūnisiyīn
UDC	Union des Diplômés Chômeurs	Union of Unemployed Graduates	اتحاد أصحاب الشهادات المُعطّلين عن العمل	Ittiḥād 'Aṣḥāb a-sh-Shahadaāt al-Mu'aṭalīn 'an al-'Amal
UDU	Union Démocratique Unioniste	Democratic Unionist Union	الاتحاد الديمقراطي الوحدوي	al-Ittiḥād ad-Dimuqrāṭī al-Wiḥdawī
UGTE	Union générale tunisienne des étudiants	General Union of Tunisian Students	الاتحاد العام التونسي للطلبة	al-Ittiḥād al-'Āmm al-Tūnisī lil-Ṭalabah

Abbreviation	French	English	Arabic	Arabic Transliteration
UGTT	Union Générale Tunisienne du Travail	Tunisian General Labour Union	الاتحاد العام التونسي للشغل	al-Ittiḥād al-ʿĀmm al-Tūnisī lil-Shughul
UNFT	L'union Nationale De La Femme Tunisienne	National Union of Tunisian Women	الاتحاد الوطني للمرأة التونسيّة	al-Ittiḥād al-Waṭanī lil-Marʾa at-Tūnisīa
USGN	Unité Spéciale de la Garde Nationale	Special Unit of the National Guard	الوحدة المختصة للحرس الوطني	al-Wiḥda al-Mukhtaṣa lil-Ḥaras al-Waṭanī
UTAP	Union Tunisienne de l'Agriculture et de la Pêche	Tunisian Union of Farmers and Fisheries	الاتحاد التونسي للفلاحة والصيد البحري	al-Ittiḥād at-Tūnisī li-Filaḥa wa-ṣ-ayd al-Baḥriī
UTICA	Union tunisienne de l'industrie, du commerce et de l'artisanat	Tunisian Union of Industrialists, Merchants, and Artisans	الاتحاد التونسي للصناعة والتجارة والصناعات التقليدية	al-Ittiḥād at-Tūnisī li-ṣ-Ṣināʿa wa-t-Tijāra wa-ṣ-Ṣināʿāt at-Taqlīdīa

Introduction to the English Edition

This book was written in the midst of the eventful and turbulent year of 2011 and published in Arabic in January 2012. One can appreciate the challenges entailed in publishing an English edition nine years later, many things having happened since then and with the events in Tunisia and across the Arab world still unfolding. Illusions of a smooth, seamless democratic transition have been shattered, but so also have illusions of a final victory for authoritarianism now that a new wave of uprisings has broken out in Arab countries since 2019. The revolutions in Sudan and Algeria (2019/2020) were more peaceful than even the Tunisian Revolution of 2011. Iraq and Lebanon also witnessed months-long peaceful uprisings against sectarian rule. Notably, the Iraqi uprisings remained peaceful despite brutal acts of repression, including targeted killings and the assassination of a number of activists.

It would be neither necessary nor helpful, ten years after the events in question, to present an English edition of the original account as it was first written. Rather, some omissions were required, as were some additions, primarily in the footnotes, in acknowledgement of at least some of the numerous publications that have appeared in the interim. Indeed, when the book was first written, no other academic resources on the Tunisian Revolution were available. A final chapter has also been added concerning Tunisia's significant – and thus far relatively successful – transition to democracy.

Opening Acts in Tunisia: Understanding a Revolution forms part of a larger project initiated by the Arab Center for Research and Policy Studies (ACRPS) to document and analyse the Arab revolutions that have occurred since December 2010. Known as the Project for the Study of Democratic Transition, this enterprise has produced a number of monographs, including three books by the author: the current work on Tunisia, a study of the Syrian Revolution and a two-volume work on the Egyptian Revolution beginning in January 2011 and continuing through the stormy period leading up to the military coup of 2013.

The aforementioned book series presents the three scenarios that played out via the revolutionary process in the Arab world between 2010 and 2013: (1) a revolution followed by a relatively successful transition to democracy (Tunisia), (2) a revolution followed by a failed democratic transition (Egypt) and (3) a revolution that led not to the hoped-for democratic transition but to a civil war (Syria).

Both the documentation of events and the combination of theoretical and applied approaches have developed and improved as the research has progressed. The author's 2020 publication entitled *Problems of Democratization: A Comparative Theoretical and Applied Study* critically reviews theories of transition, from modernization theories to the so-called transitology. In so doing, it adds a theoretical dimension to the research presented in the three previous books in the series. Hence, this project is informed at once by a critical, social-scientific approach and a comparative, historical approach to revolutions and the process of democratization. However, we can expect both the archival and theoretical elements of the project to be tested by future developments.

The present work is an attempt to retrace the course of the Tunisian Revolution, which gave rise to the legendary slogan – *al-shaʿb yurīdu isqāṭ al-niẓām* (the people want to bring down the regime) – that would later be echoed across the Arab world. It charts its transformation from a protest into a revolution and then into a process of democratic transition imposed on the existing regime. Through a multidisciplinary approach that utilizes tools from the social sciences and an investigation of 'live' history, the resulting analysis covers the most prominent junctures and elements of the revolution from the viewpoint of its internal dynamic.

Written in 2011– that is, in the immediate aftermath of the events it treats – this book is not an attempt to write the history of the Tunisian Revolution. It does, nevertheless, belong to the general domain of immediate history given its focus on the daily recording of events. This approach has come under sharp attack from the French Annales School, which advocates what is termed 'long history'. However, the question is not whether one should adopt 'immediate history' as opposed to 'long history' but, rather, which approach best suits the examination of the process of social change in the Arab world. This work adheres to a cross-disciplinary approach that combines sociological analysis, political economy, documentary history and field investigations. It also employs methods such as interviews, interactive seminars and the practice of tracing shifts in ideas and institutions. Hence, it is a sociological, economic and political analysis of an extraordinary process of transformation, as well as an attempt to convey the spirit of historical events through their daily dynamics and realities.

The advantage of this approach is that it allows one to write in temporal proximity to events through the use of objective epistemological tools which draw on the very logic of events while being close to their spirit. Despite the undeniable drawback of lacking distance from the events, this approach may pre-empt a tendency to fall for preconceived ideas, exaggeration and myth-making. The reason for this is that given this temporal proximity to the events in question, insufficient time has passed for myths to have grown up around them.

Furthermore, during a phase of social upheaval like that which was being witnessed in the Arab world in 2011 and beyond, change may occur so rapidly that there is a need for analytical and comparative research which will enable us to diagnose both ongoing and potential developments.

Of course, despite our earnest attempts at objectivity, the text was inevitably influenced by the fervent atmosphere of the year 2011. As successive 'citizens' revolutions' or 'citizenship revolutions' (as contrasted with the 'coup d'état revolutions' of previous decades) erupted in Tunisia, Egypt, Yemen, Libya and Syria, democrats worldwide believed they were witnessing a live refutation of the alleged Arab and/or Muslim exceptionalism, a breakthrough towards a new era of democracy and an affirmative answer to the question of whether the transition to democracy might be triggered, not by reforms from above but by revolution from below.

In my 2007 book, *The Arab Question*, I set out to refute the entire notion of Muslim exceptionalism but agreed that there is an Arab exceptionalism due mainly to unresolved tension between state and nation (termed the 'Arab Question') that aggravates other hurdles for democratization such as a rentier economy and culture,[1] deep cleavages concerning the state, intervention and influence by other Arab countries and elites' political culture. Specifically, I argued that the unresolved tension among contrasting ideals for society and the state could not be resolved without a sociopolitical consensus on the state on the way to form a nation of citizens in harmony with Arab and Muslim culture. Furthermore, I proposed that of all Arab countries, Tunisia and Egypt were the closest to such a consensus.

In 2011, many democrats believed that at long last, Arab countries were on their way to dismantling authoritarianism, toppling despotic regimes and embarking on true democratic transformation. As is often the case, the situation turned out to be far more complex than many had anticipated. Nevertheless, as naïve as it may sound in the midst of civil wars and bloodshed, I believe that a new stage has been set and that we are now witnessing its opening acts. The Arab world will never again be as it was before 2011.

Some of these complications were foreseen through analyses of actual Arab societies and state structures coupled with a comparative reading of history. It was clear that where ethnic, tribal and confessional cleavages have not been overcome by the modern state but rather exacerbated under authoritarianism revolutions are highly likely to lead to civil war, especially if the ruling regime ensures the fealty of security forces – the army in particular – by appealing to shared confessional, tribal, regional or ethnic affiliations. This is the regressive approach which has been taken by modern states that foster and politicize such affiliations and counter-affiliations, first in the private sphere and later in the public domain at times of revolutionary turbulence and the need to shore up an enfeebled state.

The uprisings in Tunisia, Egypt and Yemen opened the way for democratic transition by splitting the ruling elites.[2] In Yemen the split took place on a tribal/regional basis; in Egypt it was between the military and the presidency; and

1. Rentier culture exported to other Arab countries by rich oil-producing countries is a concept coined in the same book.

2. Unlike the scheme drafted by transition-to-democracy theorists, the split in the ruling elite was caused not by disputed reforms initiated by the regime but by a popular revolt. See Guillermo O'Donnell & Philippe C. Schmitter (eds.), *Transitions from Authoritarian Rule: Tentative Conclusions about Uncertain Democracies*, vol. 4 (Baltimore: Johns Hopkins University Press, 1986); Juan Linz & Alfred Stepan (eds.), *The Breakdown of Democratic Regimes* (Baltimore and London: Johns Hopkins University Press, 1978); Giuseppe Di Palma, *To Craft Democracies: An Essay on Democratic Transitions* (Berkeley: University

in Tunisia it began within the security apparatus and then spread to the army. Subsequent developments in Egypt and Tunisia depended to a great extent on the political culture of influential elites, readiness to bargain with moderate sectors of the old regime, the army's political ambitions and other factors such as foreign and regional influences and the geostrategic weight of the country concerned.

Other uprisings split not the ruling elite but the people, which led not to democratic transition but to civil war. In Syria this split took place without toppling the regime, whereas in Libya and Yemen it took place after the regime was overthrown. However, some turns of events could not have been foreseen due to contingencies, particularities of timing and location and the unpredictability of the human factor, including reactions to the new conditions on the part of those who had lived under oppression for decades. Especially difficult to anticipate was the extent to which protracted authoritarian rule had impacted the political culture of ruling elites – an element which I expect to occupy us for some time to come.

By analysing the situation in different Arab countries, we attempt to identify similar components of Arab authoritarianism across regions. In this context, we examine the development of personal dictatorships into dynasties (ruling families) even in republics, the rising role of the security apparatus in public policy, the relationship between nepotism and corruption, cartels of new businessmen, ruling families and the security apparatus and ruling parties.

The English edition of this book begins with Prologue titled 'On Revolution and Susceptibility to Revolution' which is originally an essay that was written in 2011 in reaction to negative attitudes towards the Arab uprisings on the part of intellectuals who, instead of acknowledging their failure to anticipate these developments, denied that the uprisings merited the name 'revolutions' or rationalized their fear of the 'masses' about whom they had once waxed so poetic. Furthermore, instead of recognizing the downsides of these revolutions, joining a struggle for democracy and claiming the right to criticize from within, they espoused an idealized concept of revolution that could not be applied to the Arab uprisings – nor to any other uprising for that matter. It was as if they had a readymade template for revolution to which reality had to conform. However, this *a priori* concept was itself built upon widespread myths which, though they had been debunked long before by historians, had survived from the days of the French and Bolshevik revolutions and, just possibly, from the days of the Iranian revolution as well.

As defined here, a revolution is a popular uprising with massive participation which is consistently directed at regime change. Revolutions aim for liberation and justice, which, according to the revolutionaries, can only be achieved via a change of regime. However, we must beware of rejecting the notion that a given uprising only deserves to be described as a revolution if it succeeds in bringing about a just

of California Press, 1990); and Stephan Haggard & Robert R. Kaufman, 'The Political Economy of Democratic Transition,' *Comparative Politics*, vol. 29, no. 3 (1997), pp. 263-283.

political system or a free society. Needless to say, a revolution remains incomplete or unfinished if it fails to achieve this aim. Indeed, a revolution may even lead to a counter-revolution and another repressive regime. Nevertheless, this does not mean that it was not a revolution or that those who took part in it were not striving for justice.

Revolution as defined here differs from the coup d'état. In a coup d'état, change originates from within the regime, its aim being to seize power, but without necessarily reforming the existing system. In the case of a revolution, by contrast, reform of some type is inevitable. That is to say, reform can lead to a revolution, but a revolution can only succeed in bringing a democratic regime into existence if it is accompanied and/or followed by reform. Furthermore, democratic reform requires a state and/or society that is susceptible to becoming a nation of citizens – that is a nation-state from without and a civil society from within – while influential political elites must be willing to bargain and make concessions. In other words, they must not only accept but also commit themselves to democratic procedures and joint citizenship in spite of ideological differences and diverse affiliations.

'On Revolution and Susceptibility to Revolution' was originally published separately and was not linked specifically with the Tunisian Revolution, although it was widely read and disseminated by intellectuals and activists alike. It was decided to include it in this volume.

Using a wide range of sources, the book achieves its aim of providing a narrative of the Tunisian Revolution that reconstructs the development of events alongside an in-depth analysis of the underlying factors. The primary source material proved essential, especially the interviews with activists and key players in the early days of protests in the provinces where information is scarce and/or poorly documented. The book benefitted greatly from these testimonies.[3] In addition, the research consulted a wide range of other primary sources such as Tunisian newspapers, TV channels and websites as well as official reports and documents, statistics and data from governmental and non-governmental bodies. The book also benefitted from the secondary Arabic and English literature in the form of books, journal articles and autobiographies. It is worth mentioning that in the process of updating the book and preparing the English edition, a wide range of new sources were reviewed in Arabic, English and French, especially the studies that rely on primary sources, field work, interviews and new materials that were published a few years after the revolutions and provide new details about the previous regime or the revolutionary events.

That said, I kindly request that readers view this work in its historical context, as an unfinished work and part of an open project.

3. Interviews were conducted for the purpose of this research in particular and as part of a bigger project conducted by the Arab Center for Research and Policy Studies on documenting the Arab Uprisings, including the Tunisian Revolution. Interviews gathered testimonies of key players in the Tunisian Revolution that had witnessed the evolution of the events on the ground.

Lastly, I would like to recognize the effort made by Ammar Mohsen and Abdulhadi Ayyad who initially translated some parts of the first draft of the Arabic version back in 2011 and 2012 prior to the overall substantial changes to the English version by enlarging the text, updating and rewriting some parts of it. I should thank Nancy Roberts, who edited the book including the additional parts and updates, and to my research assistants Israa al-Batayneh and Yara Nassar. Given my current research and many other responsibilities, I would never have found the time to work on a book I wrote a decade ago without their help.

PROLOGUE

ON REVOLUTION AND SUSCEPTIBILITY TO REVOLUTION

Thawrah *(revolution)*

Historically, the term 'revolution' has been applied to a broad range of phenomena, from unarmed protest movements against particular policies, to armed revolts that strive to topple and replace a ruler or a ruling magistrate, to military coups, to provincial revolts against a central government. It is difficult to define a politically disputed, value-laden term which is used so extensively and in so many varying occasions, in everyday speech, in literature and in the political sphere. However, the venture becomes indispensable when the phenomena that the term is supposed to signify become the subject of academic research.

In modern Arabic, the word *thawrah* (revolution) has been used retroactively to describe popular movements of varying forms, such as the Zanj Revolution[1] and the Revolution of the Qarmatians,[2] though they were spoken of by their contemporaries as civil strife (*fitnah*, plural *fitan*).

Influenced by the revolutions of their own times, some intellectuals would sometimes reference historical antecedents in an attempt to interpret the past through contemporary concepts and associate current developments with a supposed revolutionary legacy viewed as a history of the struggle of the oppressed. Just as the Zanj and the Qarmatians revolted, ʿUmar al-Mukhtar (1862–1931) led the Libyans in a revolution to free the country from Italian colonialism, as did Muhammad Ibn Abdulkarim al-Khaṭṭābī (1882–1963) in the armed Rif Revolt

On Revolution and Susceptibility to Revolution was originally written in Arabic and published by the Arab Center for Research and Policy Studies. This text is a shortened version of the translation.

1. The Zanj Revolution was the culmination of a series of minor revolts staged by black slaves (*al-zanj*) against the Abbasid Empire. It took place over a period of about fifteen years (869–83 CE) near the city of Basra in southern Iraq.

2. A group of Ismaili Shiis who founded the Fatimid dynasty in the tenth century, the Qarmatians first appeared in Iraq around 890 CE. Initially, the Qarmatians challenged the Abbasids in the Iraqi and Syrian deserts and were popular in Iraq, Yemen and present-day Bahrain, where they established what may be considered a 'utopian' republic in 899 CE.

against the Spanish occupation forces (later joined by the French) in northern Morocco. The Algerian and Palestinian liberation movements, the 23 July 1952 coup[3] in Egypt (1918–70) and the 14 July 1958 revolt led by Abdulkarim Qāsim (1914–63) which overthrew the Iraqi monarchy and the Iranian revolution of 1979, were all branded revolutions. Likewise, European Marxists and anarchist revolutionaries in the nineteenth and twentieth centuries freely applied the term 'revolution' to such events as the Spartacus' slave revolt in ancient Rome. Since Karl Marx and Friedrich Engels, the German Left has referred to Thomas Müntzer's millenarian messianic religious peasant rebellion as a 'peasants' revolution'.

Due to the influence of the Russian (Bolshevik), Chinese and Cuban revolutions on the discourse of revolutionaries in the second half of the twentieth century, the concept of revolution as opposition to both US hegemony and local dictatorships spread through from Latin America and became central to the political theology of left-wing intellectuals throughout the Third World.

According to *Lisān al-ʿArab*,[4] the word *thawrah* stems from the verb *thāra*, which is also used for natural phenomena such as volcanic eruptions and has the meaning of rising up in anger, disruption and upheaval. Therefore, one can deduce that in the Arabic philological conception, revolution was closely associated with notions of rage and turmoil. Such terms do not necessarily come to mind when revolution is defined as a sociopolitical phenomenon, although they should, as such associations in the daily use of the term are natural. After all, a popular revolution does not break out without elements of rage against repressive treatment by a ruling regime perceived as unjust. As Hannah Arendt rightly noted, any modern concept of revolution necessitates a radical departure from the status quo. In this sense, the connotations of the Arabic word *thawra* fall more naturally within the semantic field of the modern-day term 'revolution' than the word 'revolution' (from 'revolve') itself, which signifies neither rage nor novelty but a mere rotation.

People who meekly view oppression and injustice as the normal order of things, the way they were and will always be, are not susceptible to revolt.[5] Hence, it has been argued that in order for a sense of justice to emerge, people must conquer the illusion of inevitability. After all, people tend to justify, tolerate or at least endure patiently what seems to them inevitable suffering. However, when such

3. Although a coup, the toppling of the Egyptian monarchy in 1952 is widely referred to in the Arab world as a revolution (*thawrah*).

4. A medieval lexicon of classical Arabic, complete with etymological references.

5. According to Barrington Moore people must conquest the illusion of inevitability for a sense of injustice to emerge, which is probably a more eloquent phrasing of a fact of common sense. Barrington Moore, *Injustice: The Social Bases of Obedience and Revolt* (New York: Palgrave Macmillan, 1978), p. 462.

People tend to justify, tolerate or at least endure patiently what seems to them inevitable suffering. The same suffering becomes a cause for indignation if it seems unnecessary. Whether it leads people to revolt is a different story; it is, however, certainly a necessary condition for this kind of action.

suffering is seen as unnecessary, it becomes a cause for indignation. Furthermore, unnecessary, unjustified suffering perceived as being inflicted by others (for example, the government) becomes a cause for moral outrage. Not surprisingly, then, rage and uprising are associated with revolution in virtually any culture. We should recall here that the young revolutionary activists of Egypt's January revolution first called their movement 'The Youth Coalition of the Revolution of Rage'. And despite being unaware of the semantic link between the English words 'dignity' and 'indignation', angry Tunisians called their uprising the revolution of dignity (*thawrat al-karamah*). Indeed, the striving for human dignity is such a powerful sentiment that it can be considered the moral foundation for all human rights. As Hamid Dabashi rightly observed:

> As a moral proposition, *karāmah*, 'dignity,' is a virtue *sui generis*, irreducible to any religion, entirely contingent on its communal summoning and articulation. The innate humanism operative at the heart of an appeal to 'dignity' in effect defines the revolutionary gathering of an inaugural moment for humanity at large. Dignity is an end in itself, caused and conditioned by the revolutionary uprisings.[6]

However, revolutions are not only outbursts of rage but also politicized endeavours directed to ends that cannot be achieved without a change of regime. The idea of a revolution is related to a rapid, emotional reaction that is included in the meaning of uprising; such associations can be traced between the idea of revolution (*thawrah*) and the Arabic terms for rising (*intifāḍa, habbah*). In nineteenth-century Arab urban settings, the word used was often *qawmah* (standing up). An example of this is the Aleppo Uprising of 1850 (*qawmat Halab*), a protest against conscription and poverty during which the poor attacked rich neighbourhoods. Interestingly, there is a linguistic distinction in Arabic among different rebellions; thus, for example, a peasants' rebellion in the countryside was named *ʿāmmiyyah* (linked to the word *ʿāmmah*, meaning general public, commoners or plebeians). The most well known of these was the *ʿāmmiyyah* of Kesrouane in Mount Lebanon, which was followed by other movements in the same region.

In his *History of the Maghreb*,[7] Abdellah Laroui discusses the jihadi[8] groups that surged across Morocco, Tunisia, Algeria and Libya in the latter half of the

6. Hamid Dabashi, *The Arab Spring: The End of Postcolonialism* (London and New York: Zed Books, 2012), p. 127.

7. Abdellah Laroui, *Mujmal Tārīkh al-Maghrib [The History of the Maghreb]*, vol. 3 (Casa Blanca and Beirut: Arabic Cultural Centre, 2007).

8. Before the surge of political Islamist movements, the word *jihad* was used to refer to any struggle for a just cause, including the struggle against colonialism. It was actually the word for what we call today *niḍāl* (struggle). Thanks to its religious associations, the term 'jihad' was effective in motivating the masses to involve themselves in causes that were not themselves necessarily religious in nature.

nineteenth century. He notes that large swathes of the Maghrebi interior remained free of European occupation for a long period. He describes the movement of al-Khaṭṭābī (known commonly as the Rif War) as a 'jihadi war'. He also refers to earlier tribal revolts that were later called revolutions, such as the *thawrah* of Ibn Ghadhahum in Tunisia (1864) and of al-Miqranī of Algeria in 1871. In Laroui's opinion, however, describing the Khaṭṭābī and other movements as revolutions in the twentieth-century sense is inaccurate and inappropriate.[9] Laroui suggests that despite its having featured a number of modern elements, the Rif Revolt is best understood within a traditional context, bearing in mind that mountainous rural communities had long been in a state of perpetual revolt against the *Makhzan* (central royal authority) and foreign occupation.[10]

Much of what Laroui argues can be applied to any other local rebellion against foreign occupation or central governments. Such uprisings came to be referred to as revolutions in the twentieth century, which involved a projection of the modern sense of revolution. What remains puzzling, however, is the dogged scepticism displayed by some Arab leftist or former leftist intellectuals towards the recent Arab revolutions while at the same time imposing the term 'revolution' on all sorts of past rebellions as if to generate an imagined heritage of class struggle. Some were frightened of the 'masses' that they praised in theory, but among whom, in practice, they had no foothold; similarly, they feared free elections.

Such Arab intellectuals have insisted that the recent Arab uprisings, which they neither expected nor took part in, do not 'deserve' to be called revolutions, even as they apply the term to past revolts that had very little in common with the modern concept. In this case the model of the French, Russian (Bolshevik) and probably Iranian revolutions is applied. This narrow concept, which is mixed with the mythical memory of these revolutions, then becomes the basis on which to judge the recent Arab uprisings. But it applies neither to most recent revolutions, including the Arab uprisings, nor to the past insurrections that they dub revolutions in the context of an endeavour to create a 'revolutionary tradition' (which is, by the way, a contradiction in terms).

In order to formulate a widely acceptable, contemporary definition of revolution (*thawrah*), at least within the political sphere, we must consider historical contexts.

Revolution in this book is not necessarily what Theda Skocpol called 'social revolutions' carried out by the lower classes and leading to swift and radical changes in state, society and class structures,[11] or what Charles Tilly branded 'great revolutions'. Of course, even the so-called social revolutions or great revolutions went through the phase of struggle over political power, as Lenin understood very well. Social revolutions are a rare phenomenon in world history.[12] Nevertheless,

9. Laroui, *Mujmal Tārīkh al-Maghrib*, p. 602.

10. Ibid.

11. Theda Skocpol, *States and Social Revolutions: A Comparative Analysis of France, Russia, & China* (New York: Cambridge University Press, 1979), p. 33.

12. Ibid., p. 33, 287.

they all began as political revolutions. All revolutions are political; they all target regime change. This is their common denominator in addition to the popular dimension, the change from below that distinguishes them from both reform and military coups.

Charles Tilly defines a revolution as a

> forcible transfer of power over state in the course of which at least two distinct blocs of contenders make incompatible claims to control the state, and some significant portion of the population subject to the state's jurisdiction acquiesces in the claims of each bloc. The blocs may be single actors, such as the class of great landlords, but they often consist of coalitions among rulers, members and/ or challengers.[13]

The problem with this broad definition is that it includes civil wars but excludes phenomena like the Arab uprisings of 2010–12, which were not led by blocs of political contenders. Furthermore, Tilly's definition presupposes organized political actors who aim to seize power, and the division of the state into two blocs, which does not actually apply to most revolutions. On the other hand, the struggles between aristocrats over the state, or between the heirs of a king over the crown after the king's death, are revolutions according to Tilly's definition.[14]

Modern revolutions cannot be understood without a conception of state, state institutions and political power as sociopolitical phenomena which not only reflect the dominant economic classes and interests but, in addition, have their own interests and dynamic relationship with society. The strength and cohesion of the state and the resilience of its security apparatus can well define the outcome of a revolution.[15] Consequently, uprisings from below aiming to change a regime in a powerful, centralized bureaucratic police state are an arduous task.

As used in this book, the term 'revolution' refers to a broad popular movement that takes place outside the confines of the currently existing constitutional structure or legal legitimacy in order to change the current ruling regime in the state. Such a definition of the term differentiates a revolution from a military coup d'état on the one hand and from reform on the other – an important distinction in modern times throughout the so-called Third World. Military coups erupt from inside the regime and target the incumbent ruler, not necessarily the regime. But as in Portugal in 1976, a military coup may replace not only the ruler but the regime itself; it may also mobilize popular support in this endeavour, in which case it becomes revolutionary. This definition distinguishes a revolution from popular protests that raise demands which the existing regime is expected to accept and implement; however, it includes popular uprisings that aim at regime change even if they are not led by political blocs.

13. Charles Tilly, *European Revolutions, 1492-1992* (Oxford: Blackwell, 2013), p. 8.
14. Ibid., p. 4.
15. Ibid., p. 32.

Linguistically, there is a difference between a coup (Arabic, *inqilāb*) and a revolution (*thawrah*). As noted earlier, the traditional Arabic usage of the term *thawrah* differs from that of 'revolution' in our era. What becomes apparent when we turn to *Lisān al-ʿArab* is that, etymologically, the Arabic word *thawrah* did not have the full meaning of revolution until it was recently developed as an ideological term. The word *thawrah* also differs from that of revolution as employed in Latin and Romance languages in terms of both linguistic roots and cultural, social, and political connotations. In Arabic, the term was often invested with a limited meaning referring to 'agitation' and 'outbreak'.

Curiously, the Arabic word *inqilāb* (from the verb *inqalab*, meaning 'to turn over') has a close linguistic resonance with the word 'revolution' as it is employed in our days. The Turks and the Persians have used the word *inqilāb* to signify radical change and a shift from one state to another (for instance, from a sultan's rule to constitutional rule). Examples of this include the *inqilāb dustūrī*, which refers to Iran's 1905 Constitutional Revolution, and the *inqilāb islāmī*, otherwise known as the Islamic Revolution of 1979. As such, Persian and Turkish speakers have employed the word *inqilāb* according to its actual meaning, while in modern Arabic, as a term it is used only in its partial sense, limiting it to the notion of a military coup with the word's connotation of changing a position and turning against a superior or an ally. Consequently, the word entered the modern Arabic lexicon as a pejorative term.

This implies that in order to use 'revolution' as a conceptual term, it needs to be distinguished from terms that signify related, but distinct, phenomena that might be confused with it. These would include phenomena relating to a change in political regime or the movements leading to that outcome. From a sociological perspective, the revolutionary phenomenon can be described as a social popular chain of acts and events that lead to the change of a political regime; however, this process does not take place in isolation from other social phenomena. It is for this reason that we need to distinguish revolution from reforms, military coups, insurrections, rebellions and uprisings, though all of these phenomena are interrelated and each of them could lead to one of the others. A popular rebellion, for example, might precipitate an internal coup, either in support of it or in opposition to it, or accuse the civilian government of indolence and inaction, while an insurrection could either spur reform within a regime or result in the opposite outcome.

The concept of reform in modern political discourse has theological roots, having emerged from the sixteenth-century Protestant Reformation. The Reformation led to a series of bloody conflicts and wars that eventually undermined the Holy Roman Empire and contributed to the emergence of the European order of nation states. The intention of the Reformation was to reform the Church as an institution and alter its approach to the relationship between God, the holy scripture and the faithful. By challenging the need for a mediator between the Church and the believer, the reformists undermined the political and social stature of the clergy while disturbing church–state relations.

With the rise of Europe's labour and social-democratic movements, which vacillated in their choices between revolution and reform, the term 'reform' returned to public use and migrated fully into the realm of politics. The same duality inspired Rosa Luxembourg's (1871–1919) famous 1900 essay 'Social Reform or Revolution?', which was written as a riposte to Eduard Bernstein (1850–1932), who had been associated with Engels in London from 1896 to 1898. Bernstein published a series of articles under the heading 'Problems of Socialism' and wrote a book *The Preconditions of Socialism and the Tasks of Social Democracy*, published in 1899. These writings heralded the famous debate on Revisionism within international socialism.[16]

The debate between reform and revolution was a reflection of the crisis facing the labour movement that had been sparked by a variety of factors, including a lull in the historical process of the economic and class polarization in society; the rise of a middle class within the capitalist system; the rising power of the central state and its policing capacities; and the potential for gradual change to socialism within the confines of capitalism through the adoption of unionist demands, workers' rights and universal suffrage. The potential for reform forged a path safer and more realistic than that of revolutions, which had a dwindling chance of occurring in advanced capitalist systems. Bernstein used this approach in hopes of counteracting that of the historical leadership of German Social Democracy. Broadly speaking, it was this problem that spurred the fragmentation of the labour movements into Communist and Social Democratic parties. Within the Second International, in a controversy led then by Kautsky, this same debate continued. During this time, Lenin stood at the helm of the opposing camp and went on to form the Comintern in 1919 (also known as the Third International). In this way, the famous dichotomy between reformists (Socialists, and Social Democrats of all stripes) and revolutionaries (in their various strands, represented in particular by the Communists) was born.

Occasioned by the split that arose within Marxism, this dichotomy between reform and revolution may have been important in understanding the nature of the struggle for social justice in a developed capitalist democratic country. However, it has only marginal relevance in the case of the struggle for democracy. A revolutionary democrat has to become a reformist and ultimately lead a reform process, while a reformer's actions inside a regime could potentially lead to a revolutionary change, for example, from authoritarianism to democracy. However, a revolutionary who refuses to engage in reform, even after a regime change, will gravitate towards either nihilism or a new type of authoritarianism. From time to time reformists face the challenge of diagnosing cosmetic reforms exploited or distorted by a regime which implements them in order to improve its image or temporarily diffuse public anger, as was done in numerous Arab contexts between the early 1990s and 2005, where reforms only affected institutions that, at best, marginally influence the decision-making process.

16. The term 'revisionism' was mistakenly translated into Arabic as 'deviationism' (*taḥrīfiyah*) by the Communists and the Moscow-based *Dār al-Taqqadum*, which was the source of much of the Arabic Marxist literature being produced at the time.

The need for reform can be concluded from a regime's inability to deal with a crisis or new regional and international realities. Reformists sometimes declare their intention is not to bring about regime change but, rather, to make the existing regime more faithful to its founders' original principles. This is why reform involves returning to the supposed beginnings or points of origin and thus regards existing forms of governance as deviations from these origins. When prevailing customs and traditions become static and begin to contradict and distort their original purpose, reformists view it as necessary to abolish these structures. Hence, one might say that reform in many cases carries overtones of 'fundamentalism' since it does not dismiss founding principles of a regime or a political doctrine but instead claims that the prevailing conditions do not fulfil the real intentions underlying these principles. Reformist politicians generally seek to explain how the regime has diverged from its own core values by evoking the nation's founding period or the ruling party's initial platform. However, their actions do not lead to the imagined past but to a new reality, liberalization and/or a split in the regime.

Revolutionaries, on the other hand, seek to replace one regime with another based not on alleged origins but on new principles altogether. This distinction is, needless to say, conceptual and abstract and, therefore, does not exist in reality in its pure form. Thus, revolution may transform into a process of reform. Those who cling to the definition of revolution as the opposite of reform may argue that a revolution remains incomplete if it only reforms the current regime. However, such semantic discussions involve little more than nitpicking. Any genuine reform involves revolutionary elements as it leads to gradual regime change, and any revolution that goes beyond mere negation will also contain some reformist elements.

Hence, we can speak about revolutionary reform and reformist revolution that reflect two different phenomena, not a single one dubbed 'refolution'.[17] In a 1989 article referring to the mass uprisings in Hungary and Poland, Timothy Ash treated these uprisings as mixtures of reform and revolution, suggesting that they be called 'revorms' or perhaps 'refolutions'. In both places there was

> a strong and essential element of voluntary, deliberate reform led by an enlightened minority (but only a minority) in the still ruling Communist parties, and, in the Polish case, at the top of the military and the police. Their advance consists of an unprecedented retreat: undertaking to share power, and even – *mirabile dictu* – talk of giving it up altogether if they lose an election.[18]

17. This term was borrowed by Asef Bayat from Timothy Garton Ash to conceptualize the Arab revolutions. See Asef Bayat, 'Revolution in Bad Times', *New Left Review*, 80 (March/April 2013), accessed on 25 January 2021, at: http://bit.ly/3tkQ6vH; Timothy Garton Ash, 'Revolution: The Springtime of Two Nations', *The New York Review*, 15 June 1989, accessed on 25 January 2021, accessed at http://bit.ly/3cFE36m.

18. Ash, 'Revolution: The Springtime of Two Nations'.

Ash added that all of this would not be possible 'without Gorbachev's tolerance, his example, and the processes he has, wittingly or unwittingly, set in motion'.[19] By contrast, the Arab revolutions were not enabled by reform from above, and, unlike the Eastern European cases, the regimes did not lose their guardian (the Soviet Union's protection in the case of Eastern European states) before the people went out to the streets. The Arab revolutions were reformist in the sense of declaring the will to force the regime to change. According to Asef Bayat, because the uprisings in Egypt, Yemen and Tunisia followed a reformist trajectory, they can be called neither revolutions per se nor reforms in the strict sense. These were 'revolutions that aim to push for reforms',[20] which is also what I conclude in my book on the Egyptian Revolution.[21]

According to John Keane, the popular uprisings in the Arab world took the spirit of the 1989 non-violent uprisings in Central and Eastern Europe to a higher level, although the violence with which the Arab uprisings were met was incomparably more severe than the violence of Eastern European states in 1989.[22] The Arab uprisings are not revolutions if what is meant by the word is 'insurrectionary transformation of state power relations fueled by violent protest from the streets'. Therefore, Keane reasons, a new word is needed to conceive the radical rejection of the old choice between reform and revolution.[23]

Ash's description of the revolutions in Eastern Europe as triggered by reforms from above is realistic. Conversely, the Arab revolutions did not erupt in the context of a reform from above, nor were they protected by such a top-down reform.

In my book *On the Arab Question: An Introduction to an Arab Democratic Statement* (2007), I wrote that what leads to democracy is neither reform per se in the framework of the regime nor revolution per se as a forcible change of the regime from without, but rather, the possibility of combinations such as reformist revolution from below and revolutionary reform from above. For reform to lead from authoritarianism to a democracy, it has to be a revolutionary reform that brings about a regime change or a reformist revolution that not only breaks or dismantles state power but changes it through reforms towards a democratic system.[24]

Coups d'état, on the other hand, are a different matter. A coup d'état occurs within the confines of a given regime and is led by sections of the ruling elite or

19. Ibid.

20. Bayat, 'Revolution in Bad Times'.

21. Azmi Bishara, *Egypt's Revolution*, vol. II, *From Revolution to Coup* (Thawrat Miṣr: Min al-Thawrah ilā al-Inqilab), (Doha/Beirut: ACRPS, 2016) pp. 25–6.

22. John Keane, 'Refolution in the Arab world', *Open Democracy*, 28 April 2011, accessed on 25 January 2021, at: http://bit.ly/3oLS2d2.

23. Ibid.

24. Azmi Bishara, *Fī al-Mas'alah al-'Arabiyyah: Muqaddimah li Bayān Dīmuqrāṭī 'Arabī [On the Arab Question: A Preamble to a Democratic Arab Manifesto]*(Beirut: Center for Arab Unity Studies, 2007).

institutions, usually the military. The people are not a participant. They learn of the coup when the usual broadcasting of the national radio or TV is cut and the newly installed regime issues its communiqués. If successful, such a takeover results in a redistribution of power within the same regime. However, history gives us examples of coups that have resulted, out of necessity, in the enactment of radical changes in regime structure and which, as a consequence, have come to be called, or called themselves, revolutions.

The situation is clearer in cases of insurrection, civil disobedience and uprisings, which are broad social movements based on the rejection of specific policies, injustices or flaws in the system. Sometimes, these popular 'disturbances' have no specific demands but simply express anger and frustration in response to unsatisfactory socio-economic conditions (as in the case of the protests that prefaced the Tunisian Revolution). As is well known, such protests may escalate and call for the removal of the regime in its entirety, either because the regime refuses to make the partial changes demanded by the protesters or because those rebelling are joined by wider sections of the public to protest against the regime in general, thereby building momentum towards a demand for the regime's ouster. This was the case in the Tunisian and Egyptian Revolutions, which were not planned, led or even exploited by a political 'avant garde' determined to seize power.

Depending on how it is viewed later by historians and others, a revolution may be described after the fact with adjectives that would not have appeared to apply to it while it was actually transpiring. The French Revolution, for example, has been described as a 'democratic revolution' by some historians and researchers and as a 'bourgeois revolution' by others. Was it democratic or bourgeois in terms of who participated in it or led it? I think not. Rather, it was a combination of reform from above imposed by the third estate (bourgeois representatives of the commoners) after the estates were summoned to meet in May 1789 to raise taxes and a revolution from below on the part of the peasantry and the urban poor. The revolution started with peasant riots in the provinces. We may speculate retroactively that despite the participation of the new middle classes and the poor in the cities (*sans-culottes* and *la plèbe*), the French Revolution could have ended like the revolutions in China or Russia had it not been for the reform that was carried out in the National Assembly by enlightened representatives of the bourgeoisie.

The French Revolution was triggered by a series of events: government measures in 1786 that left many people out of work, a 1787 decree that removed restrictions on the grain trade and a disastrously short harvest in 1788, followed by an unusually harsh winter and a spring filled with severe storms and floods. In sum, a combination of natural disasters and political uncertainties led in the summer of 1789 to peasant uprisings in many parts of France.[25] The storming of the Bastille on 14 July 1789 was sparked by a fear of revenge by the royal troops surrounding Paris, while the peasants' protest the same month was motivated by a

25. Barrington Moore Jr., *Social Origins of Dictatorship and Democracy: Lord and Peasant in the Making of the Modern World* (Boston: Beacon Press, 1966), pp. 74–5.

fear of invasion and pillage.[26] Hence, the revolution was not a capitalist revolution, nor was it motivated by a bourgeois aspiration for democracy; rather, democracy emerged out of a subsequent series of reforms. In fact, some of these reforms took place prior to the French Revolution. Upon the convocation of the Estates General to approve a tax increase, deliberations on the major issues had been established: that is, the question of representation, the first and second estates' privileges and tax exemption, taking the oath to stay in session until writing a constitution in June 1789 and the establishment of the National Assembly. Thereafter, French democracy endured a lengthy series of ups and downs until the establishment of the Third Republic in 1870. Capitalism as a system benefitted from the process of liberalization that followed the French Revolution, including abolition of the privileges of the clergy and the old aristocracy.

Hannah Arendt wrote her 1963 book *On Revolution* under the influence of the modern Russian and French revolutions, though, as a German-born philosopher writing and residing in the United States, she also drew heavily on the American Revolution. She wrote, 'Revolutions are the only political events that confront us directly and inevitably with the problem of beginning. For revolutions, however we may be tempted to define them, are not mere changes.'[27] We know that revolutions are not mere changes. And maybe we do confront the question of beginning, but the contribution of this abstract statement to understanding specific revolutions is doubtful. In addition it may also apply to artistic and scientific revolutions, because the use of the term 'revolution' involves a qualitative leap.

According to their understanding of Darwin's theory of evolution, Marx and Engels contested the view that evolution can be seen only as a gradual, interconnected process, asserting instead that quantitative accumulation leads to qualitative change through intermittent leaps and mutations. Such mutations are, then, a natural phenomenon, representing, in the natural world, the equivalent of the notion of revolution in society. This was one of Marx's few philosophical attempts to find an ontological theory of society based on a reinterpretation of Darwinian concepts.

It has been argued that revolution is distinguished from a mere change of government from below by the fact that revolutions create a new economic system. This argument is associated with a Marxist perspective according to which great political revolutions are expressions of class struggle. New social-economic formations are created by the change of production relations and, with them, the revolutionizing of political and juristic ideas and structures. The emergence of new social-economic formations includes political revolutions and other turbulent changes but is not caused by a single political revolution, power seizure

26. Jack Goldstone and Charles Tilly, 'Threat (and Opportunity): Popular Action and State Response in the Dynamics of Contentious Politics', in: *Silence and Voice in the Study of Contentious Politics* (Cambridge: Cambridge University Press, 2001), p. 182.

27. Hannah Arendt, *On Revolution* (New York: Penguin, 1990 [1963]), p. 21.

and 'breaking the political power of the Bourgeois' as Lenin and many leftist revolutionaries after him had hoped.

The social and economic dimension of regime change was recognized even in pre-modern times. The ancient Greeks also saw this 'class' dimension as the basis for changes in government. It was clear to both Aristotle and Plato that the takeover of government by the rich leads to oligarchy, while democracies result from the revolt of the poor against the rich. Even in instances where tyrants reach power, their rule often enjoys legitimacy among the poor because of their desire for equality. All are equal under tyranny, whether through the provision of their basic needs or through being equally deprived of their political rights.

Social change is an ongoing historical process interspersed with 'revolutionary' leaps that undermine existing social and political structures. These instances of transformation might express themselves through political revolutions, though change does not necessarily take place in this manner either in the economy or in politics. If social change and political revolution are seen as linked, then socio-economic change may take place either over the course of more than one political revolution or very gradually without any political revolution at all.

Political revolution has to do with a change of a political regime, not of 'social-economic formation'. Protest actions turn into a revolution in response to a widely held feeling or conviction within the body politic that the current ruling regime is no longer capable of dealing with the issues and crises created by the current political structures.

Why is the term 'revolution' used in other contexts? What justifies this? When it comes to scientific revolutions, these occur when the dominant paradigm is no longer capable of explaining phenomena that it has created or to whose discovery it has led. In either case, a crisis occurs, leaving only two alternatives: ignore the new reality, or change the tools used to understand it. This necessitates a paradigm shift. The academic establishment may ignore such a crisis in science for some time, defending the old paradigm as it has often done; eventually, however, the new paradigm imposes itself as guardians of the old paradigm lose their confidence in it and refuse to come to its defence.

Just as scientific revolutions reject the justifications offered by the old scientific paradigm, political revolutions also reject the arguments and claims made in defence of the existing order and aim to change institutions in ways that are prohibited by these very institutions. No scientific paradigm, of course, is capable of defending itself in the face of a scientific paradigm shift by using its own terminology and language, since these are its own creations. Similarly, to defend a political regime in its own language is akin to a circular argument. Thus, just as a scientific revolution distances itself from the existing paradigm, waging a battle against conservatives with a terminology borne out of the new theory, a political revolution rejects the vocabulary of the prevailing constitutional and political order, validating itself via a language that emanates from a new vision.[28]

28. Thomas S. Kuhn, *The Structure of Scientific Revolutions*, 3rd edn (Chicago and London: University of Chicago Press, 1996), pp. 92–4.

When there is disagreement between those who advocate change and those who wish to maintain the existing order, any chance to arbitrate disappears unless there are agreed-upon social institutions to resolve the dispute. At this point, depending on circumstances and the historical context, the people become the final arbitrator of the conflict. If large segments of the population can no longer endure the status quo, and if the protest expands consistently (with or without the help of politically organized opposition), this gives the political opposition the opportunity to re-emphasize the issue of the nature of the regime.

In ancient Greek philosophical thought, the recurring succession ('revolution') of democratic, aristocratic and oligarchic regimes was believed to be based on a series of distinctions thought to be 'natural', such as those between the rich and the poor, the elite and the masses, rulers and the ruled. In the age of modernity, however, the possibility of breaking this cycle emerged through a widespread refusal to understand social disparities as part of the natural order. Instead, people could imagine a society free of poverty, one that would achieve equality through 'rights'. Hannah Arendt, for example, described the 'factual existence of American society prior to the outbreak of the Revolution'[29] as a society free of poverty due to the country's abundance of natural wealth. In addition, she argued that poverty could be vanquished through colonialist geographical expansion, which offered migration as an alternative to accepting one's current class position.

Arendt misses one dimension, namely that these revolutions were the by-product not solely of the 'surprising prosperity' of the New World, which permitted the imagining of a society without poverty even when they were English colonies, but also of American settlers' expansionist theology with its genocidal outcomes and peasant revolts in France.[30] On the other hand, the ability to imagine societies without poverty has manifested itself through various quests for a human utopia, though social utopias were mostly connected to an imagined new beginning in a newly discovered or not yet discovered place.

Was the American war of independence a revolution according to our definition of the term? No, it was not. Nevertheless, the process of establishing the United States was revolutionary from a historical perspective because a totally new political regime was established on new principles.

What made the American and French cases remarkable was the growth of a social sector that came to be known as the Third Estate in France and the colonial townships in the United States. These groups believed that they had the right not only to lead better lives free from tutelage but also to participate in the management of their own affairs (in the United States) or those of the nation (in France).

The idea of novelty held such powerful sway over the French revolutionaries that they proposed a new calendar that would begin with the beheading of Louis XVI and the founding of the Republic instead of Christ's birth. The same revolutionaries also planned to discard the ancient county names in favour of numbers, as though the revolution had been a cosmic event, ushering in new

29. Arendt, *On Revolution*, p. 23.

30. Moore, *Social Origins*, pp. 69, 109–10, 141–2.

names for months and a new method for counting the years. The Bolsheviks of the October 1917 revolution also sought to establish a new beginning. Taking a page out of the French revolutionary book, the Bolsheviks, and Lenin in particular, aspired to create a 'New Russia' founded upon a rational historicist design connecting the whole of Russia through railways and electricity and the reshaping of the 'new Soviet man'.

In fact, one of Edmund Burke's major objections, not only to the French Revolution but to the principle of revolutions in general, was what he viewed as mistaken revolutionaries' illusion that they can create a new beginning, and hence, their propensity for the destruction of existing institutions and the repudiation of tradition. This so-called new beginning, Burke believed, was presumptuous, conceited and ignorant of the nature of states. There are no new beginnings, and believing that states are built on contracts does not mean that they resemble commercial contracts that can simply be revoked. If states are built on contracts, then they also bind contemporaries to previous generations. Institutions incorporate the history and experience of previous generations, incarnating accumulated wisdom. Burke's second major objection to the principle of revolution was directed against French revolutionaries who, contrary to the English wisdom of grounding political principles in political experience and practices, derived their policies from abstract principles such as the natural rights of man, which implied reshaping realities according to principles and the inevitably violent destruction of existing institutions.[31]

The same Burkean distinction can be utilized in order to compare reformist and revolutionary approaches. For Burke, political wisdom means accepting the inherited institutions of the society and working according to their principles to repair and improve them and not according to an external principle. As such, Burke's concept of reform was a conservative one. Nevertheless, we know that Burke also praised the changes of 1688 that constituted 'the glorious revolution'.[32] He considered the 1688 revolution a positive development in contrast to the violent revolution of 1649, which led to the deposition and execution of England's King Charles I and which Burke compared to the French Revolution. He did not consider his positions paradoxical, perhaps because the so-called 'glorious revolution' did not contradict the monarchic principle. Nevertheless, the regime had indeed been changed, and this means that reforms can be revolutionary.

As proof that society cannot be altered for the better by imposing changes through a process of violent restructuring, Burke cited the situation of post-

31. Edmund Burke, 'Reflections on the Revolution in France' (1790), in: *Revolutionary* Writings, Iain Hampsher-Monk (ed.) (Cambridge: Cambridge University Press, 2014), esp. pp. 40–1, 100–1, 160–1, 174–5.

32. A reference to the revolution of November 1688 in which James II, King of England, Scotland and Ireland, was deposed and replaced by his daughter Mary II and her Dutch husband, William III of Orange.

revolutionary France, in which ignorant segments of the society came to power and exploited the credulity of the masses or what he termed 'an ignoble oligarchy'.[33]

Burke's forebodings were partially negated and partially confirmed by the century-long process of reform and revolutions that followed and led to democracy according to the principles of the revolution and the republic. Some of his other conservative theses were also disproved by later developments both in Britain and France. In Burke's view, the people who ought to be enfranchised are those who are economically independent, not dependent poor people who can be bribed, misled and deceived. So here we have two theses: the first is that you cannot change reality according to abstract principles, the proof being the emergence of a new oligarchy which is the real face of the so-called democracy; the second is that poor and dependent segments of the society should not have the right to vote. These theses were refuted neither by reform alone nor by revolution alone but by revolutionary reforms that did not spare the so-called principle of the existing institutions and did, in fact, give birth to new guiding principles.

Still, the rational side of the conservative critique was verified in the quest for a 'clean break', that is, a total novelty that would lead to attempts at social engineering according to 'external principles' in totalitarian states. Both Nazi and Stalinist paradigms envisioned a total revolution that would change everything by fulfilling a historicist teleological model of socio-economic development, which was perceived as the evolution of history towards its highest, final purpose by a specific elite, class, nation or race. In both cases, seizure of political power was a means to implement their ideas, the only real difference being that while one of these systems justified its repressive totalitarianism through an ideology that invoked universal values such as freedom and equality, the other ideology was based on the negation of these values.

Democratic revolution and ideological revolution

History has yet to record a case of popular revolution that demands the implementation of a pre-set programme stemming from a stated intellectual or political ideology. Even those revolutions that led ultimately to doctrinaire ideological regimes, such as those in Russia and Iran, began as demonstrations of anger, protests and revolts against injustices and oppression. The establishment of the new regimes often came about due to the appropriation of the revolution by a political party or an organized political network as the moment of success neared or shortly thereafter. In many cases, the gravitation towards a single, official ideology took place years after the revolution's seizure of power by an armed political movement. Revolution in Cuba did not initially have an ideological programme,

33. According to Burke, the ignoble oligarchy is 'founded on the destruction of the crown, the church, the nobility, and the people. Here end all the deceitful dreams and visions of the equality and rights of men'. Ibid., p. 199.

though such a programme would be formulated later in order to rationalize the shift to communism. We might also speculate that if the Vietnamese revolution had declared itself at the outset to be a Marxist movement aimed at establishing a communist regime, the Vietnamese people might not have volunteered as enthusiastically as they did. Furthermore, during revolutions, even the most ideological of parties tend to embrace a minimalist programme that can attract the broadest sectors of the population. Attempts to launch an Islamist revolution have turned usually to an insurrection or an armed revolt against the state and have never become revolutions. The only 'Islamic revolution' was called Islamic because of the forces that prevailed at the end and the regime they founded, not because it was an ideological revolution from the outset.

In some cases, a number of cultural and ideological changes may have affected broad swathes of society in modernity, without which it would be difficult to speak of a 'revolutionary way of thought' or 'revolutionary motives'. For example, during a revolution, participants consider themselves the 'people', and the government is depicted as extraneous or as a force that makes use of the state to serve the personal interests of the oligarchy. If this trend evolves into an anti-elitist populist discourse, it may threaten the process of democratization after the revolution.

Popular revolts are, by their very nature, not those of ideological parties. Demands are based on a conception of justice, freedom and 'rights' though not necessarily understood as civil liberties. All these factors notwithstanding, it is difficult to imagine consistent mass protests incurring all manner of loss in an effort to establish a system of rule based on the ideological platform of a given political party. The latter often fails to unite the people, either turning into guerrilla insurgencies or military coups. However, this does not preclude the possibility that a political party will gain control of a revolution because it is more organized, experienced and determined, in which case others may accuse it of having 'stolen' the revolution. Furthermore, while this statement is valid for most revolutions, it is especially true in the case of democratic revolutions, where the declared purpose is to overthrow an authoritarian regime and where the intended outcome by major forces should be a democratic, pluralist system of rule.

It goes without saying that not all revolutions against authoritarian rule have democracy as their aim. Nevertheless, the Arab revolutions that were ignited between December 2010 and July 2011 were directed against despotism and corruption, and the demands that were raised could be implemented only in a democratic system. Most of the grassroots organizations spoke directly about democracy. Political parties involved in these movements identified one of their goals as 'a civil state' (*dawlah madaniyah*), a term used by some as contrasted with military rule and by others as contrasted with a religious state. Not being clearly defined, 'civil state' is a political term used by some secularists against religious rule, and by some religious forces against military rule, while avoiding the use of the term 'democratic state'. Nevertheless, every activist knew that the list of demands presented, including fair elections and civil liberties, could only be implemented in a democracy, which was the only alternative to authoritarianism being proposed, even if political parties were not ideologically democratic.

During a revolution, the motivations of those who march in the streets in protest are not always clear to analysts. The most fundamental motive for the ongoing Arab uprisings may have been people's accumulated frustration towards their rulers and the social and economic stagnation and corruption which, having begun in the 1970s, reached their apex in attempts by rulers to groom their sons as their successors. This frustration had been caused by multiple factors: poverty, unemployment, a lack of social security and a dignified life; the sheer difficulty and hellishness of daily life, social deprivation, political disenfranchisement; and clientelism and nepotism running rife within the state. In addition to regular mistreatment by police and security forces, most of these factors are a source of humiliation for the Arab citizen. Restoration of human dignity thus became a supreme goal, and anger ignited by humiliation became a major stimulant for young people to act. If post-revolutionary policies and institutions are not convincing enough or capable of containing this anger, the feeling of humiliation will continue to be a source of unrest against those in power.

Participants themselves may rationalize the reasons to revolt after the success of a revolution. In the case of Tunisia, the majority did not even count ideological motivation among such reasons. Although the basic issues of concern to the religious Arabist and leftist ideological streams were certainly present in the minds of local political activists in the Tunisian Revolution, a quantitative research project conducted by the Arab Center for Research and Policy Studies (ACRPS) concludes that such issues did not appear among the slogans of the uprising in Kasserine and Sidi Bouzid, and few were mentioned in retrospect by those who took part in the early days of the revolution:

- Only 58.1 per cent of the respondents[34] considered the state's lack of respect for religion 'very important' or 'somewhat important' as a factor explaining the outbreak of the protests.
- Over 80 per cent of the respondents explained the outbreak of the revolution in terms of unemployment, corruption and nepotism.[35]
- Over 85 per cent of the respondents stated that the lack of political freedom was a 'very important' or 'somewhat important' factor explaining the outbreak of the revolution.[36]

34. A quantitative field study, directed by Tunisian sociologist Mouldi Lahmar, was conducted on a representative sample of the local population in Sidi Bouzid and Kasserine aged eighteen years and above. The sample was selected based on variables closely related to the research questions.

35. Mouldi Lahmar, 'al-Muqaddimah' [Introduction], in: Mouldi Lahmar (ed.) *The Tunisian Revolution: Examining the Triggers through the Prism of Humanities [al-Thawrah at-Tūnisiyah: al-Qādiḥ al-Maḥallī Taḥt Mijhar al-ʿUlūm al-Insāniyyah]* (Doha and Beirut: ACRPS, 2014), p. 35.

36. Ibid., p. 137.

A sociological perspective on the social movements accompanying these revolutions would be that all these factors, seen and unseen, interact and coalesce. Of this, there can now be no doubt: the Arab street had become the beating heart of opposition, expressing the mood of the Arab people – the living, enraged and mutinous expression of the marginalized and excluded majority. The street was the angry, revolting public opinion in the absence of a constitutional state that respects civil and social rights. The demand for democracy had now become a fully formed idea in the minds of many activists, the result of a process of political accumulation extending over more than three decades.

Some leftist intellectuals who sympathized with the Arab revolution were fascinated by the lack of leadership and confused it with radical democracy. However, there is no correlation between leaderlessness and democracy and certainly not between spontaneity in revolution and building a democracy after one. In fact, the opposite might be true. Asef Bayat refers to Slavoj Žižek who considers the revolutionary scene in Tahrir Square in Cairo as 'magic' and 'a miracle'; it was a new political happening that was free of 'hegemonic organizations, charismatic leaderships or party apparatuses'. Similarly, Antonio Negri and Michael Hardt considered the Arab Spring and the protests that followed in Europe (the Indignados Movement) and the United States (Occupy Wall Street) as expressions of the people's longing for a 'real democracy' in protesting a 'traditional liberal constitution that merely guarantees the division of powers and a regular electoral dynamic'.[37] Leftist intellectuals confused their longing for what they call radical or direct democracy with the temporary forms of protests in the public space and people's experience of euphoria and a sense of liberation during protests in public squares with state regimes (i.e. the way states should be run). They were fascinated and impressed by what they considered leaderless revolutions, whose central figures they described as 'modest representatives of decency and dignity'.[38]

Consequently, these sympathetic observers were blinded to the shortages and deficiencies of the Arab revolutions and to the fact that spontaneity and lack of leadership became weaknesses rather than strengths. Liberal democracy is not the manifestation of a mere idea but a product of two centuries of practical experimentation with ideas, tools and concrete realities. As appealing, attractive and charming as they can be, happenings in public squares are not a miniature democracy, nor do they necessarily portend the coming of democracy. Rather, they are simply non-violent forms of protest; they deserve to be admired for this and not for phantasies projected on them.

Leftist intellectuals also confuse the lack of central leadership in the Arab uprisings with 'their refusal of oligarchy in all its different forms … and their

37. Bayat, 'Revolution in Bad Times'; Slavoj Žižek, 'For Egypt, This Is the Miracle of Tahrir Square', *Guardian*, 10 February 2011, accessed on 25 January 2021, at: http://bit.ly/3oJBfYo; Michael Hardt and Antonio Negri, 'Arabs Are Democracy's New Pioneers', *Guardian*, 24/2/2011, accessed on 25 January 2021, at: http://bit.ly/36HvxQB.

38. Keane, 'Refolution in the Arab world'.

insistence on the political advantages of multiple leadership, on the importance of dispersing power during attempts to democratize'.[39] However, there is a difference between dispersing power, pluralism and multiple leadership in a democratic regime and dispersion during a revolution, which cannot be a dispersion of power.

In order to direct and control the transition from authoritarian rule to democracy, there must be a plan that can garner the approval of the broadest possible section of the political spectrum. A democratic revolution has specific features that distinguish it from other revolutions. It does not lead to a seizure of power by a single political force, and it does not eradicate each and every person who worked in any echelon of the old regime. Rather, opposition parties who become legalized after the revolution are ready to negotiate with moderate elements of the elites of the old regime. A bargaining process over rules of the game and procedures leading to elections is established, and attempts are made to neutralize the military even at the price of allowing it to keep some privileges until new army officers who are committed to the democratic system have been trained. No matter how long such a process takes, it must be well thought out and organized and must acquire a measure of consensus.

The overall aim of any democracy is fairly obvious; hence, it is not acceptable to engage in theoretical 'reinventions of the wheel' and assume that the Arabs are innovating a completely new phenomenon. There is an agreed-upon minimal standard that can be used to tell whether a given regime is democratic or not. The big question, however, relates to the mechanism of this transformation. This is where the specificities of any one country play a role, where creativity comes in. Historically, modern democracies developed gradually (though not necessarily peacefully) out of liberalized political systems of rule over at least a century of reforms and counter-reforms. By contrast, modern transitions from authoritarianism to democracy have to be more abrupt, as people will not wait a century for inclusive suffrage. Even so, such transitions usually begin through some reform from above that splits the ruling regime. Popular reaction to it then splits the opposition, followed by an agreement between the soft-liners on both sides to proceed towards an inclusive democracy.

Rarely will a transition to democracy be triggered by a revolution, but this can happen, and if it happens, the transition is generally more complicated than in the case of a reform followed by mass protests that demand the reform's intensification and expansion. The rules of transition remain the same, but under more difficult conditions. Nevertheless, this is what happened in Tunisia, where the process has been relatively successful so far, and in Egypt (where it has failed).[40]

39. Ibid.

40. Even in revolutions that took place in Eastern Europe, where it is claimed that civil society played a more central role in refuting the 'reform-from-above' thesis of transition theorists, the transition to democracy would have been unimaginable without the reform that began at the top of the Soviet Communist Party.

A revolution that deepens sectarian or other identity-based cleavages will clearly not lead to political pluralism but to division. Secession and infighting will ensue in an endless process of identity construction. Such an outcome is one of the potential pitfalls of revolutions in weak states, especially those in the Arab East, whose political regimes did not solve the issue of vertical social cleavages by nation-building based on citizenship and do not distinguish loyalty to the regime from patriotism and loyalty to the state.

Other worrisome possibilities also exist in the case of democratization after a revolution: (1) Protests continue by inertia, becoming the knee-jerk reaction to everything, and might obstruct stability and 'normal life'; in so doing, they alienate people from the revolution and render them more vulnerable to counter-revolutionary propaganda. (2) Populist discourse arises, exploiting the fact that democratic culture is neither widespread nor deep-rooted among the people yet. This discourse may have existed under authoritarianism but was difficult to distinguish from other oppositional strategies, whereas now it emerges as a distinct form of discourse as democracy and free speech take hold. (3) The risk of counterrevolution grows because democracy's restrain could be interpreted as weakness. (4) Power struggles between ideological and other political forces take centre stage after the revolution because, unlike reform, revolution provides neither time nor opportunity for dialogue but, rather, espouses temporary unity against the regime.

The problem lies not in the primacy of political parties in and of themselves; in some situations, such a primacy might in fact be desirable if the parties represent a modernizing tendency, embody genuine political trends within the society and present practical alternatives to authoritarianism. Rather, the problem arises when political parties rediscover their true ideological hues after having concealed them during the course of the revolution. These groups, some of which supported the revolution, may bring ideological differences to the fore as soon as the old regime falls or begins to show the first signs of weakness. Evidence of this type of behaviour is plainly visible in the cases of some religious and secular parties in both Tunisia and Egypt.

The danger is that a political party will attempt to raise ideological disputes before the nascent democratic regime has consolidated as a framework inclusive of various ideologies and conceptions of the public good, thus obstructing the transition to democracy. This peril calls for a commitment among all parties to subjugate ideology to the rules of the democratic system, which are to be respected by all major social and political forces and state institutions, particularly the army, regardless of which party wins a given election.

One of the central components of democracy is majority rule or, at least, rule by representatives of the majority who have been chosen through free and fair elections. Of equal importance, however, is for the representatives of the majority to govern according to democratic principles. These principles – epitomized in civil liberties and political rights – embody the aspirations of people who live under authoritarian regimes around the world and for whom democracy offers the promise of a better future.

Although the term 'equality' has been subcategorized and modified in modern political and ethical thought (moral equality, equality before the law, social-economic equality, equal opportunities), the ideal of democracy is generally premised on equality not only among the ruled but between the rulers and the ruled. The different conceptions of the dialectic between equality and freedom delineate different democratic schools of thought.

Revolution might fail to build democracy; however, no modern revolution could be said not to desire freedom or liberation. As Arendt astutely observed, 'the revolutionary spirit of the last centuries – the eagerness to liberate *and* to build a new house where freedom can dwell – is unprecedented and unequalled in all prior history'.[41] The freedom sought is not a freedom in the abstract but, rather, civil liberties and achievement of political rights of participation through elections and other civil channels as expressions of self-determination. On the other hand, political rights are worth little unless they are accompanied by the righting of social and economic injustices. Otherwise, what good is the revolution for the many people whose motivation to revolt was precisely the need to improve their living conditions?

Political revolution thus brings with it a revolution of expectations concerning standards of living and social justice, as well as scepticism towards elites and politicians. If the major political forces cannot cope effectively with social expectations in the times of declining growth that are virtually inevitable during a turbulent revolutionary phase (bearing in mind that nascent democracies often stand in need of foreign monetary assistance), politics comes to be perceived as the profane occupation of 'dubious' politicians rather than the 'sacred' calling of the revolutionary. When this occurs, populists and elements of the old regime, taking advantage of their freedom of speech, will be there to 'explain' this corruption to the 'deceived masses'. Indeed, Tunisia's democratically elected governments will be obliged to deal with this burning issue if they are to ensure a stable democracy.

A revolution in pursuit of freedom and liberty does not always guarantee democracy, which is a complex process that involves managing political, ethnic and religious pluralisms; checking and limiting political power; and counter-balancing the public and private spheres. The ruling majority in a democracy will consist not necessarily of a constant identity majority but, rather, a majority of opinions and interests. Consequently, ethnic and cultural minorities should be recognized without being transformed into established political minorities vis-à-vis politicized ethnic or cultural majorities.

The ideals of freedom may be lost to people amid poverty and deprivation. Any reader of history can recall situations in which the 'masses' have been mobilized to fight against concepts of civil liberties which they had come to see as luxuries of the rich. Other examples have seen the poor being marshalled in the name of some identity, be it religious or national, against the 'illusion' of freedom.

41. Arendt, p. 35.

Those who raise the concept of 'the people' above the actual people are typically the very same individuals who act with a sense of tutelage towards them, combining a sense of pity with a romantic notion of their inherent good nature and sense of justice. This supposed inherent goodness of the people, assumed by populist trends in modern history, was to replace real concern for the organization of the government and its institutions (i.e. regulating power and political freedom). Third World countries, including Arab countries, experienced such populist 'democracies' after national liberation movements and military coups that mostly turned to various forms of authoritarian regimes.

This conception of 'the people' became the foundation upon which the revolutionaries (who neglected the citizens in favour of the collective interest and failed to institutionalize the protection of civil liberties and human rights) would later construct modern forms of despotism. Individual rights and demands were subjugated to collective ones via emergency laws and similar legislation in 'the name of the people'. And what is done 'in the name of the people' against the 'enemies of the people' is, ipso facto, 'revolutionary'.

In a similar vein, national unity, initially conceived of as collective cohesion against foreign enemies, was shrunk from a cluster of institutions and consensual principles of legislation into a mere opposition to diversity and pluralism and exploited as a justification for restricting civil liberties and individual rights.

It behoves Arab democrats to learn from past experiences that if the first and necessary stage of national sovereignty is national independence, then real national sovereignty is achieved by building the nation in the form of a democratic state. Transferring sovereignty from the dictator\autocrat\despot (the sovereign) to the nation presupposes the creation of a new public space. Once the previous sources of legitimacy have been undermined, such a process requires a period of formation and coalescing, as well as the choice of a point of departure. Difficult questions that arise may include: What comes first: elections or drafting a constitution? The constitution in both Tunisia and Egypt was ultimately drafted by an elected body. However, it doesn't matter what comes first, whether elections or constitution, there is no substitute for the endorsement of democracy by major political forces before and after elections. No matter how liberal they are, drafted principles cannot guarantee the protection of civil liberties from the vicissitudes of majorities unless the leaders and influential elites of major political and social powers accept them and adhere to them until democracy reproduces itself and they become common national principles served by laws.

Revolution as a contagious phenomenon

The French Revolution, followed by the restoration of monarchy, sent shockwaves throughout Europe, especially after the end of the Napoleonic era and its occupations, which also helped spread revolutionary ideas. The process that was launched by the French Revolution spread throughout Western and Central Europe, primarily through wars and uprisings. These transformations took place as a result of the direct actions of the French Revolution, nationalist continental reactions to Napoleonic French occupation and/or a desire to emulate the French Revolution, a process that culminated in the 1848 revolutions in the majority of European countries.[42]

The current situation in the Arab world appears to be most similar to events in Europe between 1830 and 1848. Revolts were spreading like wildfire, and governments were determined to extinguish them. Contagion due to regional vicinity or cultural affinity may compensate even for the lack of what was previously called revolutionary conditions. In several cases in nineteenth-century Europe, a democratic constitution was promulgated after the failure of a revolution (i.e. after a revolution had failed to bring down the regime).

The French Revolution elaborated on the concept of the nation-state not only by bolstering the idea of a country with clear political borders and a population ruled by a single administrative legal system but also by making the state the expression of a nation representing a group bound together by a common language. This was the situation in the aftermath of the French Revolution and during the Napoleonic era. France obliterated local dialects and ethnic affiliations in order to achieve the linguistic and political unity of the French nation though, ironically, today, the same country preaches to others about the rights of minorities, lending its funding, experts and institutions to the goal of ethnicizing local cultures and religious minorities in the Arab world and elsewhere in attempts to turn them into separate nationalities.

Revolutions in Europe were not content merely to empower the nation-state; entire countries and empires withered and perished in the period between the beginning and the middle of the nineteenth century. Already towards the end of the eighteenth century, the Holy Roman Empire disintegrated, along with small Italian republics such as Genoa and Venice, while the number of German Free States and independent cities decreased. Until Napoleon's defeat in 1815, the Austrian Empire led the coalition of reactionary European powers arrayed against Napoleon and the French Revolution. Starting in 1820, this empire advocated immediate suppression of all popular movements and revolts, a position that greatly resembles that of Saudi Arabia and the UAE after the revolutions of Egypt and Tunisia and in light of the Iranian role in Syria and Iraq. Iran has also played such a role in Syria, Iraq and Lebanon.

Eric Hobsbawm writes:

> Rarely has the inability of ruling regimes to control the flow of history been so clearly displayed as in the decades following Napoleon's defeat in 1815, as his occupations and the resistance thereto them had awakened a nationalist spirit. The main aim of all the European governments that had battled the French

42. See Eric Hobsbawm, *The Age of Revolution 1789-1848* (New York: Vintage Books, 1996 [1962]); and Theda Skocpol, *States and Social Revolutions: A Comparative Analysis of France, Russia, & China* (New York: Cambridge University Press, 1979).

> Revolution between 1789 and 1815 was to prevent the eruption of another revolution elsewhere in Europe. However, revolutions came in waves: the first of these, between 1820 and 1824, was followed by the revolutionary wave of 1830, and the third was the crescendo of 1848, also known as 'the Spring of Nations'.[43]

The Arab world witnessed the emergence of a counter democracy block of states, but also a second wave of revolutions already.

Irrespective of their success, all of these movements could easily be referred to as 'revolutions' due to the memory of the French Revolution. They also took place during an era that witnessed the emergence of domestic intelligence agencies that sought to prevent such uprisings. Another key event of the mid-nineteenth century was the birth of the Chartist movement (the People's Charter) in Britain. This group published a charter containing six demands: (1) universal adult suffrage, (2) voting by ballot, (3) equal electoral districts, (4) disbursement of salaries to members of the parliament, (5) abolition of the property qualification for parliamentary candidates and (6) annual parliamentary conventions.[44]

This important British movement followed in the footsteps of the radical democrat Jacobins, as well as the English and Scottish radical liberal tradition (as opposed to conservative and conservative liberal) that called for universal suffrage and the independence of the legislature from the wealthy classes. However, it did not become a revolution because the British system reformed itself in a gradual transformation from liberalism to liberal democracy. The same era also saw the proliferation of a brand of activists who believed their mission to be the organization of political revolution through the founding of secret societies, fraternities and political parties and spreading the idea of rebellion against the old regime throughout Europe.

When nationalist and democratic sentiments overlapped, revolutionaries' driving forces were simultaneously nationalist and internationalist. In the nineteenth century, revolutionaries across Europe believed that the cause of all peoples was one. Many of these activists moved from one country to another, struggling to promote both democracy and national independence. Guissepe Mazzini (1805–72), for example, participated in the establishment of nationalist organizations such as Young Italy, Young Germany and Young Poland, hoping to group them all within the Young Europe Organization. Mazzini believed that each group had a specific mission, representing a singular contribution in realizing the broader mission of humanity. Nationalism in this sense is the specific mission of a people in the context of the greater humanistic quest. Similarities can be easily noticed in this aspect too. Each Arab revolution expressed an interest both in changing the regime for the sake of the people of

43. Hobsbawm, p. 109. 'The Spring of Nations' was an appellation later adopted in Eastern Europe, the Arab world and other parts of the globe during their respective eras of democratic revolution.

44. See Hobsbawm, p. 114.

a state (state-nation) and in integrating themselves within a regional Arab wave of change via revolution.

Revolution does not erupt somewhere simply because the factors leading to revolution in some other country have been replicated. Protests' organizers and participants do not, in these cases, seek to understand the situation sociologically or compare their circumstances with those of others. Rather, revolutions take place as a result of changes in both circumstances and mindsets. Oftentimes, revolutions spread to countries that are not prepared for them by any 'objective' measure according to a so-called theory of revolution. However, when a revolution erupts merely due to injustice, anger and hope aroused by a revolution in an adjacent country, it may succeed; it may also be undermined by its spontaneity and lack of organization. Spontaneity can be an asset for a revolution, but it can also be fatal to it.

The Syrian Revolution is a clear illustration of the fact that contagion may be very effective but also misleading. The Syrian people witnessed the fall of Mubarak and Ben Ali, yet this did not motivate them to protest Assad's regime at first. They knew all too well the difference between their regime and both the Egyptian and Tunisian regimes. It seemed that only when the Libyan Revolution broke out did many Syrians become convinced of the possibility of change. For if revolution was possible even in Libya, they probably surmise it would be possible in Syria as well. Their determination to continue in spite of the brutal repression they had to endure was then cemented by NATO's decision to intervene in Libya. However, the Syrian regime's resilience and readiness to resort to the unrestrained use of lethal force and to cow minorities into standing by the regime changed the character of the revolution.

With this in mind, it could be argued that the Arab world has been conducive to the spread of revolutions long before the contemporary upheavals. Egypt's July 1952 revolution was, in fact, a military coup that was perceived as a revolution not only because of its revolutionary outcome and the popular support given to it but because the movement took place in an environment that was susceptible to revolution. The Free Officers' coup d'état was, in reality, an extension of an ongoing revolutionary movement that had started in the 1940s and spread throughout Egypt in a variety of ways: students' and workers' associations, a rise in youth movements that rebelled against the model of the traditional political parties, a monopoly of politics and wealth by the elite and the Royal Court, the struggle against the British in the Suez Canal Zone, and a series of mutinies that brought down successive cabinets.

Free Officers movements then spread across the Arab world via revolutionary coups that aimed not just to overthrow the existing regimes but to establish new orders in their respective societies. The first and most significant of these coups was the July 1958 Revolution against the monarchy in Iraq. We could also place the surge of the Algerian struggle for independence within the same context, while keeping in mind the specificity of the Algerian case (i.e. a typical national liberation revolution against direct foreign colonization). Clearly, Egypt's July 23 revolt led to the spread of revolutionary ideals throughout other Arab countries. This spirit would be embodied through the military – the primary institution that had been inherited by these countries from their former colonial occupiers, but which was also capable of unifying the people.

One could argue that environments ripe for revolutions, as well as active revolutionary movements, were already at work in several Arab countries but were immediately aborted by the coup officers that took over following the *Nakba* in Palestine in 1948. A nuanced analysis demonstrates that the military coups both aborted and complemented these revolutionary currents. The coups did away with the democratic dimension of revolution by resorting to populist discourse devoid of popular participation in politics in addition to suppressing freedoms and exerting military rule in the name of the people. However, these coups also achieved national liberation and land reform, politically integrating the cities and the countryside and abolishing feudal privileges and free schooling. This dissemination of the idea of revolution must be explored in this Arab political and cultural environment just as the Europeans emulated the French Revolution. In 2011, Arab countries witnessed the reaction of an existing Arab revolutionary phenomenon to the model presented in Tahrir Square by the Egyptian revolutionaries, who were inspired by the success of the Tunisian Revolution after the flight of Ben Ali. With trial and error and the passage of time, the extent of this model's utility was tested in several countries and revealed that a mass demonstration and a protracted sit-in in a public square will not be sufficient to topple a regime if the army and the security apparatus remain loyal and cohesive. Moreover, other Arab regimes learnt from the experiences of Ben Ali and Mubarak.

More than at any other time, this revolutionary period has proven that common identity and culture play a role in spreading the 'contagion'. The revolution witnessed by a large Muslim country like Indonesia, though quite similar to Egypt's, prompted no imitation in the Arab world. By comparison, a revolt in tiny Arab Tunisia, situated at the historic heart of the greater Arab Maghreb, swept through the entire Arab world like an electric current that conducted hopes, fears, aspirations, concerns, agendas and ideas and was able to directly impact Egypt.

The Tunisian regime's attempts to distance Tunisia from Arab national identity drove many Tunisians in the coastal regions and the interior to emphasize this very identity, just as for many people (not necessarily Islamists), Islam became an important component of their identity as a reaction to the Tunisian regime's attempts under Bourguiba to impose French-styled secularism (*laïcité*). On the other hand, the Syrian regime turned the shared Arab cultural-ethnic identity into a political ideology, but, in reality, the regime's policies and sectarian practices split the Syrian people and Arab public opinion, while Tunisia's revolution became an inspiration for Arabs everywhere.

Some saw the protesters call for Ben Ali to '33egage' (leave) as a sign of the cultural openness and multilingual nature of the Tunisian Revolution, while others proposed that the protesters chanted in French to imply that this was the language Ben Ali would understand and were treating him as they would a colonial power. Too much was read into using a French word, which entered the daily spontaneous use in the vernacular language of people in North African countries since the

French Occupation. However, nearly all slogans of the revolution were in Arabic. The slogan, 'The people want to bring down the regime' (al-*sha'b yurīd isqāṭ al-niẓām*) was first raised during the Tunisian Revolution on Friday, 14 January 2011, and became the main mantra of Arab revolutions in 2011.

According to Emmanuel Todd, the prominent presence of French culture in Tunisia is one of the factors which, in addition to rising literacy rates and a decline in fertility, led to the Tunisian Revolution.[45] However, Nabiha Jerad rightly rejects this argument based on the fact that the centre and southern parts of Tunisia that were the home of the revolution were also the hubs of anti-colonial resistance.[46] These regions stressed the Arab and Muslim dimensions of their Tunisian identity, in part influenced by the Youssefi[47] movement and in part as a means of protesting against Bourguiba's imposed ideology. Indeed, these regions have given birth to uprisings throughout the modern history of the country. So the uprisings cannot be attributed to the influence of French culture however significant it has been in the Maghreb.

Granted, the protests bore no connection to pan-Arab ideology, Islamism or even the Palestinian cause.[48] Nor did they begin in mosques but mostly in public squares or labour unions. Rather, Tunisians throughout the country joined the uprisings motivated primarily by socio-economic issues and by concerns that they had in common with other regions. However, this does not mean that the revolutionaries were not consciously Arabs or Muslims. On the contrary, Arab identity and issues like the Palestinian cause are quite central to Tunisians, secular and religious alike, as public opinion surveys have shown.[49]

45. Eric Aeschimann, 'La Tunisie a rejoint le modèle historique general', *Libération*, 17 January 2011, accessed on 6 November 2020, at: https://bit.ly/35sQPky.

46. Nabiha Jerad, 'The Tunisian Revolution: From Universal Slogans for Democracy to the Power of Language', *Middle East Journal of Culture and Communication*, vol. 6, no. 2 (2013), pp. 242–3.

47. The Youssefi movement derived its name from Salah Ben Youssef, secretary-general of the Neo-Destour Political Party, who became Bourguiba's arch-enemy following Tunisia's independence. The Youssefists believed in the pan-Arab movement being advocated by Gamal Abdul-Nasser.

48. Ibid., p. 240.

49. For example, the latest Arab Opinion Index survey conducted in Tunisia by the Arab Center for Research and Policy Studies (ACRSP) shows that 89 per cent of Tunisians view the Palestinian cause as of concern to all Arabs and not to Palestinians alone. This attitude has remained constant since the first AOI survey in 2011. See 'The 2019-20 Arab Opinion Index Main Results in Brief', Arab Center for Research and Policy Studies, p. 54, accessed on 6 November 2020, at: https://bit.ly/3f6IIgY. This also can be observed in Tunisian Prime Minister Kais Saied's populist discourse during the last presidential race, where his platform highlighted Arab issues and the Arabic language itself. See 'Kais Saied, a University Professor, who surprised the Political Arena in Tunisia' [Qays Saeid,

On the revolutionary condition and susceptibility to revolution

When do the people make their move towards revolution? Not all of them move, and the sectors that do rarely begin with an all-out revolution; instead, they go out and protest, raising specific demands or simply expressing disaffection and anger at the conditions they face. Goals and demands may vary, as will motivations. Once people go out to protest, what are the factors that can cause a rebellion or civil disturbance to turn into a revolution? To pose such questions is not an attempt to formulate a theory of revolution, nor would such an attempt be fruitful. Nevertheless, the bulk of the theoretical literature on the subject takes inspiration from a specific historical revolution, compares it with other events that have been identified as revolutions based on this or that agreed-upon definition, and makes generalizations based on its specific findings. If analyses of this nature fail to explain how still other revolutions have erupted, the theory is modified to include them, and the modified theory then becomes the focus of further research.

In my view, none of the previous attempts to understand and contextualize past revolutions can be properly described as 'theories', because the myriad factors that lead people to rise up against their governments, and then transform these uprisings into revolutions, defy prediction. Even if these factors are enumerated and detailed, it remains difficult to determine which of them are unique to a particular situation and which apply more generally to become a base for a theory. We can, of course, study the structure of certain revolutions and draw theoretical conclusions from them. However, we should not expect such studies to yield a comprehensive theory that can predict the occurrence of a revolution in some scientific manner.

Tilly has argued that revolutions are not subject to laws, as if they were a separate phenomenon, or an interruption in the normal flux of social and political life. He likens revolutions to a traffic jam rather than to a natural phenomenon like a solar eclipse. Its components are normal and predictable, yet the phenomenon itself remains unpredictable. The combination of factors that lead to revolutions is unpredictable, as is the intensity of the phenomenon. Each factor is independent somehow from the other, and each is 'relatively predictable on its own', but the coalescence of all these factors seems like a contingency.[50] Tilly is right, although the metaphor he employs is less than successful. He is also right that what is needed is not a theory of revolution but 'a systematic, historically grounded analysis of revolutionary processes that connects them firmly to our accumulating knowledge of state formation and routine political contention'. The concept of revolutions depends on the concept of state, political regime and the 'people' as a political force. Revolutions include the act of seizing state power; hence, they are influenced by the nature of the state and also by relations between states, including

al-Ustādh al-Jamiʿī alladhī Fājaʾa as-Sāḥah al-Siyāsiyah fī Tūnis], *BBC Arabic*, 9 October 2019, accessed on 7 November 2020, at: https://bbc.in/3ku0f3K.

50. Ibid., p. 7.

peace and war.[51] For example, states defeated in a costly war are more vulnerable to revolutions.

Tilly understands the revolutionary condition as a part of his definition of the phenomenon, which includes popularly supported political blocs that contend for power in the state. Consequently, the existence of such blocs is a condition for a revolution. But if the definition is not accepted (as in the previous analysis), neither will the condition be. In Lenin's *The Collapse of the Second International*,[52] he lists the basic components of the 'revolutionary condition' that are necessary but not sufficient to bring a revolution into being: The ruling classes find it impossible to maintain their rule when there is a crisis in one form or another among the 'upper classes', leading to a fissure through which the oppressed classes erupt in discontent and indignation. The Russian Revolution was preceded by a crisis that led to a fissure in the ruling classes. However, the same kind of crisis might have led to reforms from above and not to a revolution. In Tunisia and Egypt, it was the revolution itself that caused a fissure in the ruling elite. It was not preceded by a crisis in the ruling regime.

According to Lenin's definition of the revolutionary situation, the conditions of the working class are not sufficient to engender a revolution; rather, the ruling class – the bourgeoisie – must simultaneously enter into a state of crisis. Such a crisis signifies a genuine divide within the ruling class over the perception of their class interests and leads to varying reactions in its ranks at the outset of revolution. One must remember that the October Revolution of 1917 was made possible by the March Revolution of the same year. Following the revolution in March, a duality emerged between the Kerensky[53] provisional government, or the 'bourgeois government' according to Lenin, and the 'Soviets' – councils representing the workers and the soldiers. Faced with this duality at the heart of the authority, the Soviets resorted to force in order to decisively settle the question of dual authority before the other side could do so, at which point power transferred completely to the councils, leading to the realization of the famous slogan, 'All power to the Soviets'. In fact, this was a misleading statement, as it concealed the reality that 'all power' lay not in the hands of the Soviets but the Bolsheviks, who agitated against (and later liquidated) any faction that acted independently of the party.

We cannot know what might have happened if history had taken the path of reform after the March Revolution. Perhaps the outcome would have been a democratic or a quasi-democratic system; instead, the Russian Revolution, which

51. Tilly, *European Revolutions*, pp. 5–6.

52. Vladimir Lenin, 'The Collapse of the Second International', in: *Collected Works*, vol. 21 (Moscow: Progress Publishers, 1965), p. 213; on the necessity of a split within the ruling elites and the bourgeoisie, see also Vladimir Lenin, *»Left Wing« Communism: An Infantile Disorder* (Moscow: Progress Publishers, 1950), p. 69.

53. Aleksandr Kerensky was a Russian parliamentary reformer who sided with the March Revolution but refused to hand over the authority of the state to the soviets.

settled the duality of power in Russia by force, established a totalitarian system of rule. In the framework of the revolutionary condition, we can see that the Kerensky-led government represented the split within the ruling bourgeoisie over whether to strike an alliance with the Czarist regime or to support the rebellion against the Czar.

Lenin observed that in order for a revolution to take place, it is usually insufficient simply for the lower classes not to want to live in the old way; it is also necessary that the upper classes be incapable of ruling in the old way. However, this Leninist 'theory' is largely recursive and descriptive rather than explaining why and when a revolution will take place. It also contains logical fallacies, since the outbreak of a revolution itself proves that the lower classes can no longer endure their lives as they are, and its success, or lack thereof, is what tells us whether what he calls the upper classes are, or are not, capable of continuing to rule in the 'old way'. Lenin's talk of classes is clearly a reference to economic classes, including those who do not rule directly but whose interests are served by the political regime according to Marxism. Of course, ruptures such as war and economic crises, of which Lenin had first-hand knowledge through the Russian Revolution, make ruling in the old way difficult, but only the success of the revolution proves that it had become impossible. Hence, this so-called revolutionary 'condition' is actually a diagnosis in retrospect.

A revolutionary situation takes hold when the suffering, deprivation and sense of injustice have grown more acute than usual and are associated clearly with the ruling regime. This was certainly true in Russia in the wake of the First World War. For this reason, Lenin included this factor in his discussions of the 'revolutionary situation'; it is also the sort of suffering one generally sees during and after wars, in times of drought and famine, during severe economic crises and in the aftermath of natural disasters. In the case of the Arab revolutions, people have demonstrated an awareness that their suffering is an outcome of injustice associated with the ruling regime.

A further component of Lenin's 'revolutionary situation' emerges when there is a considerable increase in the activity and restlessness of the 'oppressed masses', who are driven both by crises and the practices of the upper classes. This relates to the intensity of protest actions and levels of awareness, and it is a sensible indicator for the outbreak of some revolutions.

What must be stressed here is that suffering and awareness of the need and potential for change, or the 'susceptibility to revolution' in the terminology of this book, are, above all, a matter of consciousness. Hegel describes need itself as the awareness of *deficiency*. 'Susceptibility to revolution' can be similarly defined as the awareness that the ongoing state of suffering is an outcome of injustice, that is, the awareness that these sufferings are neither justifiable nor part of a given natural state, in addition to an awareness of the possibility of taking action against this unfairness. When the protests break out, people who believe that taking action against the regime is possible need to be there. If the regime attempts to suppress the protests, such people work to sustain and politicize them, rejecting both the regime's attempts to appease them and attempts by opposition figures to settle for the regime's concessions. The mission of such protest leaders (at least on the local level) is made easier when the protests escalate and protesters are further radicalized with each concession by the regime. The revolution wins against the regime when it can no longer be contained by either the state's attempts at repression or its offers of concessions.

The recent Arab revolutions have proven that toppling a modern dictatorship by means of peaceful demonstrations, strikes and sit-ins is extremely difficult without neutralizing the position of security forces and the army. There must be a disinclination on their part to defend the regime for whatever reason, be it reluctance to use violence against civilians beyond a certain degree, fear of a split in the army or even hidden ambitions to take over themselves. Lacking such conditions, the ruling authority remains a fortress, even if abandoned by some of its employees and officials; this occurred in Libya and Syria, where the revolutions turned into armed movements followed by civil wars whose outcomes were determined by foreign intervention.

The popular uprisings that have taken place in Arab countries were soon transformed into popular revolutions aimed at the regime and calling for its overthrow, yet without proposing a specific political force in its place. These were reformist revolutions in the sense that they demanded regime change and did not enforce the change by imposing a specific leadership. In this sense they differed from the Russian and the Iranian revolutions, whose representation was requisitioned by political forces or networks that seized power. In Tunisia the revolution led to chaos and confusion in the regime and a mutiny in the Tunisian security forces. The presidential guard was also confused (either that, or it was part of a plot), and when the army did not put down the mutiny, the president fled the country. In Egypt, the army refused to crush the popular uprising, leading the regime to relinquish its figurehead in order to save itself. Then, however, the army faced a new, revolutionary legitimacy which was consolidated by the dictator's overthrow and was forced to negotiate a transition period with the organized political movements. The revolution, along with continuous targeted political protests in its aftermath, was followed by political reform in the existing regime, which led to a democratic transition. In cases where the schism between revolutionary forces was deep enough to prevent them from giving priority to democratic procedures over political rivalries and mutual mistrust, and when, additionally, the old state was still sufficiently powerful, counter-revolutionary forces succeeded in associating revolution with chaos.

These Arab revolutions have provided the world with a new model which is not yet fully formed. They have defied explanation based on extrapolation from the revolutions in Russia and Iran. Theoretical attempts coming from Egypt before the revolution were more or less limited to broad and intuitive observations on the conditions for revolution, such as 'there must be a social and political conflict between the rulers and the ruled', 'the rulers must be incapable of resolving the conflict' and 'the people aspire to change'. Another such theorization is that there must be 'a secret or public group, party, or front that seeks to resolve the existing conflict to its advantage based on the interests of the revolutionary forces, and chooses the opportune moment, or the ripe conditions, to grab power'.[54] However, these criteria have been invalidated by the Arab uprisings, in which no organized political party initiated the mass protests or turned them into a revolution.

The Muslim Brotherhood in Egypt awaited the optimal moment to seek power, and they did so in fair elections forced by a revolution which they themselves had not called for. Indeed, they even hesitated to join in the beginning for fear of bearing responsibility for protests which did not promise to fare any better than previous ones. (A similar situation applied to Al Nahda[55] in Tunisia.) Furthermore, the time when the revolutions broke out was 'the opportune moment' only in hindsight, for the call to take to the streets had not even been made in the name of revolution. The Tunisian Revolution erupted in the form of social protests and acts of solidarity with the demonstrations taking place in Sidi Bouzid. The protests were sporadic and 'general' in the sense that they did not raise specific demands that the regime was expected to fulfil. Rather, each region had its own difficulties; hence, they all came together in a shared rage that would be difficult to placate. The protests morphed into a full-scale revolution when the urban centres joined behind the demand for regime change.

The Tunisian Revolution began as what might be termed a socio-economic uprising and a revolt of dignity against humiliation in the province of Sidi Bouzid,[56] which then spilled over into the other provinces in the southwest and central-west regions of Tunisia. There were certainly political activists involved, but the social base of the uprisings was comprised of the poor and unemployed, including wage labourers and the lower middle classes, especially in the regions that benefitted the least from the economic growth that Tunisia had witnessed in the previous two decades, and those who felt unjustly deprived by the central government. This sentiment added to a history of bitterness and politico-cultural alienation that had festered since the days of Bourguiba, when these regions had stood by his rival, Salah Ben Youssef, following the struggle for independence.

Once their waves had hit the coastal regions, the uprisings might have receded if other cities of Tunisia had not joined them. This added support came from two

54. ʿĀṣim Dasūqī (ed.), *Al-Thawrah wal-Taghyīr fī al-Waṭan al-ʿArabī ʿAbr al-ʿUṣūr [Revolution and Change in the Arab Homeland throughout History]*, Proceedings of the Symposium Held by the Egyptian Society for Historical Studies (Cairo: Center for Social Studies and Research at the Cairo University College of Arts, 2005), pp. 16–17.

55. Also known as Ennahda.

56. The outburst of anger after the humiliation of a street vendor in the context of preventing him from 'occupying the public space' illegally reminds of the interesting thesis of Asef Bayat of the 'art of presence' in the urban space as a resistance strategy of the poor and marginalized, who promote their positions in the city in the individual daily struggle for survival but can turn to a revolt when the state clamps down on them and tries to prevent the consolidation of their de facto positions and thereby reverse their achievements. Asef Bayat, *Life as Politics: How Ordinary People Change the Middle East*, 2nd edn (Stanford, CA: Stanford University Press, 2013 [2010]), pp. xi. 14–15, 18–19.

sources: (1) poor neighbourhoods and members of the middle classes in Tunis, Sfax and other cities and (2) political opposition activists, unionists and some human rights associations, especially the lawyers' union, whose members spoke out in small rallies of solidarity with the regions of the south, challenging the regime's silence, the media blackout over the uprisings in many provinces and the brutal repression. It was not until the last two days, 13 and 14 January 2011, when segments of middle classes in the capital and other cities joined the protests, and mutiny took place in some of the security agencies. So what was this? Judging by its outcomes, it was a democratic revolution.

The revolution took two main forms: peaceful rallies and demonstrations on the one hand, and violent (though unarmed) clashes with internal security forces on the other, including the burning of police stations and vehicles and ruling party local branches. These actions went on for more than three weeks, wearing down the security apparatus.[57]

Although the revolution in Tunisia did not start specifically as a pro-democracy movement, the thesis that democracy emerged merely as a contingent outcome of political struggle, as Adam Przeworski would put it,[58] does not stand in this case. The template for democracy was already there. Przeworski's thesis was based on the writings of Dankwart A. Rustow, who concluded from research on the historical emergence of democracy in Sweden that 'Democracy was not the original or primary aim; it was sought as a means to some other end, or it came as a fortuitous byproduct of the struggle'.[59] It is true that the Tunisian Revolution was not focused on introducing democracy; it nevertheless came eventually to demand it as a ready-made product. It did not emerge fortuitously.

As Przeworski notes, forces which share the aspiration to dismantle an authoritarian regime have different interests and plans. However, in order to impose their interests and implement their plans for the organization of state and society, they must 'not only dismantle the old regime but must create simultaneously conditions that would favor them in the newly established political system'.[60]

The act of achieving democracy 'by contingency' results from a peculiar balance of powers among political players who cannot determine the outcome of the struggle between them but who, at the same time, do not want to risk losing everything as an outcome of potential civil war. However, uncertainty here continues to be a pressing issue with the outcomes of the elections, how the different players react to them, and whether they will respect a peaceful

57. In Egypt's revolution this happened in only three days, since it started from the main cities.

58. Adam Przeworski, 'Democracy as a Contingent Outcome of Conflicts', in: Jon Elster and Rune Slagstad (eds.), *Constitutionalism and Democracy* (Cambridge: Cambridge University Press, 1988), pp. 59–80.

59. Dankwart A. Rustow, 'Transitions to Democracy: Toward a Dynamic Model', *Comparative Politics*, vol. 2, no. 3 (1970), p. 353.

60. Przeworski, 'Democracy as a Contingent Outcome of Conflicts', p. 63.

transition of power. Therefore, the vital thing here is to agree on the rules of the democratic game. This phenomenon was observable over the course of the nineteenth century and the beginning of the twentieth as democracies emerged in countries like Britain Sweden, the Netherlands and even France, where some liberties were already consolidated (in the course of the century that followed the revolution).

Per contra, we find that when, in the cases of Tunisia, Egypt and other countries in the region, as well as in South America and Eastern Europe, an authoritarian regime was brought down by a revolution from below and mutiny in the security forces, the major political forces in the country were clearly aware of the possibility of democracy, because liberal democracy had already developed as a model and been tested in numerous places. Whenever a comparison could be made between democracy and despotism, democracy was the more attractive option. As for other alternatives, such as Communism, they had been discredited following the collapse of the Soviet Union and the Socialist Bloc so that even radical leftist opposition did not present a viable, practical alternative to liberal democracy. The main Islamist currents were likewise obliged to demonstrate in one way or another, during the revolution, that they were favourable to democracy.

Despite its flaws, the major positive features of the democratic model are known to all. Hence, when the existing political forces negotiate alternatives to despotism – provided that no single one of them has seized power since the dictator's ouster – it will be clear from the outset that democracy is the best alternative to the old regime.

The Tunisian Revolution was an outcome of successive uprisings in specific provinces which, as they spilled over into other regions, evolved into a revolution that demanded the overthrow of the ruling regime. The ultimate outcome was democracy because no element of the revolutionary leadership seized power for itself and because the various forces in play – particularly political parties and pragmatically minded elements within the regime – had to agree on what alternative they would adopt, and the only acceptable alternative to despotism known worldwide and already tested in many countries was the democratic system. In fact, this was precisely what many political opposition forces in Tunisia had demanded under the dictatorship of Ben Ali.

The second question that might be asked here is why the revolution emerged in Tunisia in a time of economic growth, with a rising GDP per capita. There had been a drop in Tunisia's GDP per capita in 2009 following the world financial crisis of 2008; however, there had been no sharp reversal. James C. Davies has proposed that 'revolutions are most likely to occur when a prolonged period of objective economic and social development is followed by a short period of sharp reversal'.[61] This is logical and may have been true for many revolutions. In the Tunisian case, however, there had been no sharp crisis following a prolonged

61. James C. Davies, 'Toward a Theory of Revolution', *American Sociological Review*, vol. 27, no. 1 (1962), p. 5.

period of development but, rather, ongoing unemployment, marginalization and deprivation in the midst of a growing economy.

According to Alexis de Tocqueville, the French Revolution emerged at a time when the ruling regime was relatively well-off, economically speaking, and perhaps even politically, as a result of which the French people had higher expectations of those in power.[62] However, neither de Tocqueville nor any other scholar can claim that people revolt because they are doing well economically and politically. They may have higher expectations as well as other needs that transcend simple subsistence and which cannot be realized without political rights and civil liberties. Nevertheless, even these higher expectations would not be enough to launch a revolution. Rather, what launches a revolution under conditions of economic growth is the explosive combination of three interconnected factors with different impacts on different segments of society. The *first* is higher expectations and aspirations generated by growth and improved living conditions under authoritarianism; the *second* is the relative deprivation being suffered by other classes or social strata and the sense of injustice associated with this; and the *third* is the issue of dignity, whether it is expressed through a yearning for civil liberties or through outrage against the humiliation caused by the oppressive and demeaning practices of security agencies and state employees and the daily experience of unemployment and deprivation.

Tunisia's protests began in the provinces that were not benefitting equally from the country's overall economic development. Although the country's economic situation had improved in absolute numbers, residents of these provinces actually felt more deprived than before because of the development being witnessed in other parts of the country. As unemployment rates rose among university graduates, education ceased to be a means of social mobility. Furthermore, the country's economic growth was accompanied by harsher and more repressive surveillance measures by the police state, as well as by corruption, nepotism and cliental networks that stifled what remained of the meritocracy that had emerged during the post-independence phase.

Contingent factors, such as Mohamed Bouazizi's self-immolation, the strong communal ties inside Sidi Bouzid, politically conscious activists, and neighbouring areas' solidarity with Sidi Bouzid, were decisive in both the outbreak

62. Public prosperity under the reign of Louis XVI was substantial; indeed, it was increasing at an unprecedented pace, despite the flaws of the government and the unequal taxation that caused the 'mutiny' of the Third Estate's representatives. In fact, Tocqueville says that 'in no period since the Revolution has public prosperity improved more rapidly than it did in the twenty years prior to the Revolution'. However, despite the growing prosperity in France, public discontent grew more bitter. In fact, the parts of France where progress was most evident became the principal centre of the revolution, while the poor and most vulnerable regions were the ones that defended the monarchy. See Alexis de Tocqueville, *The Ancien Régime and the French Revolution*, Jon Elster (ed.), Arthur Goldhammer (trans.) (Cambridge: Cambridge University Press, 2011 [1856]), pp. 155–6.

and continuity of the uprising to the point where the poor neighbourhoods of large cities, including the capital, joined in. Over time, the uprisings also drew in people whose living standards had improved under Ben Ali and who had begun to cultivate higher expectations. And lastly, the movement was joined by members of the middle class who, although they had enjoyed a better economic situation from the start, felt that the regime was illegitimate and that they had been deceived by its promises of political reforms concerning political rights and civil liberties. For despite such promises when Ben Ali came to power in 1987, by the beginning of the 1990s he had moved to a full-scale authoritarianism. Though comfortable materially speaking, the urban middle class lived under the surveillance of an authoritarian regime that deprived its members of their civil and political liberties and whose corruption repelled them. This, then, was the coalition of forces that formed the Tunisian Revolution.

The Tunisian Revolution was instigated by neither a political force that intended to seize power nor even one that sought to make use of it for its own gain. Rather, it simply forced the regime to launch a transition to democracy, and in this sense it was a reformist revolution. Within the ruling party there were Bourguiba loyalists who had been marginalized or even persecuted by Ben Ali's regime, as well as a number of technocrats who, though employed by an authoritarian state, sought sincerely to act as civil servants. Figures such as these played an important role in the transition to democracy both before and after the election thanks to their pragmatism and readiness to bargain and make concessions to ensure the transition's success by forming coalitions with Al Nahda.

As we have seen, merely enumerating and describing the grievances and antagonisms between rulers and ruled will not suffice in the formulation of a theory capable of predicting revolutions. The questions then become: How do such grievances and antagonisms intensify to the point where they cannot be resolved within the existing regime, and how widespread is people's awareness of the impossibility of reforming this regime? There are no simple answers to such questions. Moreover, even if the answers are available, many other questions remain to be answered concerning what triggers outbursts of popular rage, the sustainability of such outbursts, the cohesiveness and resilience of the system, and the level of repression it is capable of deploying against its own people.

Chapter 1

THE ARAB AND THE TUNISIAN IN THE TUNISIAN REVOLUTION

Whichever historical perspective one adopts, the postcolonial period in the Arab world has been marked by the entrenchment of the state, which has challenged ideologies, sometimes held by its own rulers, that delegitimize its borders as artificial and colonially determined. This process, which can be traced back – depending on the country in question – to the 1970s, began in Tunisia before other Arab countries due to the state's embrace of postcolonial Tunisian nationalism.

The question is: Do events of the second decade of the twenty-first century herald the beginning of an entirely new era, or are we simply entering a new phase of the same historical period? An attempt to answer this question would be premature, since it will take decades for the outcomes of the Arab revolutions to emerge and for their structure to become clearer. However, if current events eventually yield a number of democratic Arab states, a new era of the history of the Arab world will indeed have been born.

The last, long chapter in the history of Arab states witnessed the emergence of a prominent trend in which despotic regimes in Arab republics assimilated certain novel behaviours and traits. Having consolidated the rule of a dictatorship, they shed the ideological facade previously posited as one of the sources of their legitimacy and began creating hybrid political systems around the dictator. Typically, this hybrid included the dictator's family (an 'innovation' unheard of in Arab republics), with or without the presence of a ruling party, strong security services and a group of prominent businessmen, bred by a mixture of economic liberalism, nepotism and political clientelism, who, through personal, familial or marital ties, were linked with the main figures dominating the country's political and security scene. This business elite generally thrived on its relationship with the regime and benefited from liberalization of the economy under authoritarianism. Not only do such capitalists not strive for democracy; they fear it as well.

The regime thus witnessed the emergence of a new ruling class composed of a network made up of the sons and relatives of the ruling family – an Arab variety of nepotism – along with the class of new businessmen and an ensemble of security agencies. This coalition of interests was in turn supported by a relatively broad group of intellectuals and technocrats who served as their institutional face and public image, although some of them were sincere civil servants who know the system too well to dare to express a political opinion, not to speak of a critique. With this class effectively taking the reins of power, cabinets and ministries became mere bureaucratic positions, since prime ministers and ministers, whether technocrats or politicians, generally lacked decision-making powers. Hence, ministers manage their respective domains according to policies that they do not determine, but for whose failures they may take the blame. Ministries are also used to reward loyalists and maintain their favour in a pattern similar to that of the regimes that emerged in Latin America in the latter half of the twentieth century. It is not unusual for governments to absorb and contain former opponents of the regime (mostly in monarchies like Jordan and Morocco, but less so in republics that are not so 'tolerant', in this sense Ben Ali's first decade in rule was an exception).

These regimes have varied in every other respect. Some, such as those in Tunisia, Egypt and Yemen, allowed a margin for trade unions and an official and semi-official opposition (with a relatively larger margin in Tunisia for trade unions historical reasons, and a relatively larger margin for press freedom in Egypt and Yemen), while others, such as Syria, Iraq and Libya (as well as Saudi Arabia and the UAE, albeit with monarchical dynasties and different sources of legitimacy), embodied a closed, rigid form of authoritarianism. The state structure and the degree of coherence and resolve of the authoritarian regimes affected both the character of the revolution and the probability of its outbreak.

For a relatively long period, it seemed as if this ominous, stagnant political reality, which had overshadowed the postcolonial Arab state since the 1970s, would be permanent. Even military coups have let up since then, except in Sudan and Mauritania. The self-assurance of Arab leaders was such that they showed no qualms about publicly displaying their corruption – a result of merging politics, security and economy; the lack of separation between private and public domains; and an absence of the rule of law. They openly relied on the heavy hand of the security apparatus and client networks. Corruption provokes people's rage even more than the existent socio-economic gaps, because corruption cannot be justified even in the regime's propaganda itself but only denied – lied about, that is – because it trains people's rage on certain persons (usually the ruler's relatives and entourage rather than the ruler himself). Furthermore, corruption is a favourite topic of sensationalists and rumour mongers, both in the private sphere and in social networks.

In democracies, the state may enter citizens' private domain; however, it does so through well-defined legal channels. The constant changes in the boundaries between public and private – alongside social struggles, changes in public awareness and the creation of new laws – lead to a domain that lies at the intersection between private and public, otherwise known as 'citizenship'. In democratic countries citizenship is endowed with both a private and a public element. In authoritarian regimes, on the other hand, the state can unilaterally invade the private sphere, which is more or less devoid of all sanctity, so the private becomes public. At the same time, the public becomes a private domain for the ruler, and corruption becomes the rule.

Meanwhile, across the region, as leaders' self-confidence grew and their regimes consolidated, they groomed their sons for succession, a feature not peculiar to Arab republics but a hallmark of ageing authoritarian republics across the world.[1] Ironically, the very term 'republic' is derived from the word 'public', a fact that is also conveyed literally in the Arabic translation of the term *jumhūriyah*. In the case of Arab republics like Syria and Libya, and to a lesser degree Egypt and Tunisia, however, the emergence of ruling dynasties and hereditary rule represented an official 'privatization' of republics, which were approached as if they were fiefdoms. This brought with it a conscious and subconscious ethos of subjugation of public affairs to personal interests that permeated all echelons of the system. This ethos would have been alien to the first generation of authoritarian rulers, who were not corrupt, at least not in the sense of personal enriching or greed for money, and sometimes even personally austere. These despots believed that they were serving the public interest even though they established the repressive 'infrastructure' for the corruption of a later generation of rulers who, although they possessed the tools of previous despots, did not share their goals.

It should come as no surprise, then, that the Arab revolutions erupted precisely in the republics that were witnessing attempts to establish hereditary rule (Egypt, Yemen, Libya and Syria, where the hereditary transfer of rule had already taken place). This was also the case with Tunisia, a country ruled by a dictator whose family had the power to plunder the economy but lacked a male heir. The rejection of the hereditary transfer of rule became a potent symbol of the struggle against the regime throughout the revolutions. Bequeathing the presidency constituted a breach of republican ethos (manifested by rulers like Bourguiba, Tunisia's first president, Algeria's Boumediene and Nasser of Egypt) and abandonment of its original ideological legitimacy. Proof of this legitimacy crisis lay in the fact that despite the public grooming of heirs and the broad prerogatives handed down to them before they assumed power, regimes typically denied their plans to bequeath rule to an heir. Denials and lies, nonetheless, did not deceive the people; rather, the regime's insistence on denying the obvious bespoke its recognition of the lack of legitimacy of its actions.

This is not to say that revolutions cannot erupt in monarchist regimes. On the contrary, this remains a possibility, as the eruption of revolutions goes beyond a crisis of legitimacy. The monarchist regimes in Saudi Arabia, Morocco, Jordan

1. See Jason Brownlee, 'Hereditary Succession in Modern Autocracies', *World Politics*, vol. 59, no. 4 (2007), pp. 595–628. Brownlee reviews and compares twenty-two cases of hereditary succession in republics and attempts to prove the following thesis: hereditary succession in republics occurs when there are fears that the absence of an electoral tradition within the party will lead to conflict. The process of hereditary succession tends to be more successful in cases of individual rule than in cases of party rule. This thesis appears to have been debunked, however, by the success of hereditary succession in Syria, where party rule preceded individual rule, and its failure in Egypt, where individual rule took precedence over party rule.

and elsewhere are most certainly authoritarian, though to varying degrees. And uprisings did erupt in 2011 in Bahrain, Jordan and Morocco. Undeniably, the source of a monarchy's legitimacy differs from that of a republic. In royalist regimes, the rule of the family and kin exists as a matter of course, but Arab republics and monarchies converge on many points, particularly in terms of the power granted to security services. In view of the revolts in the region, those who claim that republics are more prone to revolution than monarchies may suffer from a short memory span and should be reminded that the very idea of democratic revolution began with the rebellions against monarchist regimes in Europe and that the most notable popular revolt before the recent Arab uprisings was the Iranian revolution against the monarchist regime of the Shah, not to mention the numerous revolutions and coups against Arab monarchies that occurred during the second half of the twentieth century. Of course, the problem for despotic Arab republics is that the contradiction between their reality and their source of legitimacy is more obvious. In addition, the traditional structures that can protect individuals from the arbitrariness of the state by mediating between them are much weaker in republics than in monarchies.

A source of frustration and concern among Arabs lies in the fact that despite clear signs of decay and corruption, the features and instruments of change had yet to emerge. It seemed as if Arab societies were doomed to remain under the yoke of ruling cliques that combined economic neoliberalism with political authoritarianism, even after it became clear that these regimes were in the twilight of their reign. In circumstances of rampant nepotism and patronage, neoliberalism means little more than the sanctioning of corruption. Never before in its modern era had the Arab world experienced such a state of hopelessness caused by despotism, corruption, deprivation, growing poverty among the lower classes and rage on the part of middle classes, which felt increasingly threatened and precarious. This took place alongside the emergence of a consumerist society and lifestyle that ceaselessly created more needs and a widening gap between needs and the means of fulfilling them.

People had no need of social theories to see that there were many obstacles to organized action for regime change; however, the principal barrier was the oppressiveness of the security apparatus.

The popular revolution in Tunisia marked the end of a grim era in Arab history. More importantly, the Tunisian Revolution has shown the opportunities that come with a new era. Across the region, a new horizon has opened, and a spirit of hope has been revived.

Authoritarianism in the phase of decadence

Tunisia's modern history abounds in instances of popular protest over social and political issues. On 26 January 1969, the al-Wardanin uprising took place against the policy of collectivized agricultural land. On 10 October 1977, a protest movement erupted in Qasr Hilal, and on 26 January 1978, a general strike was announced by the General Tunisian Labor Union (UGTT). This popular protest was quelled so brutally that the day was infamously designated 'Black Thursday'. The bread uprising that flared on 3 January 1984 – the one most similar to the 2011 uprising-turned-revolution – was followed[2] in 2008 by the protracted uprising of the mining basin in Gafsa Governorate.

Tunisia's revolution was preceded by local uprisings with social demands that had been increasing in frequency over the previous five years, mostly in the country's interior, in the marginalized centre and southwest. The revolution itself started as a local uprising. This geographical division, which has historical roots, had been reinforced by government policies in modern Tunisia. Not only was there no affirmative action and development planning to close the gap, but the governments who came mostly from the coastal cities tended to favour the coastal areas for development and public allocations. Despite the unevenness of government policies throughout the country, numerous Tunisian cities and provinces joined the movement. Thanks to the perseverance and courage of the residents and political activists of Sidi Bouzid and Kasserine governorates and other peripheral provinces, the last of these uprisings lasted long enough for the cities, especially Sfax and the capital city of Tunis, to join in, along with a number of civil society activists, poor inner-city neighbourhoods and, towards the end, members of the middle classes.

For the citizens of Sidi Bouzid and Kasserine who took to the street, social demands were mixed with a sense of rage and affronted dignity, epitomized by the act of a young Tunisian man who set himself on fire in protest against the humiliation he had endured. The fact that urban areas joined in revealed the rage that had been building up in the poor peripheries of the capital. Similarly, it revealed the regime's growing isolation even from the social base of the marginalized ruling party, which could no longer provide this base with the privileges to which it had grown accustomed.

Self-immolation is the most powerful declaration of protest against injustice and helplessness. Hence, the movement began as an uprising that had been triggered not by poverty alone but by poverty and indignation. The will to restore dignity is founded upon a desire for freedom from degrading repression and for equal treatment as a human being. It was this combination of the rejection of deprivation and a repudiation of humiliation that led to such audacity.

To a large extent, the Tunisian Revolution began as a rebellion of the marginalized peripheries against the political and economic centre. It was then joined by political parties and elites who presented democracy as an alternative. Indeed, this structure of the revolution will determine the course of Tunisian politics for a long time to come.[3] Time will tell whether a democracy in a developing country can resolve

2. It is worth noting that almost all revolutions and uprisings in Tunisia have taken place during the month of January.

3. This book was drafted prior to Tunisia Constituent Assembly elections on 23 October 2011. The election results reinforce the argument that Tunisia's revolution constituted a

issues of social and interregional injustices in spite of scarcity, populism, competing political parties, protracted disagreements over social plans and growing expectations on the part of the public. This will be a major challenge for democrats.

Corruption was actually not a distinguishing feature of Arab republics' founding authoritarian rulers. The first generation of the leaders of independent Arab states was not corrupt. Nasser, Bourguiba, Ben Bella, Boumediene, Shukri al-Quwatli and Abd al-Karim Qasim were not known for their pursuit of wealth. Regardless of the faults of their reigns, greed and the desire to enrich themselves at the expense of the public were not among their failings. On the contrary, the ability to rise above such material ambitions was viewed as essential to the character of a great leader.

Meanwhile, in the absence of democracy and transparency, patriotic values are hollowed out, ideological legitimacy is tarnished and financial corruption reigns. Corruption has been bald-faced in recent years, with a majority of the business class forming close links with the likes of Mubarak (and his sons and his wife), Bashar al-Assad (and his brother, wife and cousins) and Ben Ali (and his wife and his in-laws). The events in Tunisia shed light on the impact corruption has on people. Arguably, blatant corruption has the potential to enrage people even more than poverty. People may even tolerate poverty if they believe that their situation is not the result of some injustice; however, patent, uninhibited and ostentatious corruption seems to confirm that poverty is, in fact, a direct consequence of discrimination and deliberate deprivation.

The symbol of corruption in Tunisia was the blatant manner in which the president, his wife's family and the network of businesspeople and politicians around them enriched themselves through their positions of power and privilege. This ostentation displayed a breach with the old public ethos and moral economy which the leadership of the previous ruling party had imprinted on public life. The Neo-Destour Party (renamed in 1964 the Socialist Destourian Party (PSD)) had been led by bureaucrats who mostly did not aim to enrich themselves. This old guard had been more concerned with power than money. Tunisian republican virtues under the despotic regime of Bourguiba revolved primarily around public interest (the insistence that the regime knew better than the people what was in their best interests) and promotion based on both merit and loyalty. So, in spite of the economic growth witnessed by the country under Ben Ali, the gap between rich and poor persisted, and as corruption manifested itself as the new form of enrichment, people grew increasingly prone to feelings of deprivation and injustice. In sum, the ethos of the prevailing sociopolitical and economic system plays a vital role in determining the likelihood of revolution.

Although not comparable to what the Syrian uprising faced from its inception, the Tunisian Revolution was met with severe repression at an undeniably heavy price. Once the protesters began to sense their strength and courage, it became

rebellion of the marginalized peripheries and expressed the provinces' rejection of the former regime and its dominant culture in the urban centres. Indeed, it went so far as to support the regime's political and cultural antithesis, Al Nahda Party.

clear that it would be impossible to put a stop to the revolutionary process without the brutal, consistent use of violence, including mass killings (the choice of Assad's regime in Syria).

Not every bread uprising, however, has the potential to become a revolution. The term 'bread uprising' is associated in the Arab collective memory with the Egyptian bread uprising of 1977, which, like most of its counterparts, did not develop into a revolution. This was also the case with yet another Tunisian bread uprising in 1984, which Bourguiba quelled at the cost of 143 dead and 400 injured.[4]

Tunisia is the classic example of a country that was susceptible to revolution. The protests that erupted on 17 December 2010 were the defining event that sparked the revolution and should be recognized in history as the starting point of the uprisings. One of the idiosyncrasies of the Tunisian case lies in the fact that, unlike in Egypt and other countries under revolt, the name of the revolution was derived not from the date of its outbreak but, rather, from that of Ben Ali's departure. The first revolutionaries in Sidi Bouzid may have felt that the general reluctance to call the revolution 'the December 17 revolution', referring to it instead as 'the January 14 revolution', simply epitomized the centre–periphery hierarchy. This assumption might indeed be correct. It should also be recalled, however, that the 'flight'[5] of the first Arab president was such a momentous, historic event that it prompted the population to inscribe that date in their collective memory. The departure of a dictator was the proof for many that this was, indeed, a revolution. Moreover, the stress on beginnings is not always well founded. In some cases, beginnings are understood retrospectively as if they would inevitably lead to the end point. In fact, however, many previous provincial uprisings had been more intense than that of Sidi Bouzid but without evolving into revolutions.

Susceptibility to revolution was particularly in evidence in the provinces that had demonstrated a refusal to continue living under existing conditions and a readiness to resist them. Once popular protests occur within a revolutionary setting, every response made by the state (other than consistent brutal force) contributes to their spread and increases the likelihood of their developing into a revolution. The development and spread of events show that Tunisia had become ripe for rejection of its status quo. This indignation was particularly felt by those who had been directly harmed by the absence of civil and political rights, discrimination and exploitation, and a crippled economy that lacked significant and sustainable development. Such people were becoming ever more outraged by

4. The army, though small, suppressed the uprising. Safwan M. Masri, *Tunisia: An Arab Anomaly* (New York: Columbia University Press, 2017), pp. xxvi–xxvii. Masri refers to Bourguiba's dictatorship as 'benevolent authoritarianism' which over time became less 'benevolent' and more 'authoritarian'. Actually, it was not really benevolent from the beginning, and his means of suppressing Salah ben Youssef and his supporters was no less violent than the methods he employed in 1984. Ibid., p. 23.

5. As will be explained later, Ben Ali's departure was not simply a flight as it was conceived by the people in every Arab country and elsewhere.

the monopoly enjoyed by a small clique of capitalists – often relatives, friends and partners of the regime – while the poor remained excluded.

Among the disgruntled were also those who had been harmed by the tourist and service economy, a sector that contributed to increasing the gross domestic product but developed and served only certain regions while impoverishing others. State economic policies had contributed to raising the price of real estate, which had done little to improve the well-being of most Tunisians or the general economy. In addition, the light industrial sector that exports its products to Europe lost its competitiveness when China joined the World Trade Organization in 2001, causing a decline in Tunisia's textile and garment industry and a sharp rise in unemployment.

Under such conditions, even the former regime's achievements began to regress. It would be wrong to undermine the achievements of Bourguiba and Ben Ali in the education sector, a fact that is clearly evident when comparing Tunisia's educational attainments to those of other Arab countries. However, Tunisia's educated population rapidly became a burden for the regime, which was unable to provide employment opportunities for emerging graduates at a time when citizens' expectations were on the rise.

Proportionate to the level of expectations is the level of disappointment, and with it comes an awareness that rejects injustice and corruption. Such awareness typically leads to a gap between the young, educated generation, which rejects the notion that a lack of rights is a natural fact of life, and the older generation, which seems to have made peace with it – whether this resignation is a result of despair or genuine conviction. In Tunisia, rebellion proliferated among the young generations in the marginalized peripheral provinces, rapidly engendering a sense of indignation and bitterness as young people questioned the gap between the centre and the periphery.

Such patterns, which exist to varying degrees in all Arab states, have been compounded by a youth bulge that is higher than the general population increase. When these factors are combined with weak economic growth, the outcome is an increase in unemployment due to the job market's inability to absorb both educated and non-educated job seekers. As a consequence of the ongoing economic policies in Arab societies and the consistent increase in the number of job-seeking youth, especially college graduates, instability is inevitable.

According to the following schedules, youth employment is lower in the Middle East and North Africa than in other regions in spite of the high percentage of youth in their populations (Table 1.1).

This does not mean that the revolutions in the Arab world have been exclusively youth revolutions, but that young people may become the primary social carrier of the protests. In some cases, young politicized activists (Egypt and Yemen) called for mass protests in the capital over which they had no control; in other cases, young activists in the provinces tried to politicize social rage locally, but the protests had only local leaders (Tunisia), although young activists did organize and lead the second stage of the revolution after the flight of Ben Ali.

The revolutionary condition is not a precondition for revolution but, rather, a condition that evolves as the revolution progresses. It is not a simple set of

Table 1.1 Youth Labour Force Participation Rate, by Region and Sex (2000, 2010 and 2015)

	Total (%)			Male (%)			Female (%)		
	2000	2010	2015	2000	2010	2015	2000	2010	2015
World	53.8	50.9	50.2	62.5	58.9	58.2	44.7	42.4	41.6
Developed Economies and European Union	53.1	50.2	50.2	55.9	52.6	52.5	50.3	47.7	47.9
Central and South-Eastern Europe (non-EU) and CIS	42.4	41.7	40.8	48.9	47.7	47.0	35.7	35.5	34.3
East Asia	67.2	59.2	56.9	65.8	57.0	55.0	68.7	61.6	59.2
South-East Asia and the Pacific	55.8	51.3	50.6	63.5	59.1	57.9	48.0	43.3	42.9
South Asia	48.0	46.5	46.3	66.1	64.3	64.0	28.5	27.3	27.2
Latin America and the Caribbean	54.2	52.1	51.4	66.5	61.3	59.3	41.7	42.7	43.5
Middle East	36.9	36.3	34.7	52.6	50.3	48.1	20.2	21.5	20.5
North Africa	39.4	37.9	36.5	53.4	52.5	50.2	25.1	22.9	22.3
Sub-Saharan Africa	57.8	57.5	57.4	64.1	62.7	62.1	51.4	52.2	52.7

Source: ILO, Economically Active Population Estimates and Projections, 5th Edition, revision 2009.

objective circumstances but a combination of concrete realities, political action and a sudden discovery of the possibility of regime change. This 'discovery' may take the form of an analytical outcome, or a simple insight that comes in response to the confusion of the regime and the concessions it begins to make, and/or the numbers of people who had never participated before in such activities but who find themselves joining in the protests.

Awareness of a potential for change goes beyond awareness of injustice; it implies a quest for a better reality and a belief in the realistic possibility of achieving this. Such awareness has now become widespread, albeit to different degrees, in most Arab states, since the window of hope opened by Tunisia and the gaping hole left in the defences of authoritarian Arab regimes by the Egyptian Revolution.

Despite the commonalities among authoritarian Arab states, especially republics, differences among them are also clear. Some allow the creation of parties, which may be nominal or infiltrated with regime loyalists and representatives of the security apparatus; others allow relative freedom of the press, although 'freedom' is perhaps not the most appropriate word to describe a system that has implanted the eyes and ears of its security and intelligence agencies throughout the media, even corrupting journalists. Journalism under despotism is not a true profession. Rather, it is either a mercenary pen for hire or a struggle in defence of integrity. Some regimes allow their citizenry some breathing room, while others stifle their populations, depriving them entirely of the public sphere. Some adopt a 'cause' or an ideological discourse that corresponds to the prevailing popular mood and national sentiment, but in so doing, they deny political liberties, whether the freedom of organization and assembly, or freedom of expression in the media. In cases where limited breathing room is allowed, the regime allows its people to obtain some 'training' in political, social and unionist activism, opening a steadily expanding margin for criticizing the regime. In these instances, the regime does not claim to represent an ideology and does not resort to criminalizing all forms of opposition; however, it does persecute the opposition, alternating between containment and, if certain limits are exceeded, punishment. In these cases, when a revolution erupts, it takes place against the backdrop of accumulated political experiences. Such revolutions also involve a political dialogue that presupposes a sophisticated level of awareness.

In cases where the regime keeps the population under tight control, no political, unionist or civic institutions are allowed to develop because the margin of criticism is highly restricted. Such regimes also tend to treat their opponents as traitors, depriving them of legitimacy and justifying the use of extreme violence against them. The political immaturity of the opposition and its repeated failures to engage in collective action become noticeable when revolutions break out in such countries.

It is these variations that determine, to a large extent, a country's revolutionary path. In those countries where a certain flexibility towards political activism, social participation and criticism is present, the chances of containing political activists are greater, but so also are the chances of revolt. From one demonstration to another and one arrest to another, some activists grow bolder and more weary of containment, and different forms of organization and protest emerge through trial and error, leading to demands for increased political rights and liberties.

In Tunisia, the regime was closest to the repressive end of the spectrum, being a police state where no margin of press freedom was allowed, although unionist action was somewhat tolerated within boundaries defined by the regime. A slight grey area was allowed for critical, non-parliamentary political parties, though these parties were under constant security supervision and control. The few licensed parties tolerated by the regime were allowed to gain a certain number of parliamentary seats in the elections; their representation rose from 9 per cent in 1994 to 25 per cent in 2009. Human rights, however, were constantly being violated by the security services, and the regime ignored criticisms by Tunisian and Western human rights organizations despite the long-lasting friendship between Ben Ali and Western states. Thus, third-party institutions had no way of mediating between the state and the people. In the decade before the revolution, the leadership of Tunisia's General Labor Union had been more or less accommodated by the state, even though throughout history its role had ranged from submission to opposition.

Bourguiba was a charismatic figure whose inflated narcissism bordered on megalomania. The central doctrine adopted by the ruling party during his tenure was one of national liberation, followed by modernization and nation-building. To Bourguiba, however, nation-building was primarily about the grooming and disciplining of a nation according to a secular, rational vision that he saw as the only cure for backwardness.

As for Ben Ali, democratic reforms were initially his alleged cause and source of legitimacy, especially after the repeated failure of democratic political currents that had emerged under Bourguiba's rule. However, following a rapid sidelining of democratic reform, Tunisia was left with a non-charismatic, authoritarian police state devoid of any political cause, which set Ben Ali's Tunisia (as well as Mubarak's Egypt and 'Ali Saleh's Yemen, though for different reasons) apart from other Arab dictatorships that had obtained their mass legitimacy by claiming to advance an ideological or national mission of some sort.

Ben Ali's rule was a colourless dictatorship that did not resonate with the mood on the streets or with public opinion. His despotism evolved from a promise of political reform and a limitation on presidential terms to the creation of a kleptocratic police state. He was oblivious to Arab causes, having established relations with Israel soon after the signing of the Oslo Accords in 1993. Ben Ali opposed the American war on Iraq, but he was affiliated with US and French policies, in general, despite anti-American rhetoric in the media, and with no ideological fig leaf apart from a pragmatism that focused on preserving the stability of the regime and a secularism that prompted many secular political forces and intellectuals to compromise with the regime despite its despotic nature.

Indeed, this dilemma continued to exist among many intellectuals and artists, who found themselves torn between despotism and fair elections. To them, free elections ran the risk of bringing to power Islamic movements that threatened their lifestyle and other achievements of the secular republic. As a result, many of these intellectuals ended up settling for despotism until the people rose up in revolution.

After the 1979 Iranian revolution, the Soviet occupation of Afghanistan (1979–89) and ongoing calls for jihad (especially in the 1990s after the Algerian elections, the Algerian civil war and the rise of Salafi Jihadism), despotic regimes competed to portray themselves as the bulwark preventing Islamists from coming to power. In Tunisia, this strategy was employed to curry the sympathy of Tunisian middle classes and garner support in the West. Ben Ali manipulated Western states by fostering the idea that any alternative to his regime would enable the Islamists to come to power. This strategy, which was adopted by the Tunisian, Egyptian, Jordanian, Saudi and Yemeni regimes (and later Syrian and Libyan regimes), was vindicated by the Islamists' victory in Algeria's 1991 elections following the democratic reforms that had been instituted by Chadli Bendjedid and the subsequent brutal civil war.

Where authoritarianism is concerned, the political polarization between the religious and the secular is but a fictive division. Secularism is not sufficient to define a political position, nor is it a ruling regime or a political current which advances a specific socio-economic policy. Broad segments of society, religious and secular alike, were harmed by Ben Ali's rule. In what might be termed 'a policy of double containment', the regime frequently warned against the Islamist threat in the hope of gaining the support of the West, the middle class and the country's educated sector while warding off international and internal criticisms. It should be remembered, of course, that both secular and religious movements may be against liberal democracy, although there are other reasons for many people to be wary of Islamist movements that plan to use state power to impose a particular way of life.

During an era that was witnessing a crisis of the left in the aftermath of the collapse of the Socialist Bloc, a number of leftists exchanged their political orientation for mere secularism as an ideological alternative to the rising Islamist opposition. In reality, the concept of secularism comprises both the left and the right, and the substitution of political ideals for secularism by some leftists did not put an end to political demands and sociopolitical struggles against the regime. Such struggles do not adhere to a line separating secularism from religiosity but follow other distinctions. The Tunisian Revolution was neither secularist nor religious, but this did not prevent some researchers from reading too much importance into the absence of so-called focal days as compared with other Arab revolutions which used such days to mobilize the masses. [6]

The movement towards change in the Arab region has become a movement against all authoritarian regimes in their various forms. By and large, these regimes

6. The Tunisian Revolution did not have focal days for mass mobilization, like the Fridays in the Egyptian Revolution. Ketchley and Barrie view such focal days as costly for the revolutionary movement because (1) on these focal days the revolutionary movement loses control over the mobilization process, and many sectors join from outside the organizer's

have commandeered citizens' rights and monopolized the sources of power by fusing politics with the economy and merging political influence with monetary gain, in some cases by fostering loyalty to the regime on the basis of primordial affiliations such as blood kinship, tribalism and regionalism (which can also overlap with sectarianism). The final product is a decrepit, authoritarian regime adorned with modern facades and slogans.

Arab republics have differed from monarchist states and conservative regimes by adopting an economy that bases itself on the public sector. Republics have also been distinguished by a ruling party ideology; some of them have adopted Arab nationalism and viewed the occupation of Palestine as a continuation of colonialism in the region. However, the divergences among different regime types began to lessen with the crisis of the public sector, the failure of import substitution economies, foreign debts and the financial hardships that led to state capitalism's adoption of privatization policies. Moreover, the collapse of the global bipolar superpower system has led these countries to follow the example set by Egypt and adopt a fully pragmatic strategy towards their relationship with the United States, including consenting to negotiations with Israel.

The ideological gap between the two types of Arab regimes has been narrowing for years. Arab nationalist regimes have proven to be nationalist only in discourse, with their Arab nationalism being restricted within the confines of their borders. The quest to preserve the stability of the regime merged with the ruler's desire to rule for life and transfer power to an heir, a fact that shaped the behaviour and the structure of the regime. At the same time, economic liberalization and adherence to the demands of the World Bank and the International Monetary Fund – modelled after the neoliberal principles known as the Washington Consensus (which has

sphere of influence, and (2) the movement cannot respond to the unfolding events during the week but, rather, must wait for the focal day to mobilize the masses.

The Tunisian Revolution did not revolve around particular focal days. However, there was no control over the protests, and the protesters did not emerge from the exclusive domain of an 'organizer' who, in the case of Tunisia, was not clearly identified. The authors allude to the participation of masses of people after the Friday prayer. But this has nothing to do with the character of the revolution, nor with the character of the 'organizer'. The fact that Fridays did not play a role in the Tunisian revolution does not turn the participants in the protests into a coalition of secularists and liberal democrats.

Ketchley and Barrie hold that the ability to mobilize sizable masses of a diverse 'negative coalition' of revolutionary contenders who are clearly against the regime does not necessarily mean that they agree on the alternative to the regime. This is a weak argument, as I do not believe protesters formed coalitions to take over the government. All the Arab revolutions have been a manifestation of 'negative coalitions', to use these authors' phrase. It was left to 'positive coalitions' of political forces from both the regime and the opposition to successfully reach (or fail to reach) a compromise. See Neil Ketchley & Christopher Barrie, 'Fridays of Revolution: Focal Days and Mass Protest in Egypt and Tunisia', *Political Research Quarterly*, vol. 73, no. 2 (2020), p. 322.

been revised in the meantime) – have also contributed to erasing the distinctions among different Arab regimes. Coupled with political authoritarianism, such economic liberalization has had the effect of effacing the differences among the economic systems in different Arab countries.

Economic liberalization under political despotism has aggravated the imbalances in the distribution of national income, concentrating it in the hands of a clique close to the regime and creating a form of capitalism composed of power and fortune-sharing among ruling elites and their relatives. Even in cases where growth rates have been accelerated and living standards have been raised, this formula has widened the gap between rich and poor and among different regions within each Arab country. Add to this humiliation by state agencies and a lack of freedom to criticize injustices, and you have the perfect backdrop for successive uprisings.

The social disruptions caused by the neoliberal socio-economic system led at first to cosmetic political reforms. However, these reforms were then quickly abandoned in favour of a renewed authoritarian rule in order to preserve the stability of the regime. Far from leading to democratization, privatization further entrenched authoritarianism. This selective economic liberalism, which has shown itself incapable of limiting exploitative practices or preventing monopolies, has served to eliminate competition and exacerbated the concentration of wealth in the hands of the select few in a manner that is decidedly unjust and undemocratic.

Ultimately, the outcome of this situation has been that the new bourgeoisie, the prime beneficiary of the authoritarian-style privatization and liberalization programmes, has made peace with political despotism, reinforcing its dynamic and adding a new weapon to its arsenal. The bourgeoisie's social proximity to the political and security regime meant they could openly lead their consumeristic lifestyle and flaunt the personal and social freedoms that had been handed to them in the guise of political reform.[7] Once the regime began sharing its gains with these groups – formerly critics of despotism – reconciliation with the regime proved easy. The liberal, consumeristic lifestyle afforded the new bourgeoisie under the spectre of authoritarianism was then labelled 'secularism' and even liberalism, whereas Bourguiba's republican understanding of secularism was much deeper, and he never claimed to be a liberal.

At the height of their decadence, growing sectors of Tunisia's bourgeoisie were ready to exchange secularism for a hedonistic lifestyle. Oddly, this same clique was untroubled by the fact that unlike Bourguiba, Ben Ali and some of his entourage presented a religious facade, endorsing religious preachers as long as they were pro-regime, while at the same time persecuting religious extremism in the deprived regions and poverty belts surrounding the cities. The fact that the educated, nouveau riche urban bourgeoisie had consolidated into a group of

7. This description also applies to Syria during the time of economic liberalism in the past ten years.

privileged political beneficiaries explains the trepidation that gripped this class as the revolts flared up.

Another social category that emerged in the postcolonial Arab era consisted of the sons of officials and businessmen, typically politicians, military officers and security personnel, who were keen to project a new high-class image in contrast to that of their parents. These individuals were typically immersed in the culture of consumerism that comes with a decadent lifestyle, while in the dungeons of their security forces, maltreatment and humiliation, in some cases torture, were commonplace practices. In contrast to the traditionally critical left-leaning artists and intellectuals, a cultural and entertainment sector arose around the urban culture industry, created through personal links with the rich and powerful. To those implicated in such relationships, this exchange constituted a kind of 'guaranteed enlightenment' which they believed would conceal the stench of despotism, corruption and the torture of opponents in prisons. Simultaneously, there emerged a group of intellectuals and thinkers whose sole job was to laud the regime's secularism, whether directly or indirectly, often presenting it as a pluralistic democratic regime perpetually engaged in the process of deepening democracy, reinforcing pluralism and strengthening freedom of the press.[8]

The logic justifying an alliance with despotism is the same one used when justifying colonialism. Some intellectuals have used the argument of 'enlightened despotism' to defend existing regimes against alternatives that adopt non-democratic populist ideologies, such as politicized religion. However, these individuals tend to forget that they are, in fact, defending a form of non-enlightened despotism that has lost even its modernizing historical function. This is neither the despotism of Nasser nor that of Bourguiba – keeping in mind the differences between these two regimes. Those arguing in favour of enlightened despotism address a society that has shed any illusions regarding these regimes, which no longer provide even the minimal conditions for citizens to fulfil the growing demands created by globalization and neoliberalism, still less the basic needs of the poor, whereas previous authoritarian regimes relied for their legitimacy on claims to be meeting the needs of the poor and on nationalist, anti-imperialist discourse (while simultaneously suppressing free expression).

Revolutionary change becomes more complex in states comprised of plural identity groups, some of which support the existing regime. In revolutionary scenarios, there is an imminent threat that an uprising could divide society vertically. In multi-identity states such as Syria and Iraq, reform needs to take place gradually, including efforts to mitigate the politicization of confessional and regional identities, and to embark on a peaceful transition of power with the

8. This type of literature exists in abundance in the Arabic language. A prominent example of this form of theorization in the English language, which is addressed to a Western audience and paints the image of a democratic pluralistic regime, can be found in Mohamed Nejib Hachana, 'Twenty Years of Change: Tunisia's Journey of Progress Continues', *Mediterranean Quarterly*, vol. 19, no. 2 (2008), pp. 1–4.

existing regime's participation. In such situations, the central question is: What should be done when the state rejects reform, approaching state and society as though they were the ruler's private domain and insisting on using identity politics as a means of mobilizing its supporters? This is a critical issue for political groups struggling to achieve democracy in states such as Syria, where the fragmentation of the political system may well lead to a civil war, political and sectarian radicalization and fragmentation of the political entity itself, transforming it to a battlefield between both local communities and foreign powers.[9]

The challenge here lies in founding democracy on the basis of equal citizenship and avoiding identity-driven conflict while, at the same time, taking representation of communities into consideration. In the Arab Levant, the illegitimacy of national borders due to colonized partition is compounded by the erosion of regimes' sources of legitimacy. The heterodoxy of politicized identities creates an ever-present threat that local adversaries might ally themselves with foreign powers. National institutions and identities are too weak to contain the social struggles within them. In heterogeneous societies ruled by an authoritarian regime that depends on social divisions, those leading the protest against the regime could find themselves struggling against large identity coalitions that identify with the regime. Conversely, Tunisian society is a relatively homogeneous society, in which class and political tensions do not manifest as conflict on the level of identity differences. Tunisian political factions, both secular and religious, deprive Tunisia of this advantage if they try to turn their contention into identity politics.[10]

In order for the people to dissociate themselves from the regime at the moment of a popular uprising without running the risk of cleavages among communities, there must be a national community of citizens that understands itself as a 'people', all of whose members are equal components of the state. This dissociation becomes possible when the concept of a national community develops into an imagined community to which the citizen feels a sense of belonging. As such, a democratic revolution is an instance of the people exercising their sovereignty. Any revolt that politically divides the people on the basis of identity is not a true revolution; at the very least, it is not a democratic one by this book's standards.

The same structure that allows people to rise up against the regime without the risk of fragmentation is what enables the state to distance itself from the regime without collapsing. In Tunisia and Egypt, this dynamic was evident once the main institution of the state, the army, refused to follow the regime's orders to open fire

9. This book was written before the Syrian Revolution turned into a civil war in which extremist Islamist groups dominated the armed opposition and marginalized the Free Syrian army.

10. The Tunisian people clearly expressed their rejection of this attempt during the election of the Constituent Assembly on 23 October 2011, when the people gave their vote to the religious and secular parties that called for reconciliation and tolerance, while rejecting those parties that thrived on turning tension between religious and secular groups into an identity conflict.

(in Tunisia, against a mutinying security force and against civilians, and in Egypt, against demonstrating civilians). This situation may not necessarily replicate itself in other Arab countries, where a revolution might require the crystallization of a non-sectarian national programme and where there is a search for mechanisms that can spare it having to resort to foreign intervention to quell the regime's violent repression. The most important elements of such a revolution are the oppositional elites' unity in support of a democratic national programme based on citizenship and respect for difference, and their ability to spark dissent among the elites who support the regime.

In the event that the army refuses to obey the regime's orders to suppress the revolution, the revolutionary movement will inevitably find itself, after the overthrow of the regime, faced with the dilemma of dealing with the army as a remnant of the former regime. This matter requires delicate handling in order to strike the correct balance between delaying the implementation of changes in the army itself until the democratic regime is well established, and maintaining popular pressure on the army in order to allow the democratic change to take place with the least amount of friction. Added to this is the lack of trust that is likely to develop among various political forces, a lack of consensus concerning the transition period, as well as widespread uncertainty regarding the respect for democratic rules, including questioning the commitment of others to the rules of the game. When this occurs, it often leads to the intervention of the army, which becomes dangerous if the military leadership harbours political ambitions.

The case of Tunisia is that of a centralized state with an established history. During Bourguiba's reign, it was difficult to distinguish the state from the regime (president and ruling party), as conflicts would arise among his subordinates, but never with, or about, Bourguiba himself. Bourguiba considered himself the founder of modern Tunisia as a nation-state on a republican model. However, the regime began to separate from the state towards the end of his rule as he grew old and frail. His prime minister, Ben Ali, ousted and succeeded him in accordance with the Constitution, and it was thus termed a constitutional coup.

On the other hand, Tunisians are now endowed with a heightened sense of national identity. Given its homogeneity, this Tunisian identity allowed for the spread of the uprising among provinces and regions, encouraging dynamic interactions and overcoming the traditional separation between the countryside and the city. Throughout Tunisia's modern history, Bedouin and peasants' uprisings had stopped at cities' borders. Indeed, the conflict between city and tribe was a major contradiction of the Ottoman era. The famous uprising of the tribes of Kasserine (1864) under Ali Ben Ghadhahum against the Bey rule in Tunis, referred to as *thawrat al-Aʿrāb* (revolution of the Bedouins), was not joined by city dwellers.[11]

11. Mouldi Lahmar, 'Collapse of Exchange Rates in a False Local Political Market' [Inhiyār Muʿaddalāt al-Tabādul fī Sūq Siyāsiyah Maḥalliyah Muzayyafah] in: Mouldi Lahmar (ed.), *The Tunisian Revolution: Examining the Triggers through the Prism of*

Tunisia has a sizeable, highly educated middle class which has the potential of playing an extremely significant role when it becomes aware of its needs and aspirations, including freedom, and realizes that it has few resources to fulfil them. Undoubtedly, the middle class seeks a political role for numerous reasons relating to its awareness, national consciousness and active participation in economic and social life. So, the expansion of the middle class spurs aspirations for broader political participation.[12] This was not an important factor in triggering the Tunisian Revolution. Nevertheless, it explains why such broad segments of the middle class joined it.

In 1997, I argued that the question pertaining to the system of rule (the regime) should be raised by politicized intellectuals in Arab countries.[13] In 2007, I further argued that at least a democratic political programme needed to be proposed against the regime and its intellectuals because it was obvious that Tunisia, of all Arab states, was, as Eva Bellin wrote, the one most prepared for democratic transition.[14] My argument was that Tunisian society would be prepared for democratic transition even according to the criteria of the theory of modernization. I do not hold that such criteria (i.e. economic development, industrialization, urbanization, the spread of education) are preconditions for a democratic transition; however, their importance for democratic consolidation cannot be denied.[15]

However, authoritarianism was consolidated and the regime fomented fears of an Islamist victory at the polls in order to deter the secular opposition from demanding democracy. The major factor, then, was the lack of will on the part of decision-makers. On the practical level, the Tunisian Revolution came as a surprise to everyone, including myself. Reform had lagged and the revolution had awaited the spark, which ultimately came from neither the middle class nor intellectuals.

Other writings questioned how stable Tunisia had been even before the revolution. In a 2009 article on the importance of Tunisia for Western anti-terrorism strategy and in its effort to preserve stability, the ability of the Tunisian state to maintain its own stability was questioned, especially after the Algerian experience, which had led to an armed struggle that threatened to spread beyond

the Humanities [Al-Thawrah at-Tūnisiyah: al-Qādiḥ al-Maḥallī Taḥt Mijhar al-ʿUlūm al-ʾInsāniyah] (Doha and Beirut: ACRPS, 2014), pp. 133–4. See also 'Introduction', p. 29.

12. See Gema Martin-Munoz, 'Political Reform and Social Change in the Maghreb', in: Álvaro Vasconselos & George Joffé (eds.), *The Barcelona Process* (London: Frank Cass Publishers, 2000), pp. 96–130.

13. Azmi Bishara, *al-Mujtamaʿ al-Madanī: Dirāsah Naqdiyyah [Civil Society: A Critical Study]* (Beirut: Center for Arab Unity Studies, 1998).

14. Eva Bellin, 'Civil Society: Effective Toll of Analysis for Middle East Politics?' *Political Science and Politics*, vol. 27, no. 3 (1994), pp. 509–10.

15. Azmi Bishara, *Fī al-Masʾalah al-ʿArabiyah: Muqaddimah li-Bayān Dīmuqrāṭī ʿArabī [On the Arab Question: A Preamble to a Democratic Arab Manifesto]*, 4th edn (Doha and Beirut: ACRPS, 2018 [2007]), p. 222.

its borders. While I did not dismiss the potential emergence of an armed Islamist current, I also discussed the possibility that the uprisings which have taken place in recent years in Georgia, Ukraine, Kyrgyzstan and Peru might replicate themselves. I concluded that change depends on the people of Tunisia, adding: 'Combining the repression of civil liberties with the collection of intelligence, imposed secularism, and semi-successful economic policies has thus far been a successful strategy for two Tunisian presidents. The question remains whether valid strategies of the past will remain valid in the constantly-changing post-Cold War world.'[16]

On the beginning of the revolution

This book's definition of revolution leads to a special interest in the transformation of successive acts of protests into a revolution that aims at regime change. No planning had taken place towards a revolution that would eventually overthrow the regime in Tunisia. In this sense, the revolution was spontaneous. Spontaneity after all applies to the greatest revolutions in history. The movement that led to the American Revolution was a constitutional movement demanding liberties which came out of a reformist interpretation of British Law, but it found itself turning into a revolution for independence from Great Britain, which in fact became a democratic revolution. Significantly, it was never originally planned as such. The American movement was spontaneous not because it lacked organization but because it was not organized as a revolution. Thus, Benjamin Franklin later wrote: 'I never heard in a conversation from any person, drunk or sober, the least expression of a wish for separation, or hint that such a thing would be advantageous for America.'[17]

The same applies to the French Revolution. The majority of the 1789 revolutionaries were royalists who did not seek to overthrow the king but sought a constitutional monarchy like that in England. However, as the republican movement grew, they were quick to deem monarchy a crime, especially after the king's attempt to flee. The revolutionaries began with a protest movement, an insurrection calling for specific demands. The movement ended up taking history and even itself by surprise by turning into a revolution that overturned the monarchist rule and rewrote the country's constitution several times in ten years. The French Revolution has since become the model of revolution in modern thought. However, evidence shows that the plan was not clear from the beginning.

In the same vein, the Tunisian Revolution was not planned as a revolution but evolved into one. This has also happened in countries such as the Philippines, where popular protests overthrew Ferdinand Marcos, ruler of the country from 1965 to 1986, and in Indonesia, where Suharto fell in 1998 after having ruled the

16. Alejandro Sanchez, 'Tunisia: Trading Freedom for Stability May Not Last – An International Security Perspective', *Defense Studies*, vol. 9, no. 1 (2009), pp. 85–92.

17. Quoted in Hannah Arendt, *On Revolution* (New York: Penguin, 1990 [1963]), pp. 44.

country for thirty years. Though there are certainly many differences between these cases, the resemblances between them are striking in terms of the nature of these regimes and the emergence of ruling families out of a protracted dictatorship, the role of security and corruption, and the rulers' political alliances with the West, specifically with the United States. Such parallels are even more evident when comparing the events in Tunisia and Egypt.

The popular response to Mohamed Bouazizi's self-immolation was organized by local political activists and relatives of the victim, and the transformation of these protests into a raging uprising was made possible by solidarity with the family of Bouazizi, who protested and did not keep silent, subsequent solidarity with Sidi Bouzid demonstrated by nearby districts, and planning and organization by local unionists and political activists; similar 'informal networks'[18] organized the mobilization in other districts. The fact that the organizers were not party leaders or known figures does not in and of itself mean that the acts of protest were merely spontaneous and improvised.

Unions, civil and human rights groups, activists from various political movements and student unions joined the protests. This process began provincially among the active and radical bases and then began to expand as the uprising spread, and union leaders and party organizations in several provinces found themselves trailing behind their own members who had joined the protests before them. The uprising lacked a recognizable political leadership, but this did not prevent political parties from using the revolution to advance the cause of democratic change. From the very beginning, actions included demonstrations and sit-ins during the day and intifada-like clashes with the security forces at night. Both patterns spread to other governorates, including the capital.

Revolution takes a country from ordinary time into a different temporal mode. In demonstrating this theory, Albert Einstein offered the example of a young man who leaves earth at the speed of light, returning minutes later, still a young man, only to discover that his peers have all aged in his absence. Similarly, during revolutionary temporality, events that usually take years occur in short spans of time; as such, Tunisians rode into the future at the speed of light, as it were. As events accelerated in Tunisia, the collective concept of time was altered. The president fled in a hurry, leaving behind him an upside-down pyramidal structure; in regimes such as his, the power pyramid rests on its head, so that when the head takes flight, the pyramid begins to sway and eventually falls. In institutionalized states, by contrast, the regime may collapse, but state institutions hold. This phenomenon becomes clearer through a comparison of Tunisia with neighbouring Libya after the fall

18. See Katia Pilati et al., 'Between Organization and Spontaneity of Protests: the 2010–2011 Tunisian and Egyptian Uprisings', *Social Movement Studies,* vol. 18, no. 4 (2019), p. 477. The main conclusion of this article is that 'organizations in repressive contexts become mobilizing structures by largely overlapping with informal ties'. The protests that erupted in December 2010 and January 2011 were coordinated by emerging and overlapping informal networks.

of the dictators in both countries. According to some international estimates, the security services consisted of 130,000–150,000 agents (1.3–1.5 security agents per 100 citizens).[19] Media reports estimated the security forces to number from 150,000 to 200,000.[20] However, ministry declarations tell that those numbers are exaggerated. The number of security forces that is closer to its estimation range between 40,000 and 80,000, with about half of them being part-time augmentation forces or paid informants.[21] Anyway, they could undoubtedly have fought valiantly in defence of the regime, which is what the president, who thought himself to be leaving only temporarily, expected them to do.

In spite of their evident superiority compared to the smaller and poorly equipped national army, the security services collapsed due to the loss of their internal coherence once the president had left the country on 14 January. Ben Ali fled amid an unstoppable popular uprising, and thus every security agent found himself alone, facing his fate unaided. Whereas the president could abandon the country for safety, the situation faced by the security agents who remained loyal to him was quite the opposite.

An institutionalized system such as Tunisia's keeps functioning as a state even when the leader is absent. The prime ministers of the era of independence, such as al-Bahi Ladgham, Hédi Amara Nouira and even to a certain extent Mohammed Mzali, were prominent politicians and party leaders. In the Ben Ali era, however, the prime minister became a mere functionary, a civil servant at best. In a relatively modernized state, professional, committed employees tend to be more responsible than their political leadership.

In less than twenty-four hours, the Constitutional Council re-appointed Mohammed Ghannouchi as prime minister in an interim cabinet tasked with

19. Michele Penner Angrist, 'Understanding the Success of Mass Civic Protest in Tunisia', *The Middle East Journal*, vol. 67, no. 4 (Autumn 2013), p. 550.

20. Fadhel Kaboub, 'The Making of the Tunisian Revolution', in: Ishac Diwan (ed.), *Understanding The Political Economy Of The Arab Uprisings* (Singapore: Economic Research Forum, 2014), p. 61, quoting from: Steffen Erdle, 'Tunisia: Economic and Political Restoration', in: Volker Perthes, *Arab Elites: Negotiating the Politics of Change* (Boulder, CO: Lynne Rienner Publishers, 2004), p. 214.

21. Querine Hanlon conducted interviews to conclude that 'the higher figure accords with the ministry payroll. According to Mohammad Lazhar Akremi, the minister delegate to the minister of interior in charge of reforms under the previous transitional government, internal security forces (police, National Guard, and civil defence forces) numbered 49,000 before the overthrow of the Ben Ali regime. The police subsequently recruited an additional 12,000 forces, bringing the total to 61,000. New recruits were needed to inject new untainted officers into the force, to manage the rise in crime and trafficking, and to replace the forces that disappeared after the fall of the regime. However, the training program for these new recruits has not been reformed.' Querine Hanlon, 'Security Sector Reform in Tunisia A Year after the Jasmine Revolution', *Special Report 304*, United States Institute of Peace (March 2012), p. 6.

managing the country until elections could be held. Due to the intense public legal debate at the time, all Arab countries became aware of Articles 56 and 57 of the Tunisian Constitution[22] and their differences. Informally, Tunisian citizens became a self-proclaimed legal expert. This rational constitutional debate provided the conditions for the birth of a new, citizen-based public space in which the population participated in the shaping of their present and future.

Some cities, especially those on the coasts, endured riots, looting, and aggression by unidentified armed groups and chaotic security management. The country witnessed a wave of thefts and attacks that targeted commercial establishments and public administration buildings in the capital and other major cities. Hundreds were arrested. However, in the span of four days, between 14 January, when the president fled, and 19 January, a new historical period was ushered in, while revolutionary hopes began to burgeon in other Arab countries. The transitional phase was nonetheless managed by the technocrats of the Ben Ali regime, including Prime Minister Ghannouchi, though he was a civil servant with less of an ideological bent than other members of the regime. Essebsi and Mebazaa had complete political and ideological allegiance to Bourguiba. Consequently, they had to weigh their liberal positions against their loyalty to the party, and ended up assuming security and ministerial positions under Bourguiba, including that of the interior minister. In spite of all this they played an important role in the transition period. It started with the realization that what had happened in the country was indeed a revolution, and when they were tempted to forget, they were reminded by demonstrations of young people demanding an acceleration in the reforms.

The opposition parties' stances ranged from viewing the interim cabinet as an achievement or necessary stage, and rejection of the presence of representatives

22. Article 56 of the 1959 Constitution with Amendments through 2008 states, 'In case of temporary disability, the President may, by decree, delegate his powers to the Prime Minister, to the exclusion of the power of dissolving the Chamber of Deputies. During such temporary disability of the President of the Republic, the government shall remain in place until the end of that disability, even if it is subject to a motion of censure. The President of the Republic shall inform the President of the Chamber of Deputies and the President of the Chamber of Advisors regarding such a temporary delegation of his powers.'

Article 57 states, 'Should the office of President of the Republic become vacant because of death, resignation, or absolute disability, the Constitutional Council shall meet without delay and certify the vacancy by an absolute majority of its members. It shall issue a declaration to this effect to the President of the Chamber of Advisors and to the President of the Chamber of Deputies, who shall immediately be vested with the functions of interim president of the Republic for a period of 45 to 60 days. If the definitive vacancy coincides with the dissolution of the Chamber of Deputies, the President of the Chamber of Advisors shall be vested with the functions of interim president of the Republic for the same period.' See 'Tunisia's Constitution of 1959 with Amendments through 2008', *Constitute Project,* accessed at: https://bit.ly/2KSPhZU.

of the former ruling party in government ranks. In any case, this debate took place in a civilized manner, without the use of violence. The protests continued until Ghannouchi's cabinet was disbanded and replaced by that of Essebsi. For each step the ruling establishment took back, the popular movement took a step forward, and each concession forced upon the regime was an achievement for the revolution. The fact that the popular movement did not rest after the attainment of a specific demand, but always called for further ones, should not conceal the fact that these concessions represented real achievements. It became clear that contrary to claims made by radical supporters of the revolution, figures from the old regime who managed state institutions after the revolution did not represent counter-revolution,[23] but rather played a significant, even indispensable, role in facilitating democratic reforms.

Initially, most political parties had no confidence in the revolution's triumph, let alone its longevity. Accustomed to short-term political visions under what seemed to be a 'stable' despotic regime, each accomplishment appeared sufficient in the eyes of these traditional parties. In truth, Ben Ali's third speech, on the eve of his departure, offered real concessions that, by the standards of any political party engaged in struggle, were like a dream come true. The tragedy of some parties, including some that effectively opposed the regime, was the fact that they were not in sync with the tempo of the revolution, and were unable to keep pace with the people's ongoing demands, nor were they aware of the exhaustion of the internal security services.

Despite the absence of political parties from the protests, the long years of party activism and the work of the UGTT and other unions and associations, especially human rights organizations, had left their mark on Tunisians' political consciousness. The discourse and forms of protest that emerged during the revolution revealed accumulated experience, a legacy of struggle, and an active memory of protest that had remained within the collective culture. These elements undeniably influenced the choices made during the revolution, the distinctions drawn between what was possible and what was not, the rejection of injustice, and the politicized language and behaviour adopted by the people.

Meanwhile, in a single session, the interim government under the moderate civil servant Ghannouchi issued a number of decisions that would have taken years in other states.[24] After Ben Ali's departure, the first meeting of the interim cabinet

23. See, for example, Muhamad Mukhtar Vilali & at-Taher ben Yousef, *Al-Qiwā al-Muḍāddah lil-Thawrah fī Tūnis [Counter Revolutionary Forces in Tunisia]* (Tunis: Fann at-Ṭibāʿah, 2013), pp. 47, 57.

24. This is what was meant by reformist revolution. Revolutionaries did not seek to seize power, and there was no such organized revolutionary leadership. The state reformed itself to make transition possible and to facilitate fair elections. In this sense the model suggested by Charles Tilly extrapolated from European revolutions does not take into consideration the possibility of reformist revolution, the prospects of which are clear in the Tunisian case. See Charles Tilly, *European Revolutions: 1492-1992* (London: Blackwell, 1993), p. 14.

took place on 19 January 2011 and was headed by Ghannouchi. The session was held after the resignation of four ministers representing the UGTT, and after the Democratic Forum party announced that it was also withdrawing its ministers. Prior to the session, Prime Minister Ghannouchi and interim president Fouad Mebazaa had agreed to resign from the Democratic Constitutional Rally (RCD) Party. In this one session, a general pardon was declared for political prisoners, banned parties were legalized, the state was declared separate from political parties and the assets of the ruling RCD Party were seized. On 6 February, Interior Minister Rajhi announced that all RCD Party activities would be banned in order to 'prevent the deterioration of the security situation in the country'.[25]

On 24 March 2011 the Tunisian Court of Appeals delayed a ruling on a challenge to a court decision that had ordered the disbanding of the RCD Party and the liquidation of its assets and funds. This decision was made following the request of the defence panel of the former ruling party, whose main headquarters in central Tunis had become one of the first symbolic targets of the revolution. On 15 April 2011, the Tunis Court issued a ruling disbanding the party and liquidating all its properties on the basis of the lawsuit filed against it by Interior Minister Farhat Rajhi. Rajhi had previously issued a decision suspending all RCD activities 'out of absolute necessity, to prevent the collapse of public order and to protect the supreme interests of the country'.

These cabinet decisions, historic events by any measure, constituted the second major accomplishment of the revolution after the overthrow of Ben Ali. The third achievement was the subsequent disbanding of the cabinet that had made these decisions, thereby acting from within the ruling system. The revolution forced the ruling establishment to enact policies that are typically made by newly created revolutionary institutions, without a revolutionary party or an armed group having had to occupy the government. It thus also forced the system to enact important reforms (by cabinets run by a combination of figures of the fallen regime and political figures from the historical opposition) even before new institutions were elected. This process was also replicated in Egypt. An Arab revolutionary pattern was thus established, whereby the people attempted to overthrow the regime from the outside and forced it to launch a transition. These were both reformist revolutions, as the transition was launched by the regime (though in Egypt, the transition was aborted by a military coup).

Entire segments of Tunisian society were mobilized in a manner characteristic of great revolutions, and Tunisia's own revolution will doubtlessly be remembered for this. Small uprisings erupted in individual neighbourhoods, districts and institutions. Similarly, popular committees sprang up to protect the neighbourhoods during the chaos and confusion through which the country was passing with the collapse of the security apparatus and the occurrence of looting and other acts of sabotage. Journalists rebelled, ousting the management in a number of media

25. See 'Tunisia: The Banning of the Party of Former President Ben Ali', *BBC Arabic*, 7 February 2011, accessed on 22 November 2020, at: https://bbc.in/3nNiXFv.

channels and taking over the administration of the channels themselves. Tunisian media became the site of ongoing debate among citizens, politicians and elites about Tunisia's past and future and the demands of the revolution. The monopoly of official and loyal private media was broken. A glance at the Tunisian television channels in the weeks following the revolution revealed a dynamic civil society in action, with a lively public space that encouraged communication and rational debate among the citizenry. Since these channels were undoubtedly still part of the ruling establishment, of course, some of them spread false rumours during the difficult times after the revolution, while some who had never voiced a critical word began criticizing everything in a nihilist manner that sowed confusion and distrust in democracy.

Throughout the course of the revolution, no acts of revenge took place, not even on the margins of the movement, which saw the participation of broad segments of the population. In the last few days preceding the fall of the regime on 14 January 2011, there were attacks on the residences of members of the Trabelsi family, Ben Ali's in-laws, police stations and local branches of the RCD Party. However, the few cases of violence were quickly contained, leading to still better discipline and organization among the revolutionaries and enabling the state to regain its power to enforce order in a relatively short time.

After Ben Ali's flight, Tunisians were quick to question the legitimacy of the regime as a whole. Hence, the revolutionaries demanded the departure of the entire ruling regime, not merely the president, realizing that the ruling party must be prevented from regaining control over the country. They did not, however, attempt to eradicate the former ruling elite root and branch. Attempts to completely eradicate ruling parties do not necessarily lead to democracy, as the Iraqi experience of de-Baathification testifies. Instead, they led to the disenfranchisement of many citizens who had joined the party, the police or the army for different reasons, the vast majority of them merely citizens who wanted to live in peace and who thought they are serving their country and had committed no crime.

Nevertheless, even after its disbanding, there remained the risk that the RCD Party could continue to spread its ideas with its redistribution across the different parties. This also applied to the former ruling National Democratic Party in Egypt. Once a party loses control over the state and its functions, a control that had empowered it with an unfair advantage, there would theoretically be no need to prevent its members from entering the political competition. On the other hand, security services must be prevented from harbouring loyalties towards the former ruling party and members of the former regime. In Tunisia, the tolerance went as far as allowing segments of the old ruling party who had not committed themselves to democracy and praise the old regime and even run for election, which was a dangerous undertaking indeed.

Being complex socio-historical processes, transitional periods are rarely marked by clarity or predictability, and no revolution is simply a leap from evil to good. The overall direction of change should nonetheless be clear, and the overriding aim should be the gradual deconstruction of the old regime. At the same time, the ruling elite is not to be entirely discarded. In fact, elements from this class can usefully be integrated in the process of dismantling once their influence begins to wane and new elites come to the fore. It should be noted that this typically opens a window for opportunists, including former supporters of the regime and its prime beneficiaries, as well as those who have cooperated with the security services. This phenomenon of opportunism is natural and should not cause concern. Opportunists always side with the victor; otherwise, victors would not be victorious, and opportunists would not be opportunists.

Chaos, on the other hand, is a cause for concern in any society and is generally the pretext used by conservative propagandists to stave off change. At the same time, some degree of chaos is inevitable during any post-revolution transitional phase, until influential political leaders representing major forces agree on new rules for the political game. News media which are not accustomed to free expression may actually magnify the chaos, a process which may be purposefully exploited by counter-revolutionary forces.

In the process of establishing democracy, we need a clear understanding of the purpose of the transitional phase. In the revolution phase, no concessions should be made as to the need to overthrow the despotic regime and to establish a new one. As the transition to democracy begins, however, the ability to make concessions is essential.

In democratic transition, the political players include those that were banned under the former regime but have now been formally recognized and elements from the former regime itself. It is vital to establish a consensus among the different factions on the rules of the political game. Those allowed to enter electoral competition are those who approve the rules and structure of the new system. Thus, a constitutional assembly may be needed. What is important is that the rules of democracy remain a matter of agreement among the conflicting and competing factions.

Every party that wishes to participate in the political process must acknowledge the aims of the revolution. Unlike the freedom once ballyhooed by the dictatorship, the freedom fostered by a democracy is tangible and manifested in the form of citizens' political and civil rights. Any questioning of these rights under ideological pretences is precluded. Furthermore, democracy is not just the rule of the majority. Rather, it is the rule of the majority according to democratic principles and legal rights, often obtained through popular struggles. Just as democracy was not invented by the Arab revolutions but was adopted as a popular demand against despotic regimes, so too were the successive declarations of human and citizens' rights, beginning with the French Revolution and continuing with the Universal Declaration of Human Rights adopted by the United Nations.

Overall, Tunisians are undergoing a remarkable experience – the experience of freedom. This is a period that has prompted individuals to rise above short-sightedness and personal interest – in which the public space has filled with individuals fully aware of their responsibilities as citizens. This is the moment of citizenship in Tunisia that encompasses even members of the police and the army, and that will lead Tunisia to become the first Arab civic state.

Some find it difficult to fathom the idea that Arabs could launch a popular democratic revolution; they stress the specificity of the Tunisian case, arguing that it is not likely to be replicated. Some attribute the success of Tunisia's revolution to its geographical or cultural proximity to Europe, for example.[26] Let it not be forgotten that the Tunisian intellectuals, activists and revolutionaries who filled the region's airwaves during the revolution spoke in fluent Arabic; moreover, they used an educated, politicized language which clearly demonstrated the influence of decades of opposition and activism, and which indicated no contradiction between Tunisian specificity and broader Arab causes, or between Tunisian national identity and Arab identity.

Furthermore, the democratic model is everywhere, and through it, Tunisia can be an inspiration to other states, be they Arab or non-Arab. Tunisia's sympathy with broader Arab causes is evident in its culture and language, its hosting of the Palestine Liberation Organization (PLO) after the outbreak of the war in Lebanon and its hosting of the Arab League when the Arab countries decided to move their headquarters from Cairo to Tunisia after suspending Egypt from the League in the wake of Anwar Sadat's peace agreement with Israel. Further, Tunisia's Arab identity was important in deciding the popular vote for Kais Saied against his opponent Nabil Qaroui in October 2019.

Besides, why does Tunisia have to be Arab in order to be a model for Arab countries? After all, Arab democrats have looked for inspiration to many countries in southern Europe, South America and Asia. Of course, Tunisia's success in overthrowing a dictator left a deeper impact on the Arab people than it would have had it been a non-Arab country, so we cannot ignore the matter of national identity, just as we cannot ignore the impact of the Libyan factor and international intervention there when we discuss the timing of the Syrian Revolution, for example. The decisive factors that distinguished Tunisian transition experience from the Egyptian failing transition are (1) the political culture of elites, Islamists and Secularists, concerning readiness to bargain and to compromise; (2) the political ambitions of the Egyptian army as compared with the Tunisian army's lack thereof; and (3) the greater impact of external factors in Egypt than in Tunisia due to Egypt's geostrategic importance. Other factors may be added, but the combination of Mediterranean orientation and Francophone culture is not one of them. On the contrary, it has been claimed by democracy theorists that former French colonies are less susceptive to democracy than British ex-colonies.[27] This is of course wrong, and the Tunisia–Egypt comparison supports the rebuttal of this hypothesis.

Bourguiba's pro-Western approach was explicit from the beginning of his leadership and was so radical that his Western interlocutors were often astonished

26. Masri, *Tunisia*, p. 10.

27. Seymour Martin Lipset, Kyoung-Ryung Seong & John Charles Torres, 'A Comparative Analysis of the Social Requisites of Democracy', *International Social Science Journal*, vol. 45, no. 2 (1993), pp. 159–60.

by his 'French identity'. Describing the late Tunisian president, US diplomat Robert Murphy said: 'I have never met, outside of France, a man who was more French than Bourguiba; and in the Arab world, I have never met an Arab who was less of an Arabist.'[28] In an interview with *Le Monde* on 10 July 1954, Bourguiba stated: 'It is in France's interest to accept negotiations with a party and with modern secular men who were formed by France and who take inspiration for their ideas from France's genius and culture, and from the principles that France has taught them.'[29] Even Bourguiba's trade union policies, amidst the conflict between the two poles of the Cold War, were pro-United States. For instance, in March 1951, he instructed Farhat Hached to abstain from joining the pro-Communist World Federation of Trade Unions and to be affiliated instead with the rival International Confederation of Free Trade Unions.

The landing of allied troops on North Africa's shores in November 1942, in addition to the swift establishment of US military bases in Morocco, revealed the United States' recognition of the strategic importance of North Africa for peace and security in Europe. As a result, Bourguiba staked his chances on this importance in the eyes of the United States as a means of confronting the Communist tide. In a letter to Farhat Hached, he wrote,

> Amid the undeniable conflict that is raging between the Anglo-Saxon world and the Bolshevik East, each party attempts to hold the cards of the game. North Africa is one of those winning cards in the eyes of the Anglo-Saxons, for it is the key to the Mediterranean and the ideal base facing a Europe that is heading towards Bolshevization.[30]

Bourguiba's personnel largely shared his pro-Western outlook, especially Ben Naji Salem and Hédi Amara Nouira. Beji Caid Essebsi recounts that, during a visit by US vice president Hubert Humphrey to Tunisia, a petition was published and signed by a large number of intellectuals calling for peace in Vietnam, denouncing the US bombardment and demanding acknowledgement of the Vietcong as the legitimate representative of the Vietnamese. This initiative did not arouse great embarrassment within the US delegation, but it enraged Bourguiba, who sided fully with the United States in its war on Vietnam. Bourguiba's Western preferences were thus borne out of personal ideological conviction.

Since Bourguiba's reign, Tunisian establishments have sought to minimize Arab and Islamic distinctiveness. Nevertheless, the state's policies in this regard have prompted large sections of the population to cling all the more tightly to

28. ʿUmayra ʿAlya al-Sghayyar, *al-Yūsifiyyūn wa-Taḥrīr al-Maghrib [The Yusufis and the Liberation of the Arab Maghreb]* (Tunis: al-Maghāribah lil-Ṭibāʿah, 2007), p. 72.

29. Ibid., 73.

30. Beji Caid Essebsi, *al-Ḥabīb Burqība.. al-Muhimm wal-Ahamm [Habib Bourguiba: The Important and the Most Important]*, Muḥammad Maʿālī (trans.) (Tunis: Dār al-Janūb lil-Nashr, 2011), p. 27.

their Arab and Muslim identities. This tendency has been reinforced by recent revisions and reappraisals in the domain of modern Arab thought, which has reconstructed itself as a space for diversity rather than homogeneity, and where Arab, national or regional identities have become part of a comprehensive construction of multilayered identity. While early Arab nationalists viewed the regional Arab state as devoid of legitimacy, it is now perceived as a necessary, legitimate component of Arab integration, where an Arab sense of belonging does not contradict the specific national identities of Arab states but, rather, assimilates them and enriches itself with their diversity. This is reminiscent of the argument used by Arab nationalist thinker Abū Khaldūn Sāṭiʿ al-Ḥuṣarī in his debate with Egyptian thinker Ṭaha Ḥusayn, when he stressed that Arab nationalism does not negate Egyptian identity; rather, it recognizes another dimension of it. Indeed, a strong nation-state is best equipped to regulate the conflicts that take place within it, whereas a regime that allows no distinction between loyalty to the ruler and loyalty to the state turns opposition into either treason or civil war.

In spite of his famed megalomania, Bourguiba succeeded in building nation-state institutions whose legitimacy was not subject to question and the existence of which is a precondition for democratic transition.[31]

Significantly, the thinkers who ask people to choose between their local causes and their Arab identities are the same people who tell those suffering under the yoke of repressive regimes to choose between submitting to despotism and accepting foreign intervention as the path to democracy. These efforts have failed miserably. In Tunisia, a popular revolution was able to succeed without foreign intervention. In reality, the revolution took the superpowers, which were allies of the former regime, by surprise, provoking confusion among the states that portray themselves as the 'guardians' of democracy around the world.[32]

Those who based their slogans on the Arab cause, and later attempted to impose them on specific Arab states without linking them to local agendas, marginalized the issue of democracy, neglecting people's local concerns and the unique features of the country concerned. Likewise, failure was the lot of those who saw a contradiction between their commitment to the causes of their country and the country's Arab identity. The revolution was made a success by people who wanted to be rid of despotism and who, holding simultaneously to their Tunisian, Arab and Muslim identities, raised their voices against both colonialism in Palestine and imperialist policies in the region as a whole. In the phase of transition to democracy, internal affairs prevail and political forces put forward competing claims to represent the interests of the state and the welfare of local society; this

31. See Dankwart A. Rustow, 'Transitions to Democracy: Toward a Dynamic Model', *Comparative Politics*, vol. 2, no. 3 (1970), pp. 337–63.

32. In the case of weaker national states such as Iraq, Syria and Lebanon, this is difficult to achieve. In these countries, it has been easy to employ foreign powers against domestic rivals. Conflict overrides state national sentiments, and it becomes difficult to view the state as a neutral party, leading to its marginalization or even its destruction.

is a process which inevitably impacts public discourse and identity, especially the affiliations in terms of which people define themselves.

The desire to be free from tyranny has not led to calls for foreign intervention and the violation of national sovereignty. On the contrary, it is attempts to maintain despotism that most often require foreign intervention. This is the reason Arabs throughout the Arab world identified with the Tunisian Revolution as if it were theirs, asking themselves when they could hope for change in their own countries. The Arab revolutions have revealed both the differences and the similarities in the structures of Arab societies, thereby facilitating mutual influences and creating a shared Arab sentiment that has generated solidarity, sympathy and emulation.

The desire for revolution intensified as young Arab men in several countries replicated the act of Mohamed Bouazizi by setting themselves on fire to protest prevailing conditions. Aside from the deeper significance of these acts, which clearly manifested rage, the desire to shock, the dire need for change and the emotional identification of Arabs with events in other Arab countries, this phenomenon showed that the media had promoted a superficial and naive interpretation of the Tunisian Revolution, attributing its cause to nothing but the self-immolation of a young man.

Revolution is born out of countless causes, but one young man's self-immolation is not one of them. When conditions are not ripe, revolution will not take place even if many men set themselves on fire. Mohamed Bouazizi could easily have remained another nameless young man who took his own life had the uprising in Sidi Bouzid not taken place. Similarly, the very uprising of Sidi Bouzid could have remained a local affair of the sort that has frequently flared up and died down once quelled by the regime through the pacification of local leaderships. Even a more prolonged uprising might have remained a demand-based bread uprising, which would eventually have been appeased by the regime through concessions or repressive methods.

An event such as the self-immolation of Bouazizi was simply the final event that sparked a chain reaction. The same could be said about the circumstances of the outbreak of Syria's uprising in Daraa on 18 March 2011. The arrest and torture of detained children could have passed without a popular uprising, and the Daraa revolt itself could have been stifled without spreading to other parts of Syria.

The ever-expanding uprisings, their inclusiveness and durability, evinced the desire for change among different sectors of society for reasons at once social, economic and political. The confused nature of the regime's response then turned a provincial uprising into the starting point of a popular revolution with political demands. This same dynamic manifests itself in other Arab countries in different forms, though it may be hampered by factors that did not exist in the Tunisian case. However, the suitable context, that is the popular Arab desire for change, is present elsewhere. Hence, the next decade is likely to be the decade of the 'Tunisization' of Arabs and of increased awareness of the need for freedom and change. While history does not repeat itself, the current Arab situation is, in many ways, similar to the national European revolutions of 1830–48 and the manner in which they spread in environments that had an appetite for democratic change.

Why is it usually difficult for a regime and its analysts to identify a revolution in the making? In its nascent hours, a revolution is similar to any other act of protest, demonstration or uprising; a revolution does not become a revolution based solely on its beginnings. The Tunisian regime's reaction of utter surprise remains difficult to explain. Was it due to the reassuring reports coming from its security services, who believed themselves to be capable of controlling everything? Was the regime blinded by its false sense of popularity? Was it the sense of megalomania that power and authority instil in rulers, preventing them from seeing the fragility of their rule (remember that Western economists and politicians had praised the Tunisian economy as 'the Tunisian miracle')? When the revolutionary condition takes over and when ordinary events become extraordinary, surprise and even shock take hold. Ordinary events become extraordinary in times of revolution because individuals no longer act as individuals, or even as groups of individuals, but as 'a people' (*sha'b*). Revolution is a state of popular activity in which the term 'people' shifts from being an abstract term to being a tangible reality. Security services, true to form, provide reports claiming that 'things are under control'. At this point, opinion tends to be divided over the question of whether force should be used or whether the protests should be ignored or treated with laxity, restricting arrests to the main organizers. Suddenly, the security agencies discover that there are no organizers, or rather that organizers exist but no organization, and that few of them are familiar faces from the opposition.

Once violence is used haphazardly, as a mere reaction to events, it quickly proves counterproductive, increasing the persistence, solidarity and spread of the revolution; protesters even exaggerate the numbers of the dead in order to mobilize domestic and international sympathy, with the ruler portrayed as a murderer of innocent civilians. When laxity is employed, on the other hand, such 'tolerance' encourages the protesters to persist, since they stop fearing the consequences. At this point, the regime's leader delivers an angry speech threatening protesters, which does nothing but incite more demonstrations. When advisers advance the diagnosis that the protests are a result of dissatisfaction with socio-economic conditions, the leader comes out anew, promising to fulfil some of the social demands being made. The pro-regime media is likely to applaud these 'grants' offered by the regime, which pretends to sense, like the people, the need for change. These media figures, experts and political analysts are also likely to attack the opposition, accusing it of exploiting the honest popular desire for change and of politicizing the legitimate demands of the people. However, protests continue to grow and spread, which then prompts the same advisors to argue that the regime's concessions were interpreted by the masses as a sign of weakness. After these concessions, even some elements within the regime lose confidence and start to calculate what price they would pay were the regime to fall. Here, the regime becomes implicated in a process of systematic repression, and blood is spilled. The revolution reaches a point where it can only be impeded by the use of massive force. It was at this stage, on what became the last day of the Tunisian

Revolution, that some security mutinied as they faced the possibility of shooting at mass demonstrations surrounding the Interior Ministry in Tunis.[33]

Revolution is a state of affairs in which advisors are of no use. Once the revolution begins to unfold, every action taken by the regime tends to backfire, and whether it shows flexibility or violence (short of unrestrained repression), it pours oil on the flames. The rejection of popular demands reinforces the revolt, while concessions embolden it. This is one of the characteristics of revolutionary times. Generally, when demonstrations and acts of protest rage and transform into a revolutionary torrent, the regime's leader, refusing to listen to his council of advisors anymore, comes out promising reforms that the opposition movement, before the revolution, would never have imagined in its wildest dreams. To the leader's dismay, however, he finds that the people no longer desire his reforms; they only want his departure. The tempo of revolutions rapidly accelerates as things that would have been popularly acceptable weeks earlier are rejected out of hand, and as demands are outpaced by the advance of the popular movement.

Some loyalists who are close to the regime begin to distance themselves, while the pro-regime media begins to voice criticisms. The army itself appears to be choosing between its loyalty to the nation and its loyalty to the regime.

The advantage of both the Egyptian and Tunisian revolutions was the overwhelming element of surprise. Since early 2011, however, Arab regimes have been preparing themselves for potential revolutions within their territories and drawing lessons from the past. Predictably, some leaders believed that the Tunisian and Egyptian regimes had not exercised sufficient systematic repression at the onset of the protests, causing them to lose control over events and rendering them unable to contain the protests after they surged. This seems to be the conclusion reached by the Yemeni, Libyan and, later, Syrian regimes, which resorted to extreme violence from the outset.

Undoubtedly, much ink will be spilled in the future on the subject of the Tunisian Revolution, and various social science disciplines will examine it, seeking to historicize, archive, diagnose and extract lessons from the region's first democratic revolution. It was a popular uprising that had started as a non-violent social movement which combined organization with impulsiveness, emerged from outside of the existing opposition parties and affirmed citizenship in an unprecedented manner. In Tunisia, the region also witnessed the first extensive

33. In an article published years after the Arabic version of this book, Jean-Baptiste Gallopin analyses how and when soldiers decide to disobey ('Dilemma and Cascades in the Armed Forces – The Tunisian Revolution', *Democracy and Security*, vol. 15, no. 4 (2019), pp. 328–60). See also The National Fact-Finding Commission on Abuses Committed from 17 December 2010 to the End of its Mandate, *Report by the National Fact-Finding Commission on the Abuses Committed* (Tunis: 2012), accessed on 11/3/2020, at: https://bit.ly/3kTB77t. For another description of that day's events, see Noureddine Jebnoun, 'In the shadow of power: civil–military relations and the Tunisian popular uprising', *The Journal of North African Studies*, vol. 19, no. 3 (2014), pp. 296–316.

use of social media by Tunisian bloggers, local activists and activists critical of the regime living in France, England and Canada for the benefit of foreign media outlets. Social media was used as a means of coordinating protest actions in a few cases, though its main role was to break the state monopoly over the media by disseminating information and supplying news, photos and videos for foreign satellite stations (mainly Al Jazeera and France 24) and news agencies.

Chapter 2

PRE-REVOLUTIONARY TIMES

On Tunisian authoritarianism

The Tunisian system of rule was authoritarian from the time when independence was achieved in 1956. Habib Bourguiba, who presided over party and state and considered himself not only the founder of the Tunisian state but also the creator and instructor of a nation, combined the traits of a national leader with those of a patriarchal autocrat and a modern dictator. Authoritarianism was further reinforced under Bourguiba's successor, Zine el-Abidine Ben Ali.

Unlike the rule of the monarchs (Beys) under the Ottomans and the French, modern despotism was not counterbalanced by the influence of communal groups and tribes. From early on, the Tunisian regime adopted a form of centralization that overrode communal and local structures given the country's small geographic area and high urban concentration, which deservedly caught researchers' attention.[1] Furthermore, Tunisia's intense modernization process was manifested in relatively high levels of education and literacy, as well as its religious and ethnic homogeneity.

Significantly, these were the same factors that enabled the regime to adopt certain totalitarian traits, which was a result of Bourguiba's diligent work at fusing the ruling party and government and tightening the links between the party, the government, especially after the party's 1964 congress, and civil institutions, especially the Tunisian General Labor Union (UGTT). The suggestion that Tunisia's regime was closer to modern despotism with totalitarian lineaments stems mainly from the fact that the state was endowed with modernized institutions that allowed the tools of repression to merge with the tools of control and cultural hegemony. In this case, however, no entity arose that encompassed all the functions of the state and society so as to join them into one totalitarian unity. The UGTT struggled

1. Rafik Abdessalem Bouchlaka, 'Modern Arab Authoritarianism: The Tunisian Experience as a Case Study', [al-Istibdād al-Ḥadāthī al-ʿArabī: at-Tajribah at-Tūnusiyah] in Ali Khalifa al-Kawwari (ed.), *Tyranny in Modern Arab Regimes [al-Istibdād fi Nudhum al-Ḥukm al-ʿArabiyah al-Muʿāṣirah]*, 2nd edn (Beirut: Center for Arab Unity Studies, 2006), pp. 85–108.

for its autonomy at least in relation to labour issues; political and ideological controversies in the party continued to emerge; and last but not least, Bourguiba adopted a pragmatic approach that saw no harm in flitting from one ideology to another: from liberalism, to a collectivist form of socialism and back to capitalism. These shifts were tolerated as long as the ultimate goal was to modernize the state and society, with Bourguiba maintaining his hold on power and himself remaining the founding principle of the nation.

Bourguiba attempted to establish and promote a special history for a distinguished nation, creating a long line of ancestors for Tunisian nationalism and for himself personally from Hannibal and Jugurtha[2] to Saint Augustine and Ibn Khaldūn. Bourguiba claimed that he had created the Tunisian nation out of nothing or, at least, from a motley collection of tribes and clans.[3] In fact, the national history of Tunisia was made to overlap with Bourguiba's personal history. For instance, Tunisia's National Day is not 20 March, the day Tunisia won its independence, but 1 June, the day of Bourguiba's return from exile in 1955.[4] Bourguiba's birthday, 3 August, was also a national holiday.

Tunisia featured an organized authoritarianism, yet without espousing a totalitarian ideology of the sort that typically permeates all institutions, including social and educational institutions. The regime's only declared ideology was that of Tunisian nationalism. Secularism per se is devoid of ideological potency for most Tunisians. A secularist might be a democrat, a liberal, a leftist, a fascist, an atheist or a theist; and conversely, he could be a mere opportunist who supports the existing regime simply because it is in power. The transition period witnessed the emergence of scores of secularist parties, most of which only endured for a single election cycle. Such parties were plagued by splits, factionalism and disunity, a fact that became a conundrum not only for the parties themselves but for Tunisia's nascent democracy as well.

Political life in Tunisia was entirely dominated by Bourguiba's leadership. The approach was a paternalistic one that focused on establishing patronizing relations between the leader on one hand and the people and institutions on the other. Before Tunisia's independence, Bourguiba's monopoly on power led to a

2. Meaning 'the eldest' or 'the strongest' in Amazigh, Jugurtha was a North African king who was born in 160 BC in modern-day Qasantina and died in 104 BC. Jugurtha rebelled against Roman rule, waging a guerrilla war that lasted for years against the Roman presence.

3. Tahar Belkhodja, *Habib Bourguiba: The Story of a Leader [al-Ḥabīb Būrqība: Sīrat Zaʿīm]* (Cairo: al-Dār al-Thaqāfiyah lil-Nashr, 1999), p. 33.

4. It was considered an exceptional event in the history of Tunisia which competed with the Independence Day in terms of the enormity of celebrations. Specialists considered it the most important event in the contemporary history of Tunisia after the Protection of 12 May 1881. It was named 'Victory Day' in the literature of the Constitutional Party and was celebrated annually as a paid national holiday from 1958 until the demise of Bourguiba's rule in Fall 1987. See 'June 1, 1995: An Event Tasted as Indepence', *Leaders – Tunisia*, 01/06/2019, accessed at: https://bit.ly/3eXOqSv [in Arabic].

deep split within the Tunisian independence elite of the Neo-Destour Party (from the Arabic *dustūrī*, meaning constitutional). This division was even deeper in the party's secretariat-general headed by Salah Ben Youssef. There was a struggle on leadership between Ben Yousef and Bourguiba. At the time, the reason behind the split was the question of Tunisia's self-rule, or autonomy. The notion of self-rule was rejected by Ben Youssef, who called for the national liberation resistance to continue until full independence from France and sovereignty were achieved. This stance was no doubt influenced by the Algerian revolution and Egypt's leadership at that time. In the meantime, Bourguiba persuaded the French, who at the time were facing the Algerian revolution after the defeat of Vietnam, that he represented moderation.

The dispute between the two young leaders did not emanate from Bourguiba's French education vis-á-vis the traditional education of Ben Youssef. Both had received secular modern educations, and Ben Youssef had studied law at the Sorbonne. They made different choices concerning the positioning of Tunisia after the Second World War, and concerning the post-independence alignments between rising powers, national liberation movements and previous colonizers. Personal competition also played a role in radicalizing their ideological choices.

This early political-ideological division, which was both horizontal and vertical, had important repercussions on political life and the balance of power in Tunisia. Bourguiba returned to Tunisia on 1 June 1955 (Victory Day) with the promise of self-rule and asserting his 'gradualist policy' (French, *étapisme*). Bourguiba worked to challenge Ben Youssef by allying himself with national organizations and institutions headed by a section of the party and a section of the UGTT. Ben Youssef, on the other hand, sought to strengthen his ties to the Islamic Zaytuna current (in reference to the traditionally minded Zaytuna University-Mosque in Tunisia) and traditional social forces, as well as some elements from the old Destour Party.[5]

This conflict, which turned into something akin to a civil war with armed resistance, police persecution and repression directed against the pro-Youssef camp, further narrowed the modest margin of freedom that had been gained at the time of national liberation.

After eliminating Ben Youssef's challenge (with assistance from the French army) and the crackdown on the communists, Bourguiba abolished the legitimacy of any political opposition, depicting it as sedition, strife and a splitting of national unity. Bourguiba saw politics as the work of an individual who stands at the helm and steers the country single-handedly.

5. Rafik Abdessalem Bouchlaka, 'On the Need to Build a Historical Bloc: The Tunisian Case as a Model', [al-Ḥājah ʾilā Bināʾ al-Kutlah at-Tārīkhiyah: al-Ḥālah al-Tūnisiyah Namūdhajan] in Ali Khalifa al-Kawwari (et al.) (eds.), *Towards a Historical Democratic Front in the Arab Countries [Naḥwa Kutlah Tārīkhiyah Dīmuqrāṭiyah fi al-Buldān al-ʿArabiyah]* (Beirut: Center for Arab Unity Studies, 2010), pp. 185–219.

This split left deep scars in Tunisian politics and society. However, Youssefi politics continued to influence people who opposed the regime's choices in domestic and foreign policy, especially in the country's interior and among Arab-Tunisian nationalists.

Tunisian politics was never as peaceful as some researchers attempt to portray it historically. Bourguiba crushed the party's Youssefi current, which resumed armed struggle against Bourguiba and the French presence in the country. Contrary to the way in which it is sometimes retrospectively portrayed, Bourguiba's political power was not merely a kind of intellectual hegemony. Rather, as will be further elaborated later, he never hesitated to use brutal force against his opponents and against public protests. Safi Saeed argues that within two years, more than 1,000 men were killed in this conflict, which is twice the number of Tunisians who were killed during the revolution against France.[6]

Independence came when the customs union between Tunisia and France was abolished, leading to the sudden withdrawal of foreign capital and an eventual collapse of the economy. As the nascent government attempted to reassure foreign investors by adopting a liberal economic policy, the UGTT came out of its 1956 convention with a socialist programme. This event pitted the Bourguiba regime against the UGTT and led to a confrontation between them.[7]

The UGTT's economic and social programme, adopted during its sixth convention, bore the features of a socialist economy, which took the form of state-supported agricultural cooperatives, state supervision of the industrial sector to contain the phenomenon of urban unemployment within a period of five years, the collectivization of artisans in cooperatives and the development of consumer cooperatives. The convention affirmed that the union had become 'a force whose duty is to shoulder its responsibility in the construction of the state', especially since the union at the time had partnered with four ministers in the government. In addition, hundreds of union cadres occupied important positions in the state apparatus.[8]

Bourguiba tightened control over the union. Believing that the socialist ideas of Ahmed Ben Salah, secretary-general of the UGTT from 1954 to 1956, would jeopardize Western support for his government, Bourguiba privately orchestrated

6. al–Safi Saeed, *al–Habib Bourguiba: A Forbidden Biography [al-Habib Bourqiba: Sira Shibh Muharamah]*, 2nd edn (Beirut: Riyadh al-Rayyes Publication, 2000), p. 206 [in Arabic].

According to the Truth and Dignity Commission report, post-independence period conflicts resulted in approximately 5,204 Tunisian victims. See Truth and Dignity Commission, *Final Inclusive Report* (Tunis: 2019), p. 230, 237, 239, accessed at: https://bit.ly/3eWmmyN [in Arabic].

7. See Aḥmad Najīb al-Shabbī's commentary on Bouchlaka's paper, 'Modern Arab Authoritarianism', in al-Kuwwari, et al., p. 115.

8. Salim Labyaḍ, *Identity: Islam, Arabism, Tunisization [al-Hawiyah: al-Islam, al-ʿUrūbah, at-Tawnasah]* (Beirut: Center for Arab Unity Studies, 2009), pp. 115–18.

opposition within the UGTT, with Habib Achour on the front. Eventually, in December 1956, Bourguiba managed to remove Ben Salah and replace him with Ahmed Tlili, who occupied this position until 1963, thereby ensuring Ben Salah's disappearance from the political stage, at least for a while. This development affected the work of the National Assembly's UGTT members, who, although they secured the mention of social guarantees in the final draft of the 1959 Constitution, failed to gain recognition for workers' right to strike.[9]

In reaction to the 1956 convention, the Bourguiba regime took a series of steps against the UGTT, in addition to the removal of the union's Secretary-General Ben Salah, the appointment of loyalists from the Neo-Destour Party to leading positions, placement of the union under state authority and the supervision of the ruling party. However, following the failure to attract foreign capital, the regime back-pedalled and in 1964 adopted a major portion of the union's economic and social programme.[10] This experience led the ruling party to revise its economic approach, which ended up being similar to that of the UGTT. The policy of socialist solidarity subsequently became the government line, in fact, and the implementation of the plan was handed over to Ben Salah, the union's former secretary-general who was appointed Minister of Planning and Minister of Finance, posts which he occupied from 1961 to 1969.[11] This was neither the first nor the last rehabilitation by Bourguiba of political figures he had previously discarded. Rather, it was his custom to exclude powerful figures, only to bring them back at will by his 'grace', thus demonstrating that there was only one powerful man in Tunisia.

The term 'constitutional socialism' first appeared in a document drafted by Neo-Destour Party leaders as part of protracted talks following the so-called 19 December 1962 conspiracy, which saw the participation of former pro-Youssef independence activists, army officers and some of the Neo-Destour Party's organizations. The meetings took place in January 1963 against the backdrop of a crisis following the end of French aid and as provincial demands for agrarian reform intensified and overall economic conditions worsened. Consequently, staple goods became scarce in Tunisian markets and long queues formed outside food stores. The party meeting presented a document drafted by Taieb Sahbani which included the term 'constitutional socialism', defined as the doctrine responding to social demands and the establishment of a system that could be described as solidarity-based and cooperative. From the beginning, those who coined the term made an effort to distinguish it from communism, 'scientific socialism' and other political forms. Moreover, Sahbani was careful to maintain a balance among what the Neo-Destour Party termed 'the three sectors' – the public sector, the private sector and the cooperative sector.

9. Kenneth Perkins, *A History of Modern Tunisia,* 2nd ed. (Cambridge: Cambridge University Press, 2014), p. 139.

10. Al-Shabbī, 'Modern Arab Authoritarianism', p. 115.

11. Labyaḍ, *Identity*, p. 120.

Ben Salah led the process of building the cooperative economy supported by the UGTT. It was clear that the difference between the president and the Minister of Finance was not merely an economic one. At one stage, Bourguiba sensed that Ben Salah's stature had grown substantially. He was, after all, backed by an entire current within the party, which endowed him with a popularity that exceeded his actual authority. Ben Salah faced accusations of having committed numerous transgressions during implementation of the land collectivization policy, a fact which was seized upon by political opponents. Eventually, in 1970 under the government of al-Bahi Ladgham, Ben Salah was brought to trial on charges of financial mismanagement. The aim was to cause a complete rupture with his legacy and defame those who had led these economic policies. However, at the start of the 'constitutional socialist' era, these policies faced no serious opposition except for that of a single politician, Ahmed Tlili, who was implacably opposed to cooperative economic policies.

Upon relinquishing the socialist economic course, Bourguiba showed no inclination towards democratic reform. After all, he was not a democrat. He believed in and defended autocratic decision-making while at the same time holding others accountable for the failure of his own decisions. Few officials were able to avoid punishment and personal defamation when they were blamed for the failure of policies that Bourguiba had personally approved or initiated.

The government's alliance with the UGTT during the cooperative era helped consolidate Bourguiba's rule. At the time, Bourguiba could count on both union support and the absence of other political parties. He also engineered a merger of the ruling party with state institutions, thus laying the groundwork for near-total control over all aspects of economic and political life in Tunisia.

The tables were turned in the early 1970s when, after the collapse of the cooperative economic plans and the economic crisis of 1969, the government suddenly lunged towards liberalism, opening the door to local private initiatives and foreign capital. The UGTT then distanced itself from Bourguiba. This was prompted by the flourishing of an underground political opposition, which found in the union a safe haven for action and a cover for all manner of unauthorized political views, whether liberal, leftist or nationalist.[12] This development is reminiscent of the role of the union's constituency during the social uprisings of the Ben Ali era. Even though among the main party leaders, including Bourguiba, only Ahmed Tlili opposed the cooperative policies at their inception, Bourguiba blamed Ben Salah, who, surmising what might happen to him, fled the country. From his exile in 1973, Ben Salah established the Popular Unity Movement (MUP), which consisted mainly of other Tunisians in exile.

However, opposition to this liberal policy gradually increased during its implementation, quickly turning into a demand for greater democracy within the party. Ahmed Mestiri was among the leading figures of this internal opposition. During this period, Mestiri led the reformist wave calling for the democratization

12. Bouchlaka, 'On the Need to Build a Historical Bloc', p. 205.

first of the party and then of the state. The majority of the participants in the 1971 al-Monastir Convention of the ruling party (which in 1964 was renamed the Socialist Destourian Party [PSD] – also known as the Constitutional Socialist Party since its adoption of the corporative economy) – supported this line. This same majority expressed itself in the Central Committee members' election, in which Ahmed Mestiri came in second after al-Bahi Ladgham.[13] Bourguiba, along with Hédi Amara Nouira, came in fifth place and proceeded to go against the majority within the party by using non-democratic methods. Bourguiba went on to dismiss Mestiri and to personally appoint the members of the political bureau against the wishes of the majority. The Second al-Monastir Convention, held in September 1974, pursued a campaign of dismissals within the PSD and the persecution of the democratic current, whose adherents were expelled from the party.

This Congress of the PSD was different from the previous seven party congresses as the members criticized the president, while the 1974 Congress, which offered Bourguiba presidency for life and the right to elect the party's Central Committee, was a consolidation of authoritarianism. Even those who had contributed to eliminating Ben Youssef's followers were dismissed. Bourguiba thus began to turn on his own children, as it were. In 1975, he declared himself president for life with support from the Tunisian National Assembly. Around this time also, the sequence of the national motto was modified from 'liberty, order, and justice' to 'order, liberty, and justice'. The revision was adopted in a 1976 amendment to Article 4 of the Constitution.[14]

After the al-Monastir Convention of 1974, the PSD made a final rupture with its constitutional past, transforming itself into a fully authoritarian party. In truth, the party had always been a one-leader party, particularly since the violent expulsion of Ben Youssef and his followers. Following the al-Monastir Convention, however, any illusion regarding the party's commitment to its historical liberal principles was quashed, and the party came to represent a dictatorial form of authoritarianism. Other ideological parties in the Arab region have passed through a similar transformation after years of authoritarianism (transforming an authoritarian ruling party into that of a ruling president or, in some cases, from a ruling clique into the president's entourage).

13. Tahar Belkhodja, who supported Hédi Amara Nouira against Ahmed Mestiri, claims that Bourguiba's absence was seized upon to launch a coup within the party. On the other hand, Beji Caid Essebsi, another Bourguiba biographer and an opponent of Belkhodja, claims that it was, in fact, a democratic majority and that Bourguiba missed out on the opportunity to democratize once he turned against that bloc. Both authors claim to have seen the need for democratization based on their experience with Bourguiba and that for this reason they had welcomed Ben Ali's coming to power. See Belkhodja, pp. 142–4; and Beji Caid Essebsi, *Habib Bourguiba: The Important and the More Important [al-Ḥabīb Būrqība .. al-Muhimm wal-Ahamm]*, Muḥammad Maʿālī (trans.) (Tunis: Dār al-Janūb lil-Nashr, 2011), pp. 171–80.

14. Perkins, *A History of Modern Tunisia*, p. 162.

This was the dawn of the ruling party's new direction, eventually leading to the rise of Ben Ali in the 1980s, who, from the outset, was not among the party leaders and who dealt with the party as a tool in the hands of the president. Indeed, Ben Ali would have been content with a number of obedient technocrats who executed his orders. In effect, Bourguiba prepared the groundwork for this style of rule.

With Bourguiba's blessings, Hédi Amara Nouira and his group led the persecution of the leader's opponents inside the party. Ahmed Mestiri was expelled from both the party and the Parliament despite having won more votes than Nouira. Baseless charges were fabricated against him, as would later happen to the leader of the Women's Nationalist Union Radhia Haddad, who was tried three times on a trumped-up charge of providing a loan to a union member valued at 118 dinars (around $40 in today's currency). This particular case became notorious due to its vindictive tactics. Hassib Ben Ammar was also harassed for his wish to publish the newspapers *al-Rai* (The Opinion) and *al-Democratie* (*The Democrat*).

Consequently, the party witnessed the formation of a democratic bloc composed of certain veteran leaders who did not approve of Ben Salah's economic policies and used the opportunity to criticize autocratic decision-making. These leaders were flanked by a segment of youth who had had a strong reaction to Ben Salah's trial and the manner in which he was scapegoated for Tunisia's economic failure. Conflicts among the different political currents began to take hold within the PDS, but any organized opposition found itself outside the party.

In 1976, these currents led by Mestiri founded the Tunisian Society for the Defense of Human Rights, which was officially recognized on 7 May 1977 and which became a venue for the development of numerous prominent opposition activists and future leaders. Shortly thereafter, in June 1978, Mestiri founded the Socialist Democrats Movement (MDS), which (with its progressive newspapers in Arabic and French) became a rallying point for leftist and democratic dissidents and was not officially recognized until November 1983. The official recognition of the MDS came with Mohammed Mzali's decision to legalize two moderate opposition parties (the other one being the Popular Unity Party, or PUP).

With the regime's increasingly frequent attacks on unionists and following the elimination of the opposition political currents within the PSD, the Administrative Committee of the UGTT called for a general strike on 26 January 1978.[15] A series of bloody confrontations between unionists and Tunisian security forces led to hundreds of dead and wounded, a day Tunisians remember as 'Black Thursday'. The crisis ended with the arrest of the Union leadership, including Secretary-General Habib Achour, who was tried along with 700 other unionists. The independence of the Tunisian unionist movement was thus crushed, and the union was transformed into a mere tool of the ruling party, with the creation of a new executive bureau by

15. 'January: The Month of Unpunished Massacres', '[Janvi, Shahr al-Majāzir al-Fālitah min al- ʿIqāb]', *al-Badīl* [website of the Tunisian Communist Labor Party], January 10, 2005, accessed on 12 December 2020, at: https://bit.ly/37KdybY.

representatives who were loyal to the party.[16] But local and sectorial groups inside UGTT remained vehemently opposed to the regime.

In 1980, on the second anniversary of 'Black Thursday', an armed group of Tunisians sought to spark a general uprising by attacking strategic installations in the southern phosphate mining centre of Gafsa, which had an exceptionally high unemployment rate due to a steady decline in phosphate prices. According to official estimates, thirty-seven were killed (probably many more). Tunisia rightly accused Libya's Qaddafi of training and equipping the attackers.[17]

During the early 1970s, a radical leftist political current arose on the margins of the Tunisian Communist Party (PCT). Various leftist groups put pressure on the consensus between Habib Achour and Hédi Amara Nouira, which represented the *entente* between the government and the UGTT. The director of National Security at the time wrote:

> In 1973, Tunisia saw the emergence of a leftist opposition with a radical tendency. In 1972, its activists had announced 'the creation of a workers' party that includes revolutionary intellectuals and workers. We, at the Ministry of Interior, had close knowledge of their activities . . . the police issued some arrest warrants and 33 of them were referred to court.[18]

The middle classes, which historically constituted the foundation of the national movement, were contained in the public service sector, mainly through an educational system that aimed to train the cadres and technocrats of a modern, expanding state. As a result of the economy's redirection towards the private sector, the middle classes were relegated to the bottom of the income ladder. This created a widespread sense of injustice and inequality not only in the working class but among many middle-class educated youth as well. This fact, alongside the leftist political activism that pressured the UGTT, was one of the main factors that led to the protest uprising of 1978.[19]

16. Sālim Labyaḍ, 'Socio-Political Crises and Their Management: Tunisia 1957-1987', [al-Azamāt al-Ijtimā'iyah wal-Siyāsiyah wa-Idāratuhā: Tunis 1957–1987',] *Majālāt 'Ulūm Insāniyah* (Tunis), vol. 18, no. 2 (2005), accessed on 12 December 2020, at: https://bit.ly/3qBO6hj.

17. Perkins, *A History of Modern Tunisia*, p. 169.

18. Belkhodja, p. 146. On the Tunisian labour activism of the era, see Abd al-Jaleel Bouqarra, *The Afaq Movement: From the History of the Tunisian Left, 1963-1975 [Ḥarakāt Āfāq: min Tārīkh al-Yasār at-Tūnisī, 1963–1975]* (Tunis: Dār Sras lil-Nashr, 1993).

19. Abdelbaki Hermassi, 'Protest Islam in Tunisia', [al-Islām al-Iḥtijājī fi Tūnis',] a paper presented in *Modern Islamic Movements in the Arab World* (Seminar) *[al-Ḥarakāt al- Islāmiyah al-Mu'āṣirah fi al-Waṭan al-'Arabī* (Nadwa)*]*, Maktabat al-Mustaqbalāt al-'Arabiyah al-Badīlah, al-Ittijahāt al-Ijtimā'iyah was-Siyāsiyah wal-Thaqāfiyah, 5th ed. (Beirut: Center for Arab Unity Studies, 2004), pp. 263–4.

The UGTT withdrew from its alliance with Bourguiba and his government and, starting in late 1977, began to demand its own independence. The demands of the union not only were restricted to workers' rights but also included greater union independence, especially since conflicts within the ruling structure over Bourguiba's succession had intensified. These troubles led to demands inside the PSD that called for greater political openness in order to break away from the ruling party's hegemony over political and public life.

The violent confrontations in 1978 between the state and the UGTT under Achour's leadership left a deep mark on the government, the opposition and the Tunisian political scene overall. This crisis marked the beginning of a transformation in the country's political life, which provided an opportunity to discover the capacities and legitimacy of unions in terms of popular representation. This was a time of intensive political student activity led by the student union. Unions proved to be a vital part of the social system, providing a launching pad for the work of opposition parties whose role had previously been obscured. This applied particularly to the Islamist movement, which, hoping that the UGTT could serve as an incubator for the improvement of workers' conditions, called upon its members to join the union. The union's demands contained no ideological tenets that would have prevented Islamists from participating in its activities. Hence, members of the Islamist movement were free to interact with the unionist currents and share in their popular demands without being inconsistent with their Islamic ideology.

The Islamist movement did not crystallize as a political organization on the Tunisian scene until June 1981, when it was founded by Rached Ghannouchi and Abdelfattah Mourou in response to the Islamists' absence from the 1978 protests and to break with the image of the Islamist current as existing exclusively to confront communists and leftists. Al-Ghannouchi also sought to overcome the traditionalism of the Levantine Muslim Brotherhood discourse.[20] The arrest of its leaders six weeks after the founding of the movement quickly placed it in a direct confrontation with the Bourguiba regime. Ghannouchi and Mourou were arrested along with many members of the Movement of Islamic Tendency (MTI) adherents on the eve of the 1981 elections. The secular opposition did not boycott the movement lest this be interpreted as support for the government's repression.[21] This allowed the opposition to gather support from broad sections

20. With the possible exception of the Syrian Muslim Brotherhood during the era of Mustapha al-Sibai, under whose leadership the Syrian Muslim Brotherhood went even further than the Al Nahda in terms of opening up to nationalist and leftist movements and struggles before making a gradual turn to extremism under the Ba'ath Party.

21. Gudrun Kramer, 'Integration for the Proponents of Integration: A Comparative Study between Egypt, Jordan, and Tunisia', in Ghassan Salame (ed.), *Democracy without Democrats?: Renewal of Politics in the Muslim World* (Beirut: Center for Arab Unity Studies, 2000), pp. 197–8.

of the Tunisian public, which had a noticeable effect on the uprising of 1984 and the protests of 1987.

After the January 1978 General Strike, Hédi Amara Nouira's prominence began to fade.[22] In the early 1980s, Bourguiba attempted to ease the political tensions that followed the excessive use of violence during the repression of the 1978 uprising. The president appointed Mohamed Mzali, known for his support for openness, as prime minister in 1981. Mzali, who promised to undertake comprehensive reforms, convinced Bourguiba to take initiatives to overcome the stifling crisis, such as appointing ministers who were known for defending political openness and releasing political and unionist prisoners.[23]

Although Mzali adamantly pursued economic liberalization, he nevertheless dashed the hopes of those who had considered him a political liberal; indeed, the real liberal aspect of Mzali was his economic policies. This combination of economic liberalism and political authoritarianism was then inherited by Ben Ali. Even though Mzali began his term by reintegrating some of those who had been expelled from the party and allowing a restrained form of party pluralism, the 1981 'pluralistic elections' which took place ten years after the al-Monastir Convention did not bring a single opposition party to Parliament.

Reform was thus aborted at an early stage. It later transpired that other parties were prevented from entering Parliament following a high-level debate: 'All the testimonies regarding the elections point to Interior Minister Driss Guiga's visit to Mohammed Mzali in al-Monastir on the evening of October 31, the day preceding the elections. It seems the purpose of this visit was to inform the Prime Minister of the President's decision to prevent any opposition list from succeeding, regardless of which'.[24]

Despite the criticism it received, the cooperative policy adopted in the 1960s created the basis for Tunisian phosphate, oil refining and textile industries, and even the infrastructure for tourism, through the establishment of thirteen luxury hotels via the Hospitality Society. Liberal economic policies initially contributed

22. He also had a debilitating strike.

23. It is worth stressing here that premiers and their governments came and went, either because they were blamed for failures in the economy or without any specific reason being given. In either case, such changes were mere window-dressing, a guise for an unchanging regime, while the real decision-maker, Bourguiba in this case, remained unaccountable and above critique. This was the method of governance adopted by all authoritarian regimes in the region, whether monarchies or republics.

24. Essebsi, *Habib Bourguiba*, p. 209. Belkhodja clearly agrees with Essebsi's assessment, but he claims that the reason for the ballot-stuffing in Tunisia was the weak position of Essebsi's list, and that it was imperative to undermine Mestiri's list. See Belkhodja, pp. 304–5. 'Later, in his 1987 open letter to Bourguiba, Mzali confirmed this ploy to me, saying: 'Qiqa admitted to me in 1981 that the President had ordered the full victory of the Party's lists . . . I remember that commando units were sent to the Tunis City Hall in order to tamper with the results'. Ibid., p. 306.

to limiting bureaucracy and achieving high rates of economic growth, especially in the manufacturing exports and tourism sectors. However, the country paid an exorbitant price, both socially and politically, for this turn to economic liberalism. The economic transformation shook the social structure to its foundations, widening the gap between social classes. Tunisia thus witnessed a phenomenon familiar to many other countries: authoritarian and military regimes that achieved high economic growth rates but failed to provide a just or equitable distribution of wealth. The needs rose with the awareness; therefore, though a Tunisian born in 1980 had more chances and better living standards than his father born in 1955, the majority of the population felt that it had no share in the country's economic growth.

These regimes tended to perceive growth from a purely quantitative perspective rather than focusing on the relationship between the economy and sustainable development, the right of future generations to the resources of their country and human well-being. Entrepreneurs enjoyed increased opportunities to foster economic activities and provide employment, as is typical in the early stages of accelerated economic growth. However, this was accompanied by a trend towards the rapid accumulation of wealth through monopoly privileges, speculation and rent-based economic activities as opposed to productive ones.

Mzali worked to bring closure to the events of 26 January 1978 by allowing the UGTT to hold its convention on 1 May 1981. The convention resulted in the return of the unionist leadership that had been arrested following the 1978 uprising with the exception of Habib Achour, who was eventually pardoned and returned to head the union in 1984. However, the emerging political openness in Tunisia came to an abrupt end when Bourguiba ordered the rigging of the 1981 legislative elections, in which four competing lists ran against the PSD.[25] In this way, Bourguiba sabotaged the reconciliation process attempted by Mzali, who had made this process a high-priority component of his programme of political reform targeted at the structure, principles and sociopolitical values of the PSD. However, he remained trapped in a view of reform that was exclusively political and neglected the close links between development and democracy, and between the economy and politics. To the detriment of the economy, Mzali approached the recession by treating only its symptoms and not its structural causes through ill-designed salary increases that caused an expansion in consumption at a rate far higher than the growth of output. The imbalances in the Tunisian economy existed at the macroeconomic level and could only be resolved through such measures. The resulting difficulty in creating the needed employment opportunities led to renewed protests, which started in high schools and colleges and later spread to workers' strikes. The crisis reached its apex in late 1983 when, in response to demands by the International Monetary Fund (IMF) and the World Bank, the Tunisian government lifted subsidies on

25. Abd al-Jaleel Bouqarra, 'The National State, 1956–1987', in Khalifa al-Shatir (ed.), *The National Movement and the Independent State* (Tunis: Center for Economic and Social Studies and Research, 2005), pp. 197–8.

staple foods such as wheat and semolina[26] in order to cut state expenditures, causing their prices to double.[27] This was the spark for what came to be known as the 'bread riots' of January 1984.

The bread riots began on 29 December 1983 during the weekly market in the southern city of Douz. Protests flared and led to clashes between demonstrators and security forces. The following day, the movement spread to the neighbouring city of Kebili and then took a violent turn after its expansion into the city of al-Hammah. When the decree to increase the prices of bread and derivative products went into effect on 1 January 1984, the protest movement was already in full swing in the north and centre-west regions, in al-Kef, Kasserine and Thala, and in other southern regions such as Gafsa, Gabes and Medinine. President Bourguiba then deployed the army in the streets of the capital and declared a state of emergency. On 2 January, the Ministry of Interior announced that deaths and injuries had occurred in Kebili, al-Hammah, Kasserine and Gafsa. Subsequently, a general strike was called in the industrial zone of Gabes, and massive demonstrations were organized by workers and students. In Tunis and Sfax, college and high school students took to the streets shouting their opposition to the withdrawal of bread subsidies.

On 3 January 1984, the uprising reached its climax with open confrontations between protesters and army-backed security forces. Shops, vehicles, buildings and buses were set on fire in the streets of the capital and its suburbs, as well as in other cities on the coast and in the interior. The security forces used live ammunition, causing further deaths and injuries among the protesters, with an estimated 143 killed and 400 wounded.

The intervention of the army in the 1978 and 1984 protests resulted in a catastrophic loss of human life, as well as growing distrust between the military leadership and the Interior Ministry. Additionally, the military saw that while the government refused to modernize the military's equipment, they were asked to 'waste' their resources on social conflicts originating from the civil political echelons' poor decision-making.[28] But the army did not reject involvement in repression of civil demonstrations in 1978 and 1984 uprisings. Following Prime Minister Mzali's declaration on 3 January 1984 that the decision to slash subsidies was final and irrevocable, the anti-government protests continued the next day in many Tunisian cities, as well as in the capital and its suburbs. The mandatory suspension of classes in all universities and educational institutions between 4 January and 7 January – accompanied by arrests of protesters deemed 'criminals and saboteurs' – did nothing to diminish the movement's momentum. The protests continued until President Bourguiba announced the restoration of subsidies.

26. Subsidies on wheat and semolina had been financed for fifteen years with revenues from the sale of crude oil, which dropped that year.

27. Perkins, *A History of Modern Tunisia*, p. 172.

28. Noureddine Jebnoun, 'In the shadow of power: civil–military relations and the Tunisian popular uprising', *The Journal of North African Studies*, vol. 19, no. 3 (2014), p. 300.

Protesters also demanded that the new state budget be revised within three months and that the deteriorating economic situation be taken into consideration, stressing that citizens were not to bear the brunt of the crisis.[29]

The decision to increase the price of wheat and semolina had been Bourguiba's, in fact; however, he had distanced himself from this decision, passing the blame for its consequences onto Mzali's policy. Bourguiba even went further, promising the people lower prices for staple goods, as a result of which people took to the streets, chanting 'Long live Bourguiba! Mzali, resign!'

In April 1984, Zine el-Abidine Ben Ali was appointed director-general of National Security. However, the UGTT questioned the decision to bring back Ben Ali, who had been at least partly responsible for the bloodshed of 1978 when serving in a similar position.[30] Subsequently, Ben Ali struck an alliance with Saida Sasi, Bourguiba's niece, whose sizeable influence within the Carthage Palace continued to increase as Bourguiba grew older.

Ben Ali was no amateur in security matters, having served as Tunisia's Director of Military Intelligence from 1964 to 1974. After serving as military attaché in Tunisia's embassies in Morocco and Spain, he became director-general of National Security in 1977, in which capacity he oversaw the brutal suppression of the 1978 uprising. In 1980 he was discharged for failing to anticipate and prevent the armed insurrection in Gafsa in January of the same year. Soon after the Tunisian bread riots in January 1984, Ben Ali was reappointed director of National Security, and a year later he became Tunisia's Minister of State in charge of the country's national security. In April 1986, Ben Ali was appointed interior minister and then prime-minister in October 1987.

The bread riots, which represented the starting point of Bourguiba's withdrawal from the political scene, allowed for the crystallization of a coordinated position among opposition forces, thus contributing to the creation of a solid and coherent nucleus for a movement demanding change. The détente among parties with varying political backgrounds led to significant results. For instance, the Islamist movement underwent intellectual and political changes that made it more amenable to the idea of democracy[31] and partnership with non-Islamist forces. Similarly, leftists and liberals appeared more prone than before to confront Bourguiba's regime in cooperation with the Islamists.[32]

The 1983–4 bread riots differed from the 1978 uprising in that they included marginalized societal groups. The 1978 events (Black Thursday) began as an urban strike led by the UGTT in three cities (Sfax the economic hub of Tunisia, Sousse and

29. Labyaḍ, 'Socio-Political Crises and Their Management'.

30. Perkins, *A History of Modern Tunisia*, p. 173.

31. Defined simply as the right to political participation and the choice of government by elections and majority rule, not as liberal democracy.

32. Mohammad Hilal al-Khalifi, 'The Historical Bloc on the Basis of Democracy', [al-Kutlah at-Tārikhiyah ʿalā Qāʿidat al- Dīmuqrāṭiyah] in al-Kawwari (et al.) (eds.), *Towards a Historical Democratic Front in the Arab Countries*, p. 279.

Tunis the capital) and expanded to all Tunisian cities, including the peripheries. In fact, the protests and clashes were mostly concentrated in Ben Arous, which is considered the centre of Tunis' labourers. The popular participation exceeded all expectations, as the streets of Tunis witnessed rallies by trade unionists, workers, students and the unemployed. The general strike expanded to various parts of the country, such as Kairouan, Gabes, Siliana, Tozeur, Kasserine and Zermadine, which indicated that it had turned into a general popular state. The regime fired live ammunition at the peaceful protesters. Unionist sources confirm that the number of those killed exceeded 400, while the authority at the time announced 52 dead and 365 wounded.[33] In contrast with the 1978 uprising, the bread riots were essentially an uprising of the peripheries that expanded to the cities, being similar to the uprising of 2010–11 that started in Sidi Bouzid. Also, both the uprising of 1983–4 and that of 2010–11 took place and continued despite an agreement between the government and the leadership of the UGTT (which was being led by Habib Achour in 1984), whereas the uprising of 1978 was a general strike initiated by the UGTT itself. In fact, in 1984, the people protested decisions that were being taken by the government, the ruling party and the Parliament and approved by the UGTT, which suggests that Tunisians were demonstrating against the entire political establishment.

An important difference between the events of 2010–11 and those of 1983–4 (both of which, like all major uprisings in Tunisia, broke out in December and January) is that in 2011 the army did not quell the uprising, whereas in 1984 the army had stood firmly with the regime and took an active part in the repression of the uprising. The 1984 bread riots, sparked by particular socio-economic policies, did not transform into a revolution aiming at regime change. Instead, the movement was contained and extinguished by the state through repression and promises of political reform, while the security apparatus, including the army, stood united behind the ruling authorities. Nevertheless, the growing gulf between the people and the establishment and the end of Bourguiba's total hegemony undoubtedly began with the 1984 uprising, an indication that the Bourguibist regime had aged along with its leader.

33. The disengagement between the UGTT and the Socialist Destourian Party (which began with Sfax Conference on 15 November 1955) formally occurred when the general secretary of the UGTT, Habib Achour, resigned from the Central Committee and Political Bureau of the Party. However, the UGTT's central board issued a notice on 22 January, 1978, that harshly criticized governmental policies and accused the party with dictatorship and violence. As an outcome, the UGTT called for a general strike to occur on Thursday, 26 January 1978. In response, units of security forces besieged the headquarters of the UGTT on the eve of 26 January, while the army and other groups affiliated with the ruling party were deployed in Tunisian cities. See Yassine Nabli, 'Events of January 26, 1978: A Smuggled memory from Regime's Books', *Nawaat*, 26/01/2016, accessed at: https://bit.ly/3nUyN2w [in Arabic].

The loyalty of the army and security forces had, in essence, been loyalty to Bourguiba. Ben Ali, by contrast, lacked the legitimacy that Bourguiba had enjoyed. Furthermore, Ben Ali's attempts to control the army and the security apparatus by pitting them against each other had simply produced tension and mistrust among them without securing greater loyalty to his person.

These comparisons suggest two conclusions. The first is that in order to become a revolution, it is not sufficient for an uprising to last for several days or to bear heavy sacrifices in confrontations with the regime. Rather, a general revolutionary condition must be present in the society, allowing the uprising to expand both horizontally and vertically among wide sections of the population, turning its desires into political demands which the regime is unable to contain. Another element of this 'revolutionary condition' is the existence of awareness and motivation among broad elements of society, who not only view their deteriorating living conditions (and/or the obstacle to their improvement) as the outcome of unjust policies but believe that the said policies cannot be changed under the existing regime. As for the second conclusion, it is that in order for a revolution to succeed in overthrowing the regime, a rift must be torn open between the regime and its repressive machine, or within the machine itself.

Bourguiba himself did not fully understand the significance of the social and political movement that was provoked by the bread riots of 1984. While the movement presented itself as a protest against the inflation of food prices and the unavailability of basic goods, it also reflected popular anger over the absence of social justice. Bourguiba's familiar ideological discourse had outlived its usefulness. He had failed to produce a political or intellectual response that could be deployed in the Tunisian political arena after this uprising, preferring to maintain his demagogic rhetoric.[34] He resorted to blaming those around him, accusing them of not informing him about the situation, while, in fact, it was Bourguiba himself who had insisted on slashing subsidies.[35] This situation is reminiscent of the third speech delivered by Ben Ali after the escalation of the revolution, in which he blamed his aides for hiding the truth from him. In the case of the 1983–4 bread riots, Bourguiba began to rely on the military and the leaders of the security establishment, which culminated in the appointment of then-Minister of Interior Ben Ali to the position of prime minister.[36] Similarly, Ben Ali replaced his interior minister during the last two days of his rule in the hope of containing the wave of protests that led to his overthrow.

34. Larbi Sadiki, *Rethinking Arab Democratization: Elections without Democracy*, 1st edn (Oxford: Oxford University Press, 2009), p. 200.

35. Without excluding issues of physical and mental issues Bourguiba, in his eighties, already had by then.

36. The dismissal of the Interior Minister to appease the population after uprisings is a repeated refrain in Tunisian history. Driss Guiga was asked to step down following the so-called 1962 conspiracy, and Fouad Mebazaa was discharged after the demonstrations protesting the Israeli aggression of June 1967.

Bourguiba firmly believed that maintaining his grip on power was a sacred duty, tantamount to the duty to preserve the unity of the nation. This 'sincere' narcissism on the part of autocrats who identify themselves with the state and consider the maintenance of their rule a sacred mission is not a rare phenomenon. And in keeping with this illusion, Bourguiba justified lying and sacrificing other officials for his own mistakes in order to preserve his stature and remain above suspicion as the living symbol of national consensus. Authoritarian rule transformed Bourguiba from the 'national leader' and 'the supreme warrior' (*al-mujāhid al-akbar*, as he was officially dubbed) into a man who, driven by power and vanity, refused to keep up with the changes that were taking place around him.

The logic underlying the need to secure power for the sake of post-independence state-building and modernization has frequently devolved into a justification of despotism. This is a problem symptomatic of numerous liberation leaders once they assume control of a postcolonial state. The paternalism that marks attempts to cling to power turns into an internal colonialism which views the citizenry as an ignorant lot in need of education and who lack the maturity required to know their true interests or engage in self-rule. Needless to say, the 'education' needed requires 'chastisement' and the culling of 'harmful' elements from the body politic.

Bourguiba was determined to build a modern state, which to him implied transforming the mentality of Tunisians and creating a new, modern culture.[37] Accordingly, he focused on the question of women's rights and gender equality, as well as on undermining traditional religious institutions and limiting their cultural and political influence. Bourguiba advanced a social project. His first decree, dated 31 May 1956, ordered the dismantling of the endowments association, an Islamic institution, while prohibiting the establishment of such public endowments and the transfer of any such association's assets to the state. Its lands and properties were redistributed on the market after being frozen for a long period, which subsequently opened the way for the reclamation of vast tracts of land for agriculture and construction.

One of his greatest achievements in this context is the Personal Status Code (CSP) of 13 August 1956, which prohibited unilateral divorce and allowed the initiation of divorce to both spouses equally, along with provisions for

37. Safwan Masri credits Bourguiba not only with secularizing the country and prioritizing education, to which he allocated a relatively large share of the national budget, but also with equipping generations of Tunisians with critical and analytical skills that had been denied to the rest of the Arab world. See Safwan M. Masri, *Tunisia: An Arab Anomaly*, Lisa Anderson (Foreword) (New York: Columbia University Press, 2017), p. xxxi. While the unique success of democracy in Tunisia after 2011 may be due in part to secular education and the critique of religious traditional thought, it should be remembered that secularism does not mean critical thinking by default. On the contrary, it can be as dogmatic and uncritical as any religion, especially if represents a blind imitation of French secularism (imitation is, by definition, not critical), or if it mindlessly glorifies a leader, whether Bourguiba or anyone else.

compensation in instances of grave injustice. Polygamy was also prohibited and declared a crime, and a father could no longer marry off his daughter without her consent. Family planning was enacted in 1962, which contributed to lowering the birth rate from 7.1 to 5.8 children per family in 1975. Women's education levels also soared, becoming the highest in the region, and the birth rate dropped as a result. Laws passed in the 1960s legalized abortion, encouraged birth control and allowed adoption. In 1963, Tunisia's population was almost equal to that of Syria, but by 2011, it was only slightly more than half that of Syria.

Not wanting to be perceived as turning his back on Islam, Bourguiba sought to present himself as a reformer who was reinterpreting the religion by means of *ijtihad* and reasoning, which was accepted by the ulama. Hence, after the enactment of the CSP, Bourguiba stressed that Tunisia was still deeply rooted in Arab and Islamic traditions. Similarly, then-Minister of Justice Ahmed Mestiri insisted that the Code was a reform of society within Islam. As a matter of fact, some of the basic ideas of the Code had been inspired by the writings of the Tunisian Islamic reformer Tahar Haddad; it was also defended by Shaykh Mohamed Fadhel Ben Achour. However, most of those in the religious establishment, especially the Shari'a courts, opposed the Code, and many of those who did so were dismissed from their posts.

Had these reforms been put to a popular referendum or democratic elections, they most certainly would have never been approved by the Tunisian public. Indeed, numerous major reforms made by influential historical leaders in the process of nation-building were not put to referendums but were instead enacted from above in order to transform reality by first reshaping public opinion. These reforms, born out of a belief in modernization and the inevitability of progress, helped create a new culture and public opinion that came to perceive them as achievements and that would subsequently refuse to make concessions on them.

Bourguiba stood at the helm of an authoritarian system. Revolutionary French values relating to democracy and freedom were not as influential in his education as were the radical secular principles of the French Third Republic. It is also clear that Bourguiba was influenced by Auguste Comte, as Beji Caid Essebsi recounts in his book on the Tunisian leader.[38] In this sense, Bourguiba's background and values were close to those of Mustafa Kemal Ataturk. He sought to inculcate modern French values in Tunisian society based on the notions of enlightenment and rationality. At the same time, however, he espoused an authoritarian interpretation of secularism on the basis of which the establishment of democracy was neglected in favour of achieving modernity. Just as Ataturk used his conflict with the opposing Democratic Party, whose leaders had fought on Ataturk's side in the Turkish national liberation war, as an excuse for disbanding other parties and imposing one-party dictatorship, Bourguiba adopted a similar strategy following his victory against the Youssefist wing. Furthermore, just as Ataturk made the Republican Party into a tool for the 'Turkification' of Turkey according

38. Essebsi, *Habib Bourguiba*, p. 21.

to a secular European nation-state model, Bourguiba followed in his footsteps by making the Neo-Destour Party (later named the Socialist Destourian Party) into the centre of a bureaucratic-political formation of the Tunisian nation and the Western-oriented 'Tunisification' of Tunisians. The measure of success in the case of Tunisia, however, is to compare it with the performance of other Arab states rather than to Turkey.

Bourguiba derived his historical legitimacy from his link to the struggle for independence and the construction of a modern nation-state. Hence, some who adopt a patriarchal view of leadership call him 'the father of the nation'. Moreover, Bourguiba's charisma and strong presence, along with his widely respected legacy in the leadership of the Tunisian nationalist movement, frequently allowed him to employ his ever-present paternalistic authority to guarantee loyalty to his person. Nonetheless, one must not forget that he employed violence against the Tunisian people in numerous instances, including militia-like violence against the enemies of the Neo-Destour Party, and within the party itself during his repression of the Youssefis. During the era of self-rule, a time when the Minister of Interior did not own a police force, Bourguiba relied upon veterans of the independence struggle, as well as youth unions, to enforce security and repress Youssefi partisans. During that period, violence was used in excess, and elements that would today be termed 'militias' or 'thugs' were sent out to disperse gatherings of the Youssefi current.

However 'liberal' Bourguiba may have been, he viewed his people as insufficiently 'mature' to enjoy liberal rights. He was deeply influenced by French culture; however, he internalized this culture along with its colonial sense of superiority towards his people. Bourguiba perceived national liberation, state-building and politics as his own personal missions and responsibilities. Monopolizing decision-making and repressing opponents were, therefore, natural parts of the political game. His dictatorial tendencies were revealed from the onset, especially within his own party. No party was allowed to organize outside the Neo-Destour Party, and no alternative political currents were to be formed within it. Indeed, from 1955 onwards, he had no compunctions about assassinating Youssefi supporters; these included three pro-Youssef members of the old Destour Party,[39] one of them being Abdel Karim Qamh, a teacher and a member of the party's Central Command. Students were also murdered during party meetings. Later, in 1977 and 1978, special Riʿāyah (providence) units were used to persecute activists who supported Achour during the conflict between the party and the union following the declaration of the general strike.[40]

39. The old Destour Party was founded in 1920. In 1934, the party split when Habib Bourguiba founded the Neo-Destour Party.

40. According to an anecdote recounted by Tahar Belkhodja, a man notorious for his crimes named Mabrouk Wardani appeared in November 1977 brandishing a pistol in a Sousse hotel, threatening to liquidate Achour with the same weapon that had killed Ben Youssef. See Belkhodja, p. 167.

On questions of security, Bourguiba was not satisfied with the 'laxity' shown towards the demonstrations against the Israeli aggression in June 1967, which had been accompanied by attacks on both the American Cultural Center and the synagogue in Tunis. Subsequently, Bourguiba set up professional internal security forces with the help of US experts. Under his successor Ben Ali, the regime became a police state with stifling security control after a short phase of openness and political reforms. The police state model then became an entrenched characteristic of the Tunisian management of politics and society. The official discourse of the state under Ben Ali was that of democracy, human rights and civil society; nevertheless, the most mundane political and procedural matters came under the authority of the security and intelligence apparatus. It was during this time that US–Tunisian relations became stronger.[41]

As soon as Ben Ali, a head of security who personally supervised the interrogation and torture of detainees, became president, he declared his intention to enact long-awaited democratic reforms in order to acquire legitimacy during a period of popular unrest, and his declaration succeeded in deluding liberals, leftist politicians and intellectuals alike. (Ben Ali was neither the first nor the last despot to legitimize his assumption of power by claiming to be a reformer, of course.[42]) Particularly after the Algerian Islamists' electoral victory of 1991, Tunisia witnessed a major decline in public and individual freedoms as the state did its utmost to destroy its Islamist opponents under the guise of 'extinguishing the fundamentalist threat'. Following 9/11, Ben Ali further doubled down on his efforts to link his policies to the United States' so-called war on terrorism.[43]

41. In December 1959 President Eisenhower visited Tunisia, and in the 1960s the United States armed the Tunisian army when France refused to do so. US influence in Tunisia was manifested during the uprising of 1984, when General Vernon Walters arrived as an envoy to Tunisia with a mandate of support for the Tunisian government. This delegation prefaced many others to come, as the United States persevered in enhancing its military and security cooperation with Tunisia. Joint US–Tunisian military training programmes had been known to all since independence but only became public during the 1990s. Tunisian officers, among them Ben Ali himself early in his career, regularly received training in the United States, much of it focusing on the use and maintenance of modern weaponry. US forces were also sent, along with their aircraft, on 'military missions' to Tunisia at least once a year beginning in 2000. See al-Tahir al-Aswad, 'The Pillars of Tunisian-American Relations', The Africa Center for Studies and Political Research, 8 December 2007, at: https://bit.ly/2Lraxpj.

42. Bashar al-Assad claimed to be a modernist in a crusade against corruption; Husni Mubarak inaugurated his term with a fair degree of openness, and intended heir Jamal Mubarak presented himself as a reformist 'crown prince'.

43. Improved US-Tunisian relations led to increased military and security coordination thanks to the United States' focus on combating terrorism as a foreign policy doctrine in the Arab region and in Southwest Asia after 11 September 2001. Already embroiled in a struggle with Islamist movements, Tunisia was an ideal candidate for closer ties. The alleged

The regime took several steps to tighten its grip on state and society.[44] Firstly, a key tool of domination consisted of bringing the UGTT back under the control of the state following the removal of its historic leader Habib Achour and the appointment of a new executive director who was amenable to containment.

Distrustful of the army, Ben Ali did not brief its top commander on his planned coup attempt but instead coordinated his seizure of power with the National Guard. The army commander was informed only on the eve of the coup, on 6–7 November 1987. Ben Ali informed the Army Chief of Staff, Major-General Youssef Barakat, and the director of the General Directorate of Military Security (DGSM) (or Military Intelligence), Colonel Youssef Ben Soliman, only after the coup was a fait accompli. Nevertheless, they were all promoted after Ben Ali assumed power.[45] Within twenty days, he had founded the National Council for Security, primarily to address issues of domestic security. Following the announcement of its establishment, the council declared that it had uncovered a network of seventy-three individuals from the banned Movement of Islamic Tendency (MTI), who were charged with conspiracy against the state. Ben Ali used this announcement both internally and externally, mainly in the United States and France, to add legitimacy to his coup and his security state and to present himself as protector of Tunisia against the Islamist threat.[46]

Early in 1988 – still in his reform phase – Ben Ali freed imprisoned Islamists and allowed Al Nahda to participate in the dialogues around the national pact. Once this façade of reformism had served its purpose, however, Ben Ali readopted the policy of wiping out Islamists, referring to it as 'drying up the springs'. After purging disloyal Bourguibist elements, Ben Ali targeted the army in 1991 by

presence of al-Qaeda in North Africa and its claim of responsibility for a suicide attack that had targeted a synagogue on the Tunisian island of Jerba in 2003, killing twenty-two people, was a convenient justification for increased cooperation. Participation by Tunisia, along with the African states bordering the Great Sahara, in annual military exercises held by the United States increased. In 2004, Tunisia participated in 'the Trans-Saharan Counterterrorism Initiative', and in early 2007, the US Secretary of Defense founded the US command in Africa, AFRICOM. American researcher Alejandro Sanchez wrote that because Tunisia was viewed as a secular, Westernized and economically competitive country that combats terrorism and extremism, it was given carte blanche to do whatever the government deemed necessary to keep the country 'clean' of extremists (Sanchez, 'Tunisia: Trading Freedom for Stability', 86). It goes without saying that this carte blanche included turning a blind eye to human rights violations by the Tunisian state. After the developments following the aborted democratization in Algeria, the growing possibility of Islamists coming to power through the ballot box, and the civil war, the stability of North African regimes became an objective in and of itself, and the phrase 'combating extremist Islamists' became synonymous with maintaining stability.

44. Bouchlaka, 'Modern Arab Authoritarianism, p. 208.

45. Jebnoun, 'In the shadow of power', p. 300.

46. Ibid., pp. 301–2.

arresting officers on suspicion of belonging to the banned Al Nahda Movement and for conspiracy against the regime.

With the civil unrest in neighbouring Algeria in the beginning of the 1990s, Ben Ali changed the mission of the Tunisian army from simple defence to patrolling the borders with Algeria to prevent any infiltration by armed groups. At the same time, he limited and weakened the military with an underfunded budget, allocating insufficient resources for the maintenance and upgradation of its equipment. This studied neglect led to a number of incidents in which army personnel were needlessly killed. For instance, on 20 April 2002, Army Chief of Staff Abdelaziz Skik, together with twelve military officers, died in a helicopter crash. The helicopter was reported to have been old and improperly maintained; however, Ben Ali kept the investigations into the crash secret and failed to address this issue with the families of the victims or the Tunisian public.[47]

In addition, the Tunisian government flirted with leftist, liberal and nationalist opposition movements under the rubric of secularism and on the pretext of confronting the Islamist threat using the Muslim brotherhood as a scarecrow. Such tactics gave the regime political cover to isolate Islamists from the other political forces. This strategy grew more effective with the spread of violence between the state and the Islamists in Algeria. As the Algerian democratic experiment became tarnished with blood and death squads, democracy was presented as a system that would only bring the Islamists to power, allowing them to impose their programme of Islamizing state and society. Two decades later, the bloody history of the region provided additional tools for dictators to frighten people away from democracy and cow them into submission, especially in the years following the US occupation of Iraq and its tragic consequences.[48] Tunisia's key allies, the United States and France, countenanced this policy and approved Ben Ali's tactics by ignoring his authoritarian practices.

When the coup took place on 7 November 1987, Paris appeared hesitant to approve the removal of France's favourite president. However, Ben Ali offered France guarantees that French–Tunisian relations would continue and prosper. Lionel Jospin, secretary-general of the Socialist Party at the time, was the first French politician to be received in Carthage Palace. He could have asked for a meeting with the ousted president but chose not to.[49]

During a visit to Tunisia in 1992 while still mayor of Paris, Jacques Chirac coined the term 'Tunisian Miracle', a phrase he reaffirmed when he became president of the French Republic.[50] Prior to the mid-1990s, France had been unconcerned with human rights violations in Tunisia. By the mid-1990s, however, the French media and public opinion were increasingly critical of what was

47. Ibid., pp. 302–3.

48. Not to mention the violence in Syria and the rise of ISIS, both of which have been heavily exploited by anti-democracy forces in the region since 2013.

49. Beau and Tuquoi, *Our Friend Ben Ali*, p. 206.

50. Ibid., p. 304.

taking place in Tunisia, forcing the French government to alter its public tone in dealing with the Tunisian government. Nonetheless, French diplomacy missed no opportunity to praise the Tunisian regime. During that time, Ben Ali waged a media campaign boasting of his long war against Islamic terrorism while claiming that European states were offering refuge to Islamist terrorists, a case in point being the political exile granted by the United Kingdom to Rached Ghannouchi.[51] After the 11 September 2001 attacks, Chirac visited both Tunisia and Morocco to coordinate counterterrorism efforts, publicly praising the Tunisian president for combating terrorism due to 'his deep convictions' and for Tunisia's 'astonishing economic and social achievements'.[52]

Another of Ben Ali's key allies was the former speaker of the French National Assembly, Philip Seguin, a de Gaullist who was keen to compare Ben Ali to Charles de Gaulle. Sagan once described Ben Ali as 'a modern politician who defends the principles of humanity and freedom'. During the November 1998 convention of the ruling party, the Democratic Constitutional Rally, Sagan said unabashedly to Ben Ali, 'This is an opportunity for me to publicly reiterate my admiration for your party, which I never miss an opportunity to mention as a model to the members of my own party.'[53]

Nicolas Sarkozy was no different from his predecessors, especially the de Gaullists among them. During his May 2008 visit to Tunisia, and following the signing of sizeable economic agreements worth more than EUR 2 billion, Sarkozy claimed that Tunisia was making advances in the field of personal freedoms and commended Ben Ali for not leaving the field open to 'extremists', 'conservatives' and 'tyrants' who were trying to drag the country backwards.[54]

The French Right tried to pursue a 'superpower' policy, that is, to act in the interest of France as a superpower aside from human rights considerations. The dictator benefitted from a French diplomacy that was even less sensitive to questions of human rights than the policies of the United States, especially in Africa. Nevertheless, the French Left continued to support the Tunisian regime given its secularism and its 'moderate' position on Israel.

For French policy makers, it was critical that France retain and invest its influence in its former colonies in order to compete with the United States in Africa and the Mediterranean Basin. To this end, France not only ignored but even violated the values heralded officially by the Republic. This approach is similar to that of Europe in general, where criticism of human rights violations is left to the European Parliament, while in practice human rights concerns are not allowed to

51. Pia Christina Wood, 'French Foreign Policy and Tunisia: Do Human Rights Matter?' *Middle East Policy*, vol. 4, no. 2 (June 2002), pp. 92–110, esp. 102.

52. Ibid., p. 107.

53. Beau & Tuquoi, pp. 174–5.

54. 'Sarkozy responds to those criticizing his support for Ben Ali: Tunisia is a model to be followed', *al-Sharq al-Awsat*, 1 May 2008, at: https://bit.ly/37ckAXJ.

interfere with strategic political and economic interests.[55] The other side of the deal with the West (support for an authoritarian ally who could guarantee stability and block an Islamist alternative) was the bargain suggested to the regime's citizens, namely to give up their freedom in return for security and preservation of the lifestyle that would be threatened by Islamist rule.[56] The problematic issue in this bargain is that many sectors of Tunisian society had never achieved the 'lifestyle' promised by the regime; on the contrary, they were struggling to meet their basic needs, while other Tunisians were unwilling to give up their freedoms at any cost.

Exploitation of the 'Islamist threat' was never enough, of course, to quench people's demand for civil liberties. In a rather happy irony, the repressive practices of the police state led indirectly to a rapprochement among Tunisia's opposition forces despite their ideological differences. This rapprochement culminated in successful dialogue initiatives between secular and religious opposition groups in 2003 in France's Aix en Provence and on a larger scale in the 18 October 2005 Committee, to be addressed subsequently.

Socio-economic background

Prior to the spread of open-market economies, which began in the 1970s and culminated in the 1980s and 1990s in comprehensive structural reforms dictated by the World Bank and the IMF, numerous Third World countries adopted economic policies that aimed to build up their national economies through investment in the public sector. These policies, which attempted to spur industrialization and self-sufficiency in consumption instead of relying on imports, became known in economic literature as policies of import substitution industrialization (ISI). The decisions were based on the needs of the local economy rather than on standard Western consumption patterns or export-oriented industries. Countries that adopted ISI strategies tended to become less reliant on the importation of consumer and basic goods, focusing their imports instead on equipment, production tools, and other specialized goods. These policies were accompanied by a process of nation-building, agrarian reforms, universalized education, and other modernization measures. However, the policies required to create national consensus and expand the social base of the political regime necessitated higher levels of public spending, which exceeded the sources of income available to the state, thus driving up their external debt.

In some of these countries, the problem was aggravated by the failures of development programmes, the overwhelming weight of debt compared to GDP, and the hasty entry into grandiose projects whose purposes and feasibility had not been well thought out. Ultimately, the tragedy lay in the transformation of the

55. Wood, 'French Foreign Policy and Tunisia', pp. 107–8.

56. See also: Beatrice Hibbou, *The Force of Obedience: the Political Economy of Repression in Tunisia* (Cambridge and Malden, MA: Polity Press, 2011).

so-called popular democracies of nationalist modernizing regimes in the newly independent states into despotic regimes which prioritized political loyalty over merit. In the absence of transparency, these regimes became hotbeds of political and financial corruption that aggravated class differences through the creation of nouveau riche classes favoured by those in power. Thus, relations of loyalty were converted into political capital, and political capital into economic capital.

In the 1960s, Tunisia adopted a socialist variation of state capitalism that was widespread in the Third World. Open to the West, this model was based on increasing the role of the public sector in the national development plan in order to effect socio-economic transformations. Five years after independence, Bourguiba abandoned his liberal economic agenda and adopted the model of a centralized economy. It was also at this time that the ruling Neo-Destour Party changed its name to the Socialist Destourian Party, and Ahmed Ben Salah was appointed Minister of Finance. This economic choice was undoubtedly based on the need of the state to intervene in the economy, which could only be done by expanding the public sector, enacting tariff protection and investing in infrastructure. This policy was especially evident in the imposition of strict controls on imports, prices and interest rates, as well as the establishment of agricultural cooperatives. By 1969, the public sector dominated the banking, transportation, energy, mining and wholesale and retail trading sectors. It also controlled 70 per cent of industries, 90 per cent of agriculture and even a portion of artisanal professions.[57] Collectivization likewise encompassed colonial farms and Muslim endowments, which had been confiscated by the state in 1957.

The main crisis of this model in Tunisia occurred in 1968 with the failure of agricultural plans based on the transfer of land to cooperatives. The seizure of the collective properties that were cultivated by families was faced by owners' resistance. In the mid-1970s, the failures in agriculture became apparent when 'farm exports to mainly European markets did not even cover 50 percent of the cost of imported food'.[58] Anger in the countryside was likewise fuelled by three consecutive years of drought.

It was in 1964 that a budget deficit appeared for the first time as a result of the general level of spending and the depreciation of the currency. Nevertheless, these policies were pursued until 1970, achieving a growth rate that averaged 5 per cent annually. In order to finance its projects, the state relied on oil exports, foreign investment and remittances from Tunisian emigrants. Nonetheless, the frequent increases in wages and the expansion of the public sector led to a rise in the public deficit. The private sector was also incapable of keeping up with the increases in

57. Myriam Blin, 'The Political Economy of IMF and World Bank Interventions: Is Tunisia Really a Model Student?' in Hamed El-Said & Jane Harrigan (eds.), *Aid and Power in the Arab World: IMF and World Bank Policy-Based Lending in the Middle East and North Africa* (New York: Palgrave Macmillan, 2009), p. 107.

58. Julia Clancy-Smith, *Tunisian Revolutions: Reflections on Seas, Coasts, and Interiors* (Washington D.C.: Georgetown University Press, 2014), p. 12.

wages in the public sector. In 1967, annual debt service came to 26.1 per cent of total export revenue as compared to 1.6 per cent in 1961; the ratio of external debt to the GDP nearly doubled during the same period.[59]

The year 1969 witnessed the replacement of Ahmed Ben Salah by Hédi Amara Nouira and the start of the first era of economic liberalization. However, it should be remembered that privatization in Tunisia never meant weakening the state's grip on the economy.[60] One should be cautious here not to be misguided by the Western understanding of economic liberalization, for in Tunisia liberalization was controlled from above for political reasons. Under Nouira, more than 500 foreign-owned factories were opened. At the same time, many state-owned companies, mostly heavy industries, were established and state funding of the public sector almost doubled between the years 1972 and 1984.[61] Government spending[62] decreased from 17.6 per cent of GDP in 1969 to as little as 13.23 per cent in 1974, and ended the decade with 14.47 per cent of GDP, which was still below that registered in 1969.[63] Liberalization led to the diversification of interest groups in the Tunisian economy and especially to the emergence of a class of businessmen who were close to political decision-makers. Also, during this era, the external debt rose from 43.70 per cent of the GNI in 1970 to 74.03 per cent in 1987.[64] This was a vivid illustration of the falsity of the thesis that liberalization of the economy and reduction of public spending reduce external debt.

The government adopted a strategy whereby it combined import substitution, private sector development and export promotion. The year 1973 saw the establishment of new institutions such as the Industry Promotion Agency (API) and the Export Promotion Centre (CEPEX) to serve this new strategy, while the Investment Law of 1972 granted special advantages and incentives to exporting manufacturing companies.[65]

The new policies consisted of encouraging exports by developing the private sector, limiting cooperatives and returning some confiscated lands to their original owners while maintaining protectionist policies in relation to agricultural goods

59. Blin, 'The Political Economy of IMF and World Bank Interventions', p. 107.

60. This legacy, which has lingered since the revolution, represents one of the major obstacles hindering investment and growth. The balance between a free-market economy and the state's guarantee of social services, fair taxation, and social justice has yet to be achieved a full decade after the revolution.

61. Perkins, *A History of Modern Tunisia*, p. 163.

62. Government spending includes purchases of goods and services, compensation of employees, grants and social benefits.

63. 'Tunisia: Government spending, percent of GDP', *The Global Economy*, accessed at: https://bit.ly/33TSoH4

64. 'External debt stocks (% of GNI) – Tunisia', *The World Bank Data*, accessed at: https://bit.ly/3mY2MFt

65. Mohamed Ayadi and Wided Mattoussi, 'Scoping of the Tunisian Economy', Working Paper no. 17, *Brookings Institution* (2016), p. 3.

and, finally, abandoning some state investments. In 1983, after a drop in oil and phosphate prices, the state attempted to lift the subsidies that it had extended to basic commodities. The price of bread was doubled (though the popular uprising led to the retraction of the decision), and economic deterioration continued on the microeconomic level. This period also witnessed the sudden deportation of 30,000 Tunisian labourers from Libya in 1985. These were the conditions that prefaced Ben Ali's 1987 coup d'état and the decision to allow international monetary institutions to interfere in the Tunisian economy.

The privatization of land in the 1990s was a crucial stage in the dismantling of Tunisia's public sector, a process that began in the 1970s following the political and economic crisis of 1968–9. Rich landlords benefitted from the privatizations, and a large number of them became businessmen in the cities. These individuals were already linked through close ties to the ruling regime and attempted to further consolidate their ties to the 'ruling family' in search of more personal gains. Land privatization provides a good example of a process of economic liberalization that does not lead to democracy but instead revives traditional political arrangements and the creation of personal fiefdoms in the countryside. As members of the labouring class lost their property, their political power shrank, as did their influence over the regime's plans and socio-economic policies. In Bourguiba's era, political and economic planning was synchronized with the populism of a regime that relied on the support of the sections of society that benefitted from the public sector and from the social policies of the state.[66]

The Tunisian economy's shift towards privatization between 1971 and 1986 resembled a similar process in Egypt, with the difference that this change took place without shifts in foreign policy or changing international alignments and was directed by the same leadership throughout. Indeed, this era could be seen as the second, and final, phase of Bourguiba's rule. However, the comprehensive structural adjustments to the Tunisian economy took place only after 1986 under IMF supervision, which included financial austerity to lower budget deficits, restriction of the role of the state in the economy and the liberalization of foreign trade as stipulated by the 'Washington Consensus'.[67] Joseph Stiglitz described this perspective as a form of 'market fundamentalism' in the sense that it represented a return to the fundamentals of the market economy.[68] Washington Consensus

66. On this theme, see Stephen J. King, *Liberalization against Democracy: The Local Politics of Economic Reform in Tunisia* (Bloomington: Indiana University Press, 2003).

67. The term was first used by John Williamson in 1989 to describe the agreement reached between World Bank, the IMF and the US Treasury concerning the role of the two institutions in Third World economies. John Williamson, 'A Short History of the Washington Consensus', in Narcís Serra and Joseph E. Stiglitz (eds.), *The Washington Consensus Reconsidered: Towards a New Global Governance* (Oxford: Oxford University Press, 2008), pp. 16–17.

68. Joseph E. Stiglitz, 'Is There a Post Washington Consensus?' in Serra & Stiglitz, pp. 41–2.

policies consisted of economic reforms to be implemented by countries undergoing financial and economic crises caused by a lack of discipline in public finance, a ballooning and inefficient public sector, the use of tariff barriers as part of national development plans, lowering prices for basic goods through direct and indirect government subsidies, and the attempt to build a national import substitution industry. All of these 'ailments', according to the Washington Consensus, led to a decline in the growth rate, an expansion of debt, budget deficits, corruption and other problems.

The 'consensus' principles call for amending these policies by focusing on macroeconomic stability by limiting budget deficits through spending cuts, inflation control, floating or fixing the value of the local currency in a manner that reflects the balance of external payments and abolition of state intervention in the pricing of goods and services through subsidies. Taken together, these policies constitute the so-called neoliberal reform package, which combines structural adjustment policies with strategies of monetary stabilization.

Generally speaking, the majority of these reforms tend to harm the poorer segments of society that benefit most from the subsidization of consumer goods and state-imposed price controls. These policies also create new wealthy classes born out of the coalition between political decision-makers and the new businesses that have benefitted from privatization and liberalization, and who receive favourable treatment in the licencing of private projects, the distribution of public contracts and so on. Under despotism, these economically liberal reforms do not lead to democratization but, rather, to rampant corruption. Furthermore, capitalists are not influential enough in countries like Tunisia to demand a share in political decision-making and are dependent on the state through cliental links. In this Bonapartist division of roles, their access to privileges is made possible by the ruling regime (through the ruling party and nepotism during Ben Ali's rule).

Joseph Stiglitz has offered a useful comparison between two different paths. On one hand, we have the Latin American countries that dutifully applied the principles of the Washington Consensus. This application led to high rates of growth for a period of seven years during the early 1990s followed by a recession in the mid-1990s. The result was an average growth rate for the decade that was only half of that achieved by the same countries during the 1950s and 1970s when the opposite policies were in place. In comparison, the countries of East Asia achieved massive advances in development and growth by maintaining monetary stability and policies that limited public spending, while remaining more cautious about privatization. A group of international economists and finance experts therefore created the so-called Barcelona Principles as a form of self-criticism. These principles focus on the necessity of achieving a balance between the role of the state and that of the market: the state is required to intervene against monopolies even on the microeconomic level. The state must likewise intervene when the market fails to regulate the economy at times of crisis, as well as in matters relating to consumer protection, environmental protection, the fight against poverty and the equitable distribution of national wealth.[69] All these elements were reiterated with further emphasis after the financial crisis of 2008–9.

The Arab world also underwent neoliberal policy shifts, which in the cases of Egypt, Tunisia and others were referred to as economic 'reforms' but were roundly criticized by a number of Arab economists. Indeed, the damage done to the economies of Latin America and the poverty resulting from these policies in some Third World countries, especially in Africa, have exposed these reform packages to sound criticism at the global level.[70] Later, this critical reflection led to the development of more credible economic alternatives, and the World Bank itself was forced to implement some of the recommendations made by its critics during the 1990s. The World Bank later amended its structural adjustment models with a new approach of 'shared growth', which proposes a strategy that allows people to participate in, and benefit from, growth.

The shared growth approach seeks to convince the beneficiaries of growth to freely share the fruits of development with others, and to view sharing as a necessary condition for maintaining growth and profit. This is to be done through targeted assistance to the poorest societal groups rather than subsidizing consumer goods for everyone and by encouraging government spending that supports universal social well-being. However, critics of the shared growth approach insist that an equitable distribution of income must form the very basis of economic policy through state human development policies, and not a mere 'conviction' or decision by the beneficiaries of growth to share their wealth. The equitable distribution of wealth requires a specific, dedicated policy, in addition to the policies fostering growth. In general, this requires state investment in fields such as education and health, the adoption of a progressive tax policy, and equality of access to capital, land property, and other resources.[71] A number of proponents of this 'New Southern Consensus', in opposition to the 'Washington Consensus', believe that inequality in access to economic resources eventually hampers growth itself, because these inequalities limit human development. The economic liberalization policies as applied in Tunisia did create a new social base in favour of economic change; however, they led simultaneously to the tightening of authoritarian policies and a rise in corruption.

The relationship of the Ben Ali family and that of his wife with the Tunisian Union for Trade, Industry, and Artisanal Professions (UTICA) was one of the primary symbols and tools of corruption, a fact which was completely ignored by the European Union and the international financial institutions that heaped praise

69. Paul Krugman, 'Inequality and Redistribution', in Serra and Stiglitz, *The Washington Consensus Reconsidered*, pp. 31–40; Stiglitz, pp. 41–56.

70. See Douglas A. Chalmers, et al., *The New Politics of Inequality in Latin America: Rethinking Participation and Representation* (Oxford: Oxford University Press, 1997).

71. Andrés Solimano, 'Beyond Unequal Development', in Andrés Solimano, Eduardo Aninat and Nancy Birdsall (eds.), *Distributive Justice and Economic Development* (Ann Arbor: University of Michigan Press, 1999).

upon Tunisia's economic policies. The fusion of business with politics through UTICA and other entities is what led industrialists and businessmen to remain silent even on policy issues.

The struggle that arose against economic liberalization policies generated a social reaction that carried democratic demands. It could be argued that all struggles against social inequality caused by economic policies in despotic states include some democratic demands, as well as those that preceded the era of liberalization.[72] The critique of the cooperative policies of the 1960s, formulated by Mestiri's current within the PSD, likewise took the form of calls for more democratic practices and structures. The struggles during the era of economic liberalization generally took a leftist and unionist character. Islamist groups began also to organize politically during the 1970s as the idea spread that the left could replace the regime. All of these movements articulated demands for democracy in the sense of political participation, even before introducing democracy as a political programme.

After Bourguiba's overthrow in 1987 in what became known as 'the medical coup' (declaring the president unfit to rule based on a diagnosis made by a team of physicians), or 'the constitutional coup" carried out by Ben Ali, the latter adopted the slogans of economic liberalism and political democratization, promising openness and reform. After the 1988 national pact and the 1989 elections, the general impression was that Tunisia was undergoing an important process of democratic transformation. However, this impression was challenged during the 1994 elections, and over the following decade, stepped-up economic liberalism went hand in hand with growing authoritarianism and repression.[73] After 1989, and with the waning of labour's political power due to privatization, the UGTT was afflicted by the same weakness as other unions had been in similar conditions: it shifted from waging unionist struggles that promoted democratic political slogans to collaborating with the regime, content to conduct seasonal wage negotiations based on the price index. During this era, union leaders were contained by the regime and worked in an environment that distanced them from their constituencies on the ground. However, some of the unions' local branches maintained greater independence and loyalty to their mandate, prompting them to cooperate with local activists.

72. Christopher Alexander, 'State, Labor, and the New Global Economy', in Dirk Vandewalle (ed.), *North Africa: Development and Reform in a Changing Global Economy* (London: Palgrave Macmillan, 1996), p. 183.

73. In the beginning, at least, it was believed by many, including Al Nahda's leaders, that Ben Ali was launching genuine democratic reforms. This belief may have been justified during the early years of his rule in the late 1980s. However, such a perspective was unwarranted in the late 1990s, when despotism became blatantly obvious. See Georgie Anne Geyer, 'Tunisia: A Country that Works', *The Washington Quarterly*, vol. 21, no. 4 (1998), p. 98.

Despite all these problems, the Tunisian economy has indeed achieved some measure of success on the macroeconomic level in a country devoid of natural resources, and whose success is dependent on investment in education and modern administration. While it was right to critique the glowing World Bank and IMF reports that presented Tunisia as a 'model student' of these international institutions, one should not judge the Tunisian experience as an unmitigated failure. Out of all the Middle Eastern and North African countries that implemented structural adjustment reforms proposed by the World Bank and the IMF, Tunisia was the only one that achieved any semblance of success, at least in terms of general macroeconomic indexes. Poverty rates declined at least in absolute numbers, the relative size of the external debt was reduced, a reasonable growth rate was maintained and inflation was kept under control. The question remains whether this success was actually due to the economic liberalization proposed by the World Bank and the IMF, or whether it was because the Tunisian government applied some of these institutions' recommendations and rejected others. I believe that more credit should be given to the Tunisian technocrats and administrative bureaus, who insisted on gradualism, defended the role of the state, insisted on partial privatization and resisted the comprehensive privatization programme mandated by the neoliberal policies of international financial institutions.

As noted earlier, change in Tunisia did not come all at once. Tunisia began the process of economic reform in 1970, well before the extensive intervention of international financial institutions in 1986 and the Tunisian economists and public officials who negotiated with international institutions insisted on maintaining Tunisia's own pace in privatization. At any rate, while Tunisia did show some positive outcomes, it did not achieve the great success ascribed to it by international institutions: unemployment rates remained relatively high, especially among educated youth, rates of private investment remained low, regional discrepancies in development were reproduced[74] and the income inequality gap steadily increased in tandem with growing political repression. Thus, the flow of funds and loans into Tunisia from international financial institutions was out of proportion to the size of the Tunisian economy and its modest successes.

The steady flow of foreign capital into the country can be explained based on political causes, such as the acquiescence of the Tunisian government to the language and policies of the IMF and World Bank, in addition to its 'moderate' stances on regional policies and on issues of interest to Western powers, such as combating terrorism, the peace process with Israel and so on. In many instances, in fact, these factors appear to have been more important to the international financial

74. Even three years after the revolution in 2014, 80 per cent of the national production was produced in coastal areas, and only 20 per cent of the growth domestic product was produced in the interior (south-west and centre-west), which is home to 11 million Tunisians. These discrepancies remain a major problem to be addressed. See Clancy-Smith, *Tunisian Revolutions*, p. 5.

institutions than the Tunisian economy itself.[75] It should also be mentioned that only Egypt and Jordan have received more foreign aid per capita than Tunisia has, which is due to the fact that these countries rely on sources other than financial institutions, such as the US government, which provides large grants for political and strategic reasons.

Despite the authoritarian rule that combined neoliberal economics with a demagoguery that claimed enlightened modernity while prohibiting civil and political liberties and real popular engagement in politics, Tunisia partnered with the European Union through migration agreements formulated according to the EU motto: 'Yes to cooperation; no to migration'. These agreements provided temporary contractual work opportunities for skilled labour with the aim of preventing migration and permanent resettlement in European countries. Under Ben Ali, Tunisia thus found a golden opportunity to benefit from Mediterranean cooperation with Europe through temporary migration contracts for its burgeoning workforce.

In 1969, Tunisia became an associate member of the European Economic Community, which guaranteed preferential treatment for Tunisia in trade with Europe. By the mid-1990s, Europe was supplying Tunisia with 70 per cent of its imports while purchasing 80 per cent of its exports, turning the EU into the Tunisia's most important commercial partner. The free trade agreement was the only means of breaking into the EU market, as the General Agreement on Tariffs and Trade (GATT), to which Tunisia had adhered in 1990, 'banned discriminatory trade practices of the kind from which Tunisia had previously benefited'.[76] Foreign investors, mostly Europeans, were pumping nearly DT 1 billion annually into the Tunisian economy. Textiles sold by Tunisia to Europe made up 42 per cent of Tunisia's total exports, which made the Tunisian economy vulnerable to economic crises in this sector and to the instability of the international market. This was especially true following the entry of Chinese goods into the European textile market, which further exacerbated the unemployment crisis.

Investments were linked to privatization measures which the IMF and the World Bank insisted on implementing in the late 1990s; around seventy-eight state enterprises were privatized between 1997 and 2001. The tourism industry was vital for the livelihood of Tunisians, 12 per cent of whom depended on this sector.[77] However, already reeling from the aftermath of the September 11 attacks, Tunisia's tourism sector faced another challenge with the April 2002 attack on a historic synagogue on the island of Jerba.[78]

On the social level, half of Tunisia's annual budget was allotted to education, health care and other similar services. Tunisia witnessed population growth at 1.1

75. Blin, 'The Political Economy of IMF and World Bank Interventions', p. 141.

76. Perkins, *A History of Modern Tunisia*, p. 203.

77. Ibid., p. 212.

78. The attack left twenty-one dead and fourteen wounded, most of them German tourists. Ibid., p. 212.

per cent a year, literacy rates reached 75 per cent and life expectancy rose to almost seventy-three years.[79]

During Ben Ali's reign, Tunisia's GDP increased fivefold, from USD 9,018 million in 1986 to USD 44,050 in 2010. After 1987, the GDP annual growth averaged nearly 5 per cent. The GNI per capita almost doubled in the two decades between 1990 and 2010. Though the inflation rate fluctuated, it was generally low compared to the last years of Bourguiba's reign. The highest inflation rate in Tunisia was reported in 1984 at 8.9 per cent, while the lowest was in 2001 at 1.98 per cent. During the last years of Ben Ali's reign, specifically after 2003, Tunisia witnessed a decrease in its government debt in relation to GDP. In fact, the country's lowest government debt (39.2% of GDP) was recorded in 2010. Tunisia's Human Development Index (HDI) score for 1990 was 0.569, while in 2010, at the end of Ben Ali's reign, it reached 0.717 (0 = the lowest level of development and 1 = the highest level of development). Unemployment rates during Ben Ali's reign declined overall, from 16.20 per cent in 1990 to 13.05 per cent in 2010. The lowest rate was achieved in 2007 with 12.36 per cent, right before the global economic crisis of 2008–9. Poverty rates (as defined by the government) declined from 25.4 per cent in 2000 to 20.5 per cent in 2010, with a drop in extreme poverty rates from 7.7 per cent in 2000 to 6.0 per cent in 2010 (Figures 2.1–2.4).[80]

However, neither Ben Ali nor the international powers that supported his policies recognized the three major challenges to these policies, all of which were linked to human dignity, namely: (1) higher living standards and broader access to education, which led to rising expectations regarding living standards, quality of

79. Ibid., pp. 211–12.

80. 'GDP (current US$) – Tunisia', *The World Bank Data*, accessed at: https://bit.ly/3dCeDFf; 'GDP growth (annual %) – Tunisia', *The World Bank Data*, accessed at: https://bit.ly/33HdkRu; 'Tunisia GDP Annual Growth Rate', *Trading Economics*, accessed at: http://bit.ly/32Tc0bV; 'GNI per capita in thousands of US$ (2011 PPP)', *Global Data Lab*, accessed at: https://bit.ly/37qOp5P; 'Inflation, consumer prices (annual %) – Tunisia', *The World Bank Data*, accessed at: https://bit.ly/37xtuhA; 'Tunisia Government Debt to GDP', *Trading Economics*, accessed at: https://bit.ly/33CDWTR; 'Tunisia: Human Development Indicators', *United Nations Development Programme: Human Development Reports*, accessed at: https://bit.ly/373Bfg3; 'Sub-national HDI', *Global Data Lab*, accessed at: https://bit.ly/2LnCPBc; 'The National Survey of Population and Employment for the year 2010', *Republic of Tunisia: The Ministry of Development, Investment and International Cooperation*, (National Institute of Statistics NSI - June 2011), p. 28, accessed at: https://bit.ly/37xN2lY; 'Tunisie en Chiffres 2018', *Institut National de la Statistique. Statistiques Tunisie*, p. 20, accessed at: https://bit.ly/36Iyp05; 'Unemployment, total (% of total labor force) (national estimate) – Tunisia', *The World Bank Data*, accessed at: https://bit.ly/3gcAzrU; 'Tunisia Unemployment Rate2005–2020 Data', *Trading Economics*, accessed at: https://bit.ly/37MZBtx; 'IMF: World Economic Outlook (WEO) Database, October 2020', *knoema*, accessed at: https://bit.ly/3gq6jKf; 'Households and living conditions: Poverty', *Statistiques Tunisie*, accessed at: https://bit.ly/33X5Gmp.

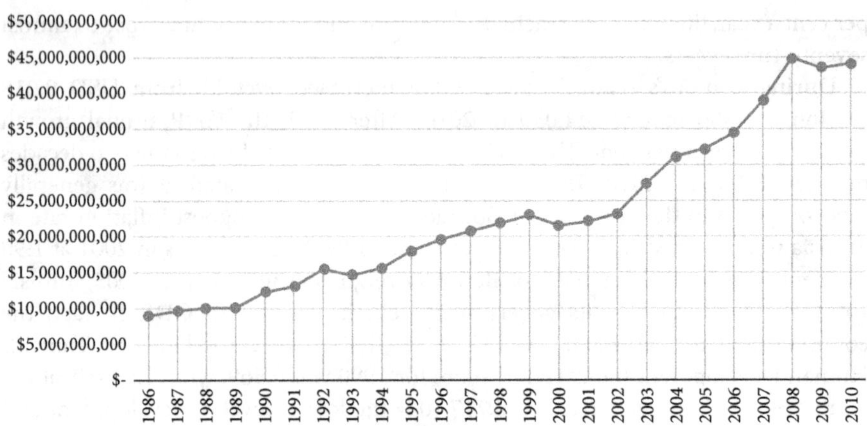

Figure 2.1 GDP (current US$) (1986–2010). *Source*: The World Bank Data.

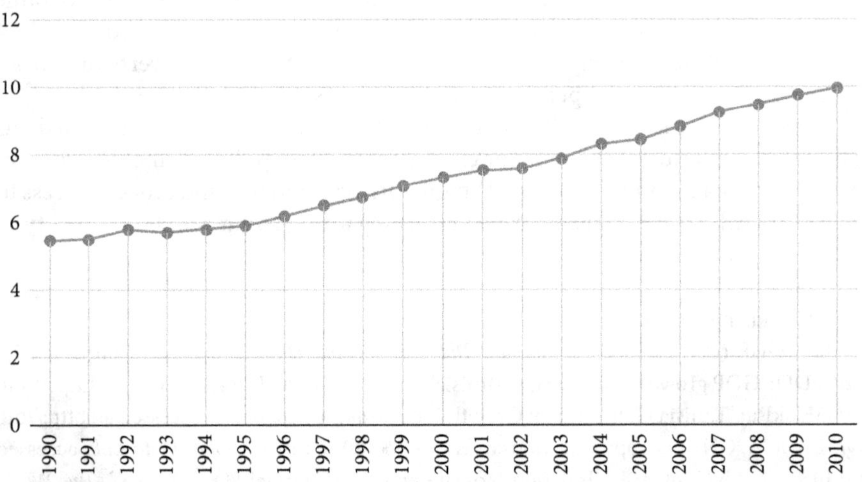

Figure 2.2 GNI per capita in thousands of US$ (2011 PPP) (1990–2010). *Source*: Global Data Lab.

life, status and the need for freedom; (2) greater awareness of relative deprivation due to unequal distribution of the benefits of growth and the inevitable corruption in neoliberal economies under authoritarianism; and (3) worsening unemployment in the country's interior and among its educated youth overall, with an industrial and service economy that produced unskilled jobs (Figures 2.5–2.7).

Modernists argue that economic liberalism diversifies sources of economic power, therefore preparing the country for a process of political democratization. It has been proven, however, that neoliberal policies in developing states under conditions of authoritarianism do not lead to democracy. At the same time, we now know that the repercussions of these policies can lead to growth, but also to worsening social gaps, higher expectations, feelings of relative deprivation, social

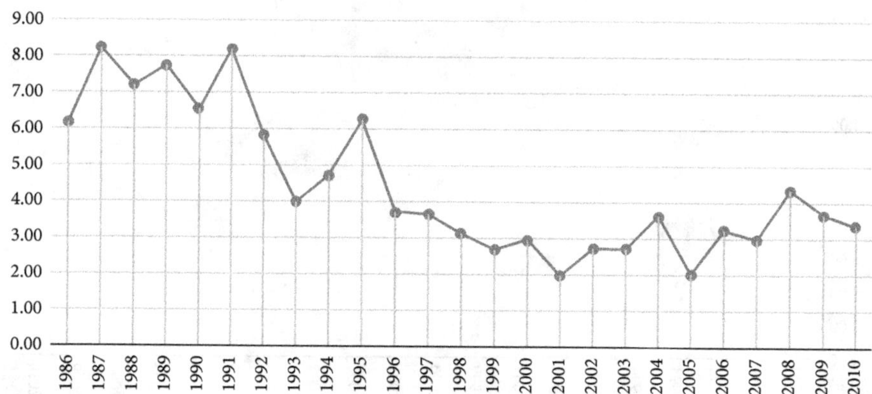

Figure 2.3 Inflation, consumer prices (annual %) (1986–2010). *Source*: The World Bank Data.

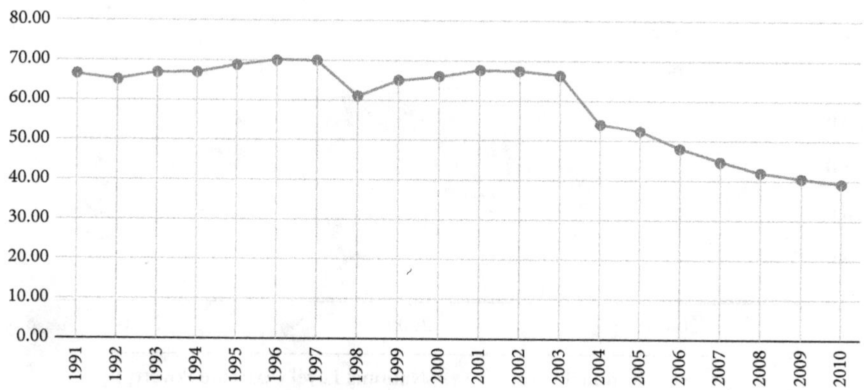

Figure 2.4 Government debt to GDP (1991–2010). *Source*: Trading Economics: Central Bank of Tunisia.

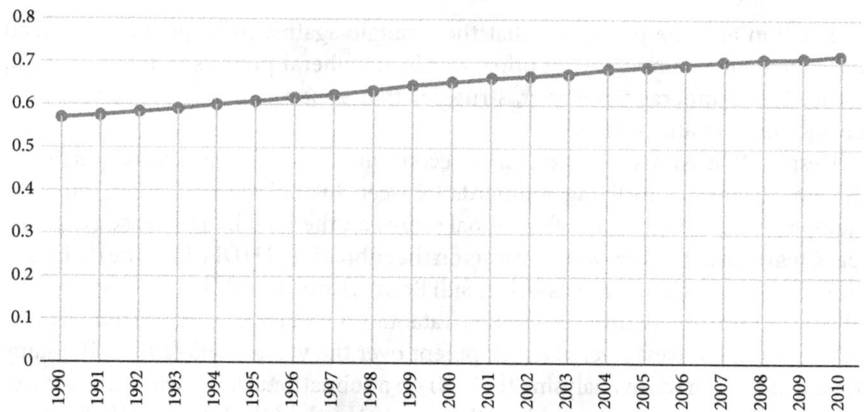

Figure 2.5 HDI scores (1990–2010). *Source*: United Nations Development Programme (UNDP); Global Data Labs.

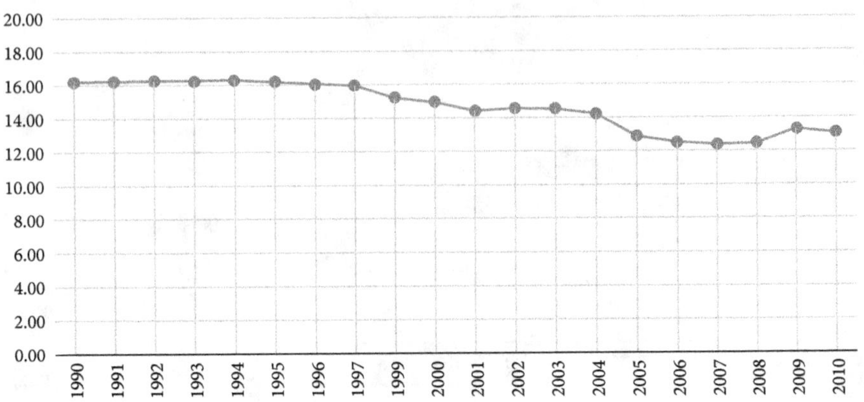

Figure 2.6 Unemployment rate (%) (1990–2010). *Source*: National Institute of Statistics NSI – Tunisia; Trading Economics: NSI, The World Bank Data; IMF Database.

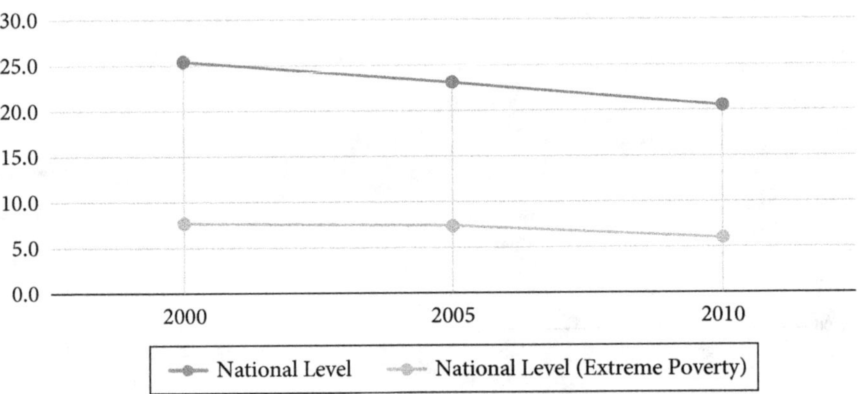

Figure 2.7 Poverty rate (%) (2000–10). *Source*: Statistiques Tunisie.

indignation and the possibility that the struggle against these policies may lead to demands for democracy. In other words, neoliberal policies in themselves do not lead to democracy; however, struggles that arise against them may possibly advance democratic demands.

Despite Ben Ali's success on many economic fronts, Tunisia faced persistent regional disparities in living standards between inland and coastal regions. For example, even though Tunisia's national scores on the HDI had increased over the years, regional disparities were obvious on the subnational HDI where the regions of the centre-west (Kairouan, Kasserine, Sidi Bouzid), northwest (Baja, Jendouba, Kef, Siliana), south-east (Gabes, Medinine, Tataouine) and south-west (Gafsa, Tozeur, Kebili) had the lowest level of development over the years (1990–2010). The same trend can be seen when analysing the GNI on a subnational level, where the centre-west, north-west, south-east and south-west regions had the lowest GNI per capita over the years, compared with the coastal regions of Tunisia. Unemployment rates

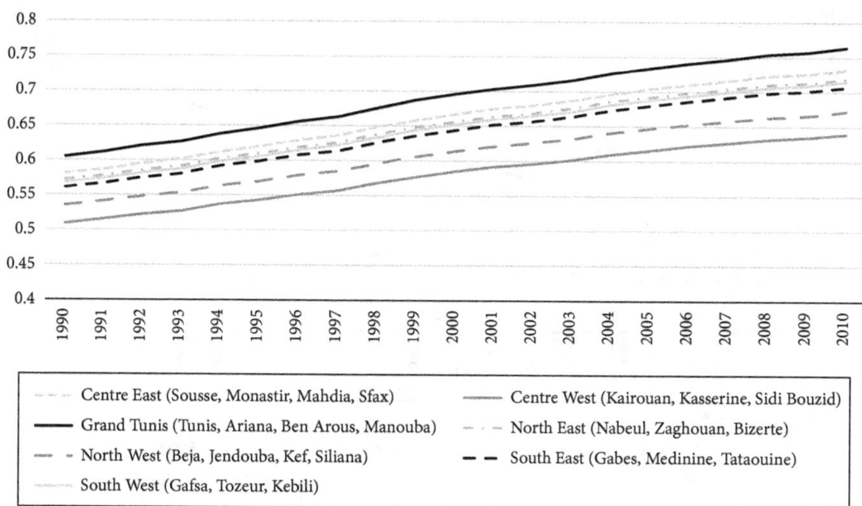

Figure 2.8 Subnational HDI scores (1990–2010). *Source*: Global Data Lab.

also varied by region. In the year before the revolution, unemployment rates in the south-west and south-east were the highest (at 23.4 per cent and 16.8 per cent respectively), with all governorates in these two regions recording unemployment rates above the national level of 13.05 per cent. Subnational poverty rates also vary considerably, and the highest poverty rates (both Poverty Line and Extreme Poverty Line) across the years (2000–10) were also recorded in the centre-west, north-west, south-east and south-west (Figures 2.8–2.10) (Table 2.1).[81]

In describing the evolution of economic policies in Tunisia between 1986 and the outbreak of the Tunisian Revolution, economists divided this phase into several stages, which could be in turn further categorized according to the successive agreements signed with the World Bank and the IMF. Broadly speaking, financial stabilization was achieved and a plan was implemented to gradually depreciate the Tunisian dinar. The depreciation took place in two stages, and efforts were made to lower the budget deficit and the inflation rate while increasing the rate of growth. These were the macroeconomic elements of stability addressed by the Tunisian economic reforms. Other structural reforms included liberalizing foreign trade

81. 'Sub-national HDI', *Global Data Lab,* accessed at: https://bit.ly/2LnCPBc; 'GNI per capita in thousands of US$ (2011 PPP)', *Global Data Lab*, accessed at: https://bit.ly/37qOp5P; 'The National Survey of Population and Employment for the year 2010', p. 154; Republic of Tunisia: Ministry of Development and International Cooperation, 'General Census of Population and Housing for the Year 2004 – First Issue: First Results', (National Institute of Statistics, March 2005), p. 45, accessed at: https://bit.ly/3mRmWRj; 'Measuring Poverty, Inequalities and Polarization in Tunisia: 2000–2010', *Statistiques Tunisie* (November 2012), p. 16, accessed at: https://bit.ly/2KbRnDg.

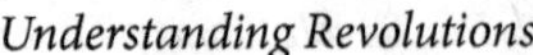

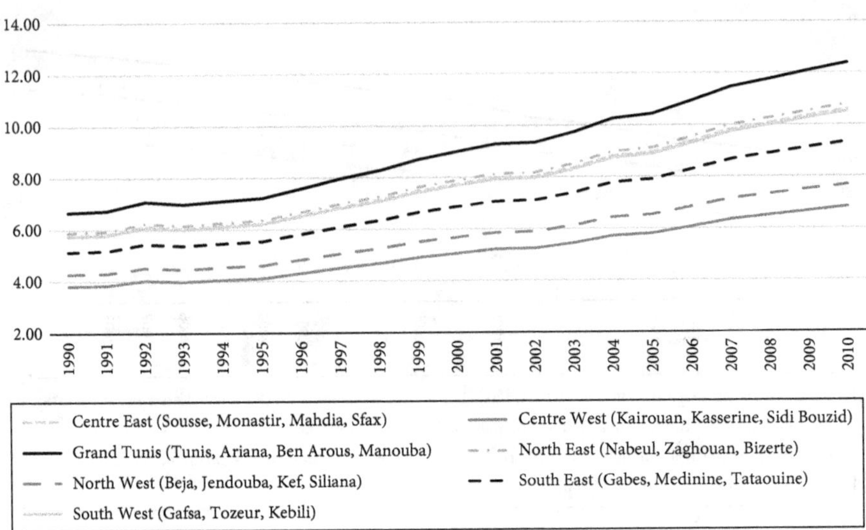

Figure 2.9 Subnational GNI per capita in thousands of US$ (2011 PPP) (1990–2010). *Source*: Global Data Lab.

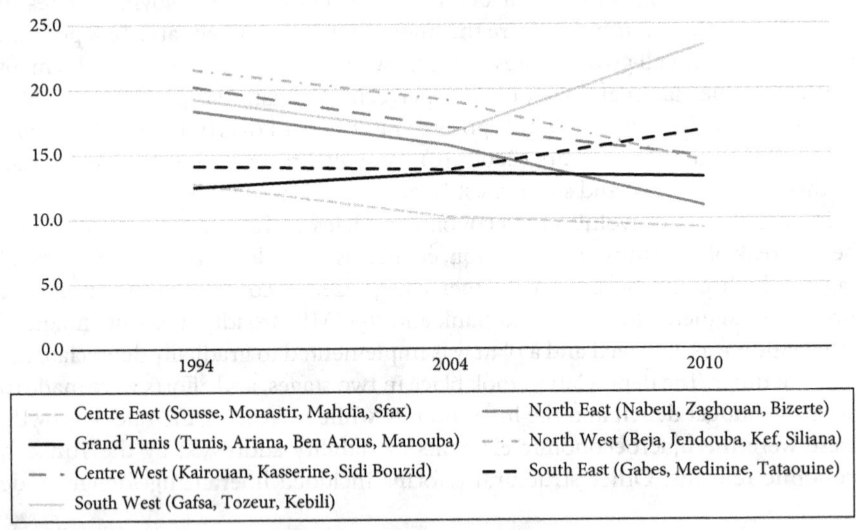

Figure 2.10 Unemployment rate (%) by region (1994–2010). *Source*: National Institute of Statistics.

by facilitating export and import licences, creating incentives to attract foreign investment, floating interest rates and implementing a gradual privatization programme.

The policies of stabilization and structural adjustment were accompanied by loans provided by international financial institutions over successive stages; these

Table 2.1 Poverty and Extreme Poverty Rates by Region (2000–10)

	Poverty Line			**Extreme Poverty Line**		
	2000	**2005**	**2010**	**2000**	**2005**	**2010**
Centre-east (Sousse, Monastir, Mahdia, Sfax)	21.4	12.6	8.0	6.4	2.6	1.6
North-east (Nabeul, Zaghouan, Bizerte)	32.1	21.6	10.3	10.5	5.4	1.8
Grand Tunis (Tunis, Ariana, Ben Arous, Mannouba)	21.0	14.6	9.1	4.3	2.3	1.1
North-west (Baja, Jendouba, Kef, Siliana)	35.3	26.9	25.7	12.1	8.9	8.8
Centre-west (Kairouan, Kasserine, Sidi Bouzid)	49.3	46.5	32.3	25.5	23.2	14.3
South-east (Gabes, Medinine, Tataouine)	44.3	29.0	17.9	17.5	9.6	4.9
South-west (Gafsa, Tozeur, Kebili)	47.8	33.2	21.5	21.7	12.1	6.4

'Measuring Poverty, Inequalities and Polarization in Tunisia: 2000–2010', *Statistiques Tunisie* (November 2012), p. 16, accessed at: https://bit.ly/2KbRnDg.

loans covered the restructuring plans in all economic fields including industry, agriculture, banking and commerce. When Tunisia joined the World Trade Organization in 1989, it began to privatize the hospitality and textile sectors. Unfortunately, however, this phase saw the emergence of privatization profiteers with close ties to the government.[82]

The Tunisian government, however, resisted the privatization of major national companies and industries, such as the phosphate industry, petrochemicals, cement, communications, oil and gas, and infrastructure projects. This reticence was influenced by the professional economic opinion among Tunisian experts and state officials. While the reasons not to privatize the vital sectors detailed by these experts were economic in nature, the regime took their advice due to political considerations related to its control over the economy and society.

According to the economic data, advances continued as the poverty rate fell to 4.1 per cent of the population in 2006 compared to 11.2 per cent in 1975. In that same year, the size of the middle class was estimated at 80 per cent of the population,[83] which is an arbitrary number obtained by subtracting the highest and lowest and 10 per cent in terms of income. However, there is evidence to suggest that poverty statistics were underreported while the middle-class data was exaggerated. Despite these official numbers, the class gap began to widen perceptibly between a relatively small wealthy class on the one hand and a broad middle class on the other. Thus, wide sectors of the 'middle' class were close

82. Blin, 'The Political Economy of IMF and World Bank Interventions', p. 121; see also Abdelsatar Grissa, 'The Tunisian State Enterprises and Privatization Policy', in Ira William Zartman (ed.), *Tunisia: The Political Economy of Reform* (Boulder and London: Lynne Rienner, 1991).

83. Blin, 'The Political Economy of IMF and World Bank Interventions', p. 129.

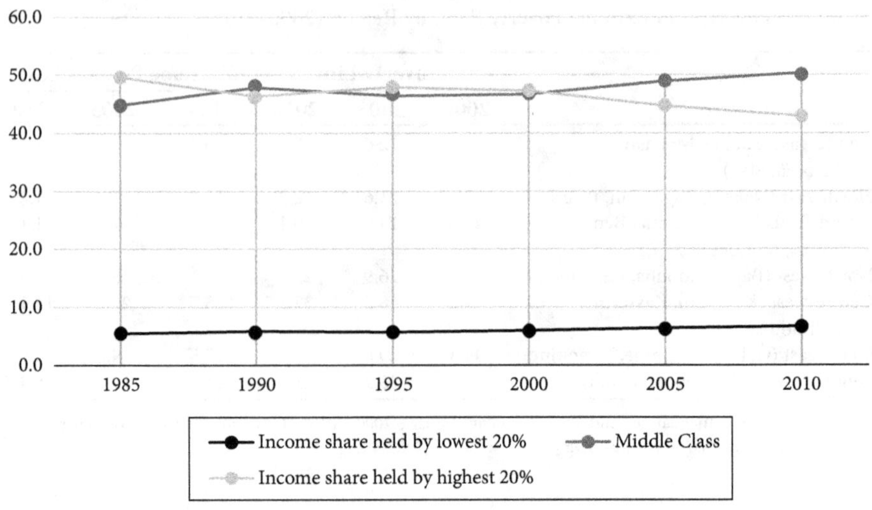

Figure 2.11 Tunisian middle-class share of income compared to the highest and lowest 20% (1985–2010).

to poverty given their low standard of living, despite maintaining the level of education, awareness, and needs typical of the middle class (Figure 2.11).

The distribution of the national income shows an extreme contrast, since the poorest 20 per cent of the population receives around 5–7 per cent of the total income, while the wealthiest 20 per cent receive around 45–50 per cent, which is almost equal to the share received by the remaining 60 per cent. In other words, nearly half of the country's total income goes to the richest 20 per cent of the population, while 55 per cent of this income is distributed among the remaining 80 per cent of the population.

Following the military coup in Algeria in response to the elections there and the outbreak of a quasi-civil war, the Tunisian regime's ability to maintain security and to defend the secular way of life became major concerns for a larger section of the public, who were exposed to regime propaganda touting a bargain to exchange their civil liberties and political rights for security. In this context, security and economic success became the regime's primary sources of legitimacy.[84]

The state also made strides in developing education, diversifying the national economy and training state officials according to the French model of the *Ecole Nationale de l'Administration* (ENA) since the Bourguiba era. On the downside, the state–society relationship was managed via the channels of political repression in order to guarantee the stability of the regime and enforce the economic programme.

84. Eva Bellin, 'Tunisian Industrialists and the State', in Zartman, p. 450; Eva Bellin, 'The Politics of Profit in Tunisia: Utility of the rentier paradigm?' *World Development*, vol. 22, no. 3 (March 1994), pp. 427–36.

State–society relations also took the form of clientelism, which benefitted regime loyalists, especially those bound to the regime through nepotism or economic partnerships. This was especially true during the regime's later years, when what remained of the state's resistance to the privatization process began to wane. A number of authors have documented the phenomenon of structural corruption that resulted from this economic and political clientelism.[85]

A look into the economic situation in Tunisia just prior to the Revolution would prove useful at this point. International reports indicate that the Tunisian economy was relatively strong in December 2010 when the protests that led to the Revolution broke out (as we showed earlier in Figures 2.1–2.7). However, although the country had achieved some progress in limiting poverty during the previous two decades, there was a continuous rise in unemployment among the educated. In 2010, the effective unemployment rate reached 30 per cent among those aged fifteen to twenty-four and stood at 23 per cent among college graduates.[86] Three factors had contributed to increasing the level of unemployment among the educated. First, large numbers of college graduates had entered the job market, thus leading to a sharp increase in the supply of skilled labour. Second, large economic sectors such as the agriculture, textile, and automotive industries tended to hire only unskilled labour; and, third, knowledge-intensive companies in the Tunisian economy were rare (Figure 2.12).

A discussion of the role of youth in triggering the Tunisian Revolution necessitates an examination of the kinds of changes that had taken place prior to this in Sidi Bouzid and Kasserine, one of which was an improvement in education on all levels. Whereas in the past, education had augmented social mobility and contributed to improving Tunisians' living standards, it later became a source of frustration, as it led to what was termed 'contradictory unemployment',[87] that is,

85. See the critical assessment of Béatrice Hibou, 'Domination and Control in Tunisia: Economic Levers for the Exercise of Authoritarian Power', *Review of African Political Economy*, vol. 33, no. 108 (2006), pp. 185–206. Even welfare projects were not spared the corruption of greed. For instance, the Tunisian National Solidarity Fund (also known as the 26–26 Fund after its postal number), founded in 1993 and tasked with helping needy citizens, funnelled money through the ruling party (RCD), which used funds to reward friends and coerce 'foes', who were accused of tax code violations if they failed to contribute to the fund. State-owned enterprises were privatized by the government, which then transferred their assets to Ben Ali's family members. See Christopher Alexander, *Tunisia: From Stability to Revolution in the Maghreb* (Abingdon: Routledge, 2016), p. 72–3.

86. 'Unemployment, youth total (% of total labor force ages 15–24) (modeled ILO estimate) – Tunisia', *The World Bank Data*, accessed at: https://bit.ly/3oCKutE; 'The National Survey of Population and Employment for the year 2010', p. 29.

87. Muḥammad Ali Bin Zīna, 'The Generation of the Revolution: The Sociodemographic Transformations in the Reality of Youth in Sidi Bouzid and Kasserine and their Role in the Tunisian Revolution' [Qirāʾah Sūsyū-Tārīkhiyah fī Taḥawwulāt Wāqiʿ al-Shabāb fī Sīdī Bū Zīd wal-Qaṣrīn wa Dawrihā fī Qiyām al-Thawrah al-Tūnisiyah] in Mouldi Lahmar (ed.),

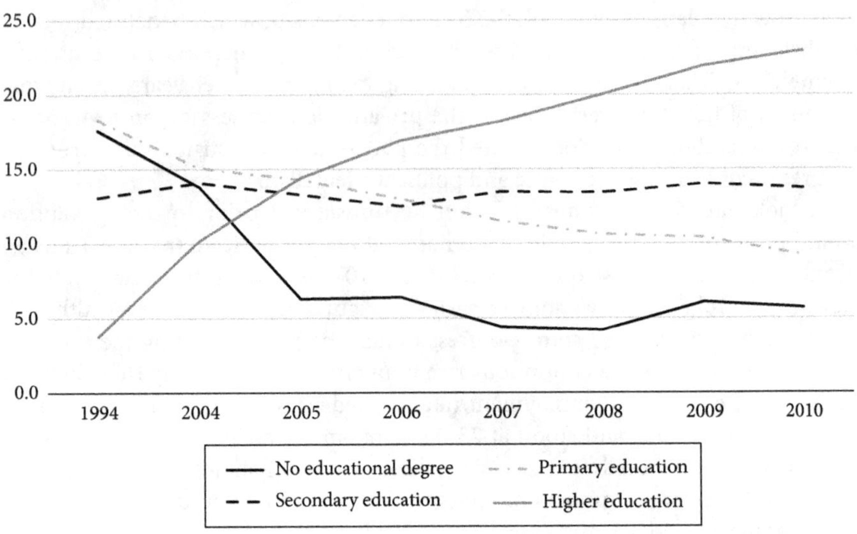

Figure 2.12 Unemployment rate (%) by education attainment (1994–2010). *Source*: National Institute of Statistics NSI – Tunisia.

the phenomenon by which unemployment rates actually went up among those with more advanced educations.[88] Obtaining a higher education is no longer a guarantee of enhanced employment opportunities; on the contrary, a new, opposing trend has now been established.

Although the rate of university graduates in Kasserine and Sidi Bouzid regions is lower than the national average, the rate of unemployment among them is higher than the national average due to relative underdevelopment. The unemployment rate among those with university certificates in Kasserine and Sidi Bouzid was 39 per cent and 40 per cent, respectively, while at the national level, the rate stood at 22.9 per cent. Also, in Kebili and Gafsa in the south-west region, unemployment among those with higher degrees was the highest in 2010 (41 per cent and 47 per cent, respectively) (Figure 2.13).[89]

GDP per capita nearly doubled twice between 1987 and 2010, rising from USD 1,259 to USD 4,141.[90] Despite economic growth, unemployment rates among

The Tunisian Revolution: Examining the Triggers through the Prism of Humanities [Al-Thawrah al-Tūnisiyah: al-Qādiḥ al-Maḥallī Taḥt Mijhar al-ʿUlūm al-Insāniyah] (Doha and Beirut: ACRPS, 2014), pp. 149–50.

88. Bin Zīna, p. 162.

89. Ibid., p. 161; 'The National Survey of Population and Employment for the year 2010', p. 154.

90. 'GDP per capita (current US$) – Tunisia', *The World Bank Data*, accessed at: https://bit.ly/3nomuuh.

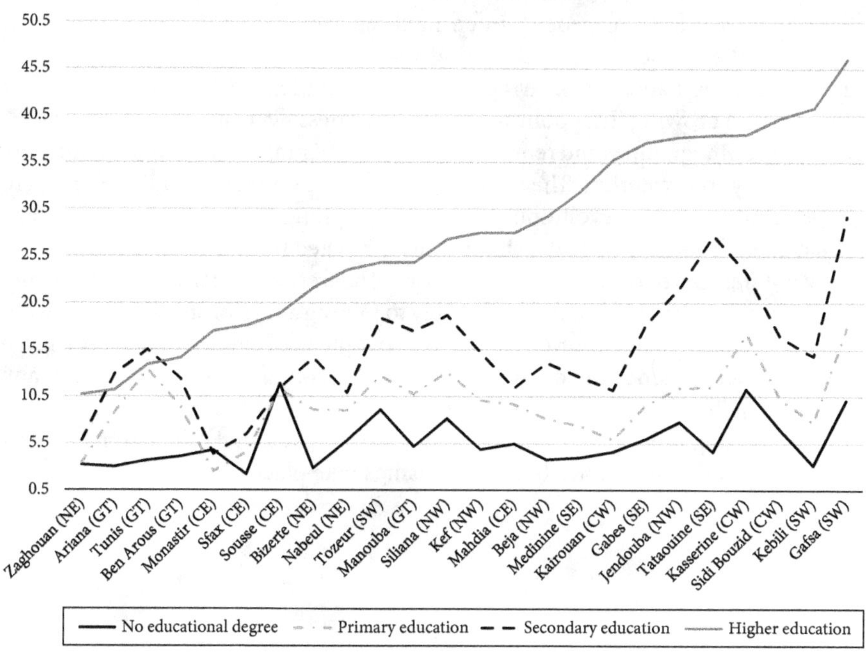

Figure 2.13 Unemployment rate by governorate and education (2010). *Source*: National Institute of Statistics NSI – Tunisia.

college graduates rose from 3.8 per cent in 1994 to 22.9 per cent in 2010.[91] This increase was highly significant given the frustration generated by the rising expectations and aspirations of thousands of educated young Tunisians. Also, unemployment rates varied significantly by region; thus, for example, the official unemployment rate in the north and Central East regions, including the capital, was 12 per cent in 2007 but was as high as 18 per cent during the same year in the interior regions. Establishment of the Union of Unemployed Graduates (UDC) in the central region of the country in 2007 played an important role in the 2008 mining basin protest in Gafsa.

Tunisia's susceptibility to revolution was not due simply to a deterioration in life conditions after a long period of social and economic improvement. The economy did undergo a downturn in the wake of the international financial crisis of 2008. However, this downturn would not have been enough to explain a revolution, nor was there an escalation in oppressive policies in 2009–10. Rather, what catalysed

91. 'The National Survey of Population and Employment for the year 2010', *Republic of Tunisia: The Ministry of Development, Investment and International Cooperation* (National Institute of Statistics NSI – June 2011), p. 28, accessed at: https://bit.ly/37xN2lY; 'Census results by topics: Presentation', *Institut National de la Statistique. Statistiques Tunisie,* slide 29, accessed at: https://bit.ly/3mIgZ9p.

the revolution at last was people's intensified sense of deprivation and frustration in spite of the economic growth taking place around them, including relative improvement in standards of living, higher expectations, a keener awareness of injustices and growing disappointment and bitterness over the absence of jobs.

Economic inequalities and repression are fundamental components of a society's susceptibility to revolution. The volatile protests that erupted in Sidi Bouzid were not premeditated as a revolution. Rather, they sprang from a spontaneous rage against acts of humiliation and feelings of accumulated frustration and deprivation that went far beyond rational calculation. Theoretical statements concerning rational win-lose calculations[92] hardly apply to joining angry protests.[93] Under what appears to be a stable authoritarian regime, people are highly unlikely to engage in political action, since the costs will be deemed too high. For this reason, many organized political opposition parties and groups hesitate to join a spontaneous popular uprising unless it overpowers them. In short, rational calculations suggest inaction or moderate actions, but still uprisings take place.

92. Take, for example, this statement: 'The steady accumulation of economic inequalities coupled with the use of repressive force meant that the costs of not acting had accumulated to a point where action against the regime was conceivable.' Thomas O'Brien, 'The Primacy of Political Security: Contentious Politics and Insecurity in the Tunisian Revolution', *Democratization*, vol. 22, no. 7 (December 2015), p. 1212.

93. Ibid., p. 1217, 1221. See also Jack A. Goldstone and Charles Tilly, 'Threat (and Opportunity): Popular Action and State Response in the Dynamics of Contentious Action', in Ronald A. Aminzade, et.al. (eds.), *Silence and Voice in the Study of Contentious Politics* (Cambridge: Cambridge University Press, 2001), pp. 179–94.

Chapter 3

FROM GAFSA TO SIDI BOUZID

On poverty, unemployment and protest

The Tunisian government's economic policies led to high growth rates, particularly in the industry and tourism sectors (Map 3.1) (Table 3.1). Still, its reliance on a market economy absent political rights or institutions promoting transparency and competition led to the accumulation of capital in the hands of a privileged elite. Rampant monopolistic practices resulted from conjoining personal wealth with politics, while the porous boundaries between the political sector and the business sector caused large sections of the middle class to fall to the bottom of the social hierarchy. Calculation of the size of the middle class by subtracting the upper and lower fifths or tenths of the population stratified according to income is a mechanical calculation that only parodies real life. Many people who make up the remaining 60 or 80 per cent are actually poor; others are middle class in terms of education but not income, and still others could be included in the category of middle class in terms of income but not in terms of social status.

The impact of neoliberal economic policies and the government's inability to provide graduates with new employment opportunities led to profound discontent among educated but unemployed youth. The decline of the public sector that constituted the main generator for the modern middle class in developing countries directly impacted these classes. From independence right up to the mid-1980s, the public sector outgrew the private sector, especially in the domains of infrastructure, transportation, energy and banking, with the private sector taking over the construction sector, public works, services and consumerist industries. Wages in the public sector were generally higher than in the private sector with an educational system that geared a large portion of its graduates towards state employment. This was also a time when unions were strengthened and when, during the 1970s or, more specifically, after 1973, the overall economic situation of most Arab countries was improving due to the rise in oil prices and labour remittances.

Tunisia had undergone the same experience as other Third World countries, including a rapid expansion of the public sector with a glut of civil servants and a decrease in their salaries. The result was a middle class that encompassed educated graduates who did not earn sufficient income to cover their basic needs and were forced either to resign themselves to poverty or take on multiple jobs to make ends

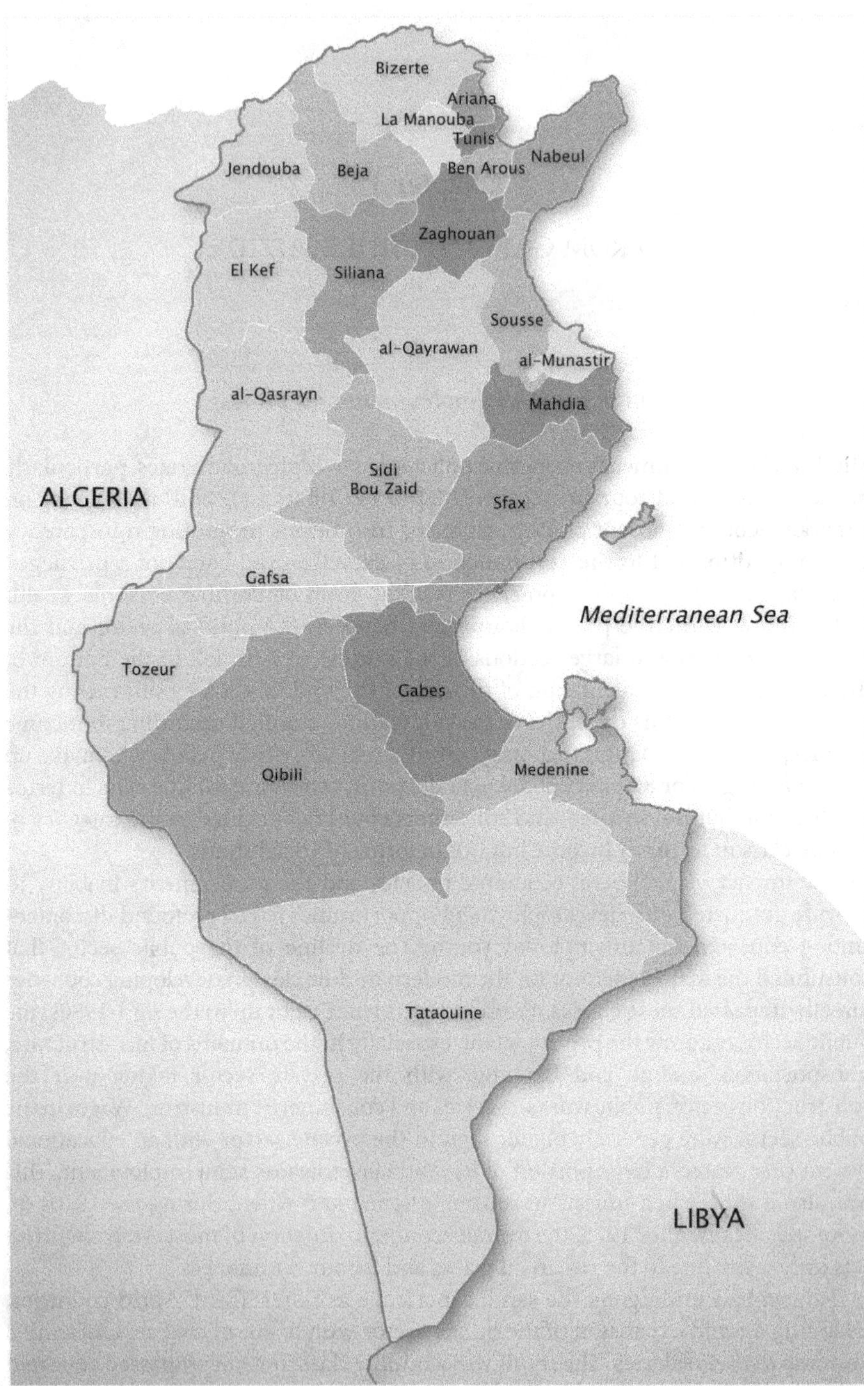

Map 3.1 Administrative map of governorates in Tunisia.

Table 3.1 Tunisian Population by Governorate and Region (2010)

Region	Governorate	Population (Thousand)	Total Population of the Geographic Region (Thousand)
North-east	Tunis	1000.3	3914.4
	Ariana	498.0	
	Ben Arous	577.5	
	Mannouba	368.7	
	Nabeul	752.8	
	Zaghouan	170.5	
	Bizerte	546.6	
North-west	Baja	306.2	1220
	Jendouba	423.2	
	al-Kef	256.6	
	Siliana	234.0	
Central-west	Kairouan	559.7	1404.5
	Kasserine	432.3	
	Sidi Bouzid	412.5	
Central-east	Sousse	611.8	2454.4
	Monastir	515.3	
	Mahdia	396.3	
	Sfax	931.0	
South	Gafsa	338.1	1555.9
	Tozeur	103.5	
	Kebili	150.7	
	Gabes	361.5	
	Medinine	455.9	
	Tataouine	146.2	
Total		**10549.1**	**10549.1**

Tunisia's National Institute of Statistics, 2010, at: https://bit.ly/3oMs89y.

meet. Rather than diminishing people's demands and expectations, however, this collapse of significant segments of the middle class simply fuelled their grievances, while their political awareness and expectations became a source of festering discontent and social tension. Their expectations of a decent material life and their yearning for civil liberties reinforced each other, morphing into a broader quest for dignity. Such tensions may manifest themselves in a number of ways: from collusion with the regime in the hope of landing opportunities, to migration, to acts of protests and political struggle. The potential for popular discontent to be transformed into broad and effective popular political action exists, therefore; however, this transformation is not the norm. Full-blown revolutions materialize only when conditions are ripe for the politicization of what was once perceived as mere 'grumbling' within narrow circles and in the private sphere.

The year 2010 produced more than 80,000 college graduates in Tunisia. In the same year, the estimated number of unemployed college graduates ranged from 157,000 (according to official statistics) to 300,000 (according to the Tunisian press). Investment in education was thus no longer a guarantee of personal and social advancement, and given rising unemployment among college graduates, this investment had become a growing burden on the state. Investment in education as a means of achieving higher income also proved problematic due to the rising costs of living. This reality was clearly reflected in trends in Tunisian migration numbers before and after 1999. While Tunisia witnessed a period of net positive migration from 1994 to 1999, it went through a critical period of negative net migration from 1999 to 2004 though the rate of demographic growth remained stable. This shift pointed to a new era in the Tunisian economy. [1]

Another clear indication of a changing economy was the increase in the numbers of middle-class families needing to take out loans in order to build a house, fund college education and meet daily needs. In 2003, debts in Tunisia approached TD 5.1 billion, equivalent to 43 per cent of total wages, compared to 1997 when debt represented 29 per cent of total wages at TD 2.2 billion. Severe debt causes social anxiety and family instability and is one of the prime indications of a weakening and impoverished middle class frustrated by its inability to maintain its accustomed lifestyle as globalization and consumer culture continue generating ever-increasing 'needs'. Tunisians' reliance on remittances from relatives living abroad increased more than sixfold in less than twenty-five years: from TD 350 per family in 1974 to TD 2,000 in 1997.[2]

Tunisian migrant remittances continue to make up for a significant portion of the trade deficit, as well as the GNP, improving the levels of human development for migrants' families and alleviating the burden of employing young graduates, who constitute a significant portion of the demographic pyramid.

According to the ESCR, 14.8 per cent of Tunisia's population suffered from an 'above-average' deprivation of their rights in the year 2000. A measure index of social, economic and cultural rights that measures the levels of deprivation in the following fields: malnutrition among children, unemployment, lack of employment security, rates of premature death, lack of social services, water contamination, lack of sewage infrastructure, illiteracy, and school attrition rates; the ESCR index is highest in the central-west provinces, which are home to a quarter of the population with poverty rates ranging between 22 and 25 per cent; following these are the north-west provinces, which constitute 19.3 per cent of the total population. The rates of deprivation are also higher than average in the south-eastern and central provinces.

Thus, three out of seven regions and fifteen out of twenty-three provinces have experienced a state of deprivation that is considerably higher than the Tunisian average. In these provinces, the rates of deprivation ranged between a seventh of the population in the least-deprived provinces (the rate of extreme poverty was 15.6 per cent in Gabes, in the south-east) and a quarter in the most deprived

1. Tunisia's National Institute of Statistics, 'Population Census 2004: Economic Characteristics of the Population', at: https://bit.ly/3nbWYIk.

2. This increase can be attributed both to an increase in migration and to the Tunisian Dinar's depreciation against the Euro. See Hussein al-Dimasi, 'The Social and Political Significance of Tunisia's Middle Class' [al-ahammiyah al-ijtimāʿiyah wal-siyāsiyah lil-ṭabaqah al-wusṭā], in: *Tunisia's Revolution [Thawrat Tunis]* (Doha and Beirut: ACRPS, 2012).

Table 3.2 Poverty and Unemployment Rates in Tunisia per Region (2010)

Region	Poverty Rate (Per cent)	Extreme Poverty Line	Unemployment Rate (Per cent)
South-west	21.5	6.4	23.4
South-east	17.9	4.9	16.8
Centre-west	32.3	14.3	14.8
North-west	25.7	8.8	14.4
Grand Tunis	9.1	1.1	13.2
North-east	10.3	1.8	11.0
Centre-east	8.0	1.6	9.3
General rate	**20.5**	**6.0**	**13.05**

'The National Survey of Population and Employment for the Year 2010', p. 154; 'Measuring Poverty, Inequalities and Polarization in Tunisia: 2000-2010', *Statistiques Tunisie* (November 2012), p. 16, accessed on 12 December 2020, at: https://bit.ly/2KbRnDg.

provinces; for example, in the central-west province of Kasserine, the percentage of absolute deprivation came to 24.8 per cent.

In 2010, the adult illiteracy rate was the highest in the central-west region (Kasserine, Kairouan, Sidi Bouzid), where it came to 30.3 per cent. The north-west region (Jendouba, al-Kef, Siliana and Baja) had an illiteracy rate of 29.9 per cent, with a staggering 25 per cent illiteracy rate in the city of Zaghouan (in the north-east region) in the year 2010 (Tables 3.2–3.4).[3]

The statistics given are based on data from Tunisia's National Institute of Statistics, which was reorganized according to ESCR standards.[4] The statistics may not be accurate or objective and may, therefore, not constitute scientific data, but they are sufficient to show a certain variation in percentages among Tunisian regions, for even when doubtful data is corrected, the variation among different regions remains.

After the revolution, Minister of Social Affairs Mohamed Ennaceur declared through an official news agency that the poverty rate in Tunisia was 24.7 per cent, far above the official rate.[5] If this constituted the average poverty rate in Tunisia as a whole, it is not difficult to imagine the real rates of poverty in the peripheral areas, given the wide variation between the periphery and the national average.

There is no theoretical model that accounts for the influence of poverty on political action within a clear conceptual structure that allows for objective prediction. Marxist theories, which have been amended throughout the years, stress the role of class, emphasizing the ability of the proletariat to organize and create a political leadership. This does not necessarily mean, of course, that the

3. 'The National Survey of Population and Employment for the Year 2010' [al-Masḥ al-Waṭanī ḥawl al-Sukkān wa al-Tashghīl li-sanat 2010], Republic of Tunisia: The Ministry of Development, Investment and International Cooperation (National Institute of Statistics NSI – 2010), p. 65, accessed at: https://bit.ly/3gF8kC8.

4. Azzam Mahjoub, 'Economic, Social and Cultural Rights in Tunisia: An Assessment', *Mediterranean Politics*, vol. 9, no. 3 (2004), pp. 509–12.

5. 'The Poverty Rate in Tunisia Reaches 24.7 Percent: New Protests and Demonstrations Expected', *Tunisia Africa News Agency*, 27 May 2011.

Table 3.3 Illiteracy Rate in Tunisia per Region and Governorate (2008, 2010)

Region	2008[a]	2010[b]
Kairouan	32	29.3
Kasserine	32.8	30.5
Sidi Bouzid	30.3	31.3
Central-west	**31.7**	**30.3**
Baja	31.3	30.4
Jendouba	33.9	31.2
al-Kef	29	27.7
Siliana	32.3	29.2
North-west	**31.9**	**29.9**
Gabes	18.6	16.2
Medinine	17.8	15.5
Tataouine	17.1	17.2
South-east	**18**	**16**
Gafsa	20.9	18.2
Tozeur	15.7	14.1
Kebili	21	17.7
South-west	**20**	**17.4**
Nabeul	17.9	18
Zaghouan	27.2	25
Bizerte	20.5	17.5
North-east	**19.9**	**18.6**
Sousse	14.6	13.3
Monastir	12.5	11.1
Mahdia	22	22.9
Sfax	16.3	16.7
Central-east	**16**	**15.7**
Tunis	12.5	12
Ariana	11.9	11.9
Bin Arous	11.6	10.4
Mannouba	18	17.6
Grand Tunis	**13**	**12.5**

[a] 'The National Survey of Population and Employment for the Year 2008' [al-Masḥ al-Waṭanī ḥawl al-Sukkān wa-al-Tashghīl li-sanat 2008], Republic of Tunisia: The Ministry of Development, Investment and International Cooperation (National Institute of Statistics NSI – 2008), p. 65, accessed at: https://bit.ly/37cOuv9.
[b] 'The National Survey of Population and Employment for the Year 2010' [al-Masḥ al-Waṭanī ḥawl al-Sukkān wa-al-Tashghīl li-sanat 2010], Republic of Tunisia: The Ministry of Development, Investment and International Cooperation (National Institute of Statistics NSI – 2010), p. 65, accessed at: https://bit.ly/3gF8kC8.

poorer classes are endowed with a revolutionary role and that they are destined to have a revolutionary function. However, the theoretical controversies over the influence of poverty on politics have affected the debate on the social and political effects of the Washington Consensus policies in developing countries.[6]

6. On this theme, see the theoretical contributions of Mike Davis, *Planet of Slums* (Brooklyn: VERSO, 2006); and Stephen Gill, 'Globalization, Democratization and Politics of Indifference', *Globalization: Critical Reflections* (1996), pp. 205–28.

Table 3.4 Poverty Rate in Tunisia per Region (2000–10)

	Poverty Rate (Per cent)			Extreme Poverty Line		
Region	**2000**	**2005**	**2010**	**2000**	**2005**	**2010**
Centre-east (Sousse, Monastir, Mahdia, Sfax)	21.4	12.6	8.0	6.4	2.6	1.6
North-east (Nabeul, Zaghouan, Bizerte)	32.1	21.6	10.3	10.5	5.4	1.8
Grand Tunis (Tunis, Ariana, Ben Arous, Mannouba)	21.0	14.6	9.1	4.3	2.3	1.1
North-west (Baja, Jendouba, Kef, Siliana)	35.3	26.9	25.7	12.1	8.9	8.8
Centre-west (Kairouan, Kasserine, Sidi Bouzid)	49.3	46.5	32.3	25.5	23.2	14.3
South-east (Gabes, Medinine, Tataouine)	44.3	29.0	17.9	17.5	9.6	4.9
Southwest (Gafsa, Tozeur, Kebili)	47.8	33.2	21.5	21.7	12.1	6.4
Overall rate	**25.4**	**23.1**	**20.5**	**7.7**	**7.4**	**6.0**

'Measuring Poverty, Inequalities and Polarization in Tunisia: 2000–2010', *Statistiques Tunisie* (November 2012), p. 16, accessed on 12 December 2020, at: https://bit.ly/2KbRnDg.

The same debate has influenced the human development reports published by the United Nations Development Program (UNDP). Indeed, ample evidence exists to support the claim that poverty marginalizes wide sectors of the population, removing them from public affairs and from the political sphere while pushing them into cultural stasis and inaction. This in turn promotes allegiance to the existing regime due to people's preoccupation with meeting daily needs and their susceptibility to manipulation by state service 'providers' and 'mediators' with power of different kinds. However, even in the absence of a theoretical model, officials and others involved in public affairs cannot avoid the possibility that poverty may generate bursts of anger and protest that are not necessarily organized and politicized, but which might, within a certain constellation of events, magnify organized politicized action. It is true that the poor may rise up, but such movements are often repressed and tend to disappear without a trace, except for the investigation commissions that are quickly forgotten along with their recommendations. Of interest, however, are the instances where, within the margins allowed for organization, politically conscious elements of the poor or activists from other classes have been able to mobilize the poor on the basis of identity, class or simply anger and frustration.

Among the most important factors is the existence of a marginalized and impoverished periphery in contrast to an economically and politically powerful centre. These peripheries are also endowed with regional centres that produce political elites capable of leading. The revolutions of Tunisia and Syria began in provincial centres like these (Sidi Bouzid and Kasserine in the first case and Dar`aa and Homs in the second). They played a decisive role in triggering, organizing and maintaining the protests. As for the peripheral areas near the capital and the poverty belts surrounding the large cities, the rules guiding political action change completely: activity is directly influenced by the political and economic centre and its activists, including those of the regime and the opposition. These peripheries tend to be demographically heterogeneous since they are composed of waves of immigration into the city (and from the city to the near periphery, in the case of the impoverishment of the middle class). Sami Zemni notes, for example, that the privatization of agricultural lands that began in the 1970s and intensified in the 1990s pushed thousands of farmers off their lands, forcing them to migrate to the cities.[7]

As such, these peripheries are not composed of communal groups; on the contrary, alienation from the centre may prompt the alienated newcomers to the city, political activists of the lower middle classes, unemployed university graduates and other sectors to form substitute groups to compensate for their lost communities; this need may also be exploited by religious extremist groups.

When peripheries of the centre (slums, poor suburbs) cannot identify with a political opposition movement, they tend to develop three models of political action. First, they can act as a social base for the existing regime, supplying votes in the case of elections, and as human resources used by the regime in case of crackdown on dissenters. Second, they can form a social base for identity politics or religious political movements and may thus find common cause with sections of the middle class in the centre. And third, they can opt for a complete exit from politics and public affairs coupled with recurrent bursts of rage. When the revolution spread from the central and south-western regions of Tunisia to the coastal cities, the transition went through poor neighbourhoods, many of whose residents originate from these regions.

This equation is different in the case of marginalized peripheries located in the provinces far from the country's economic and political centre. These regions are often endowed with urban centres which are themselves marginalized, and which tend to be homogeneous, since they repel rather than attract immigrants. These homogeneous communities with their shared histories exist within a social framework of mutual commitments and communal solidarity.[8]

The Tunisian and Syrian Revolutions began as popular uprisings springing from peripheral centres as in the model described here, while the Egyptian Revolution represented a different revolutionary model that began in the large cities of Cairo and Alexandria, attracting huge segments of the slum's population. When the uprising flared up in the provincial outskirts of the city of Sidi Bouzid and in Kasserine, the entire province followed; in the case of the city of Dar`aa in Syria, the countryside also followed the city in rebellion.

7. Sami Zemni, 'The Tunisian Revolution: Neoliberalism, Urban Contentious Politics and the Right to the City', *International Journal of Urban and Regional Research*, vol. 41, no. 1 (January 2017), p. 75.

8. The same is not true for the Syrian peripheral urban centres, where rural migration towards peripheral cities, such as Latakia and Homs, led to the creation of a heterogeneous demography on the sectarian and religious levels, which became the basis for sectarian frictions. This has resulted from the ease with which political and social tensions can be transformed into identity-based conflicts.

Some researchers have predicted that, with the emergence of poverty due to neoliberal policies, the role of broad popular protest and trade union action will be reduced in favour of non-governmental welfare organizations and Islamic social action, which often serve as a social network of Islamist movements.[9] The Tunisian Revolution has disproven this line of analysis, showing that there is no exclusive model for the mobilization of the poor in the process of political change.

The endeavour to predict the political behaviour of the poorer classes has led to an attempt to divide the poor into different categories, each displaying a different political behaviour. Proponents of this practice often claim that in order to facilitate predictions, they are in need of accurate empirical data on the distribution of the poor among the unemployed, daily workers, occasional workers, small business owners surviving on low profit margins, workers in corporatist sectors – such as the public sector, government companies and others – and employees in capitalist companies. However, no socio-economic group can be isolated and associated with a predictable pattern of political behaviour. Mutual influences exist among these different societal components, and the emergence of political movements in the right conditions can open unexpected horizons for the mobilization of the poor.[10]

What occurred in Tunisia was an uprising of the peripheries which, aided by simple communal solidarity, labour union activists, grassroots opposition parties and social media (as a source of TV coverage), expanded to involve actors in the provinces as the revolution made its way towards the capital. In the capital, the movement was initially joined by spontaneous protests in the impoverished periphery in the form of 'riots' and by small rallies of organized political and civil activists in the city itself. The social protest arising in the periphery then encountered broad sections of the politically conscious middle class with some freedom to organize in unions, federations and illegal and semi-legal political parties. These two social groups constituted both the Tunisian Revolution and the Egyptian Revolution, although their involvement came about in opposite orders.

Coastal Tunisia eventually joined in the demand for regime change; however, it remained in the seat of power. The post-revolutionary political system has so far been unable to find a formula allowing not only political expression but also empowerment of the peripheries that began the revolution. As a result, the political and social tension in Tunisia continues. The elites of the economic and political centre still hold the reins of government, politics and the economy, while the centre, the south and south-west are underrepresented, suffering from floundering development policies. Consequently, they can easily become an angry political

9. See, for example, Stephen Hurt, Karim Knio and Magnus Ryner, 'Social Forces and the Effects of (Post) Washington Consensus Policy in Africa: Comparing Tunisia and South Africa', *The Round Table*, vol. 98, no. 403 (June 2009), p. 304.

10. Robert W. Cox, *Production Power and World Order* (New York: Columbia University Press, 1987); and Jeffrey Harrod, *Power, Production, and the Unprotected Worker* (New York: Columbia University Press, 1987).

base for populist propaganda against political elites in general. The question thus remains: Will the evolution of Tunisian democracy resolve this dilemma? The answer to this question will be a major factor determining the nature of coming political struggles, forms of political organization and the demands that will accompany them.

Rising unemployment has been behind many of Tunisia's protest movements, most notably the 2008 protests in the Redeyef district of Gafsa and the Ben Gardane protests of 2010.[11] The mining basin protests in Redeyef began following the announcement that entry exam results would be used to select employees for the Gafsa Phosphate Company, whose selection process was tainted by corruption, nepotism and a preference for workers recruited from outside the region, thereby stripping the locals of job opportunities. The demonstrations subsequently spread to the cities of Um al-Arais, Mdhila and later Gafsa. The company's announcement detonated an already-explosive situation borne out of the escalation of poverty and police repression against Tunisia's regional unemployment committees. Rising prices of food and basic goods coupled with reduced purchasing power further added to the spread of the protests.[12]

The Mining Basin Uprising lasted approximately five months and resulted in a series of demonstrations, protests and strikes, which were met with a violent crackdown and the imprisonment of dozens of citizens and unionists. At the time, the complicity between the General Tunisian Labor Union and the ruling regime was blatant. The union aided the state in stifling the uprising by stripping the unionists leading the protests of their union membership and banning any unionist initiative from supporting the uprising in the other branches.[13]

A 2010 report by Amnesty International highlighted the events of the Mining Basin Uprising and the repressive measures adopted, which left two dead and many others wounded. Hundreds of protesters were arrested with no fewer than 200 individuals brought to trial. (Some were indicted and sentenced to up to ten years in prison.) Eyewitnesses reported that security forces opened fire without warning and that many of the injured received gunshot wounds in their backs and legs. In June 2008, Adnan al-Hajji, secretary-general of the Redeyef branch of the General Tunisian Labor Union, was arrested along with thirty-seven others and accused of leading the protest, forming a criminal gang, belonging to a group seeking to sabotage property and other similar charges. The accused stood trial in December with thirty-three of them given prison sentences of up to ten years.

The Mining Basin Uprising was not only the largest and lengthiest insurrection since the 1984 bread riots, which effectively paved Ben Ali's road to power, and

11. The latter was limited and had more to do with smuggling networks across the Libyan Tunisian Borders.

12. Ammar Amrussia, 'The Mining Basin Uprising . . . an attempt at assessment', *al-Badīl: The Tunisian Communist Workers' Party*, 7 April 2008.

13. Bachir al-Hamidi, 'Two Years after the Repression of the Mining Basin Uprising', *al-Hiwar al-Mutamaddin* (Civilized Debate), 7 June 2010.

although it was suppressed and didn't go beyond the basin, it should be remarked that it also raised political demands and prefaced a chain of protests that eventually led to Tunisia's revolution.

A closer look at developments in the Gafsa governorate, home to the 2008 mining basin protests, and corresponding unemployment figures (around 21 per cent in 2004 according to official figures, compared to 28.3 in 2010, which was the highest rate compared to other governorates in that year) is instructive.[14] On 6 January 2008, protesters against the Gafsa Phosphate Company took to the streets, chanting slogans condemning the violations taking place during the selection process and demanding the right to work. On the same day, nineteen unemployed protesters announced a hunger strike at the headquarters of the local labour union. The next day, the protest movement in Redeyef grew stronger, garnering the support of more citizens and the local unions. This prompted local authorities to negotiate with actors representing the unemployed, but the talks failed to reach an agreement.

On 10 January, protests flared in the district of Um al-Arais, where demonstrations took off with a massive assembly of students, unemployed youth and municipal workers on strike. The local branch of the Union of Unemployed Graduates announced a sit-in, and a number of citizens put up tents, besieging the Gafsa Phosphate Company and disrupting its operations. The protesters also blocked the railroad tracks, preventing the company from transporting its merchandise. On 12 January, the al-Mitlawi District joined its neighbours, putting up tents in the centre of town and on the railroad tracks while workers halted the production process in the phosphate refineries. The protests successfully halted work in the company's largest production centres but ended following promises by officials and state representatives to provide more employment opportunities for the residents of the protesting towns.[15]

As Table 3.5 shows, 2004 unemployment figures for Redeyef, Mdhila, Um al-Arais and al-Mitlawi range between 21 and 38 per cent. These are peripheral districts within the governorate of Gafsa, which includes districts that can be considered central, such as Northern Gafsa and Sidi Aich, where unemployment figures were 6.3 and 7.5 per cent, respectively. The latter did not participate in the protests.

In analysing these trends, one can compare the events of the mining basin in 2008, which ended with broken promises of change from the authorities, and the events in Sidi Bouzid in 2010, which evolved into a full-fledged revolution (Map 3.2).

14. Tunisia's National Institute of Statistics, 'Population Census 2004'; and, 'The National Survey of Population and Employment for the Year 2010', p. 154.

15. Bachir al-Hamidi, 'This Is What Is Happening in Tunisia: Citizen Protests in the Mining Basin in the Gafsa Region . . . a Battle for the Right to Work and to a Dignified Life', *Democratic Unionist Website*, 11 April 2008, at: http://www.kifah-nakabi.org (site discontinued).

Table 3.5 Unemployment Rates in the Gafsa Governorate (2004)

District	Unemployment Rate (Percentage)
Gafsa North	6.3
Sidi Aich	7.5
Ksar	21.4
Gafsa South	15.7
Um al-Arais	38.0
Redeyef	27.0
al-Mitlawi	20.9
Mdhila	27.9
Guetar	20.0
Belkhir	17.1
Sened	27.6
Overall rate	**21.1**

Tunisia's National Institute of Statistics, 'Population Census 2004'.

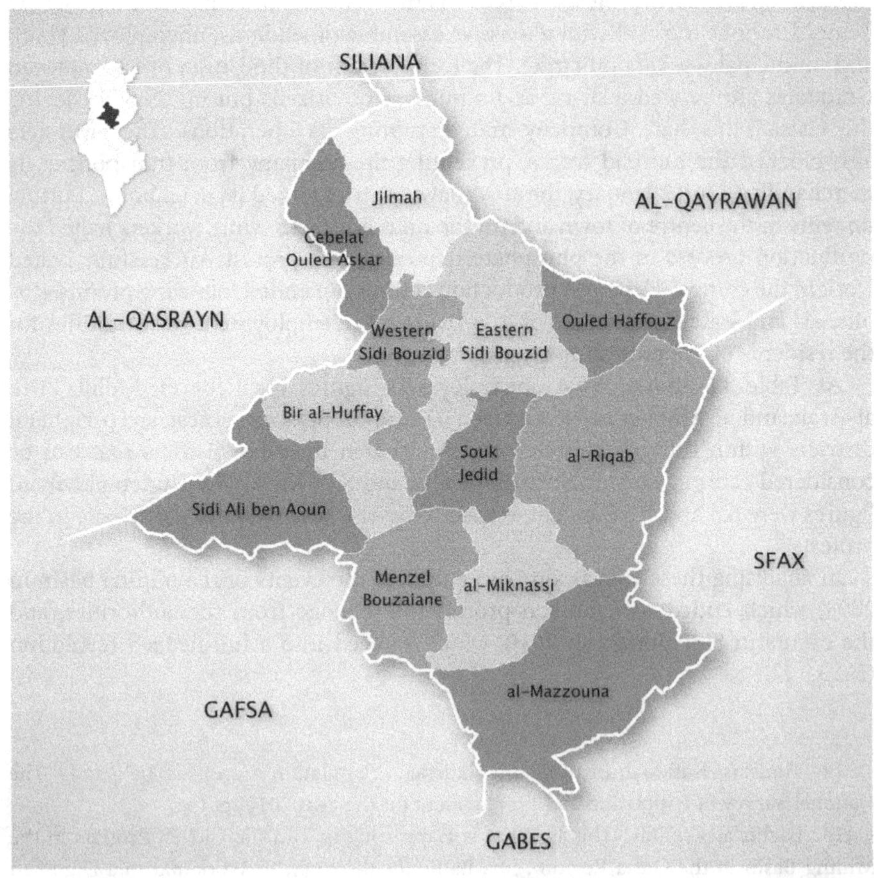

Map 3.2 Administrative divisions of the Sidi Bouzid governorate.

Table 3.6 Unemployment Rates in the Sidi Bouzid Governorate (2004)

District	Unemployment Rate (Percentage)
Western Sidi Bouzid	11.7
Eastern Sidi Bouzid	11.1
Jilmah	19.5
Cebelat Ouled Askar	19.7
Bir al Huffay	10.8
Sidi Ali bin Aoun	10.4
Manzil Bouzian	23
al-Meknes	30.5
Souk al-Jadid	27.3
al-Mazzunah	14.3
al-Riqab	5.9
Ouled Haffouz	13.4
Overall rate	**14.1**

National Institute of Statistics, 'Population census 2004'.

Table 3.7 Unemployment Rates in the Sidi Bouzid Governorate (1994–2010)

	1994	2004	2010
Sidi Bouzid	17.0	14.1	14.7

'General Census of Population and Housing for the Year 2004 – First Issue: First Results', p. 45; 'The National Survey of Population and Employment for the Year 2010', p. 154.

The spark igniting the Tunisian Revolution took place on 17 December 2010 in the district of Eastern Sidi Bouzid, the governorate's administrative and economic centre. The district's unemployment rate, at 11.1 per cent, was lower than the governorate's overall average of 14.1 per cent. In comparison with the unemployment rates in peripheral districts, such as al-Meknes (30.5 per cent) and Souq al-Jadid (27.3 per cent), the rates in Eastern Sidi Bouzid were far lower (Table 3.6). Such disparities among districts in the rate of unemployment reflect the injustice created by unequal growth, which is a source of social tensions across Tunisia (Table 3.7).

Based on the diaries included later in this book, the district of al-Meknes joined the protests on 20 December 2010 (day 4 of the Revolution) after events had spiralled out of control in Sidi Bouzid. Once the protests had broken out in the province's centre, they quickly spread throughout the governorate of Sidi Bouzid and overflowed into the peripheries, giving rise to a ripple effect in other peripheral provinces. The same scenario unfolding in Sidi Bouzid took hold in Kasserine. The first revolutionary cities in the Kasserine governorate – Kasserine and Thala – were located in its centre.

At the very start of the events, the revolution spread to the provinces' periphery following their success in the provincial centres. Amnesty International's February 2011 report details that 'the majority of deaths in greater Tunis took place between 12 and 16 January in working class neighborhoods such as Tadhamoun, Sijoumi

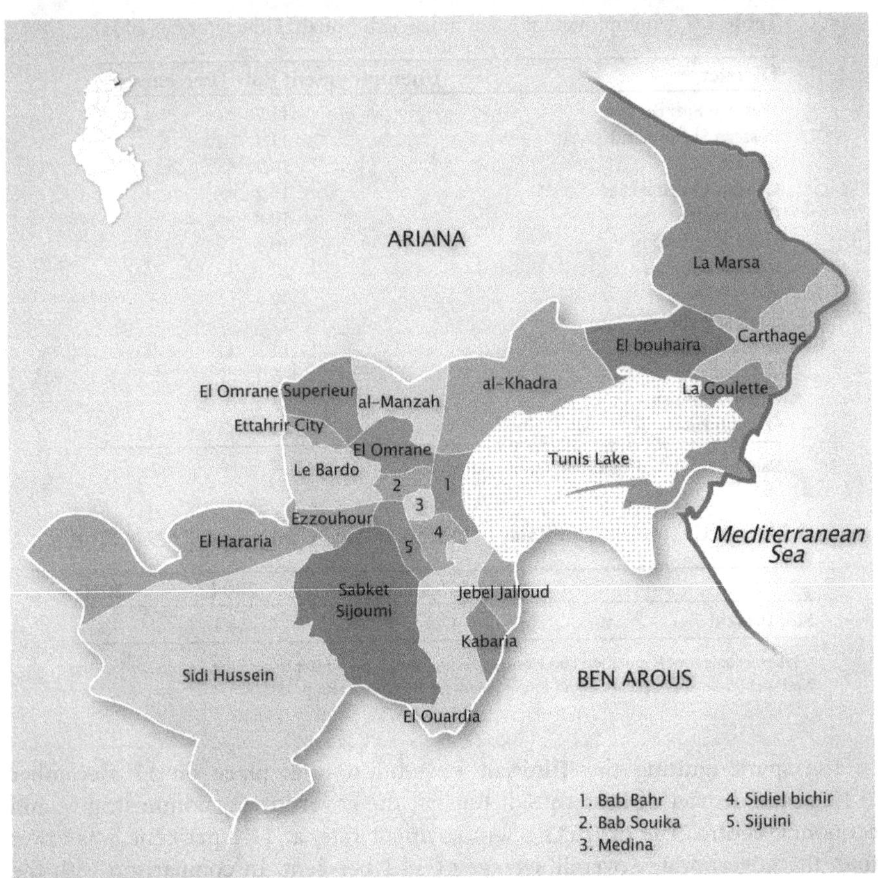

Map 3.3 Administrative divisions of the Tunis governorate.

and Mallassine'.[16] The unemployment rate was 24.9 per cent in the district of Sijoumi which, along with the district of Sidi Ḥusayn, had witnessed a multitude of local protests since the late 1990s, including a major uprising in 2004 after the flooding of several neighbourhoods by marsh water rendered 150 families homeless (Map 3.3).[17]

16. *Tunisia in Revolt: State Violence during Anti-Government* Protests (London: Amnesty International, 2011), p. 23.

17. 'The Authorities Confront the Legitimate Demands of the Protesters of Sidi Ḥusayn and al-Saijumi with Brutal Repression' [al-Sulṭah Tuwājih al-Maṭālib al-Mashrūʿah li-Mutaẓāhirī Sīdī Ḥusayn al-Sayjūmī bil-Qamʿ al-Waḥshī], *Tunisian Communist Workers Party - al-Badeel*, 10 January 2004, accessed on 12 December 2020, at: https://bit.ly/3oKgufn.

Equally desperate conditions obtained in the neighbourhood of al-Tadhamoun, located in the central province of Ariana north of the Tunisian capital. Al-Tadhamoun featured the highest unemployment rate in the province, at 16.8 per cent, compared to the city's unemployment rate of 6 per cent. Likewise, the neighbourhood of Mallassine had been so thoroughly marginalized that Tunisia's National Institute of Statistics abstained from reporting its figures and excluded it from the administrative map of the Tunis governorate. Mallassine provides a good reference point for the study of poverty in Tunisia, particularly given its gruelling conditions and the radicalism and brutishness of its language of protest.[18]

In August 2010, just a few months before the young Mohamed Bouazizi set himself on fire, protests erupted in Tunisia's south-east, where the residents of Ben Gardane had risen up in protest against the authorities' decision to restrict commercial trade with Libya, effectively ending the role of middlemen in the border crossing of Ben Gardane and, therefore, the primary source of income for local residents. The crisis took a dangerous turn after Libya decided to impose an entry fee on vehicles and prohibit the sale of all Tunisian goods that lacked an export/import licence. Confrontations between the locals and the Tunisian security forces occurred after the decision to close down the border crossing of Ras Ajdir. The protests expanded after rumours spread alleging that influential Tunisian figures were behind the decree.[19] Subsequently, Ben Gardane witnessed violent confrontations between the protesters and the security forces until an agreement was reached between Tunisia and Libya to reopen the crossing. The success of this uprising fuelled further protest, increasing the numbers and boldness of politicized activists. This was the last uprising prior to the one at Sidi Bouzid.

It will be seen, then, that Tunisia has witnessed multiple waves of protests set off by socio-economic factors, including significant popular uprisings. It goes without saying that these waves of protest have heightened the population's political awareness and their grasp of the importance of dissent. As for the authorities, their ability to contain protests through violence has done nothing to make them more amenable to reform in the long run; on the contrary, it has engendered a sense of overconfidence on their part. Eventually, however, as regimes exhaust their tools of repression and containment, waves of protest escalate into a torrent that cannot be quelled by familiar means of repression. The totally different scale of repression needed to suppress a revolution faces security forces with the dilemma of loyalty – whether to fulfil their duty to the government or to face punishment, knowing the uncertainty of the outcome and the consequences of the regime's potential fall.

18. Mohsen Bouazizi, *Expressions of Protest and the Social Sphere [al-Ta'birāt al-Iḥtijājiyah wal-Majāl al-Ijtimā'ī]* (Tunis: ad-Dār al-'Arabia lil-Kitāb, 2009).

19. 'Tunis: A Chain of Protests' [Tunis: Silsilah min al-Iḥtijājāt], *AlJazeera.net*, 26 December 2010, accessed on 12 December 2020, at: https://bit.ly/3gHui7S.

Sidi Bouzid in context

Disproportionate regional development reproduced and reinforced already-existing disparities among the various areas of the country. Investment poured into the coastal regions, which contained 84 per cent of its industrial zones and absorbed 80 per cent of its industrial labour.[20] By contrast, the total value of investments in the north-east of Tunisia came to DT 16.583 million, while the south-west, including Sidi Bouzid, received less than DT 1.948 million, with around half of these investments coming from the public sector.[21] As Tunisia continued to be labelled an 'economic miracle', its development policies entailed forms of unjust distribution, thus leading to an increase in social unrest. This dynamic was reflected in the uprising on 26 January 1978, the bread riots of December 1983–January 1984, the 2008 Gafsa Uprising and again the events of the uprising in December 2010–January 2011. The 1984 and 2011 uprisings both occurred on a national scale; the second, however, could not be contained by the regime.

Sidi Bouzid was considered one of the bulwarks of the ruling party in terms of membership, as Dar`aa, the southern city in which the Syrian Revolution broke out, was for the Ba'th party in Syria. At one time, the regime had relied on party networks to mediate between itself and local constituencies. State services and employment in which the party network had a say empowered the party among its constituencies throughout different regions and allowed it to maintain their loyalty.[22] With time, however, the party lost this middleman role as its status weakened inside the regime. Membership in the ruling Neo-Destour Party under Bourguiba's rule had once given local leaders a sense of pride and power because it enabled them to broker relations between kin, other local networks and the state. During the final decade of Ben Ali's rule, however, it became apparent that the party's status had deteriorated, its functions had changed and new cliental networks had emerged. In addition, the party was unable to accommodate the demands and expectations of rising numbers of young unemployed academics who did not believe in the party's line, but who had no other channels to the state, were unable to make it on their own, and lacked the means to be a part of the new cliental networks.

At the same time, the state was prepared to use more repressive measures to impose submission. Impoverished segments of society needed the party's services more than others, as a result of which they appeared more loyal than those who were better off. However, they would also be more inclined to join popular protests once they had broken out due to their socio-economic conditions.

20. General Tunisian Labor Union, 'Employment and Development in . . . Gafsa', pp. 16–17 and 164.

21. Ibid., pp. 64 and 168.

22. The redistribution policies implemented by the Tunisian regime through services and employment were changed by the 1986 Structural Adjustment Program (SAP) imposed by the International Monetary Fund and the World Bank.

When Tunisia's ruling party could no longer deliver its former services because of its weakened position in the regime, it frustrated its own members. This may help to explain the fact that the two regions in which the Tunisian Revolution broke out (Sidi Bouzid and Kasserine) had the largest number of locals involved in the ruling political party (the Democratic Constitutional Rally).[23] Mouldi Lahmar maintains that the conflagration that was ignited so dramatically and violently by the Bouazizi incident in Sidi Buzid, and whose impact quickly spread to Kasserine, was an expression of extreme disillusionment in a local political economy within which the rates and mechanisms of exchange that had been entrenched since independence had collapsed. Lahmar states,

> In this society, where the Bedouin-peasant culture had been eroded, this phenomenon gradually stripped away what remained of people's confidence in the work of the ruling party's local political activists. At the same time, it revealed the opportunistic nature of their work which, in this context, demonstrators viewed as the root of despotism, cronyism, violation of individual dignity, and disregard for the values of justice and equality.[24]

Four main changes befell the political market according to Lahmar: (1) The new elites that had joined the Democratic Constitutional Rally (RCD) during the early 1980s had not obtained their legitimacy from the history of the national struggle movement or from prioritizing the public interest over private benefit; on the contrary, their partisanship was conspicuously opportunistic. (2) The state labour market could no longer provide jobs to university graduates. (3) New leaders in the party and elites in the state became essentially technocrats who superficially respected the law yet ignored the social and economic conflicts between the public interest and the policies they promoted. This coincided with the regime's persecution of its opponents by pursuing a comprehensive technical security policy. (4) The number of educated rural elites who sought to obtain resources from the political market increased. Consequently, the RCD sought to attract them for fear that they would join the opposition, but it was unable to accommodate their demands or address their needs. Fifty per cent of the party members in Sidi Bouzid were unemployed men and women; this included disabled and senior citizens, one of whom was Bouazizi's mother.[25]

Occurring just two years prior to the protests in the border town Ben Gardane in the summer of 2010 and the uprising of Sidi Bouzid in December of the same year, the mining basin protests paved the way for a revolution. This is not to assume a direct causal link between the two uprisings but simply to acknowledge that they

23. Mouldi Lahmar, 'Collapse of Exchange Rates in a False Local Political Market' [Inhiyār Muʿaddalāt al-Tabādul fī Sūq Siyāsiyah Maḥalliyah Muzayyafah] in: Lahmar (ed.), p. 94.

24. Ibid., p. 99.

25. Ibid., pp. 114–17.

were both peripheral uprisings with the potential to evolve into a revolution. These rebellions, together with pro-Palestinian demonstrations that started with the second Intifada, in 2000, the acts of solidarity with Iraq (2003) and with the Palestinians during the Gaza War (2008–9), trained many seasoned activists. The central and southern regions thus saw the creation of a nucleus of politicized social protest that was maintained by a small number of conscientious activists who joined legal opposition parties and the General Tunisian Labor Union, either in order to seek them out as protection for their cause or to employ them directly in local struggles.

Aside from the importance of political activists, one should consider the importance of communal groups and kinship in peripheral regions. In this context, Sidi Bouzid constituted a traditional province with a rural way of life commonly associated with a cohesive familial and clan structure. Communal groups and blood relations played a crucial role as sanctuaries for the individual. Sidi Bouzid's community proved efficient in mobilizing social solidarity with the Bouazizi family, a large extended family even by provincial standards; it became clear that such familial and communal relations existed among the activists themselves, which undoubtedly contributed to their solidarity. However, it would be misleading to ignore the role of organizers, political activists and unionists in coordinating protest actions. Ben Ali's official press had initially accused activists and unionists of being responsible for these events and transforming a demands-based movement into a political one. This, precisely, is the definition of revolutionary effort – an effort that transforms protests that have arisen out of anger and/or specific demands into political causes that target the ruling regime itself. For authoritarian regimes, politicization is an offence, since it questions the existing system of rule and political power. The revolution had no centralized national leadership but rather valiant field activists and local leaders. These activists and local leaders enjoyed the popularity and credibility needed to effectuate such a process, but they never controlled the course of the events because the mass movement developed its own spontaneous internal dynamic. When the revolution was victorious, the very political forces that had condemned the activists' politicization of popular rage began to deny the role of these activists under the pretext that the revolution had been impulsive and unplanned. Activist Lamine Al-Bouazizi states:[26]

> Here, we should turn to the press that was controlled by the authorities and which claimed that a group of extremists and radical parties were attempting to blow a mere incident up into something bigger. Following the revolution's success, the claim was spread that it was a revolution without leadership. Had the fates willed differently and had the revolution failed, this group of activists would have been hunted down, imprisoned, and executed.

Prior to the success of Tunisia's revolution, the regime attempted to minimize the protests as a regional and even a familial issue or, in this case, an issue peculiar

26. Arab Center for Research and Policy Studies' researchers Hamzeh al-Moustafa and Rami Salameh, in a personal interview with Lamine Al-Bouazizi on 19 April 2011, in Doha.

to the Bouazizi family, implying that such matters could have been resolved internally by the regime were it not for the incitement of political activists. This is characteristic of regime intelligentsia; once they admit to the existence of a problem, they proceed to attack all those who politicize it and dub them as extremists. Forces that are otherwise deemed extremist become mainstream during revolutionary times. Following a revolution's success, the main concern for former regime affiliates is to prevent those who tried to politicize popular rage from claiming the right to safeguard the aims of the revolution and speak on its behalf. Attributing a revolution to mere spontaneity assures that no one can take credit for it. This is a purpose-driven diagnostic that aims not only to exclude revolutionary forces from influencing the course of events after the revolution but also to silence the people's voice retroactively in order to distort or misrepresent the revolution's true motives and goals.

Realistically speaking, it would be impossible to explain a transformation of this magnitude on the basis of a single event. Nonetheless, it is possible to identify a period that separates the beginning of a popular uprising from the moment of its transformation into a full-fledged revolution. In determining the beginning of the Tunisian Revolution, we will rely on the chronology of the revolution's diaries beginning with the self-immolation of the young Mohamed Bouazizi. With this in mind, it should be stressed that Ben Ali's departure was followed by the demand that his entire apparatus and regime be ousted.

Bouazizi's desperate act was marked by anger against injustice, a sentiment shared by many of his generation. Unable to stop his oppressors or change his condition, Bouazizi decided to declare his frustration to the world by an ultimate act of rejection of the reality he was being forced to endure. Suicide under these circumstances was not carried out behind closed doors but in a public space, which transformed the act from a mere expression of desperation into a desperate protest, a tool by which to shock the public. This shock then transformed his individual act of desperation into a call for others to confront injustice as a collective choice rather than languish in individual isolation and impotence. In this respect, suicide was brought closer to the notion of martyrdom in its popular conception though not necessarily according to its religious definition. Thus, when asked for a legal ruling on the matter, the Mufti of the Tunisian Republic issued a bizarre fatwa declaring Bouazizi's self-immolation to be religiously prohibited.

Bouazizi's dramatic act sparked a revolution though it could have led to nothing but a peripheral protest. Similarly, the protests in Sidi Bouzid could have culminated in an understanding with the regime or, as previous cases, simply have been repressed. However, the revolutionary condition, which had matured behind the facade of stasis, transformed these events into triggers of a revolutionary movement.[27]

27. Azmi Bishara, 'The Great Popular Tunisian Revolution', *Commentary*, ACRPS, 26 January 2011,https://bit.ly/2K2Rl0J.

The media boom preceding the popular revolution

Despite its advances in culture and education and the existence of private media outlets, including television, Tunisia enjoyed no freedom of the press prior to the 2011 revolution, even when compared to Egypt under Mubarak. In Egypt, the creation of private media channels had been accompanied by limited freedom to criticize the authorities. Such freedom was kept in check through security and control and by planting pro-regime journalists in all media channels. Even so, Egypt had enjoyed a degree of press freedom for two decades; in fact, the critical media activism allowed within this margin was one of the elements that paved the way for the Egyptian Revolution. Tunisia, on the other hand, represented a unique model in which the state controlled the media and where the existence of private media did not necessarily equate with the existence of an independent or free press.

Ben Ali's accession to power in 1987 was accompanied by a new press code which eased restrictions on the media and, in 1993, allowed the appearance of newspapers of licenced opposition parties. This phase was short-lived, however, and was followed by a return to tight government control. In 2003, privately owned radio and satellite television channels, mainly in entertainment and sports, were permitted though without allowing any diversification in content. The regime ruthlessly controlled state-owned and private media alike.[28] When the revolution broke out, 'professional' journalists not only did not cover the revolution, but many of them played a counter-revolutionary role due to their ongoing allegiances to owners of the private media. Others justified their counter-revolutionary stances by emphasizing the chaos that had ensued following the uprising or by highlighting the misdeeds of the revolutionaries.

Besides the limited space afforded to private media, an internet boom took place under Ben Ali. Indeed, Tunisia was described as 'an Internet pioneer in the Arab world'.[29] It was also, however, a pioneer at restricting internet access. Web filtering and monitoring technologies had been implemented since 2000 so that while Egypt was loosening control over expression, Tunisia was tightening it[30] by means of surveillance, threats and repression for critics and rewards for loyalists.

In 2002, Zouhair Yahyaoui, a Tunisian journalist, cyber-activist and founder of the satirical website 'TUNeZINE', was sentenced to thirty months in prison for

28. Edward Webb, *Media in Egypt and Tunisia: From Control to Transition*? (New York: Palgrave Macmillan, 2014), pp. 50, 55.

29. Barney Warf and Peter Vincent, 'Multiple Geographies of the Arab Internet', *Area*, vol. 39, no. 1 (2007), pp. 83–96. Tunisia's first internet access was achieved in 1991, and by 30 September 2020, the number of internet users in the country had reached about 7.8 million with a 66.8 per cent penetration, while Facebook subscribers totalled nearly 7.5 million. See 'Internet Users Statistics for Africa', *Internet World Stats*, accessed on 17 November 2020, at: https://bit.ly/3pyxKpc.

30. Webb, p. 55.

criticizing the judiciary and police and satirizing the Ben Ali regime. After surviving three hunger strikes, torture and other mistreatment in prison, Yahyaoui died of a heart attack in 2005 not long after his release. Yahyaoui thus became an icon of cyber activism in Tunisia, and the period between 2005 and 2009 witnessed an exponential increase in the number of blogs in Tunisia, many of which, including 'Nawaat' and 'Tunisia News', were blocked by the authorities.[31]

Meanwhile, Abdelwahab Abdallah, Ben Ali's media adviser, oversaw the corruption of the press through Tunisian Agency for External Communication (ATCE), 'an agency formed to promote Tunisia internationally but also responsible for advertising by government entities', and which rewarded and punished media outlets through the selective deployment of money.[32] Detailed ATCE reports on its dealings outside the country and internally were released after the revolution.

Despite its significance, the Gafsa Mining Basin Uprising of 2008 was not reported by the media, and Tunisians barely followed its extensive events. However, when uprisings erupted in 2010, they began to capture international attention, primarily because social media coverage was so much more active and effective in 2010 than it had been in 2008. Moreover, although the majority of Tunisians, especially those in rural areas, watched TV, Facebook and blogging had by this time become significant locally and internationally, and more young people were regularly connected to both blogs and social media.

In the year preceding the revolution, a Human Rights Watch report on freedom of the press in Tunisia revealed that none of the publications and local media outlets offered critical coverage of government policies, with the exception of a small number of magazines that had a limited distribution, such as *al-Mawqif*, the occasionally banned and confiscated mouthpiece of the Progressive Democratic Party (PDS). The government also restricted access to political and legal internet websites that featured critical coverage of the Tunisian regime.

On 4 May 2009, the National Union for Tunisian Journalists (SNJT) issued a report criticizing the government's repression of the media and the absence of journalistic freedoms in Tunisia. On 15 August of the same year, in an effort to defame the former, democratically elected members of SNJT's executive bureau were terminated by pro-government journalists. A pro-government council was then 'elected' in its place, and Jamal el-Karmawy, media advisor to the secretary-general of Ben Ali's ruling party, was elected the new SNJT president. In October of the same year, Tunisian authorities prevented the North African correspondent for *Le Monde* from entering the country, accusing her of 'exhibiting extreme prejudice and systemic aggressive bias against Tunisia'.[33]

31. Aymen Rezgui, 'Les jeunes facebookeurs et la révolution du 14 janvier', in: *La Transition démocratique en Tunisie: Etat des lieux* (Tunis: Diwan Éditions, 2012), pp. 235–7, 241.

32. Ibid., p. 63.

33. 'Tunisia: Events of 2009', *Human Rights Watch*, accessed on 12 December 2020, at: https://bit.ly/2W4Erlk.

According to the 2009 Amnesty International report on Tunisia, those who criticized the Tunisian government or uncovered corruption and human rights abuses in the public administration had been subject to harassment, intimidation and physical assault by state security officers. Some were tried or imprisoned on trumped-up charges, becoming the target of smear campaigns in the pro-government media. As for those guilty of corruption and/or human rights violations, they enjoyed impunity, and complaints against them were rarely investigated. Some government critics were subjected to repressive surveillance, having their phone lines disconnected, their communications eavesdropped on and their internet blocked. The authorities also took down a number of internet websites, maintaining tight control over media outlets.

On 30 January 2009, the authorities closed down Kalimat Tunis Radio (Kalima Tunisie), an independent satellite radio station, four days after it began broadcasting from abroad. The police besieged the station's headquarters and harassed its employees. Sihem Bensedrine,[34] the station's editor-in-chief, was interrogated on charges of using a broadcast frequency without a licence.

In November of the same year, opposition journalist Taoufik Ben Brik was issued a six-month prison sentence after a sham trial based on a politically motivated accusation. Though the struggle for freedom of expression has a long history in Tunisia, these incidents attracted the attention of international human rights organizations in the year preceding the Tunisian Revolution.

In situations in which media is fully controlled, satellite channels, together with social networks, play an important role in disseminating criticisms and protests. Social media networks are not simply a medium of communication; they are a virtual public space where people can assemble without need of a permit, and public affairs can be discussed with a dynamism and persistence exceeding that of a traditional setting. These facts are particularly relevant to the revolutions of Tunisia and Egypt. In Syria, this type of media was utilized not only by the youth but also by the regime's supporters, who disseminated pro-regime propaganda and waged campaigns against the revolution. However, despite the importance of social media networks and their role in connecting activists and disseminating their ideas, Western media has exaggerated their role, scale and influence among the millions who participated in the revolutions.[35]

Despite the prominent and important role of electronic media in Arab revolutions, it should be remembered that every historical phase has had its own distinctive medium of communication. For instance, the influence of cassette tapes in the case of the Iranian Revolution cannot be ignored, since it was through

34. After the revolution she became head of the Truth and Dignity Commission.

35. See Egyptian researcher Rabab El-Mahdi's analysis of this Western exaggeration of the role of the social media that turns activists into a Western product rather than sympathizing with them and downplays the role of the poor in the Egyptian Revolution. Rabab El-Mahdi , 'Orientalising the Egyptian Uprising', *Jadaliyya*, 11 April 2011, accessed on 7 February 2021, at: http://bit.ly/3aHoLeF.

these tapes that Khomeini's speeches were disseminated among Iranians when he was in exile, while the transistor radio was key to spreading the ideas of the July 1952 Revolution in the Arab world, particularly in regions where electricity had not yet arrived. Similarly, one cannot ignore the role of the newspaper and the railway in the 1917 Russian Revolution and in revolutions that preceded it during what is referred to as the 'Springtime of the Peoples' between 1830 and 1848. Examples of such contemporary protests in which the social media did not play a role include the Tiananmen Square Protests in China in 1989, the Student Revolt in Indonesia in 1998 and the Saffron Revolution in Myanmar in 2007. Only in the Green Movement in Iran in 2009 and 2010[36] did the social media play an important role (Twitter, specifically), not in organization but by enabling activists in exile and other sympathizers to transmit the news of the uprising (the green revolution) to the outside world.

The majority of respondents in surveys conducted after the revolution said that the main means of communication they used was face-to-face or phone conversations with family and friends. Other sources were the internet, including social media.[37]

The online social networks made a marked contribution to facilitating coordination between activists and in providing reports, photos and videos to traditional media outlets, especially TV networks. In Egypt they also played a role in spreading calls for protest actions before the revolution and in its aftermath. These means of communication are extremely difficult for any regime to control unless the internet is banned completely, a step that can only be maintained for a very short time, if at all.

Through virtual networks, activists were transformed into private journalists. Accordingly, they documented, filmed and broadcast events and images via social media to be used by foreign media channels. Even when correspondents were prevented from entering a city or village, it became impossible to put a lid on an event once new media had accessed it. Any citizen with a third- or fourth-generation mobile phone and internet connectivity could broadcast images and videos of a quality fit for television broadcasts – a possibility that had not been available at the time of the Gafsa uprising two years before.

Virtual communities are not fictional but represent genuine social entities that emerge within a virtual space. Social media networks are distinguished by the fact that they are a dynamic tool for communicating news that is creatively reported,

36. Anita Breuer, Todd Landman and Dorothea Farquhar, 'Social Media and Protest Mobilization: Evidence from the Tunisian Revolution', *Democratization*, vol. 22, no. 4 (June 2015), p. 767.

37. Andrea Kavanaugh et al., 'Media Use by Young Tunisians during the 2011 Revolution vs. 2014 Elections', *Information Polity*, vol. 22, no. 2–3 (2017), p. 155.

With introducing media pluralism and freedom of speech after the revolution the vast majority of Tunisians turned from foreign channels like France 24 and Al Jazeera to watching local Tunisian TV channels.

even if there is the potential for sensationalizing and exaggerating facts. Truths and lies circulate equally on these networks, and news items are reported freely, often with critical commentaries, without following the editorial rules of traditional media. As such, they generate a communication space that is free from the rules that govern the act of publishing, creating a situation that is simultaneously advantageous and disadvantageous in comparison with traditional publishing and broadcasting.

Journalists and activists who broadcast via social media platforms are generally committed to specific causes and stances and may not even claim neutrality or accuracy. However, they are capable of highlighting what does not get broadcast by institutionalized media either because such items remain under the radar of traditional media or because of the mainstream media's biases. In the beginning, social media was not as popular a political tool; hence, it had yet to be infiltrated by organized political and economic forces as it is now. The interactive nature of the online social media also allows the exchange of opinions on public affairs and the crystallization of shared values. The unique nature of this type of media lies in the fact that it serves as a meeting space between individuals who are interested in public affairs, as well as non-engaged individuals who develop an interest in public affairs due to these encounters. The creation of this new virtual space provides a 'place' for individuals who would not have been able to congregate anywhere else, even if they enjoyed the freedom of assembly.

It goes without saying that these new developments should be factored into any attempt to explain social transformations, be they democratic or otherwise. Just as in the 1960s, European and US campuses were viewed as a sphere for protest against the system, social media platforms now perform a similar function, although they are 'thinner', faster, more easily accessible and much more diverse and inclusive.[38] Complete with both advantages and disadvantages, social media networks and the new media in general represent a new domain for the formation of social and political forces capable of rising above the conditions of material life. At the same time, they do not create a revolutionary situation or revolutionary individuals; they would not have had such a decisive impact had there been no susceptibility to revolution in Egypt and Tunisia and no individuals and groups to make use of them.

Reliance on social networks as an alternative source of information is the result not only of state monopolies on the media but of the spread of personal computers and 'smartphones'. Prior to the revolution, the Tunisian regime had implemented a project to provide 'a computer for every family' and facilitated the purchase

38. See Mathieu Rousselin, 'Modern Communication Technologies and the Extension of the Territory of Struggle: Conceptualizing Tunisia's Jasmine Revolution', *New Media and Society*, vol. 18, no. 7 (August 2016), pp, 1201–18. 'Thin' territories are more exclusive than thick territories. However, thick territories, which are in fact identity-based or communities of shared values and other frames of identification, are more determining for political attitudes for the subject.

of personal computers through instalments. In the 1990s, Ben Ali's regime invested intensively in the telecom sector, and Tunisia had eleven internet service providers competing among themselves in a market economy, an unprecedented phenomenon in the Arab world. The fact that President Ben Ali himself was interested in IT and surrounded by advisers who pushed in that direction, and his daughters also owned one of these internet companies, may have prompted the state to encourage internet subscription, eventually leading to about 2 million Tunisian users of Facebook alone in a country with the highest internet penetration rate (34 per cent in 2009 and 36.8 per cent as of 2010 when the uprising began) in the Arab world with the exception of the Gulf states.[39] Facebook penetration at the outbreak of the revolution was 17–18 per cent,[40] which was even greater than that in more developed countries such as Russia, Great Britain, Brazil, China and Germany.

The Internet World Stats Website indicates that in 2009, the number of internet users in Tunisia had reached 2.8 million. Table 3.8 shows the spread of the internet between 2000 and 2009 for each Arab country and the Arab region as a whole.

Lamine Al-Bouazizi, a prominent activist in Sidi Bouzid, explains the influence of these developments on political activists in his region:

> To counter the intentional delays in the provision of phone lines, people resorted to cyber cafes. Despite the fact that there were only two licensed Internet cafes, there were over 20 illegal ones, and political websites were unblocked in these establishments. . . . Facebook quickly became the supplier for major media channels, and the role of the journalist was reduced to filming with a mobile phone costing no more than $40. Facebook played a notable and dynamic role in breaking the siege via its coverage of events in Sidi Bouzid. In fact, Tunisian newspapers made no mention of Sidi Bouzid during the first week, with many believing that the scenes of billowing smoke and others were actually taking place in Fallujah. Had the locals not recognized the area, they would not have believed that the events were taking place in Sidi Bouzid.[41]

Acknowledging the significance of such shifts is important though it is equally important to avoid falling into the trap of mythologizing new media. Mere participation in these virtual associations is not a revolutionary act, nor is it an

39. Sherry Lawrence, 'Was the Revolution Tweeted? Social Media and Jasmin Revolution in Tunisia', *Digest of Middle East Studies*, vol. 25, no. 1 (2016), p. 158.

40. Breuer, Landman and Faruqhar, p. 773. By the beginning of 2008, the number of Facebook users in Tunisia had reached 16,000; by August of that year, it had risen to 28,313; by February 2009 it was 304,084; by July 2009 it was 640,661; by late August 2010 it had grown to more than 1,600,000 users, and after Ben Ali was deposed, the number hit 2 million. Rezgui, 'Les jeunes facebookeurs et la révolution du 14 janvier', pp. 242, 244, 247, 255, 256.

41. Lamine Al-Bouazizi, Interview, 19 April 2011.

Table 3.8 Rates of Internet Usage in Arab Countries

	Country	Population (2009)	Internet Users (December 2000)	Internet Users (2009)	Per cent Change (2000–09)
1	Egypt	78,866,635	450,000	12,568,900	2693.1
2	Morocco	31,285,174	100,000	10,300,000	10200.0
3	Saudi Arabia	28,686,633	200,000	7,700,000	3750.0
4	Sudan	41,087,825	30,000	4,200,000	13900.0
5	Algeria	34,178,188	50,000	4,100,000	8100.0
6	Syria	21,762,978	30,000	3,565,000	11783.3
7	UAE	4,798,491	735,000	2,922,000	297.6
8	Tunisia	10,486,339	100,000	2,800,000	2700.0
9	Jordan	6,269,285	127,300	1,500,500	1078.7
10	Kuwait	2,692,526	150,000	1,000,000	566.7
11	Lebanon	4,017,095	300,000	945,000	215.0
12	Oman	3,418,085	90,000	465,000	416.7
13	Qatar	833,285	30,000	436,000	1353.3
14	Bahrain	728,709	40,000	402,900	907.3
15	Yemen	22,858,238	15,000	370,000	2366.7
16	Palestine (West Bank)	2,461,267	35,000	355,500	915.7
17	Libya	6,324,357	10,000	323,000	3130.0
18	Iraq	28,945,569	12,500	300,000	2300.0
19	Eritrea	5,647,168	5,000	200,000	3900.0
20	Somalia	9,832,017	200	102,000	50900.0
21	Mauritania	3,129,486	5,000	60,000	1100.0
Total/Average		**349,861,209**	**2,515,000**	**54,615,800**	**5836.9**

Miniwatts Marketing Group, 'Arabic Speaking Internet Users' Statistics: Internet User Statistics in Population Stats for the Countries and Regions with Arab Speaking Internet Users', *Internet World Stats*, 23 March 2012, accessed on 12 December 2020, at: https://bit.ly/2JWnFT3.

act of protest that could bring down a regime. As mentioned earlier, the majority of the population not only had no social media accounts but did not treat social media as a major source of information. Its information had to pass through the traditional media. At that time, social media had not yet reached the stage of becoming a comprehensive social space that encompasses communication, news, power relations and so forth.

In Tunisia, one particular image went viral and proved to be an effective ingredient of the campaign: that of Bouazizi setting himself on fire. Eventually, the image turned out to be that of a young Korean committing suicide; nevertheless, this iconic picture spread, as did the images of anger and protest in Sidi Bouzid. Solidarity emerged as each region saw the protests and steadfastness of other regions in real time. As a result, they sensed that they were not alone but part of a popular national movement with the courage and boldness to move mountains. Traditional media channels, including Al Jazeera and some French and European channels that closely followed the evolution of events, constituted a major source of information for most of the population, including the protesters, the majority of whom did not own Facebook accounts. At the same time, videos and texts of social media activists were a main supplier of media coverage due to the fact that TV crews were not allowed on the ground. In tandem, social networks, news websites and private forums contributed to spreading the details of events and revealing truths that the regime sought to hide, thereby creating a symbiosis between new and 'traditional' media.

It has been argued that the Tunisian regime's tightening internet censorship led inadvertently to both the growth and popularization of social media use, particularly Facebook. By the time the revolution broke out,[42] half of the 34 per cent of the population who had access to the internet owned a Facebook account.[43]

Prior to the revolution, Facebook had not posed a threat to the regime as long as its users remained distanced from politics. In fact, the regime viewed Facebook as a depoliticizing factor that would divert young people's attention from public affairs. It was 'more the epitome of a lifestyle for a predominantly young population than a tool for political activism'.[44] However, when it began penetrating the political sphere, it first transformed it into a subculture relatively free of restrictions.[45] Attempts at digital activism during the Gafsa uprising led to a state ban on Facebook, the blocking of accounts and a policy of tight surveillance. However, after Ben Ali lifted the block, which lasted from 24 August to 2 September 2009, 300,000 new users joined this social network.

42. Mohamed Zayani, *Networked Publics and Digital Contention: The Politics of Everyday Life in Tunisia* (Oxford: Oxford University Press, 2015), pp. 169–70.

43. For statistics on Internet usage in Tunisia, see 'Tunisia', *Internet World Stats*, accessed on 2 November 2020, at: https://bit.ly/34MYRUZ; and, 'Tunisia Internet Users', *Internet Live Stats*, accessed on 2 November 2020, at: https://bit.ly/3jIAwEg.

44. Zayani, *Networked Publics and Digital Contention*, p. 171.

45. Ibid., pp. 171–2.

The unblocking of Facebook marked a shift towards intensified state surveillance, and security services ordered Tunisian ISPs to intercept the details of Tunisian Facebook users. These details were then relayed to the Tunisian Internet Agency (ATI), which used them either to block the accounts entirely or to threaten users.[46] The regime's internet censorship and its attempts to suppress cyber activities were counterproductive, however. An online petition protesting these measures attracted more than 10,000 signatures in 2010.[47] And unlike other Arab regimes which learned from the Tunisian experience, the Tunisian regime censored and controlled the social media as thoroughly as it could although it stopped short of digital counter-activism.[48]

Cyber activism, or digital activism, appeared in Tunisia long time before the revolution, as a matter of fact. It started in 1998 when two anonymous activists by the names of 'Foetus' and 'Waterman' founded a group called Takriz as a cyber resistance network. After Takriz was blocked in August 2000, a new collective blog, 'Nawaat', was founded in 2004 by exiled activists. The new blog's goal was to 'provide a public platform for Tunisian dissident voices and publish information about the regime's corruption and human rights violations'. Some Facebook pages functioned as the organ of the revolution, an online space for bloggers and human rights activists; Nawaat functioned as an organ of the revolution abroad. Radio Kalima and other blogs reached thousands of people inside and outside Tunisia.

The testimony of blogger Ramadan ben Umar, one of the first Tunisian political bloggers, reveals how the 2008 Mining Basin Uprising contributed to the creation of what came to be called the bloggers' community, which took it upon itself to report the protest movement in the peripheries to the different centres. He says:

> The blogger phenomenon existed prior to 2008, but it was not associated with politics; the real beginning of the transformation of the blogger into a political and social activist was with the uprising in the mining basin districts.[49] On a personal level, I used my blog at the time to upload video footage and news reports on the protests and to send them to the media channels. The blogging

46. Breuer, Landman and Farquhar, p. 771.

47. Michael J. Willis, 'Revolt for Dignity: Tunisia's Revolution and Civil Resistance', in: Adam Roberts et al. (eds.), *Civil Resistance in the Arab Spring: Triumphs and Disasters* (Oxford: Oxford University Press, 2016), p. 43.

48. Mathieu Rousselin considers social media to be a 'space–provider', an instrument of territorialization, a cyber territory which brings people together in immaterial 'territories of struggle'. Concerned primarily with 'thick' (material) territories, the Tunisian regime made little attempt to dispute the 'thin' (immaterial) realms of struggle. In this way it differed from the other Arab regimes that learned from the Tunisian experience. See Rousselin, 'Modern Communication Technologies and the Extension of the Territory of Struggle', p. 1207.

49. A phenomenon very similar to the role of Egyptian bloggers who engaged with the ongoing social protests, especially during the workers' strike at Ghazl al-Mahalla in September 2007.

> phenomenon continued and expanded to the point where the regime devoted a specialized unit, referred to by bloggers as 'Ammar 404', to the pursuit of political bloggers. The experience we gained from that phase undoubtedly bore fruit in December 2010. There is also no doubt that the rise of the new social media platforms such as Facebook and Twitter gave bloggers a broader space in which to interact with each other.[50]

Some digital activists interested in cultural or entertainment topics turned their platforms into political ones. An example is Lina Ben Mhenni, who launched 'Nightclubbeuse', a blog that was initially dedicated to nightlife in Tunisia but which, in 2009, was politicized in reaction to the regime's growing repressiveness and began to report increasingly on social and political issues. Tunisian authorities blocked Mhenni's site in early 2010, but she later relaunched another version of her blog under the name, 'A Tunisian Girl' dedicated to political issues.[51]

Before 2007, Tunisian internet activist sites such as Tunezine, Takriz and Nawaat were based outside the country. After that year, local cyber activism through blogging also became noticeable. The presidential and legislative elections of October 2009 and the arrest of blogger and activist Fatima Riahi on 2 November of the same year were contributing factors to the intensification of cyber activism. After Riahi's arrest, a Facebook page was created demanding her freedom, and her release within a single week further empowered internet activists. The following spring, the regime escalated its censorship campaign, and Facebook began increasingly to advocate for bloggers.[52] The first call for anti-censorship demonstrations came from Facebook pages: Sayeb Sale7 and Nhar 3la 3ammar.[53] The demonstration planned for 22 May 2010 was not carried out, but a group led by Slim Amamou and Yassine Ayari switched to writing letters to members of Parliament. Some of its members were also active in the information campaign against the regime during the revolution.[54]

Online activists interacted with the Ben Gardane protests on the Tunisian-Libyan border in August 2010 after the closure of the Ras Ajdir border crossing through which goods were imported into Tunisia and sold at low prices. However,

50. Personal Interview conducted with Ramadan ben Umar via Skype, 15 October 2011. To view the videos uploaded by Ben Umar, see 'Romdhane Ben Amor', *Facebook*, accessed at: https://bit.ly/3qJ9uBg.

51. Breuer, Landman and Farquhar, pp. 771–2. See also Nesrine Romdhani, 'Les blogueurs', in: *La Transition démocratique en Tunisie*, p. 266.

52. Tarek Kahlouni, 'The Powers of Social Media', in: Nouri Gana (ed.), *The Making of the Tunisian Revolution: Contexts, Architects, Prospects* (Edinburgh: Edinburgh University Press, 2013), p. 150.

53. Derived from the name of former Tunisian Minister of Interior Habib Ammar, the first to issue norms for internet surveillance, "3mmar404" is the nickname Tunisian internet surfers use to refer to the internet censorship authority. See Nesrine Romdhani, pp. 261–2.

54. Kahlouni, 'The Powers of Social Media', p. 151.

the reopening of the crossing ended the online campaign. With the outbreak of the protests in Sidi Bouzid on 17 December, online campaigns were reactivated. Despite the arrest of a number of activists, this activity continued.[55]

By then, the number of Facebook users had already exceeded 1,700,000. The first days of the revolution had witnessed online participation by opposition party leaders on Facebook. They engaged in campaigns exposing and defaming the regime. Rezgui mentioned opposition figures such as Moncef Marzouki, Hamma Hammami, Tarak Mekki, Ahmed Brahim, Ahmed Najib Chebbi, Naceur Laouini, Chokri Belaid and others. Al Jazeera quoted posts and comments of those leaders and shared photos, videos and news about the revolution from the most famous pages. The media exposure stimulated coverage competition among Facebook pages.[56] Two Facebook pages, 'Ma Tunisie' (500,000 members) and 'Tunisia_تونس_Tunisie' (300,000 members) – both of them connected to the Sidi Bouzid activists – provided a platform for sharing information regarding protests.[57]

In November 2010, just a month before the outbreak of the revolution, activists began translating and disseminating Wikileaks cables involving communications with the US ambassador to Tunisia which provided detailed information on the corruption within Ben Ali's entourage.[58] The significance of these leaked documents lay in the fact that, since their source was an ally of the Tunisian government, they provided conclusive evidence of the corruption within the Ben Ali regime.

55. Rezgui, 'Les jeunes facebookeurs et la révolution du 14 janvier', pp. 238–9.

56. Ibid., p. 250.

57. Kahlouni, 'The Powers of Social Media', p. 153.

58. Michael J. Willis , 'Revolt for Dignity: Tunisia's Revolution and Civil Resistance', in: *Civil Resistance in the Arab Spring: Triumphs and Disasters*, Adam Roberts, Michael J. Willis, Rory McCarthy, and Timothy Garton Ash (eds.) (Oxford: Oxford University Press, 2016), pp. 43–4. The author's assumption that Tunisians who took part in the 2011 revolution knew ahead of time that the United States would not come to Ben Ali's rescue – as if this had been a premeditated calculation – is farfetched. Rather, the Wikileaks documents simply confirmed the already widespread image of the Ben Ali government as a corrupt regime.

Chapter 4

PARTIES AND OTHER ASSOCIATIONS BEFORE THE UPHEAVAL

Ben Ali came to power promising democracy, national reconciliation and limits on presidential powers. In addition, he combined endorsement of the World Bank's structural adjustment programme (SAP) with liberal political reforms, which included limiting himself to three five-year consecutive terms. He also freed political prisoners and led a national dialogue which in 1988 led to a national pact with sixteen political parties and organizations.

In the beginning, Ben Ali made certain changes in order to placate the religious sentiments of particular sectors; for example, he allowed the call to prayer to be broadcast on radio and TV and legalized the Islamic Tendency Movement (MTI) student organization. Unlike Bourguiba, Ben Ali was not a convinced secularist; he was simply a secular autocrat. Hence, he was not willing to engage in a debate with the Zaituna clerics over the fast of Ramadan and its damage to the economy as had Bourguiba, who actually discouraged Tunisians from fasting. Instead, he presented himself as a believer who abided by his religious duties, built El-Abidine Mosque in Carthage, even claimed the title 'protector of homeland and religion' (hami el-hima wal-din) and encouraged fasting and other traditional religious practices. However, he had no compunctions about censoring the Friday sermon.

In its turn, the MTI made a concession by signing the 1988 National Pact, which stated that the secular Personal Status Code should remain unassailable. However, the Pact also acknowledged the centrality of Tunisia's Arab and Islamic heritages, calling for closer ties between Tunisia and the rest of the Arab world,[1] and recognizing the importance of Tunisia's nineteenth- and twentieth-century Islamic reform and modernization movements.[2] The Pact stipulated a multiparty system, limited presidential terms, promised civil liberties and freedom of the press, and adhered to the achievements of the modern state, including the Personal Status Code and women's rights; it also, and simultaneously, emphasized the centrality of Tunisia's Muslim and Arab heritage. Consequently, the Pact was accepted by secular and religious participants alike.

1. Ties whose value Bourguiba had disparaged even when he was forced to acknowledge them.

2. Kenneth Perkins, *A History of Modern Tunisia*, 2nd edn (Cambridge: Cambridge University Press, 2014), pp. 192, 194.

Ben Ali renamed Bourguiba's Neo-Destour Party as the Democratic Constitutional Rally (RCD). He needed the approval of the party and public opinion, of course, because he was busy purging Bourguiba loyalists in both the party and the state, a task he carried out successfully by containing some, neutralizing others and dismissing the rest.

Ben Ali's image as a reformist lasted only until the end of the 1980s, at which time he gradually went back on his promises of reform and began implementing more repressive policies against the opposition, mainly the Islamists. Ben Ali's crackdown coincided with the outbreak of violence in Algeria after the Algerian state cancelled national parliamentary elections.[3]

The 1988 National Pact gave the impression that Ben Ali would transition Tunisia from a one-party state to a multiparty state. During this time, following popular 'bread uprisings' that spread across the region, similar reforms were attempted in Egypt, Jordan, Morocco and other Arab countries. Undeniably, reform had opened a channel for restricted political debate and the exchange of opinion in these countries, but the regimes in place still maintained their grip on power.[4] Although these reforms did not limit presidential powers and were essentially cosmetic in nature, they nevertheless provided an opportunity for the traditional opposition to express itself through parliamentary elections and even participate in cabinets. (After all, neither the government nor parliament is an independent decision-maker in a dictatorship.)

Tunisia appeared to hold more promise of democratic transformation given the existence of relatively developed state institutions, a broad middle class, extensive women's rights, and a fairly advanced education system. Behind these reforms, however, lay Ben Ali's need to build a popular legitimacy following his coup. Many scholars interpreted these steps as the dawn of a democratic transition and went so far as to compare them to Spain's democratic transformation following the death of Franco and the introduction of the Moncloa Pact.[5] Change in Tunisia, however,

3. The Islamic Salvation Front (FIS) party had been projected to defeat the ruling National Liberation Front (FLN) party after winning the first round in December 1991. However, this was followed by a military coup and, eventually, a ruthless civil war that lasted nearly a decade.

4. The most radical, genuinely democratic-seeming reforms to take place were those implemented in Algeria in the late 1980s. However, it was for this very reason that such reforms were countered by the military, which led to a protracted civil conflict that cost the lives of over 100,000 Algerians.

5. Larbi Sadiki, 'Political Liberalization in Ben Ali's Tunisia: Façade Democracy', *Democratization*, vol. 9, no. 4 (September 2010), p. 133. In his article, Sadiki maintains a measure of optimism, but offers a critical review of the reform era, claiming that the existing party pluralism in Tunisia is a mere façade. Also, as I previously noted in Chapter One, Lisa Andersen was optimistic about the 1988 National Pact of Tunisia, but she later admitted that her enthusiasm had been 'uncalled for' after Ben Ali became one of 'the most despotic kleptocracies in the world'. See Lisa Anderson, 'Political Pacts, Liberalism, and

hardly amounted to democratic transition. Rather, it bore a greater resemblance to the measures taken by Anwar Sadat to manufacture personal legitimacy following the charismatic rule of Gamal Abdel Nasser or the reforms of Mubarak in 1984 and King Hussein in the late 1980s.

Ben Ali's decision to relax his grip on the press was especially promising. To his advantage, this increased press freedom served as evidence that he was serious about his reforms. To the opposition's advantage, however, press freedom could be exploited to force Ben Ali to be serious about his reforms.[6] Nevertheless, the opposition was sufficiently marginalized that it could not prevent Ben Ali from rescinding his reforms and reinstating authoritarian measures. Meanwhile, the rise of the Islamist movement in neighbouring Algeria enabled Ben Ali to present himself to the international community as the protector of Tunisian modernism against Islamism. Add to this the economic growth and prosperity that Tunisia witnessed after Ben Ali's economic reforms, which primarily benefitted major cities, including the business community and some segments of the middle class.

Three secular parties were legalized in 1988: the Democratic Unionist Union (UDU), the Social Progress Party (PSP) and the Progressive Socialist Rally (RSP). Neither these parties nor the pre-existing secular parties managed to present candidates in more than a quarter of the districts during the 1989 elections. Only about 5 per cent of the vote went to secular opposition parties. By contrast, the RCD won nearly 80 per cent of the vote, acquiring all of the parliamentary seats. Al Nahda candidates who ran as 'independents' won about 15 per cent of the vote; they enjoyed massive support in the capital's suburbs as well as in some inland districts where they obtained more than 30 per cent of the vote. In the 1994 parliamentary elections, the regime guaranteed the opposition a 12 per cent quota of parliament seats, so that candidates representing legal secular parties could compete for a share in this quota.

In his attempt to forge a new legitimacy, Ben Ali readily played the role of a strongman capable of leading the transition. Up until Tunisia's 1994 elections, and even until the electoral contest in 1999 when the regime volunteered to grant the opposition parties a number of seats, few observers remained optimistic, although Ben Ali ran unopposed in the presidential elections and won 99 per cent of the vote.[7] In April 2002, Ben Ali amended the constitution to allow himself to run for more than three terms. Even then, some 'optimists' insisted that the democratic transition was not threatened by the re-emerging autocracy.

Democracy: The Tunisian National Pact of 1988', *Government and Opposition*, vol. 26, no. 2 (1991), pp. 251–7; Lisa Anderson, 'Forward', in Safwan M. Masri, *Tunisia: An Arab Anomaly*, Foreword by Lisa Anderson (New York: Columbia University Press, 2017), pp. xvi–xvii.

6. Eoghan Stafford, 'Stop the Presses! Media Freedom in Authoritarian Regimes: A Case Study of Ben Ali's Tunisia', *The Journal of the Middle East and Africa*, vol. 8, no. 4 (October-December 2017), pp. 351–385.

7. Perkins, *A History of Modern Tunisia*, p. 195.

The loyal parties ('décor' parties as they were called in Tunisia) were intended to keep up an appearance of party pluralism while concurrently justifying the policies and measures of the regime. Even though they might voice harsh criticisms on occasion, the legal and semi-legal opposition parties had internalized the role of a malleable opposition that adheres to a script pre-determined by the ruling regime. These parties were largely convinced that the Islamist threat was real and that it was more dangerous than the regime itself.

An opposition that is content to criticize without questioning the authoritarian system at its core or striving to reach power itself is a cog in the wheel of the established regime rather than a meaningful challenger. However, it may start to behave like an opposition if the regime is shaken by forces that do not abide by the rules of the game, like a revolution. The illegal opposition, by contrast, was severely persecuted, and because its actions were closely monitored, it could not surprise the regime or launch a planned revolt. Most of the regime's intelligence work was targeted against the organized political opposition, especially the illegal. No wonder, then, that the surprise came from a different direction.

The Tunisian Party Law promulgated on 10 April 1999 mandated that a political party must function within the bounds of constitutional legitimacy and the law, defend the Arab Muslim identity of Tunisia (an emphasis that marked some of Ben Ali's reforms) and human rights as defined by the Constitution, and respect the international agreements signed by the Tunisian Republic.[8] The law also required that parties reject all forms of violence, extremism, racism and other forms of discrimination and avoid any activity that might threaten national security, the general order, and the rights and freedoms of others. Accordingly, each party's founding statement was required to state that the party was based not on religion, language, gender or region but on democratic foundations and principles.

According to the aforementioned law, a political party will be considered illegal if its principles, choices or programmes are not distinguished from the principles and programmes of other legally recognized parties. A Tunisian political party may not, whether directly or indirectly, receive financial support from a foreign entity or from foreigners residing in Tunisia, regardless of their nature and purpose. The law also grants the Minister of the Interior the power to order the courts to disband a political party if its activities and programmes contradict any of the earlier principles.[9]

Most of these principles and conditions appear to be standard and acceptable in a democratic system. In countries ruled by authoritarian regimes, however, they become mere formalities because, given the threat they may pose to the regime, political parties are subjected to intense political scrutiny. In Tunisia, the state was inordinately concerned with a party's internal democratic structure – a domain that should be outside the purview of the state and solely within the domain of the

8. 'The Law of Political Parties in Tunisia', *UNDP-POGAR*, 10 April 1999, accessed at: https://bit.ly/383MXqa.

9. Ibid.

citizenry. A party is a voluntary, preferably democratic, association and obliged by law to respect its declared charter. It does not, however, have an obligation to be democratic, since a citizen can opt to leave the party at any time. The state, on the other hand, is not a voluntary association, and democracy is, above all, a system of rule within the state. It is, therefore, ironic that a non-democratic state feigned concern for its political parties' internal democracy.

The following is a brief description of the political parties relevant to this study, bearing in mind that the history of political parties in Tunisia is richer than what can be presented in this chapter.

The revolution was neither triggered nor led by political parties. Nevertheless, the presence of organized political parties and a political tradition was to become vital for the transition to democracy after the revolution, albeit only for a short period of time. The décor parties disappeared and most of the old opposition parties were defeated in the second democratic elections held in 2014. The attempts to fill the vacuum left by the dissolution of the RCD worked only for a short period of time, and the resulting chaos continued to debilitate the young parliamentarian democracy and alienate the people from political elites, thus fertilizing the soil for populism. One of the reasons for the collapse of the regime lies in the fact that the RCD was corroded and emptied of any content in its transformation from a ruling party to the party of the ruler (the president); it had thus been reduced to a tool of the regime and one of its cliental networks.

Parties represented in Parliament on the eve of the revolution

Until the revolution, the Tunisian Parliament (when it was elected) was composed of 214 seats occupied by elected party candidates, in addition to 25 seats for appointed members.

The Democratic Constitutional Rally (RCD): 161 seats

The RCD has ruled Tunisian politics since Tunisia's independence in 1956. The party was founded by Abdelaziz Thâalbi in 1920 under the name the Tunisian Constitutional Party, or the Constitution Party (*ḥizb al-dustūr*). The choice of the name was meant to be associated with the constitutional legacy of Tunisia before colonialism and because the promulgation of a national constitution was one of the main demands of the anti-colonial movement. In 1861, when the Tunisian monarchy was still an Ottoman protectorate, it became the first Muslim country in modernity to promulgate a constitution.[10] The Arabic word *dustūr* (constitution)

10. The first constitutional era in Tunisia was between the years of 1857 and 1864. It began with *ʿAhd al-Amān* (the Security Covenant) of 1857 followed by the Constitution of 1861.

was kept when the name was changed to the Neo-Destour Party (1934), to the Socialist Destourian Party (1964), and to the Democratic Destourian Rally (1988).

Despite having been drafted under foreign pressure, the Constitution was a source of pride for Tunisians, as it provided a way to combine their national liberation from French colonialism with the modern discourse of constitutional rights and a proven capacity to manage a sovereign state. The modernist tradition, which was apparent in the national liberation movement against colonialism, continued not only in the regime itself but also within Tunisia's various liberal, nationalist and socialist movements. This can be seen within the party in figures such as Ahmed Mestiri and Hassib Ben Ammar, who established the Tunisian Human Rights League (LTDH), as well as within other parties like the Congress for the Republic (CPR), the Progressive Democratic Party (PDS), the Democratic Forum for Labor and Liberties also known as Ettakatol (FDTL) and leftist entities such as the Workers' Party and the Democratic Patriots' Unified Party.[11]

In its early days, the RCD was concerned with independence and Arab liberation and unity. However, despite these pan-Arab leanings, it initially stood against the movement of Sharif Ḥusayn Ibn Ali and his sons in the Hijaz on the pretext that the movement had collaborated with the British against the Ottomans and, therefore, could not achieve the promised Arab state. At the same time Thâalbi believed that Arab 'backwardness' was a result of the 'tyranny of the Turks'.[12] In its ideology, the party had Arabist and Islamic beginnings, reflecting Thâalbi's arguments from his book *Martyred Tunisia*.[13] In March 1934, the party changed its name to the New Constitutional Party (*al-ḥizb al-dustūrī al-jadīd*), which led the liberation struggle and steered the negotiations for independence from France. The negotiations phase gave rise to internal party conflicts (see Chapter 2) that ended with Bourguiba's victory as head of government. In 1957, the parliament declared the end of the monarchist regime and the emergence of the republican system. Then, following the Bizerte Convention of October 1964, the party's name was changed to the Socialist Constitutional Party (*al-ḥizb al-ishtirākī al-dustūrī*).

Transformations within the party began with the arrival of French-educated Tunisians, ultimately leading to the founding of the Neo-Destour Party. After assuming power, Bourguiba led the party to focus so heavily on Tunisia's identity as a nation that the term 'Tunisian nation' came to be equated with Tunisian nationalism. Thâalbi's pan-Arab vision did not conform to that promoted by members of the new, French-educated generation, including Habib Bourguiba,

11. Yadh Ben Achour, *Tunisia: A Revolution in an Islamic Country [Tūnis: thawrah fī bilād al-islām]*, Fathi Ben al-Haj Yahya (trans.) (Tunis: Tunisian Institute for Translation/ Cérès for Publications, 2018), pp. 70–1.

12. Salim Labyad, *Identity: Islam, Arabism, and Tunisification [al-Hawiyah: al-Islām, al-ʿUrūbah, al-Tawnasah]* (Beirut: Center for Arab Unity Studies, 2009), p. 65.

13. Mohamed al-Fadil Ben Ashour, *The Literary and Intellectual Movement in Tunisia [al-Ḥarakah al-adabiyah wal-fikriyah fī tūnis]*, 3rd ed. (Tunis: al-Dār at-Tūnisiyah lil-Nashr, 1972), pp. 444–6.

Tahar Sfar, Bahri Guiga, Mahmoud El Materi and others who joined the party in 1933.

The new Destouri elite further distinguished itself by its radical secularist position after independence, which went beyond the call for a separation of religion and state to the position which, similar to the French *Laic* model, held that religion should be limited to the private sphere. The Destouri elite thus adopted the radical French conception of secularism while at the same time advocating Tunisian state control over religion. In this way, the Destouri elite simultaneously distanced themselves from the position of the founders of the party who had adhered to the reformist ideal of adapting Islam to modernity and from the views of some of new-generation figures such as Secretary-General Salah Ben Youssef.

Even when Bourguiba was still embroiled in conflict with the previous Destouri elite who followed Thâalbi's legacy, Salah Ben Youssef and the Zaituna Sheikhs, he maintained steadfast support for the Maghreb's struggle for liberation from colonialism.

The conflict that took place between Salah Ben Youssef and Habib Bourguiba at the time was the continuation of an old ideological conflict within the Neo-Destour Party. However, following the 3 June 1955 agreements that granted Tunisia self-rule, these conflicts led to a struggle over leadership. Bourguiba was openly pro-Western and secular, leading him to opt for an alliance with the West after the end of the Second World War. Salah Ben Youssef, on the other hand, believed that Tunisia's place was with the nationalist Arab movement and the non-aligned countries following Nasser's Egypt. The conflict between the two men began to surface publicly following the speech delivered in July 1954 by French prime minister Pierre Mendés-France, who supported Tunisian self-rule without political independence. Bourguiba welcomed the speech, viewing it as a step forward and as a radical shift in the French position, noting: 'Our country is small and we cannot live in isolation; we wish to remain an independent country in the orbits of both France and the Arab world.'[14] Ben Youssef, on the other hand, believed that Tunisia's independence was possible without the need for an alliance with France, particularly since colonialism was entering a state of retreat. He also believed in the unification of North Africa's resistance movement and in Moroccan, Tunisian and Algerian independence.

One might argue that Bourguiba's insistence on Tunisian nation-building seemed more pronounced throughout this conflict. In other words, Ben Youssef's stances and ongoing conflict within the party, which eventually led to his intellectual, and even physical, liquidation, made Bourguiba elevate nation-building in Tunisia to the level of an ideology. This position received France's support, and because France saw Bourguiba as a suitable partner, his position within the Tunisian national movement was strengthened. Ben Youssef, on the other hand, considered

14. Umayra Aliyya Al-Sghayyar, *The Youssefis and the Liberation of the Arab Maghreb [al-Yūsifiyūn wa-Taḥarrur al-Maghrib al- ʿArabī]*, (Tunis: al-Maghāribiyah lil-Ṭibāʿah wal-Nashr wal-ishhār, 2007), p. 19.

Bourguiba's signing of the autonomy agreement on 21 April 1955 while he (Ben Youssef) was attending the Non-Alignment Conference in Bandung to be an act of treason. He was especially harsh in his criticism of the negotiator al-Munji Salim.[15]

In reality, neither of these men was more nationalistic than the other, or more insistent on resisting colonialism. Pro-Youssef figures participated effectively in the resistance, but they advocated different paths for Tunisia. Following independence, there was an attempt to defame Salah Ben Youssef, his movement, and their role in the resistance and struggle. Pro-Western Bourguiba employed Stalinist methods to erase any mention of Ben Youssef from Tunisian history except in relation to his role as leader of a so-called sabotage movement. Yet despite all these conflicts, the pro-Youssef opposition engaged in an armed struggle against the French that started before 1955 and was cautioned by the leadership, including and Bourguiba. When Ben Youssef broke with Bourguiba, his followers continued fighting, while Bourguiba's deposed their weapons. The struggle continued after independence (from late 1955 to mid-1956) along the entire border area with Algeria (centre-west and south-west of Tunisia). This armed resistance, alongside Bourguiba's negotiations, was one of the main reasons France granted Tunisia full independence. Official history neglects this role, and Ben Youssef is hardly mentioned, but people in the Tunisian interior most certainly remembered him. In his book, Essebsi has only a single reference to Ben Youssef: 'Salah Ben Youssef occasionally visited Paris and would always contact our branch; relations were supposed to grow tighter . . . but Salah Ben Youssef struck me as a gruff and authoritarian personality.'[16] This aversion to Ben Youssef's 'authoritarian' personality was expressed, notably, by a politician who was a loyal disciple of Bourguiba.

Ben Youssef became the Tunisian representative for the Committee for the Liberation of North Africa, where he was an ally of the Arab nationalist current and Abdel Nasser.[17] As noted earlier, Bourguiba welcomed France's acceptance of Tunisia's autonomy, and on 23 November 1954, he ordered the Tunisian armed resistance to surrender its weapons to the Tunisian government. The disarming of the resistance faced opposition from Ben Youssef's supporters, and on 14 October 1955, Bourguiba was expelled from the Committee for the Liberation of North Africa. In the same month, Ben Youssef refused to attend the Sfax Party Convention, whereupon there ensued a violent struggle against the pro-Youssef current. The leaders of the pro-Youssef movement were arrested in early 1956, and

15. See Tawfiq al-Mdeini, *Tunisian Opposition: Emergence and Evolution [al-Muʿāraḍa at-Tūnisiyya: Nashʾatuha wa-Taṭawuruha]* (Damascus: Arab Writers Union Publications, 2001), p. 19 [in Arabic]; 'A Focus on the Fifth Conference of the Constitutional Liberal Party: Sfax 15-19 November 1955', *Leaders – Arabic*, 3/11/2015, accessed at: https://bit.ly/3vFjdu8 [in Arabic].

16. Beji Caid Essebsi, *al-Habib Bourguiba: The Important and the Most Important [al-Ḥabīb Būrqība . . . al-Muhimm wal-Ahamm]* Muḥammad Maʿālī (trans.) (Tunis: Dār aj-Janūb lil-Nashr, 2011), p. 15.

17. The Committee was headquartered in Cairo and headed by Moroccan Allal al-Fasi.

Ben Youssef fled to Libya. The conflict continued even after Tunisia's Declaration of Independence on 20 March 1956, exacerbated by international alliances. Nevertheless, Ben Youssef became an adamant defender of Tunisia's Arab and Muslim identity in opposition to Bourguiba's chosen path.

Under Bourguiba's leadership, the Neo-Destour Party exerted considerable ideological effort in an attempt to ethnicize Tunisian identity whereby Tunisians would not only be citizens of Tunisia whose ethnic nationality was Arab but, rather, have a separate ethnic national identity. In pursuit of a Bourguibist populism opposed to the populist Nasserist and Tunisian Arabist movements, the party asserted its vision by glorifying the Phoenician and Roman epochs of North African history. This question of identity, which became one of the axes of conflict between Bourguibism and Youssefism,[18] gave rise to the party's 'Francophone' elites (Bourguiba among them), who were, in general, deeply influenced by the radical republican secularist models of the Third French Republic.

Prior to the outbreak of the 2011 Revolution, several popular uprisings had erupted under the party's rule, the most famous of which were the uprisings of 1978, 1984 and 1985, apart from the 1962 the coup attempt by the Youssefis. Numerous political forces, including the Nasserites, the Baathists and the Youssefis, were persecuted and imprisoned. Leftists also suffered persecution and arrests, including the trials of the 'Socialist Studies and Action Group', known as the 1960s *Afaq* (Horizons), and its 1970s offshoot *Majmūʿat al-ʿAmal al-Tūnisī* (the Tunisian Labor Group). The same treatment was accorded to the secret People's Organization in 1979, the Progressive Socialist Coalition in 1986, the Communist Workers' Party in 1978 and the Islamist movement, whose confrontation with the regime began with the MTI in 1981. Moreover, even the Tunisian General Labour Union (UGTT), which contributed to founding the Republic as part of the National Front in 1956, suffered persecution whenever anti-regime social sentiments emerged.

Between 1955 and 1986, the official party ideology focused on patriotic themes such as 'national unity' and 'Tunisian identity'. The purpose of the political elite was to shape a self-sufficient Tunisian nation independent from Arab and Muslim influences and affiliations, demonstrated through the ruling regime's adoption of distinctive policies towards 'Arab' causes, such as Palestine and Arab unity.[19]

18. The so-called Youssefi movement goes back to 1952, before it became associated with Youssef's name, and was tied to the appearance of groups that advocated armed struggle against French colonialism. The most prominent early advocate of armed resistance to French colonialism was al-Tahir Laswad, leader of the Popular Liberation Army, which solidified after the signing of the autonomy agreement of 1955. As a political current, Youssefism carries a Maghrebin, Arab, and Islamic identity; it can be linked to the mood, ideas, and aspirations that went along with the Nasserist phenomenon at the time. The Youssefis enjoyed broad support among the Tunisian people and even within the party itself. Therefore, Tunisia's history after Ben Youssef must be read as the outcome of the victory won by Bourguiba, in part due to his alliance with the French colonial administration.

19. Labyad, *Identity*, p. 70.

Despite the gap between the government's stances and those of the people, Tunisia was more or less successful in establishing a nation-state and state institutions. Until the 1970s, Tunisia was the only Arab republic (with the possible exception of Lebanon) that did not adopt an Arab nationalist ideology and whose foreign policy and alliances were closer to those of the Arab monarchies. The regime's main problem lay in the fact that despite its emphasis on Tunisian nationalism, this nationalism did not provide, in its view, a sufficient basis for Tunisians' sovereignty as a democratic nation. In fact, it had become a barrier to democratic change. Hence, the struggle against authoritarianism in Tunisia came to be associated with outlooks opposed to that of the regime and with pan-Arab and Islamist positions.

In July 1988, the ruling party held the Salvation Convention, one of whose stated principles was 'the preservation of Tunisian identity with its Arab and Islamic features'. Like other reforms touted by Ben Ali, this was merely a cosmetic change, a ploy to garner mass appeal at a time when the people held high expectations for the new era. In reality, however, the party continued to be led by elites who openly acknowledged their affiliation with the Francophone tradition.[20]

As a rule, members of the party's political bureau are chosen by the leader of the party from among the members of the Central Committee and elected through a general national convention. The committee is convened by the head of the party once every six months and oversees the execution of party policies. In Ben Ali's later years, the number of businessmen appointed to the Central Committee exhibited a notable increase; new members also included Belhassen Trabelsi and Sakher el-Materi, both in-laws of the president. In short, the party became a tool not only of the regime but of the extended ruling family. The identity of the leading members of the party thus signalled the regime's complete transition to economic neoliberalism.

The party's Central Committee was composed of 350 members, 250 of whom were elected. The party's secretary-general oversaw 28 coordination committees distributed throughout Tunisia, with one committee in each governorate with the exception of Tunis, which had five. There were a total of 358 coordination committees, divided into 8,100 domestic branches, including 40 branches for professors of higher learning and 509 branches abroad.

The RCD, which permeated society and state, was deeply rooted in Tunisia's history and national struggle. Prior to the revolution, the party had enjoyed a loyal popular base; before long, however, it began catering to government officials and interest groups, and by the time the revolution erupted, it was indistinguishable, and inseparable, from the regime. Moreover, the party had lost its responsiveness to the residents of poor regions due to the clout of big business, the ruling family and other cliental networks. After the revolution, numerous activists attempted to evoke the party's ideological past by claiming that it had a philosophy and a tradition that could constitute a basis for new parties. Nonetheless, the RCD had lost its one remaining source of strength – namely, the fact of its being the party

20. Ibid., p. 74.

of the president, and in that sense it had already been on its deathbed prior to the revolution.

After the revolution, the combination of state nationalism, secularism and economic liberalism that this party had represented found no vehicle capable of carrying them forward. The leftist parties could not fill the vacuum, and the secularist parties that had been founded upon the Destouri legacy could not survive the internal power struggles, disunity and the need to form coalitions due to the fact that no one party held a monopoly on power any longer. Nevertheless, in a relatively short time its legacy bred not only liberal nationalist right-wing parties (which were unsuited to play the role of the opposition) which were ready to bargain and make concessions in order to share power in a pluralist democracy but, in addition, populist, right-wing, anti-democratic parties which sought to exploit the consecutive crises of a young democracy by evoking nostalgia for the days of 'law and order' and the so-called prosperity they had brought.

The Movement of Socialist Democrats (sixteen seats)

The Movement of Socialist Democrats (MDS) began forming in the early 1970s at the height of the conflicts that had erupted within the Destouri Party. The Movement eventually seceded from the Destouri Party, demanding respect for individual and public freedoms and freedom of expression, in reaction to the dispute that arose between Ahmed Mestiri and Bourguiba during and after the Monastir Convention of 1971.[21]

From its inception, the Movement attempted to distance itself from traditional Destouri discourse. For instance, during their first national convention held in August 1981, Movement members announced their intention 'to support the cultural personality of Tunisia as part of the Arab nation and the Muslim community'. The Movement was also vocal in its stances on the Palestinian cause and the Arab-Israeli conflict.[22] It published *al-Ra'i*,[23] a political weekly edited by Moncef Marzouki[24] and Naziha Rejiba, which contributed in a major way to the 1977 founding of the Tunisian League of Human Rights, the first such association of its kind in the Arab world.

After a past plagued by confrontations with the regime, the Movement came to be perceived during Ben Ali's rule as one of the 'official parties', which created the illusion of party pluralism. This shift began as a result of the Movement's support for the transition of power following the coup carried out by Ben Ali in 1987. Despite

21. Aliya al-Alani, 'The Movement of Socialist Democrats: From Foundation to the First Conference')Faculty of Social Sciences, Department of History, Tunis University, Tunisia 1986).

22. Labyad, *Identity*, pp. 76–7.

23. The magazine was permanently shut down by the authorities in December 1987.

24. Marzouki became Tunisia's first president after the revolution.

Mestiri's liberal, socialist and democratic leanings, Ben Ali exploited Mestiri's frustration at Bourguiba as a means of winning his sympathy and preventing his party from siding with the opposition. After Mestiri withdrew from public life in 1990, his successor, Mohamed Moadda, was harassed (jailed and exiled), and MDS was for years an opposition party before being co-opted after Moadda accepted the regime's conditions. He openly sided with Ben Ali, praising his policies and adapting his party's platform to conform more closely to that of the RCD.[25] This development coincided with Ben Ali's tactics to contain the liberal and democratic oppositional parties.

Prior to the revolution, the MDS was the second largest legal party in Tunisia after the ruling party and supported Ben Ali in all of his presidential bids until 2009; it won sixteen seats in the 2004 parliamentary elections.

Other parties

The National Unity Party (twelve seats – among those reserved for the opposition)

The National Unity Party is rooted in the Popular Unity Movement founded by Ahmed Ben Salah. In the late 1970s, a group separated from the Popular Unity Movement, dubbing itself the Popular Unity Movement under the leadership of Mohamed Belhaj Amor.

The Unionist Democratic Federation (nine seats)

The Unionist Democratic Federation was founded on 23 November 1988 and legally recognized and licensed three days after its declaration. One of its prominent founders was Abderrahmane Tlili, former leader and Central Committee member in the ruling RCD during the Ben Ali era. Al-Tlili split from the party to found the federation, which was never an opposition party and which he led until 2003 when he was imprisoned on corruption charges. Ahmed Inoubli succeeded Tlili and remained at the party's helm until the revolution.

The Social Liberal Party (eight seats)

Founded in 1988 by Mounir Beji, the Social Liberal Party is based on a liberal philosophy that promotes freedom, political pluralism and national dialogue. Led by Mondher Thabet, the party gained little popularity despite its leaders' efforts to expand its base.

25. Stafford, 'Stop the Presses! Media Freedom in Authoritarian Regimes', p. 374, 376.

The Green Party for Progress (eight seats)

Founded in 2005 with an emphasis on environmental concerns after splitting from the Social Liberal Party, the Green Party was formally recognized in 2006. El-Munji el-Khamasi served as the party's secretary-general and oversaw its weekly publication *al-Tunisi*.

The Renewal Movement (two seats)

Following the collapse of the Soviet Union in April 1993, the Tunisian Communist Party renamed itself the Renewal Movement. The Tunisian Communist Party was founded in the 1920s as an extension of the French Communist Party. Like some other Communist parties in the Arab region, the Tunisian Communist Party took up the burden of its colonial origins. It thus remained an affiliate of the French Communist Party until the decision to 'Tunisify' the party in 1939, at which time it became the Communist Party for the Tunisian Homeland and elected Ali Jrad as its secretary-general. For a long time, the party adhered to a Communist-Leftist French discourse, viewing Tunisian liberation as a consequence of France's hoped-for liberation from capitalism and 'class exploitation'. Despite the fact that Tunisia went through a phase of national liberation struggle, the real shift in the party's political platform towards Tunisification was established only after independence. The party reformed its line in the congress of 1957 under the leadership of Ali Jarad, Morris Nizar, Muhammad al-Nafea gerge Adda and Khamis alKa'bi. The party, which was an opposition party that struggled against the French and Bourguiba, was disbanded in 1962 when political pluralism was abolished, but it resumed its public activism in 1982 as part of Mohamed Mzali's openness policy.[26]

During Ben Ali's era, and under the leadership of Mohamed Harmal, the Renewal Movement supported the regime's policies. However, when, to everyone's surprise, its and the opposition's presidential candidate, Mohammed Ali El Halwani, won less than 1 per cent of the total vote in 2004, it was already critical of the regime and revised its policies under the leadership of Ahmed Brahim and adopt more critical stances. In 2008, together with two unlicensed leftist parties (the National Democratic Action Party and the Socialist Party), the Renewal Movement announced the formation of a political initiative for coordination and cooperation under the name 'the national initiative for democracy and progress'.

26. Azzedine Layachi claims that due to the clashes between the Communist Party (and the Tunisian left in general) and the regime in the 1960s and 1970s, 'the political arena [was left] wide open for the Islamist tendency to make headways as a popular movement seeking radical change in Tunisia'. Therefore, Layachi adds, Bourguiba followed the same methods as in Algeria and Morocco, in which he used 'the religious current to face off the leftist challenge'. See Azzedine Layachi, 'Islam and Politics in North Africa', in *Islam and Politics Around the World*, John L. Esposito, Emad El-Din Shahin (eds.) (New York: Oxford University Press, 2018), p. 183. However, Layachi here gives an opinion without giving a concrete evidence on this.

During the revolution, the Renewal Movement committed the same mistake as the Progressive Democratic Party, which, in the past, had adopted even more radical positions against dictatorship. The Movement issued a statement approving the formation of a national unity cabinet to be led by Ben Ali following his last speech on 13 January 2011. Following Ben Ali's removal, it participated in Mohammed Ghannouchi's cabinet.

The Movement was officially acknowledged during Ben Ali's time, and in some phases it represented one of the most prominent advocates of reconciliation with the regime due to its secular character. In fact, the state of accord between the Movement and the authority goes back to the early days of independence. The secularization measures taken by Bourguiba were all supported by the Tunisian Communist Party. The Movement was steadfast in its support for the *Laic* secular policies of the regime, which led to an acute conflict, especially during the days of the growing Islamic tide in Tunisia in the late 1980s. The Movement or the Communist Party's newspaper *al-Ṭarīq al-Jadīd* became a forum for secular intellectuals to vent against the Islamists and the regime in the 2000s.[27] However, like other parties that allowed themselves to be co-opted by dictatorships, the Communist Party paid a price for this stance in terms of popularity, poor electoral performance and the loss of its social base, especially after the revolution.

Licensed parties unrepresented in Parliament

The Progressive Democratic Party

The Progressive Democratic Party was founded in 1983 and licensed by the state in 1988. In 2006, Maya Jribi was elected secretary-general, succeeding the party's founder, Ahmad Najib al-Shabbi. The Progressive Democratic Party frequently opposed Ben Ali, challenging his policies and decisions, such as the constitutional amendments that allowed him to run for a fourth presidential term.

27. After the revolution, the Communist Party helped found the Democratic Modernist Pole, which ran in the Constituent Assembly elections. The group focused its electoral campaign on attacking the Islamists, painting them as a threat to democracy and Tunisia's social achievements, although experience has shown that most ex-communists and the radical left were actually not committed to democracy, especially as they had not fared well in elections. The Modernist Pole performed poorly in the elections, gaining a mere five seats in the 217-seat Constituent Assembly. It gained a single seat in the Tunis 2 district (8 per cent of the vote), but it gained no more than 2 per cent of the total vote in the Tunis 1 district, where it also won a single seat, largely because of the elitist character of the upscale Tunis 2 district. The group also won 5 per cent of the votes cast in Aryana, and a slightly lower percentage in Ben Arous, which shows that its popularity is concentrated in the Greater Tunis region, although it received 8 per cent of the vote among all except among Tunisians residing in Paris, France.

The Progressive Democratic Party's stances against Ben Ali's despotism earned it heavy persecution. However, al-Shabbi welcomed the concessions announced by Ben Ali in his speech on 13 January 2011, and following the autocrat's overthrow, he readily agreed to participate in Ghannouchi's cabinet. In retrospect, this step turned out to be a serious mistake which cost the party its historical reputation as a steadfast opponent of tyranny, despite the fact that it had supported the uprising from its very beginning.

Under Ben Ali, the Progressive Democratic Party was known for its frequent hunger strikes and sit-ins and the persecution it suffered. The PDP was one of the major components of the October 18 Collective for Rights and Freedoms. Its hasty decisions during the revolution, however, led to its being dismissed as a submissive party, which was not true. Upon examination, one would see that the party's stance towards Ben Ali's last speech was not the result of political opportunism; rather, it was actually consistent with the party's previous positions. The tragedy of such parties is that they did not understand the changes that often occur in popular political moods as the result of a revolution.

Prior to the revolution, many Tunisian activists had fought tirelessly for their demands, refusing to become a decorative façade for the regime. Nonetheless, once the regime backed down under popular pressure, acquiescing to the people's demands in a single speech, those who had struggled for years viewed this event as a major accomplishment. They failed to perceive the regime's weakness and the futility of these concessions. Similarly, they failed to appreciate the adamant stance being taken by a growing majority of people who insisted on nothing less than the regime's dismantling. This majority realized that the moment the revolution ceased in exchange for empty promises, these same promises would be abandoned and a campaign of persecution against presumed organizers and instigators would be launched.

At this point, a paradox was clearly emerging: many of those who had never previously engaged in struggle were unmoved by the regime's concessions while genuine, lifelong activists seemed satisfied with the concessions provided and viewed them as a worthy outcome of their activism rather than suspecting the regime of engaging in artful authoritarian ploys. At the same time, it should be noted that the Progressive Democratic Party's willingness to give credence to Ben Ali's promises of reform does not necessarily equate with giving up their principles. Rather, their behaviour was an understandable reaction, as they had struggled for decades without popular support. This type of activism requires courage and realism and should not be mistaken for opportunism. The same paradox emerged as a pattern across other Arab countries that went through revolutions: seasoned activists who had struggled under extremely difficult conditions began to appear less revolutionary than the new activists who took to the streets during the revolutionary tide. The latter were no longer content with reforms, demanding an entire regime change.[28]

28. The outcome of this paradox (and the party's forceful agitation against the Islamists in the hopes of gaining the support of the secular camp) was manifested in the meagre (and

Democratic Forum for Labor and Liberties

Headed by Tunisian politician Mustapha Ben Jaafar, the FDTL was founded on 9 April 1994 by a group of activists from a variety of political backgrounds, including unionists and human rights activists, who advanced slogans of freedom, democracy and progress. However, the FDTL was not licensed until 25 October 2002.

Following Ben Ali's accession to power, Tunisian parties and movements signed the National Pact document, which endorsed 'the principle of democracy based on the multiplicity of political parties'. As a result, a flurry of permits was granted to political movements, including previously illegal ones. The parties licensed in 1988 became part of the 'loyal opposition', and no new permits were granted until 2002.

The FDTL was also one of the major components of the October 18 Collective, which brought reformist, secular and Islamist parties and figures together in defence of public liberties in order to debate the horizons of democratic transformation in Tunisia. The FDTL became famous for its role in the hunger strike of October 2005, as well as its agreement to cooperate with the Islamists. The controversy over cooperation with Islamists eventually led to a split within the FDTL when its official leadership endorsed a policy calling for the assimilation of the Islamic movement within the process of democratic change. The FDTL presented a comprehensive democratic programme that also stressed the Arab and Muslim identity of Tunisia. In this context, it presented a new model for a modern centrist party that takes clear stances against tyranny and in favour of assimilating the main stream Islamist Al Nahda as warranted by a democracy. Following the victory of the Tunisian Revolution, the FDTL entered the ruling coalition (or the so-called Troika) after the election together with Al Nahda and the Congress for the republic party led by Marzouki. Ben Jaafar became the head of the National Constituent Assembly, which acted as the first elected parliament after the revolution.

Not being viewed as 'authentic' representatives of Tunisia's hard-core secular nationalist bloc because of their alliance with Ennhada, the two moderate secular parties of the Troika were marginalized by the secular-religious polarization that followed. However, the transitional democratic process was prevented from collapsing in 2013 by an agreement that was reached with the secularist nationalist bloc led by pragmatic old-school figures such as Essebsi.

Banned political parties: Al Nahda

The secularization of Tunisia did not evolve in a vacuum but, rather, in a Muslim country that encompassed numerous popular expressions of religiosity, both rural

surprising) results achieved by the party during the Constituent Assembly elections after the revolution. The party received no more than 17 of the Assembly's 217 seats, placing it in fifth place. It also came in third among secular parties, trailing two parties who had not agitated against the Islamist movement and who had proven themselves to be radical opponents of the regime.

and urban, the religiosity of the ulama, both conservative and reformist, and the interaction between reformist religiosity and modern political forces like the Destour Party. Muslim renewal had been manifested since 1950 in movements such as the Muslim Youth Society headed by Muhammad Salih Nayfar, the community of Zaituna students, the Islamic Union magazine and *Zaituna* magazine.[29] But the transition to Islamist ideology on the part of a political movement took place with the establishment of MTI.

What became Al Nahda was created in the late 1960s by a young Rached Ghannouchi and lawyer Abdelfattah Mourou, among others, under the name the Islamic Community (*al-Jamāʿah al-Islāmiyah*).[30] More of a religious and political society than a political party, the Islamic Community held its first organizational meetings secretly in April 1972. The community's activities were initially limited to the intellectual domain, such as religious classes and involvement in Quran memorization societies. Numerous religious organizations emerged in the 1970s, most significant of which was the Association for the Preservation of the Qur'an, established in 1970 by a group of Ez-Zitouna University students seeking to preserve the Muslim identity of Tunisia and Tunisians and to deal with the repercussions of secularization and Westernization manifested in what they saw as 'deteriorating morals'. Despite Al Nahda's critical view of government policies, the regime did not suppress it as it had other critical movements, even liberal ones, nor did it interfere in any way with its activities, hoping that this leniency would lessen the tension between the state and religious leaders.[31]

By the late 1970s the MTI had emerged and, as mentioned before, was declared in 1981 to be a political movement which aspired to place Islam at the centre of both public and private life. MTI's cofounders, Ghannouchi and Mourou, demanded an end to the single-party system. MTI gained followers among the poor, the post-independence generation of youth who regarded the Socialist Destour Party as an 'anachronism' and middle-class sectors who valued their Islamic heritage.[32] The movement had thus come a long way: from being an Islamist political movement resembling the Muslim Brotherhood to the declaration after 2011 that it had become a political, democratic and civil party based on Muslim and modern cultural values.[33]

29. Ben Achour, *Tunisia: A Revolution in an Islamic Country*, p. 72.

30. On 6 June 1981, al-Jamāʿah al-Islāmiyah officially changed its name to 'The Islamic Tendency Movement (MTI)'.

31. Perkins, *A History of Modern Tunisia*, p. 162.

32. Kenneth Perkins, 'Playing the Islamic Card: The Use and Abuse of Religion in Tunisian Politics', in Nouri Gana (ed.), *The Making of the Tunisian Revolution: Contexts, Architects, Prospects* (Edinburgh: Edinburgh University Press, 2013), p. 59.

Ibid., pp. 64–5.

33. The trend was consolidated later and this is how Ghannouchi defined the movement in a 2016 interview with *Le Monde*. Ghannouchi added, 'We are moving towards a party devoted solely to political activities. . . . We need to identify the difference between political

After Al Nahda's licence application was denied, it proceeded with its activities illegally. Ghannouchi was then imprisoned and was not released until 1984. The mid-1980s witnessed intensified Al Nahda activity and more and more confrontations with the authorities.

The first struggles of the MTI were directed against both the secularism of the regime and the left, which controlled the opposition against Bourguiba and led the 1978 protests organized by the UGTT and university student movements. This was a time of conflict not only between the left and the regime but between the left and the Islamists (as in Egypt), especially after 1979 when the Islamic movement gained momentum thanks to the Iranian revolution and the establishment of the Islamic Republic of Iran.[34]

When Al Nahda proposed the idea of seeking formal authorization as a political party in 1981, this sparked intense internal debate over the movement's image and mission. There was, not surprisingly, opposition from within Al Nahda to registering the movement as a political party. Traditionally, this kind of Islamic movement had believed in changing society by 'Islamizing individuals and society' before changing the state, which is in essence a reformist activity. Even though the Muslim Brotherhood had decided to run in parliamentary elections, it never gave up its mission of being a religious community whose primary role was to reform society by directing it to the authentic sources of Islam,[35] a mission which, in the Brotherhood's view, could only be completed through the exercise of political power by establishing an Islamic state in keeping with the *Shar'ia*.

activities and religious activities. The place for political activities is not in the mosque. The mosque is a place for people to come together, so there is no justification for using it for the activities of one party. We want religion to be a source of unity, not division. . . . We want religious activity to be completely separate from political activity. This is good for politics because, in this way, [political activists] can no longer be accused of manipulating religion for political ends. It is also good for religion, which can no longer be held hostage by politics. [. . .] The 2011 revolution brought an end not only to dictatorship, but to secular extremism. Tunisia now lives in a democracy. The 2014 Constitution imposes the same limits on secular extremism as it does on religious extremism. Therefore, there is no longer any justification for political Islam in Tunisia. [. . .] We are allowing political Islam to enter Muslim democracy. We are Muslim democrats who no longer preach political Islam.' Frédéric Bobin, 'Rached Ghannouchi: «Il n'y a plus de justification à l'islam politique en Tunisie»', *Le Monde*, 18 May 2016, accessed at: http://bit.ly/37IFUVh.

34. Rory McCarthy, *Inside Tunisia's al-Nahda: Between Politics and Preaching* (Cambridge: Cambridge University Press, 2018), p. 42.

35. I agree in part with Asef Bayat's statement that the main thrust of the Muslim Brotherhood's approach as laid down by Hassan al-Banna is actually a Gramscian strategy, as it practices manoeuvre and hegemony before controlling the state. Asef Bayat, *Life as Politics: How Ordinary People Change the Middle East*, 2nd ed. (Stanford, CA: Stanford University Press, 2013 [2010]), p. 250.

If Al Nahda was going to transform itself into a political party, this would require it to give up its all-or-nothing approach to religion in society and state and acknowledge its mundane status as simply one political party among others. Otherwise, it would have to accept the consequences of its comprehensive or totalitarian religious approach, and seek to take over the state so as to impose its vision of Islam on the entire society. There was also a third possibility, namely, to remain at the crossroads by participating in elections and, at the same time, claiming not to be a typical party but, rather, a messenger with a sanctified calling and an exclusive grasp of religious truth whose rivals are necessarily infidels.

This third option, however, is a duplicitous game that evokes fear and mistrust. Ultimately, Al Nahda evolved in the direction of the first option and was pragmatic enough to bear the consequences. For example, when it tried to register as a party in 1988, it was ready not only to change its name, but also to accept Tunisia's secular Personal Status Code, which was clearly in conflict with any traditional understanding of the *Shari'a*. Exploiting Tunisia's economic crisis and high unemployment rates, the MTI campaigned in 1985 for a referendum to reject the Personal Status Code, which they viewed as the reason behind women entering the public sphere and, thus, taking jobs once occupied by men.[36] Al Nahda continues to oscillate between a demand for rule by the *Shari'a* and accepting laws and norms which interpret the Shari`a in less restrictive ways.

After a spate of demonstrations in 1987, Bourguiba arrested Ghannouchi and other prominent MTI figures on charges of 'fomenting a plot to overthrow the government and create an Islamic state'.[37] Thousands of activists and suspects were arrested and Ghannouchi was sentenced to life imprisonment after Al Nahda was accused of targeting four hotels in the cities of Sousse and Monastir on the eve of Bourguiba's birthday. Though the MTI denied any link to the incident, Bourguiba reacted by ordering mass arrests and the executions of many detainees. As interior minister, Ben Ali convinced Bourguiba not to carry out the death penalty against the suspects for fear that it might make the Islamists into martyrs. In fact, Ben Ali ignored the order until an ageing and cantankerous Bourguiba changed his mind again.

Unlike the Muslim Brotherhood, Al Nahda never presented a consistent doctrine, but drew instead on a mishmash of Islamic resources. Similarly (at least after the MTI phase), Al Nahda presented no explicit programme for an Islamic state or the rule of the Shar'ia. They spoke of the revival of Arab Islamic culture and identity, but never officially challenged women's rights.[38]

36. Perkins, *A History of Modern Tunisia*, p. 175.

37. Ibid., p. 177.

38. Monica Marks, 'Purists and Pluralists: Cross-Ideological Coalition Building in Tunisia's Democratic Transition', in Alfred Stepan (ed.), *Democratic Transition in the Muslim World: A Global Perspective*, Religion, Culture, and Public Life (New York: Columbia University Press, 2018), p. 93.

Al Nahda was initially inspired by Hassan al-Banna, founder of the Muslim Brotherhood, Sayyid Qutb, whose radical fundamentalism left its mark on Muslim Brotherhood thought, Shi'i thinker Ali Shariati, and Shi'i cleric Mohamed Baqir al-Sadr. In its founding statement on 6 June 1981, the MTI (which would later become Al Nahda) included a number of points: the principled rejection of secularism, its link to Muslim causes throughout the world, the rejection of Arab nationalism, and an understanding of the Palestinian cause as being the result of Arabs' deviation from the righteous religious path. The statement argued that the Palestinian issue could be resolved by establishing governments that represented the masses. It also spoke in favour of reinvigorating Tunisia's Islamic identity, adopting Islamic principles in economic life, and distributing wealth based on Islamic principles.[39] Al Nahda's radical fundamentalist beginning[40] was partially shaped by the radical secularism of the Tunisian regime. However, influenced by a pragmatic determination not to be marginalized, but instead to become a major political force in a deeply secularized society and state, it grew increasingly moderate, and even cooperated with secular opposition forces. People tend to view ideology as the moving force behind praxis; however, praxis can change the ideology of those who engage in it. Similarly, politics is not a passive tool of ideology but, rather, itself influences and shapes ideology.

Led by Ghannouchi and Mourou, Al Nahda spread its ideas through sermons delivered in mosques and religious schools criticizing the government for its failure to respect Islamic culture in Tunisian society. Its speakers also called for re-Islamizing society to remedy the effects of the regime's policies. Hence, the group welcomed the overthrow of Bourguiba on 7 November 1987, which ushered in improved relations between the regime and Islamic movements. As a result, the movement participated in the 1989 legislative elections with independent lists, coming in second (ahead of all licensed parties with the exception of the ruling party) with 17 per cent of the vote. Subsequently, the movement changed its name to Al Nahda in order to comply with the provisions of the law regulating political parties, which prohibited 'the establishment of parties on a religious basis'. Nevertheless, the party's request for a licence was rejected by the authorities, bringing the two sides to an impasse.

Following the unification of several Islamist factions within Al Nahda, its leaders attempted to make it more compatible with a secularized state and society. In this sense, Al Nahda was the precursor of the post-Brotherhood era for Islamic

39. Sara Fayez, *Parties and Political Movements in Tunisia 1932-1984 [al-Aḥzāb wal-Ḥarakāt al-Siyāsiyah fī Tūnis]* (Damascus: Maktab Khadamāt al-Ṭibāʿah, 1986), pp. 212–14. See also: Abdelbaki Hermassi, 'Islamic Protest in Tunisia', [al-Islām al-Iḥtijājī fī Tūnis], a paper presented at a seminar entitled, *Modern Islamic Movements in the Arab World [al-Ḥarakāt al-Islāmiyah al-Muʿāṣirah fī al-Waṭan al-ʿArabī* (Nadwa)*]*, Maktabat al-Mustaqbalāt al-ʿArabiyah al-Badīlah, al-Ittijahāt al-Ijtimāʿiyah wal-Siyāsiyah wal-Thaqāfiyah, 5th ed. (Beirut: Center for Arab Unity Studies, 2004), pp. 247–300.

40. In 1989, the Islamic tendency movement changed its name to Al Nahda.

movements, with their experience preceding that of the Turkish Justice and Development Party. Ghannouchi codified this 'post-Brotherhood' vision for the Islamic movement in a series of books, including *Public Liberties in the Islamic State*, *Approaches to Secularism and Civil Society*, and *The Islamic Movement and the Question of Change*.

Following the 1989 parliamentary elections, the Tunisian government launched a comprehensive campaign against Al Nahda, ultimately banning it in 1990, followed by a campaign of incitement and persecution in 1991. At that time, all known MTI members were persecuted and arrested, causing thousands of its supporters to flee the country, and with some seeking exile in Europe.

As a means of restricting Al Nahda's presence in the public sphere, the regime surrounded it with a wall of silence. A total ban was imposed on any statements relating to the movement, whether for or against it. The movement was subjected to four rounds of trials in the years 1981, 1984, 1987, and, lastly, 1992–3, leading to the imprisonment of tens of thousands of its members and supporters.

Nevertheless, despite the paralysis that afflicted Al Nahda due to prolonged persecution, especially in the final years of Ben Ali's rule, it nevertheless maintained its popularity,[41] particularly among social sectors that opposed the blatantly secular regime. The movement was not always united politically and ideologically; on the contrary, it was shaken by intense internal debate following the revolution over issues of pragmatism vs. loyalty to principles, and moderation vs. fundamentalism. These issues had been controversial since the start, of course, but the secretive nature of the movement's activity had more or less suppressed lively debate.

Al Nahda lacked the welfare networks and associations of other Muslim movements, and unlike the Muslim Brotherhood in Mubarak's Egypt, it had no margin whatsoever for political work under Ben Ali. Nevertheless, Al Nahda rebuilt itself after the revolution into a large and organized political movement in Tunisia. Rory McCarthy attributes Al Nahda's resilience to the existence of deep informal networks, the willingness to reimagine the Islamist project, and activism on the movement's intellectual and structural periphery.[42] The special aura which Al Nahda enjoyed following the revolution can possibly be explained based on three factors: (1) the suffering and persecution it had endured at the hands of a

41. Katarína Pevná, 'Revolutions in Tunisia and Egypt and Political Participation of Islamists', *International Issues & Slovak Foreign Policy Affairs*, vol. 20, no. 2 (2011), pp. 42–4. Contrary to the title, the article does not examine the role of the Islamist movements in the revolutions of Egypt and Tunisia; instead, it repeats widespread and familiar generalizations on Islamic movements, arguing that tyranny breeds extremism and that democracy alone is capable of transforming these movements into organizations similar to the Turkish Justice and Development Party.

42. Rory McCarthy, *Inside Tunisia's al-Nahda: Between Politics and Preaching* (Cambridge: Cambridge University Press, 2018), p. 3.

despised regime, (2) its 'authentic' Muslim and Arab identity and (3) its distance from corruption and party politics.

Large sectors of the population were naturally inclined to support a movement which was so different, both ideologically and practically, from the Ben Ali regime. Al Nahda had been persecuted so badly under Ben Ali's rule that observers thought it had disappeared inside Tunisia. Imprisonment was a formative experience for members of Al Nahda, in some cases granting them all the more psychological resilience, and prompting them to engage in constructive self-critiques.[43] Depending on the individual prisoner, his movement and its leadership, and the prison itself, prison experiences can either radicalize detainees, turning them into hardened terrorists, or catalyse revisions and self-criticism that further mature their pragmatic political approach. Hence, the repression phase produced both radical Salafi Jihadi Islamists and a second generation of post-revolution Islamists who viewed Al Nahda as a renegade movement. And exile was no less formative.[44] The persecution and repression endured by Al Nahda contributed to its image as a victim, which attracted others' sympathy and solidarity in the post-2011 phase. Conversely, the movement also lost some of its popularity after taking part in the actual governing process, bearing responsibility for the country's affairs, and being embroiled in the inevitable bargaining and compromises of party politics.

Support for Al Nahda is greater among the working classes than among the middle classes.[45] When, after the revolution, Al Nahda and other Islamist parties had been registered and permitted to operate, many people began to question the extent to which Islamist movements would be able to establish a societal presence and influence politics and society. This question was particularly pertinent given

43. Ibid., p. 69.

44. This analysis obviously questions Shadi Hamid's argument, which opposes the thesis that 'more democracy makes for more moderate Islamists', and that limiting political opportunities increases the risk of Islamist radicalization. Hamid argues that 'repression can force the moderation of Islamist parties – and often did, particularly during the 1990s and 2000s'. Shadi Hamid, *Temptations of Power: Islamists and Illiberal Democracy in a New Middle East* (New York: Oxford University Press, 2014), p. 4, 36, 38. He applies this thesis also to Al Nahda's moderation process, especially after the persecution campaign against it in 1984. In fact, it is not so hard to point at individuals and movements who were radicalized under repression and in prisons; some emerged under harsh oppression, some even split in prisons from the mother organization of Muslim Brothers due to its 'lenient' positions. On the other hand, Al Nahda's moderation took place both under repression, in prisons and exile, and under democracy due to the necessities of government, pragmatism, public opinion and commitments to coalitions that required openness and moderation, thereby bolstering the reformist trend that was there in the movement. Myriad factors determine the so-called 'moderation/radicalization' processes. There is no one formula that will enable researchers or governments to predict the outcome of repression pertaining to radicalism or moderation. In this sense, Hamid's thesis may be exploited by some governments to justify repression on the pretext that it leads to 'moderation'.

45. Hermassi, 'Islamic Protest in Tunisia', p. 293.

that many Tunisians adopt a largely modern, secular lifestyle, with a liberal notion of individual freedoms and equality between men and women, and where women have access to most occupations.

The movement responded by affirming its respect for Tunisian national institutions and their achievements, and acknowledging that Tunisia cannot be ruled by a single movement or ideology. In the Constituent Assembly elections that took place after the revolution, Al Nahda won eighty-nine seats, emerging as the main victor of the contest, although it failed to secure a majority in parliament. Following this achievement, Al Nahda's deputy Sadok Chourou and others drafted a bill that identified the *Shari'a* as a principal source of legislation. However, the bill was not approved. Thereafter, Al Nahda released a number of statements reaffirming its conciliatory principles. However, these statements came only in response to secular parties that had been seeking to promote scepticism concerning the movement's credibility by leaking controversial statements addressed by Ghannouchi to his Islamist constituency. In short, despite its long process of reform, Al Nahda nevertheless remains an Islamist political party. It should be remembered that in his writings on public liberties in the Islamic state, Ghannouchi has expressed opinions which range from sharp criticisms of extremist Islamist sects and persuasions, to similarly vehement stances against secularism.

As a result of its active involvement in state affairs and political and economic life following the revolution, the movement came to accept its status as one of many political parties, albeit distinguished by its religious values, and by political programmes that it viewed as more sublime or sacred than those of other parties. At the same time, Al Nahda decided to separate the propagation of the Islamic faith (*da'wah*) from its duties as a party. This decision was made after a month of workshops and debates during the Tenth Conference held in May 2016. In a speech he delivered at this conference, Ghannouchi described Al Nahda as

> a party that evolves and reforms itself ... from an ideological movement engaged in the struggle for identity . . . to a comprehensive protest movement against an authoritarian regime, to a national democratic party devoted to reform, ... thus consolidating the clear and definitive line between Muslim democrats and extremist and violent trends that falsely identify themselves with Islam.

In this same statement, Ghannouchi stressed that the decision to draw a distinction between political and social action on one hand, and the spiritual and religious dimension on the other, had not come about suddenly or in capitulation to temporary pressures, but rather, as the culmination of a historical evolution in which the political, the social, the cultural and the religious were recognized increasingly as both conceptually interdependent, and distinct in practice.[46]

46. 'Transcript of #an-Nahdha president @r_ghannouchi's speech at the opening ceremony of the tenth party conference', *Ennahda International Page (Official) on Facebook*, 21 May 2016, accessed on 18 November 2020, at: https://bit.ly/38Shrh6.

The reason this chapter does not discuss extremist Islamists is that they were not organized as political movements. Extremist religious violence broke out in Tunisia before it did in Algeria, a fact often missed by researchers, although the civil war in Algeria drew in Jihadist young Tunisians, as did the campaigns for Jihad in Afghanistan. The country's interior and the peripheries of the capital and other coastal cities had produced many bitter, frustrated and alienated young people. The reaction to the extreme secularist ideology of the regime injected Tunisian Islamist extremism with a special blend of ire and determination. Unlike the Egyptian regime, the Tunisian regime refused to allow even quietist Salafi movements and associations to act freely, its purpose being to weaken the Muslim Brotherhood (Al Nahda in this case). So, at the time when Al Nahda was being persecuted, non-political, non-Jihadi Salafis were also being repressed.[47]

After the revolution prisoners, including those indicted for violent actions, were freed. Salafi groups were allowed to register in political parties, two Salafi parties were established, though they did not make it to the Constituent Assembly, and nearly 100 Salafi preaching associations began to act openly with different degrees of intrusion into people's private lives. Jihadi groups escalated their activities, and after a violent demonstration that attacked the US Embassy (14 September 2012), killing four people, the 'Ansar Ash-Shari'a' movement was outlawed and is still held to be responsible for the assassinations of secular politicians and terrorist actions. Al Nahda believed that granting freedom of action and integrating radical movements into the political process was the way to de-radicalize these groups, although Al Nahda itself had been deradicalized under ruthless persecution. As noted earlier, there is no magic formula for either radicalization or deradicalization. Nevertheless, Al Nahda was both blamed by secular parties for its tolerance of religious extremists and accused by extremists (to whom its lost some of its support) of 'submission' to secularism and 'collaboration' with the old regime, and even with the United States!

The Congress for the Republic Party

The Congress for the Republic was founded in 2001 headed by Moncef Marzouki. An intellectual, a veteran in Tunisia's struggle and a radical opponent of the former Tunisian regime, Marzouki headed the Tunisian League for the Defense of Human Rights (LTDH) from 1989 until he was forced out of the country in 1994. During his exile in Europe, Marzouki gained a reputation as a human rights activist and

47. But like other Muslim countries during that phase, Tunisia witnessed terrorist actions that appear to have reached their peak in an open confrontation with security forces in Suleiman district south of the capital in January 2007, when twelve armed extremists and two security forces were killed, and in the wake of which thirty members of the organization called 'Jund Assad ibn al-Furat' were sentenced to prison.

developed extensive relations with democratic forces in European countries. The Congress Party did not receive an official licence prior to the revolution but was one of the first parties to receive a permit in its wake.

The Congress Party participated in the October 18 Collective, thereby making a complete break with the regime, and was distinguished by combining a democratic orientation with Arab nationalist positions. Furthermore, Marzouki expressed his unwavering support for the right of Al Nahda to participate in the political life of the country.

On 18 January 2011, after Ben Ali's removal, Marzouki returned to Tunisia from Paris and called for a transitional national unity government that would represent all political parties with the exception of the RCD. The Congress Party took second place in the October 2011 elections, having won 29 seats in the Constituent Assembly; it thus seemed natural that an alliance would emerge between the Congress, Al Nahda and the Democratic Forum, forming a majority within the Assembly and the Troika that would lead the country through the first phase of the transition.

Rather than strengthening the party, however, Marzouki's election as president only marginalized it. The Congress Party also faced acute internal controversies and splits and, like the Democratic Forum, was unable to survive the religious–secular polarization taking place. During the political crisis of the Troika Coalition in 2013, following the assassination of two opposition parties' leaders, the Congress Party was already weakened by its coalition with the Islamists despite having rejected Al Nahda's bargains with figures from the old regime. Meanwhile, the radical leftists and nationalists rejected any compromise whatsoever with Al Nahda, as a result of which Al Nahda cut a deal with the right-wing nationalist secular bloc.

The Tunisian Communist Workers' Party

The Tunisian Communist Workers' Party (PCOT) was founded in 1986 by a group of former activists from the Organization of the Tunisian Laborer and went on to become the largest of the active Marxist-Leninist parties in Tunisia. The party has an important presence in the student community, although prior to the revolution it was illegal and functioned clandestinely. The PCOT made a clear stance against Ben Ali's November 1987 coup and later called for his overthrow.

The PCOT is considered ideologically and politically radical, particularly at a time when Marxism-Leninism has faded as a partisan ideology, with only marginal parties remaining in its orbit. Nevertheless, it offered an accurate diagnosis of the state of the Tunisian regime in the age of neoliberal reforms. Yet, despite the party's radical stances towards the dictatorship and the struggles its leadership faced as it was relentlessly pursued by the authorities, it was not truly committed to democracy, a fact which is made obvious by its political stances and conduct after the revolution.

Although the PCOT's popular base remained limited, it nevertheless played a prominent role in disseminating the events of the Tunisian Revolution in the media, and the party activists and journalists who reported and documented these events were pursued by the regime. The party's media personnel were also able to connect with local and Arab media outlets, while its daily editorial, the 'Uprising of the Poor', became increasingly popular. Its coverage throughout the revolution was widely trusted, since its activists were embedded with the protesters in the streets.

The PCOT participated in the dialogue with the Islamists and joined the October 18 Collective. However, it adopted a hard line against the Troika government after the elections and played a central role in forming the popular front that led the demonstrations against it. Although the PCOT was one if the winners of the 2014 election and its president came third in the presidential elections, with its radical ideology and uncompromising stances, its electoral power diminished gradually from one round of elections to the next until it was effectively marginalized in Tunisia's democratic political process.

October 18 Collective for Rights and Freedoms (Collectif du 18 Octobre)

This coalition of opposition parties and forces was formed in 2005 following protest demonstrations involving lawyers, judges and human rights activists triggered by the Tunisian government's prevention of the LTDH and the Union of Tunisian Journalists from holding their conventions, as well as the overthrow of the leadership of the Association of Tunisian Judges (Association des Magistrats Tunisiens – AMT).[48] The activists' demands included freedom of expression, freedom of the press, the freedom to organize political parties, the release of political prisoners and the enactment of a general pardon law. A hunger strike waged on 18 October 2005 received extensive media coverage from various Arab and international media outlets because the International Summit for the Information Society was being held in Tunisia at the time.[49] The public was enraged by the fact that an invitation to attend the Summit had been extended to Israeli prime minister Ariel Sharon. The event, which constituted an official affront to Tunisian national and Arab sensitivities, thus became an occasion for protest by the opposition forces while further provoking the public's aversion to the regime.[50]

48. Najib al-Shabbi, 'al-ʿAlaqa bayn al-ʾIslāmiyīn wa al-ʿIlmāniyīn: Tajribat 18 Uktūbar fī Tūnis [The Relationship between the Islamists and the Secularists: October 18's Experience in Tunisia],' *al-Adab*, vol. 58, nos 11–12, 2010.

49. Ibid.

50. Convinced that Zionist circles controlled political decision-making in the United States, some Arab regimes courted Western favour by establishing relations with Israel on different levels. In an effort to keep US criticisms of human rights at bay, the Tunisian government played this infamous Israeli card in February 2005 by inviting Israeli prime minister Ariel Sharon to Tunisia. Close security cooperation between the US and Tunisia permitted the regime to skirt international criticism on human rights issues, even during

The October 18 Collective for Rights and Freedoms was established after the October 18 hunger strike, which lasted 32 days, and through which Islamists, Arab nationalists, leftists and socialist activists protested against the police state and the repression of civil liberties. The October 18 Collective grew out of a national committee that had been established to support the hunger strike. Four documents, drafted by four different subcommittees, discussed the relationship between the state and religion, women's rights and gender equality, elections and freedom of conscience.[51] The compromises reached thus preserved the secular character of the state while affirming Islamists' participation in the democratic process. In this dialogue, the Islamists acknowledged the secularization of the state and the achievements of modernization, while all partners recognized democracy as a desirable alternative to authoritarianism.

The October 18 Collective was joined by the majority of opposition movements and parties, as well as legal and unionist organizations, including Al Nahda, the Congress for the Republic, the Democratic Forum for Labour and Liberties, the PCOT, the Progressive Democratic Party, the Renewal Movement, the National Democratic Action Party, the Green Tunisia Party and a number of smaller leftist parties.[52] It also received support from a number of legal and human rights associations, including the LTDH, the National Council for Liberties, the League of Free Writers, the Center for the Independence of the Judiciary and Attorneys, Amnesty International's Tunisia branch and the Union of Tunisians in Cinema and Audiovisual Fields. Regarding union organizations, support came from the general student unions; regional labour unions in Sfax, Mdhila, Kairouan and Jendouba; and members of the Regional Labor Union in Tunis.[53] Union support thus revealed a complete separation between regional bases and the central leadership of the UGTT, which was consistent with unions' subsequent positions on the revolution.

Delegates participating in the Information Society Summit visited the site of the strike, with a number of international figures urging strikers to suspend the

the period of the so-called Neocons' influence in the US Administration, when George W. Bush criticized his allies' violations of human rights and civil liberties and demanded reforms. US Secretary of State Colin Powell reiterated a similar message during his visit to Tunisia in October 2003. This criticism, however, was mere lip-service to human rights, as US-Tunisia relations became even tighter following Tunisia's acknowledgement of the US-appointed Interim Governing Council in Iraq.

51. Ben Achour notes that these matters became the central issues inside the Higher Authority for Realization of the Objectives of the Revolution, Political Reform and Democratic Transition (HIROR), and during the phase of formulating the constitution. Achour, *Tunisia: A Revolution in an Islamic Country*, pp. 222–3.

52. 'Parties, associations, and unions support the October 18 movement', [al-Aḥzāb wal-Jamʿiyāt wal-Naqābāt Tusānid Ḥarakat 18 Uktūbar], *Tunisian Communist Workers' Party - al-Badil*, 14 November 2005, accessed on 13 December 2020, at: https://bit.ly/2Kls1Tw.

53. Ibid.

strike and vowing to push for the fulfilment of their demands. The strike was suspended on 18 November 2005.[54]

Subsequently, the members of the collective divided into two camps. The first camp favoured secular-Islamist cooperation, while the second camp opposed such cooperation. Those who advocated cooperation with the Islamists included the PCOT, the Progressive Democratic Party (which changed its position after the revolution) and the Congress for the Republic. Those who refused to cooperate with the Islamists included secularist intellectuals and leftist organizations, including the Renewal Party.[55] In their view, Islamists represented an equally insidious form of authoritarianism due to their totalitarian tendencies.[56] After the revolution, the Democratic Modernist Pole, which ran in the Constituent Assembly elections, became an extension of this political position and cultural tradition. The Troika government that was composed in 2011 from the Congress for the Republic (CPR), the Democratic Forum for Labour and Liberties (FDTL) and Al Nahda could be considered an extension of the October 18 Collective. The three parties met after the approval of the constitutional amendments that would allow Ben Ali to run for a fourth presidential term, demanding a new constitution that would guarantee the principles of democracy, the sovereignty of the people as the only source of political power and guarantees of the rights and liberties set forth in the International Declaration of Human Rights.

In subsequent years, the Collective's committee continued to meet, but its activism quickly faded following the dispersal of its constituents. Still, this experience heralded the political future of Tunisia, having established rules for democratic cooperation between secularists and Islamists on the basis of Tunisia's Arab identity. As noted earlier, subcommittees drafted papers articulating a joint position on the major issues of a future democracy in Tunisia – issues that would also face the drafters of the Tunisian Constitution.

It goes without saying that the Tunisian political scene has witnessed radical shifts since the revolution, including the granting of legal permits to previously unlicensed parties such as Al Nahda and the disbanding of the former ruling party. Before the revolution, legal parties were, for the most part, little more than 'décor', their sole purpose being to maintain the illusion of political pluralism in the country. Under those circumstances, numerous parties which learned to organize and function in the difficult 'grey zone' between quasi-legality and illegality successfully educated and trained many of their cadres in political activism.

The importance of the October 18 Collective stems from four important facts: (1) It penetrated the barrier of fear by organizing political actions when

54. al-Shabbi, 'The Relationship between the Islamists and the Secularists'.

55. This must be distinguished from the Communist Workers' Party, which took principled stands against dictatorship and in favour of Tunisia's Arab identity. The Communist Party, by contrast, was historically a Francophile organization.

56. al-Shabbi, 'The Relationship between the Islamists and the Secularists'.

the regime appeared stable and strong. (2) Collective participants challenged the Islamist-secularist divide that the regime had toiled to preserve. (3) An organized opposition succeeded in introducing a democratic alternative to authoritarianism which was accepted by both secularists and Islamists. (4) The controversy among the parties who were supposed to join it on the cooperation with the Islamists from the beginning and other debates in the collective after its formation were the issues that, in effect, split the Tunisian political society after the revolution.

One might argue that the votes of Tunisians after the revolution bolstered the political forces that persisted within the October 18 Collective, especially following the withdrawal of several secular parties that refused to cooperate with the Islamists. An exception, however, was the Progressive Democratic Party, which forcefully defended the legitimacy of the alliance with the Islamists. After the revolution, however, the party changed course, having decided that the goal of the Collective had been achieved and that thenceforth it (the Progressive Democratic Party) should stress its secular character. It also decided that, in the absence of dictatorship, Al Nahda should be perceived not as an ally but as a rival party.

Associations and non-governmental organizations and a note on civil society

Civil society is often identified with the term 'non-governmental organization' (NGO), that is to say, a voluntary association engaged neither in profit-making nor in politics. Some extend the term 'civil society' to include social movements as well. However, this approach strips the concept of civil society of its analytical value given that it developed historically through the dialectic of state, society and individual in modernity. The term 'civil society' was once applied to a society's emancipation from the so-called state of nature through association among individuals; it was then used to refer to the reproduction of bourgeois society through market economy mechanisms without the coercive power of the state. With the development of modern society, the term 'civil society' came to refer to the reproduction of an increasingly differentiated unity of state and society through more inclusive representation of individuals via parliaments, trade unions, public opinion's influence on politics, women's movements, civil rights movements, citizen initiatives to mitigate the free market's negative repercussions on health and the environment and, at a later stage, designation of a public space that would be regulated neither by the coercive force of the state nor by profit-driven action. The concept was imported to Third World countries in its latest form without the rich dialectic that it had left behind, including many phases of state–society differentiation and the formations that emerged in the process, such as parliaments, political parties and trade unions. However, employing the concept of 'civil society' as nothing but a designation for NGOs reduces it to a mere term with positive connotations, but without the analytical and critical potentials of the associated concept.[57]

This dwarfing of the term may justify the notion, proposed by some researchers, that the revolution in Tunisia was not triggered by an awakening or a call from civil society for political rights but, rather, was a revolt of the marginalized centre and south regions against the coastal economic centre.[58]

Tunisia's major national associations, most of them self-financed, such as the UGTT, the LTDH and others, are not simply NGOs but organizations with grassroots foundations. These organizations are actually closer to the concept of civil society than are NGOs, which are sustained by foreign funding[59] and, therefore, are not integral components of the state–society–individual dialectic that make up civil society.

Despite not being controlled by the ruling party (the RCD), Tunisian national associations have played an important role in empowering Tunisian society, frequently insisting on an autonomous role. In the final decade of Ben Ali's rule, the labour union was contained by the government, whereas the grassroots were permeated by political parties, especially from the opposition. This in itself poses the question: What remains of the idea of civil society if it is separated from the so-called political community?

It is true that the leaders of the most important Tunisian associations (UGTT, UTICA, UTAP, UNFT, UGTE) were led by supporters of Ben Ali,[60] and that the UGTT not only failed to participate in the 2008 Gafsa Mining Basin uprisings but even stood with the regime.[61] However, the ongoing struggle between the union's grassroots and leadership is important for understanding both the causes of the revolution and its triumph. Thus, arguing for a separation between civil society and politics not only is unrealistic but also obstructs and distorts the analysis of the events that happened in Tunisia as the revolution began. Moreover, on many occasions the aforementioned associations struggled for their autonomy while at

57. This is a condensed version of the thesis I propose in my *Civil Society: A Critical Study [al-Mujtama' al-Madanī: Dirāsah Naqdiyah]* (Beirut: Center for Arab Unity Studies, 1998).

58. Niklas Plaetzer, 'Civil Society as Domestication: Egyptian and Tunisian Uprisings Beyond Liberal Transitology', *Journal of International Affairs*, vol. 68, no. 1 (Fall/Winter 2014), p. 295. See Joel Beinin and Frédéric Vairel (eds.), *Social Movements, Mobilization, and Contestation in the Middle East and North Africa* (Redwood City, CA: Stanford University Press, 2011), p. 238.

59. This in itself is not a criticism of these organizations, nor does it mean that they do not perform significant functions.

60. Fadhel Kaboub, 'The Making of the Tunisian Revolution', *Middle East Development Journal*, vol. 5, no. 1 (March 2013), pp. 1350003–5.

61. Plaetzer, p. 259. See also: Kasper Ly Netterstrøm, 'The Tunisian General Labor Union and the Advent of Democracy', Middle East Journal, vol. 70, no. 3 (Summer 2016), pp. 392, accessed at: https://bit.ly/2RzEBSX

the same time accumulating a civil tradition that enabled them to play an important role in maintaining the cohesion of society at times of political polarization. Their commitment to pluralist democracy after the revolution was crucial. In Egypt, by contrast, such a coalition of powerful civil bodies organized on the national level was not available. Instead, the army claimed to represent the unity of the nation after the revolution; however, it was not committed to democracy but had its own political agenda.

Tunisian General Labour Union

Established by Mohamed Ali El Hammi (who initially formed the General Confederation of the Workers of Tunisia in 1925), the UGTT is one of Tunisia's most important civic associations. Independent unions were later launched by Tunisian labourers led by Farhat Hachad in 1944. These groups created the basis for what would come to be known as the UGTT, founded in 1946.[62] The Tunisian experience with unionist activism and the field of human rights is the oldest and arguably the most authentic in the Arab world; nevertheless, the labour movement was excluded and marginalized. Under Ben Ali, it was transformed into a subsidiary of the state and its policies, a common practice in authoritarian and totalitarian regimes. In Tunisia, however, there remained a margin within which branches of the General Labor Union were able to operate. This constituted a vital channel for political forces to build bridges with the people and the workers and to advocate for their demands before state leadership with a flexibility that could not be emulated by a political party.

The UGTT's founding convention was held in Tunis in 1946, and Farhat Hachad was elected secretary-general not long thereafter. From its early days, the UGTT played a pioneering role in society at the national level. Between its founding in 1946 and Tunisia's independence in 1955, the UGTT was engaged in a series of struggles and strikes that threatened French interests in the country, which led to Hachad's assassination by the French 'Red Hand' organization on 5 December 1952.[63] In January 1952, Tunisia's national resistance was launched, and the resulting protest movements and assassinations turned into bloody confrontations with French occupation authorities. The UGTT contributed to building the modern Tunisian nation-state by participating in the elections of the Founding National Council and developing an economic and social programme.

Though the UGTT's activism waned in the 1990s, it rebounded after the year 2000 and contributed consistently to nationalist and political struggles: presenting a discourse that radically and unquestionably supported the Palestinian cause and condemning the Tunisian government's interference in the activities of the

62. For a further discussion, see ʿAbd as-Salām bin Ḥamīdah, *The History of the Unionist Labor Movement in Tunisia [Tārīkh al-Ḥarakah al-Niqābiyah al-Waṭaniyah lil-Shaghghīlah bi Tūnis (1924-1956)]*, vol. 2 (Sfax: Dār Muhammad ʿAlī, 1984).

63. Labyad, *Identity*, p. 114.

Human Rights Association. In general, however, the UGTT leadership more or less went along with state policies under Ben Ali; it even supported his nomination for the presidency in 2004 and 2009. It would be safe to say that the Arab world has never witnessed a union organization with the political and national weight of the UGTT. Within Tunisia, the UGTT is composed of numerous committees and councils led by the National Convention, its highest authority, which meets once every five years; the National Council, the UGTT's second-highest authority, meets once every two years; and the National Administrative Commission, the UGTT's third-highest authority, convenes at the invitation of the National Executive Office once every three months, with extraordinary meetings held whenever the need arises.

The Tunisian Union of Industry, Trade and Handicrafts

The Tunisian Union of Industry, Trade and Handicrafts (UTICA) was established in 1947 by businessmen and traders. The UTICA as an organizational body follows an administrative and political territorial division. It is more of a confederation that combines 17 professional federations, 24 regional unions, 216 local unions, 370 national trade chambers and 1,700 regional trade chambers. In 1990, UTICA also created a women's chamber, as well as a youth section.[64]

Since its founding, UTICA not only represented the interests of its members but also gained the right to distribute raw materials, such as cotton, silk, wool and leather. With the adoption of a corporative policy in the early 1960s, UTICA and its constituency plunged into a crisis that was only overcome when economic liberalization was pursued by the government of Hédi Nouira's.

Under the Ben Ali's regime, particularly throughout the 1980s and 1990s, UTICA's role was bolstered by the increased liberalization of the economy. In fact, the private sector in the Tunisian landscape was largely dominated by the UTICA, with 150,000 private companies enjoying a membership. At the international level, the UTICA has '30 country-dedicated business councils that help develop bilateral cooperation and adhered to multiple organizations including the International Organization of Employers (IOE)'. Over time, the structure of the UTICA became even more complex.[65] It backed the transition from centralized economy directed by the state to a competitive and open economy[66] and opening Tunisia to European markets, especially following the signing of the Association Agreement with the European Union in 1995

All the governments that ruled since the revolution needed the association's cooperation together with the UGTT, as the government's ability to undertake

64. 'Mapping of Business Organizations in the MENA Regions', *Background Notes*, OECD (2019), pp. 8–9, 23–4, accessed at: https://bit.ly/3b0B9au

65. 'al-Ittiḥād at-Tūnisī lil-ṣināʿa wal-Tijāra wal-ḥiraf al-Yadawiyya', *Ittiḥād al-Ghuraf al-ʿArabiyya*, accessed at: https://bit.ly/33cyRAT [in Arabic].

66. Ibid.

economic reforms was limited. In some cases both organizations had veto power over some governmental decisions.

Tunisian Bar Association (ONAT)

On 15 March 1958, a law governing the legal profession was passed. It was not substantially different from laws that had existed under the protectorate despite being adapted to the Tunisian situation. Éric Gobe argued that the law only '"Tunisified" and unified the profession by merging the Tunisian proxies exclusively practicing within the local judiciary and lawyers attached to the French judiciary, while reproducing the decentralized French model of allocating lawyers to the local Bar Associations practicing within the Tunisian courts of appeal'. Each applicant to the Bar was required to pass an exam that was organized by the Ministry of Justice and to submit a certificate of aptitude for the profession of advocate.[67]

The association was dominated by the regime's opponents during the late 1950s and the early 1960s, but Bourguiba was able to neutralize the associations after the July 1961 confrontation between French and Tunisian troops at the Bizerte military air base.[68]

In 1963, a law was passed to create the Tunisian Bar Association, TBA. And despite that internal struggle on the leadership of the bar and many lawyers' firmness in issues of civil rights in effect, most TBA presidents belonged to the Neo-Destour Party or aligned with the regime.

Ben Ali's regime exerted pressure on the parliament to pass a bill in 1989 limiting the profession's autonomy. Following a TBA general meeting, Tunisian lawyers were called to strike for two hours on 1 November 1990 against the repeated violations of lawyers' rights. However, the TBA was unable to stop government violations against lawyers or to amend the 1989 law. Furthermore, the 1990s witnessed a tightened grip over TBA and other associations.

In the two decades between 1991 and 2011, membership to the Bar increased from about 1,400 members to 7,759 members. Women became noticeable in the profession during this period, with female members soaring from just 5 per cent in 1980 to 25 per cent in 2001, and to 43 per cent in 2015.

67. Éric Gobe, 'Tunisia Lawyers: A Political Profession?', in Richard Abel et al. (eds.), *Lawyers in 21st Century Societies*, vol. 1: National Reports (London: Hart, 2020), pp. 657–8; See also: Éric Gobe, 'Lawyers Mobilizing in the Tunisian Uprising: A Matter of 'Generations'?' in Mark Muhannad Ayyash and Ratiba Hadj-Moussa (eds.), *Protests and Generations: Legacies and Emergences in the Middle East, North Africa and the Mediterranean*, vol. 5: Youth in a Globalizing World (Leiden: Brill, 2017), pp. 73–95, accessed at: https://bit.ly/2QQblXO

68. Gobe, 'Tunisia Lawyers', pp. 659.

When the Bar Association Council decided to call for a strike in 2002, the authorities tried to intimidate it, and pro-government lawyers challenged in court the legality of the strike.[69]

After the outbreak of the revolution, individual lawyers took part in the protests in their own way, but the TBA remained inactive. This did not last long as the protests quickly spread. The TBA called for a general strike on 6 January 2011 to protest against what they described as an 'unprecedented use of force against lawyers' during their 31 December 2010 sit-in at the Justice Palace,[70] and finally decided to formally join the protests after the UGTT called for a general strike on 12 January. The TBA later participated in creating the National Council for Safeguarding the Revolution in February 2011.

Tunisian Association of the Democratic Women

In early 1980s, the Tahar Haddad Club for the Study of Women's Condition became the platform for the women's movement. It is this club which set up women's organizations such as Tunisian Association of the Democratic Women (ATFD) and Association of Tunisian Women for Research and Development (AFTURD).[71] Those two organizations began to take an activist approach during the 1980s.[72] However, ATFD was granted a legal status in 1989 but remained under strict surveillance and even harassment in some cases.[73] Nevertheless, it carried on working with state-sponsored women's organizations that received state funding.

Ben Ali was not really interested in developing women's rights. In August 1994, ATFD denounced the ambiguity of the regimes and its use of religion to sustain women's oppression especially in during the populist phase of Ben Ali when he tried to appear as protector of religion. Ben Ali was also accused of instrumentalizing women's rights to strengthen his alliance with the West and to cover up his human rights violations.[74] The regime fiercely rejected the interference of the AFTD in legislation and governmental decisions. The AFTD's charter states

69. 'Independent Voices and Stifled in Tunisia', *Amnesty International* (July 2010), p. 17, accessed at: https://bit.ly/3tlVc9H

70. 'The Role of Lawyers as Transitional Actors in Tunisia', *Lawyers, Conflict & Transition* (August 2015), p. 1, accessed at: https://bit.ly/2QTnZoX

71. Lilia Labidi, 'The Nature of Transnational Alliances in Women's Associations in the Maghreb: The Case of AFTURD and ATFD in Tunisia', *Journal of Middle East Women's Studies*, vol. 3, no. 1 (Winter 2007), p. 19, accessed at: https://bit.ly/3gWrmGt

72. Ibid., p. 15.

73. Maaike Voorhoeve, 'Women's Rights in Tunisia and the Democratic Renegotiation of an Authoritarian Legacy', *New Middle Eastern Studies*, vol. 5 (2015), p. 7, accessed at: https://bit.ly/3vEJtVl

74. Imen Yacoubi, 'Sovereignty from Below: State from Feminism and Politics of Women Against Women in Tunisia', *The Arab Studies Journal*, vol. 24, no. 1 (Spring 2016), p. 263, accessed at: https://bit.ly/3h3livQ

its struggle against all forms of discrimination but also the inevitable struggle for real democracy in both public and private spheres. Hence, when AFTD interfered in the regime's policy, it was considered a serious encroachment of the general rules of NGOs. Ben Ali warned the ATFD and ordered it to restrict its activities to women's issues. In 1993, it created a centre in Tunis for assisting female victims of violence and offering legal counselling. In 2000, it launched a campaign against sexual harassment of women. On 8 March 2004, it presented a bill to parliament that criminalizes sexual harassment. The law passed but with a very limited definition of sexual harassment and with a high burden of proof on the claimant.[75]

Fifteen days after Ben Ali's ouster, the ATFD organized a 'March for citizenship and equality'. The demonstration took place on the eve of Rached Ghannouchi's return from exile and was understood as a message to the Islamic political forces. It continued to mobilize its social base to protect women's right in the Constitution and in later legislation.

The National Union of Tunisian Women (UNFT)

It was the DRCD Party's women's organization under Ben Ali's regime. It encompassed 120,000 members and offered services for women and ran local offices and women health clinics throughout Tunisia.[76] When it was formed in 1956 the UNFT was the only women's organization in the post-independence era. It formed a framework of partnerships with governmental structures and national organizations. The UNFT acted as the only channel through which women could be elected to the RCD or appointed in decision-making positions.[77] Through the UNFT Bourguiba's authoritarian regime contained the women movement and curtailed the feminist trends.[78]

Feminist organizations that belonged to the opposition during Ben Ali's regime, such as the ANFT, opposed the UNFT too.[79] Nevertheless, they needed to cooperate with it in order to keep access to funding ongoing. Secularist women's groups worked with the authoritarian regime because it was perceived as the

75. Raoudha Kammoun, 'NGOs and Women's Rights in Tunisia: the Case of ATFD', in Galia Golan & Walid Salem, Non-State Actors in the Middle East (Abingdon: Routledge, 2013), pp. 7–8, accessed at: https://bit.ly/3xOz37u

76. 'Gender Equality Policy in Tunisia', *European Parliament* (2012), p. 7, accessed at: https://bit.ly/3b0pybv

77. Mari Norbakk, 'The Women's Rights Championship: Tunisia's Potential for Furthering Women's Rights', *Report no. 5,* CMI (October 2016), p. 11, accessed at: https://bit.ly/3ucEzyF

78. Ibid., p. 15.

79. 'Gender Equality Policy in Tunisia', *European Parliament* (2012), p. 7, accessed at: https://bit.ly/3b0pybv

guarantor of women's rights.[80] But , the UNFT was conceived as an extended arm of the state.

Human rights organizations played a significant role under Ben Ali's regime. Of these, the most important is the LTDH, founded in 1977. This and other organizations reflected a growing awareness of the need for non-partisan civil advocacy for human rights, as well as resistance against the practices of the regime inside and outside Tunisia. These organizations also introduced new modes of action, opted for by leftist and liberal political forces, for resisting authoritarianism. The Movement of Social Democrats was a key political influence on the association's work from the time of its founding, but Tunisian factions of all types, legal and illegal, quickly flocked into the organization and its managing committee, including the Islamist MTI and the PCOT. Although the regime attempted to stifle and marginalize the association, it persevered in its defence of human rights. The repression and persecution by Ben Ali's regime led to the establishment of various initiatives and associations, such as the Higher Council for Liberties, whose members included a broad variety of Islamists, secularists, and others.

In the heat of the events preceding Ben Ali's overthrow, unions and political movements had five main demands: removal of the government, the formation of a transitional government that would prepare for early legislative elections, accountability for those who had fired at the demonstrators, release of the detainees and the opening of a new political page that would involve a dialogue regarding the political future of the country. On Wednesday, 12 January, three weeks after its outbreak, the labour union's central leadership issued a statement supporting the uprising. This gave further momentum to the protests, which escalated on 13 and 14 January and led to the overthrow of Ben Ali and his government. After the conclusion of these events, the union also played an important role in adopting initiatives meant to preserve the achievements of the revolution, complete the dismantling of the regime and prevent the return of its leading figures. In the absence of clear leadership for the revolution, the union greatly benefitted from its role as an umbrella organization for a large number of political factions.

Other forms of citizen initiatives appeared after the revolution, such as community associations and neighbourhood committees that contributed to local security, guarding state institutions, and aiding the army at times of chaos and poor coordination between the army and other security forces.

80. Kira Jinkinson, 'State Feminism and the Islamist-Secularist Binary: Women's Rights in Tunisia', *E-International Relations*, 27/7/2020, accessed at: https://bit.ly/3uq0CCg

Chapter 5

DIARY ENTRIES

FROM UPRISING TO REVOLUTION

Stage one: Protests leading up to the revolution

Among citizens who see themselves as disadvantaged or oppressed, periods of relative stability in authoritarian regimes are often perceived as times of stagnation and hopelessness. The material situation may be worsening, but the prospect of organized protest against the regime appears remote and the chances of changing the regime remoter still. This period of false calm is the time in which public anger gradually builds up.

Protests by the unemployed, clashes with security forces such as those that took place in Gafsa and Ben Gardane, and boats of African immigrants sinking off the Tunisian coast, may appear to have gone unnoticed.[1] However, the calm appearance of the era of decay often conceals a mounting popular rage against the regime until

1. Impressions of rising suicide rate were conveyed to me by many Tunisian. However, the data on the subject shows that Tunisia is ranked 159th among of 183 states in suicide mortality rate. The gap between the spread impressions and the results of the comparison of the severity of the problem with other countries is telling concerning the relative nature of impressions and the role they play.

Suicide mortality rate is the number of suicide deaths in a year per 100,000 population. See 'Tunisia Suicide Rate 2000–15'.

Year	Total	Male	Female
2015	3.40%	4.50%	2.30%
2010	3.60%	5.00%	2.30%
2005	3.60%	5.10%	2.20%
2000	3.50%	4.90%	2.10%

Source: World Bank

'Suicide mortality rate (per 100,000 population) – Tunisia', *The World Bank Data*, accessed on 16/2/2021, at: https://bit.ly/37kMEYB; 'Suicide mortality rate, female (per 100,000 female population) – Tunisia', *The World Bank Data*, accessed on 16/2/2021, at: https://bit.ly/

a single, seemingly minor, incident triggers an uprising, and the anger that has been accumulating beneath the surface erupts. History has witnessed many instances of uprisings that never evolve into anything greater until, quite unexpectedly, a single event detonates mass protests through a particular confluence of contingencies.

Particularly when they represent an injustice, tragic events may turn into political symbols that have a major impact on the public. Such calamities are often the result of longstanding negligence, mismanagement, or corruption. To their victims, however, these mishaps connote one thing: that the deprived and disinherited always pay the price. In Tunisia, such symbolic events came to include repeated suicides by young people, which had become a form of protest for aggrieved and frustrated Tunisians. Mohamed Bouazizi's self-immolation was by no means an isolated incident. On the contrary, Tunisia's suicide rate was already high when Bouazizi's suicide took place, and statistics gathered by human right organizations show that suicide among Tunisian youth had been a notable phenomenon since 2005. One Tunisian sociologist who devoted a study to the phenomenon of indifference among youth wrote saying that young Tunisians were 'sinking in the mire of conformity', adding that 'they barely speak, and, if they do, they hardly say anything meaningful due to an absence of vision and authoritative points of reference'.[2]

Just one month prior to Bouazizi's self-immolation, another unemployed young man in the central province of al-Monastir had committed suicide in a similar fashion. However, his death had provoked little public reaction, thereby underlining Sidi Bouzid's critical role as an incubator of the uprising through the way in which it reacted to Bouazizi's suicide.

A 'practice run' of sorts had in fact already taken place in Sidi Bouzid, when protests flared in nearby Regueb. Just two months prior to Bouazizi's desperate act, members of his extended family had staged a protest in reaction to the judiciary's silence on the seizure of their agricultural land by Tunisian banks and businessmen. Investors were given the green light to seize the lands of farmers who were unable to repay their loans, a devastating consequence after the droughts that had hit the region in previous years. In reaction, a sit-in was organized in Regueb, and it spread rapidly to the provincial capital. All age groups participated in the protest; witnesses claimed to see an illiterate old woman collaring a policeman, and an old man in his seventies attacking another policeman with his cane.

The news of Bouazizi's suicide furthered political organization which had begun that same year, and was instrumental in the promptness of the protest reaction.

3aqSYQu; 'Suicide mortality rate, male (per 100,000 male population) – Tunisia', *The World Bank Data*, accessed on 16/2/2021, at: http://bit.ly/3u2K9nE

2. Mohsen Bouazizi, 'The Sociology of Indifference: A Study of Silent Expressions of Tunisian Youths', [Sūsiyūlujiyat al-Lāmubālāh: Dirāsah fī al-Taʿbirāt al-Ṣamiṭah ladā al-Shabāb al-Tūnisī] in Sari Hanafi (ed.), *The State of Exception and Resistance in the Arab World [Ḥalat al-Istithnāʾ wal-Muqāwamah fī al-Waṭan al-ʿArabī]* (Beirut: Center for Arab Unity Studies, 2010), pp. 207–28.

It will be remembered that in June 2010, following the 31 May Israeli attack on the Turkish ship 'Marmara' in the Mediterranean to prevent the 'Freedom Flotilla' from reaching besieged Gaza, a demonstration had marched through the streets of Sidi Bouzid (and in many other cities) in solidarity with Gaza. Here, two currents could be observed. Many of the demonstrations were content to chant: 'Gaza, the symbol of dignity!' and pan-Arab slogans. In Tunisia, demonstrations in support of Arab causes were tolerated as long as they did not target the regime, which allowed local branches of the UGTT to channel popular anger through Arab nationalist causes. However, the demonstrators' slogans linked broader Arab issues to people's local demands. Arab nationalist activities were, after all, legal and tolerated in Tunisia, and support for national causes became an occasion to expose Tunisians' concerns and demands.[3]

Long-time activist Ali Bouazizi, who participated in the protests from the inception of the uprising, is typical of the kind of young politicized activist found in local branches of Tunisian opposition parties. Ali Bouazizi's testimony reveals the role performed by local political activists:

> I have been active in the Progressive Democratic Party for over three years. . . . We gathered a nucleus that rapidly expanded and attracted more followers. For more than three years, we had been holding sit-ins and protests in front of City Hall. Some of these were political, while others sought to achieve social demands for the people of Sidi Bouzid. . . . We launched our first sit-in with six participating members on 20 November 2008 in front of the governorate's hall, and demanded the release of an activist in the Progressive Democratic Party who had been sentenced to two years and four months in prison under the anti-terrorism law.
>
> Another event took place prior to 17 December 2010, when residents and farmers of Regueb protested against the theft of their lands, the abuse of the law, and the ties between those in power and members of the bourgeoisie. Our friends, who were active in civil society, legal rights, and political struggle, all stood with the farmers. We provided them with support, attended their protests, and documented the process by posting photos online and writing articles in newspapers run by radical opposition parties.[4]

Amin Bouazizi adds:

> The farmers of Regueb – men, women, and elderly alike – confronted security officials. The Meknes district was reputed for its history of struggle during the period of national liberation (from French colonialism). . . . The land the State

3. From several testimonies collected by the team of the Arab Center for Research and Policy Studies (ACRPS).

4. Ali Bouazizi, interview conducted in Doha for this book by two ACRPS researchers, Hamzeh al-Moustafa and Rami Salameh, 22 April 2011.

> had attempted to seize from farmers had been granted to them by Bourguiba following Tunisia's independence in recognition of their legacy of struggle against colonialism.[5] After holding these plots of land for over 50 years, these farmers were informed by the authorities that they were no longer the proprietors. According to reports posted on Facebook, more than 2,500 farmers started an uprising in reaction to this news and set up tents on their plots. The Regueb uprising, however, hardly received any mention in the media.
>
> Similarly, during the Fall, teachers' union activists in primary, and particularly in secondary education, would hold a sit-in at a different educational institution nearly every day in defense of the right to organize unions in educational institutions. . . . A group of roughly 50 unionists and activists who turned the sit-ins into a daily affair were mocked by skeptics, who called them 'sit-in specialists.' At the time, nobody knew that these intense activities would break the barrier of fear.[6]

Protests in Sidi Bouzid were met by a remarkable sense of popular solidarity, the same form of solidarity shown in cases such as the mining basin and the Ben Gardane protests. Protesters also received support from unions, sit-ins and Facebook campaigns, which little by little became the voice of those without a voice. The link between the Mining Basin Uprising and that of Sidi Bouzid is interesting, particularly since the former did not, at first, garner much solidarity in Sidi Bouzid. It began after a number of young men from Sidi Bouzid passed the employment examination administered by the local phosphate company. According to Sidi Bouzid locals, the events were sparked by locals from Gafsa, who were protesting against local unemployment and non-transparent employment procedures. They questioned how 'strangers' (i.e. people from Sidi Bouzid) could be hired over locals, noting the fact that the director of the phosphates company in the mining basin originated from Sidi Bouzid. Regional sensitivities were thus aroused, which dampened sympathy in Sidi Bouzid for the mining basin and the Gafsa uprising despite the scale of the protests.

The uprising that began in Sidi Bouzid reflected the dire socio-economic conditions faced by Tunisians everywhere; it also highlighted their political awareness and their sense of injustice and deprivation of their political liberties. Tunisians were no longer willing to be ruled in this manner, the question being whether the regime could continue to impose such rule on them by force. Beginning in Tunisia's economically deprived regions, the uprising gradually spread to the capital. The diaries of the revolution validate the hypothesis, proposed in earlier chapters, that the Tunisian Revolution was an uprising of the peripheries, in which urban centres carried their entire provinces with them, and in which unemployment, regional and class disparities and feelings of deprivation despite

5. It happened in the context of collectivization in the era of the cooperatives.

6. Lamine Al-Bouazizi, interview conducted in Doha for this book by two ACRPS researchers, Hamzeh al-Moustafa and Rami Salameh, 19 April 2011.

overall economic growth played a major role. Only later did the wealthier regions of Tunisia join the protests, with some taking part only after Ben Ali's departure.

The documentation in this chapter relies on critically evaluated sources from interviews, mostly with activists, social media and other 'new media' tools, such as YouTube. The data gleaned, including dates and locations, have been carefully verified and compared to other information available, as well as official reports released after the revolution.[7] Interviews with witnesses, along with other methods, were employed to verify the information below, including reliance on local Tunisian media outlets, primarily the website of 'Kalimat Tunis' radio station and the online newspaper *al-Badil* published by the Tunisian Communist Workers' Party. The local opposition media, which broadcast its reports abroad and used its websites to disseminate news, played a central role in introducing the revolution to the world. Activists and bloggers also posted news of the protests on their personal websites, thus counteracting the regime's attempts at censorship. This was all taking place at a time when Arab and international media still struggled to comprehend the events in Tunisia. It was also clear that the opposition media played an active role in propagating the mood of protest by linking protests across the country and by countering regime propaganda. In so doing, the opposition media undoubtedly concealed some facts while exaggerating others, which will be evident below when events in the capital city and in some north-western provinces are thoroughly reviewed. Special emphasis will be placed on the events of the first days and on the sources of the uprising's persistence, without which this unprecedented historical event would not have been possible.

Day 1: 17 December 2010

In a tragic act of protest against humiliation, injustice and deprivation, 26-year-old Mohamed Bouazizi set himself on fire in front of the Sidi Bouzid governorate building after his fruit and vegetable cart had been confiscated by municipality officers. Rumours spread that he had been slapped by a policewoman in the governor's office, and that he was an unemployed college graduate. (The latter claim is not accurate; nevertheless, the rumour spread and impacted tens of thousands of unemployed college graduates.) It seems that Bouazizi committed suicide after being prevented from meeting a municipal official to present a complaint, which casts doubt on the claim that he was infuriated by an affront to his manhood by being slapped by a female officer.[8] Assuming that Bouazizi was indeed slapped by the policewoman in question, he did not commit suicide directly following the alleged incident. He attempted to file a formal complaint concerning his cart, and when nobody in the governor's office showed any concern for his plight,

7. Some information became available only after publication of the Arabic edition of this book.

8. *The Tunisian Observatory for Unionist Rights and Liberties*, 17 December 2010, accessed at: https://bit.ly/3a5Sqjb.

he set himself on fire. This was the chain of events; however, the precise cause of the suicide matters little in this context. Understanding the revolution does not require an understanding of the reasons behind such a drastic act of self-destruction; it does, however, require an investigation into what made this specific act so significant.

Following the incident, Bouazizi's family rallied support, and a group of unionists and political activists responded. At the beginning of the protests, activists distributed a photo of Bouazizi in flames, though it was later ascertained that no one had photographed him as he burned, and that the photo was that of a South Korean man. Even so, the photograph was used to mobilize and sensitize the public. This was a demonstration of the importance of the visual image and media 'spectacle' in mobilizing and shaping public opinion. The image used for the mobilization was not of Bouazizi himself; nevertheless, it was an image of an event that had in fact taken place. This should be distinguished from manufactured images of a sham event. In the latter case, the image is not a tool of simulation but rather an instrument of forgery.

Bouazizi's suicide prompted local political activists and unionists to stage a large sit-in along with the family of the deceased young man and the residents of Sidi Bouzid, thereby igniting a protest that quickly morphed into a movement against unemployment and the marginalization of their community.

> At the moment of Bouazizi's self-immolation, two things took place: his family rallied support, and a core group of political activists and unionists showed up. The slogans raised following Bouazizi's death carried specific symbolism because the anger was directed at the State. Activists, some of whom were engaged in political parties like the Democratic Progressive Party, and others who were not, worked to increase solidarity between the unions, parties and Bouazizi's family.[9]

The movement in Sidi Bouzid has often been mischaracterized by understating the role of politicians and unionists while exaggerating the role of traditional communal solidarity. While traditional community ties were, and remain, important,[10] what transformed the event into a major scandal was the efforts of unionists and political activists. Around one o'clock in the afternoon, activists assembled in front of the hospital, and large numbers began to show up at the Bouazizi family residence. By three o'clock, many unionists and activists had also assembled in the main square of Sidi Bouzid, which prompted the security forces to gather around the protesters, though they did not intervene. In a provincial setting such as that of Sidi Bouzid, it is extremely difficult to distinguish the role of the local community from that of political activists, and any such attempts could be misleading. An analysis that focuses exclusively on communal and clan loyalties fails to explain the phenomenon, because such communal and tribal relations can be used either

9. From the testimony of Amin Bouazizi.
10. This was equally proven during the Constituent Assembly elections in Sidi Bouzid.

to calm protests and mediate with the authorities, or to mobilize support for the political opposition.

In response to questions about why such a sharp response emerged, Amin Bouazizi states:

> The only legal opposition party with activists on the ground was the Democratic Progressive Party, whose local activists were aware of the mood in Sidi Bouzid, while underground political parties were headed by the Marxist and Arab nationalist currents. Despite Al Nahda's popularity, it lacked known unionist and political figures, most of whom belonged to pan-Arab nationalist (i.e., Baathist and Nasserite) and leftist (i.e., Communist currents. . . . The first sit-in included the family of Bouazizi, his friends, unionists, and political activists, with around 350 attendees in total.[11]

The role of the local community in this situation was prominent. Communal groups tend to be employed as a shield for the individual in the face of tyranny when he or she does not feel protected by notions of citizenship or the law. This function is most pronounced in the distant peripheral regions which, unlike industrial and economic centres, tend to be demographically homogeneous and stable, with little internal migration. The Bouazizi family, together with a core group of activists most of whom belonged to the extended family, played an instrumental role in mobilizing and sustaining the protest movement for over a week. The movement gained the support of the people in the district, after which other Tunisians – citizens, political movements and syndical unions alike – joined in as well. Activists were thus able to politicize solidarity.

It later transpired that a number of political activists, journalists and human rights activists contributed to organizing the protests in the city by taking on multiple roles. In the provinces in particular, an activist can be a member of a human rights association and a self-appointed correspondent for newspapers and internet websites, transmitting news, images and information from distant regions that are little known to the press. The press often lacks the local knowledge required to navigate the region, including the names of its towns, families and landmarks, and the existing links among individuals and communities.

Testimonies speak not only to the presence of this type of community-party-union activism but also to the national level communications with opposition leaders in the capital and coordinated media activism. Again, the political activist here is often a 'local' who simultaneously performs the role of activist, journalist, analyst, and so forth. Naturally, experienced activists, such as Ali and Amin Bouazizi, did not imagine that this day would turn into a historic moment in Tunisia. It is impossible to know what would have happened had it not been for this turn of events. Would the protest have lasted long enough to turn into

11. From the testimony of Lamine Al-Bouazizi.

an uprising? Would that uprising have persisted long enough to transform into a revolution? Would major cities have joined the protest this time?

In describing his activities on that day, Ali Bouazizi recounts:

> Half an hour after the incident, Mohamed Bouazizi's uncle, Saleh, contacted me, knowing that I was active in the field of human rights. He informed me that a young man had set himself on fire opposite City Hall. He asked that I come to the scene and organize a group of protesters in an attempt to sensitize the public and mobilize it in protest over the tragic incident. . . . I contacted Amin Bouazizi and some friends and political and legal activists. We began by supporting the family's presence in front of the municipality headquarters.[12] A farewell letter from Mohamed Bouazizi to his mother was widely published on Facebook, but the letter was a hoax, though.
>
> Khalid al-Owayni, a lawyer, and a number of political activists joined Bouazizi's family in protest; initially, the demands were social, including an end to corruption, the right to work, the rejection of clientelism and bribery, and action to address the miserable situation in Sidi Bouzid. . . . A critical move was our decision to turn to the media since, prior to 17 December, most Tunisians had never heard of Sidi Bouzid, a small agricultural town in the Tunisian interior. We taped the events of the first day with the help of activist Wail el-Iffi, a specialist in montage, to upload the videos onto my Facebook account. Half an hour later a massive media response took place, and activist Zouhair Makhloufcalled me and told me that Al Jazeera wanted to use the link and use the video. He invited me to appear as a guest on *al-Ḥaṣād al-Maghāribī* (a political nightly show focusing on the Maghreb) on 17 December. I agreed, of course.

At this early stage, the importance of satellite channels was not that they transmitted information outside of Tunisia but that they informed the residents of other provinces, and perhaps other districts within the same province, of the happenings in Sidi Bouzid. Ali Bouazizi continues:

> In my commentary on 17 December, I was very cautious about what I said. I tried to play the role of the journalist, objectively reporting on events in spite of my political affiliation. I spoke without revealing that I was part of a group leading and coordinating the events because we did not believe that the movement would remove the dictator; we merely hoped that it would lead to 'something big'. The words coming out of my mouth could be used as evidence against us and could lead to us being legally indicted – if you watch the video, you will notice this concern. I blamed the authorities for the troubles, arguing that the authorities must act responsibly, hold wrongdoers accountable, and not resort to

12. The video tapes from the first day of protest show Bouazizi's immediate family, surrounded by political activists, demonstrating in front of the entrance to the governorate's hall. The rest of the people of Sidi Bouzid were effectively watching from behind.

security solutions. Following my appearance on Al Jazeera, the official Tunisia-Africa news agency published a mere three lines, claiming that no exceptional events had taken place in Sidi Bouzid and that certain exaggerated reports had been exploited by some political parties described as an 'extremist minority.' The official news agency added that the Sidi Bouzid governorate had received its fair share of development with over TND 300 million allocated for the region,[13] and questioned why they would protest. The next day, the same statement was published in official newspapers. On the first day, only the local security units of Sidi Bouzid were present. The young men hurled stones at City Hall and attempted to break into the building; some jumped over the fence. Brawls erupted between the protesters and security forces. On the first day, a number of young protesters were detained, but none of the political activists.

Objective press reports in such a case are an impossibility. Neutrality is not an option, nor is objectivity, as images and news produced by activists in an attempt to transmit the facts and mobilize people to stand with the weak and disenfranchised are bound to be obfuscated by the official media. Objectivity in this case means that the news and the images must serve the purposes of the struggle, including the transmission of facts concealed by the official media, though these same facts are undeniably manipulated and selectively used by the revolution's media as well. 'Journalists' in such a situation are actually political activists on the ground. They generally hold strong opinions, and do not deem it their duty to conduct analytical, behind-the-scenes reportage that investigates the alignment of political positions within the ruling establishment. The same phenomenon took place in Syria, Libya, Yemen and Egypt once the authorities had prevented the media from covering events live; local activists were thus turned into media correspondents.

The reaction to the first day was to be expected; no party issued a statement describing the events as an 'uprising.' For the next two days, statements focused on the topic of Mohamed Bouazizi. The organization was local, as was the will to escalate events, which were later described by the Tunis media and its intellectuals as 'spontaneous.'

Our party leadership often referred to us prior to the revolution as 'hotheads,' and described us as the 'Sidi Bouzid Republic,' because we would speak to international correspondents and the world media without consulting them. The Progressive Party is a radical and official opposition party, but its role was reformist; they had no plans to overthrow the regime. The party hoped that reforms would lead to a democratic and civic state where all liberties are provided. Meanwhile, on that first day, limited clashes and arrests took place, but without loss of life. The protest dispersed at sundown, and Bouazizi was transported to a hospital in Sfax since the Sidi Bouzid hospital did not have the

13. The figure is a huge exaggeration in a state whose entire annual budget comes to no more than TND 20 billion.

> equipment and expertise to treat severe burns. Subsequently, he was moved to the hospital of the Ben Arous governorate adjacent to the capital Tunis, as it had a specialized hospital for severe burns.[14]

Some may question the validity or value of such testimonies, but one could argue that these young men did not merely watch events; they participated in bringing them about while possessing a political awareness and a distinctive perspective on the issue. These are not neutral political analysts but heavily politicized activists. From this perspective, the narration of their views forms an important aspect of the reality in Sidi Bouzid and represents an important factor in the escalation of the protests.

The events began at 11 o'clock in the morning, and rallies continued from 1:00 to 5:00 p.m., especially between 3:00 and 5:00 p.m. The majority of the crowd was composed of angry youth, unionists, and Mohamed Bouazizi's immediate family. The security forces attempted to restrain them, being fully aware of the scale of anger and tension in the air. These young protesters first tried to remove the helmets of the security forces, who evinced no reaction. In fact, the highest-ranking officer present was shoved to the ground, and none of the security forces reacted. The security apparatus wanted to curb the state of anger, knowing full well that things would escalate. 17 December was later considered the beginning of a revolution, but to activists and unionists, it was simply a day that witnessed an escalation of the protests.

> During the night, 100 officers belonging to the intervention units were transferred from Kasserine and Gafsa to Sidi Bouzid.[15]

Day 2: 18 December 2010

The act of suicide went viral on social media networks and youth groups were formed online. Steadily growing public interest in the event drew the attention of satellite channels, similar to what had happened in Egypt after the death of Khalid Saʿid under torture by Egyptian security officers in Alexandria on 6 June 2010.

> Saturday, the second day, is usually the day of the weekly local market for small cities such as Sidi Bouzid, which usually means that the city's population density doubles or triples. By noon, the people had assembled. Unionists and political

14. From the testimony of Ali al-Bouazizi.

15. 'Report by the National Fact-Finding Commission on Abuses and Violations Committed from 17 December 2010 to the End of Its Mandate' [Taqrīr al-Lajnah al-Waṭaniyah li istiqṣāʾ al-Ḥaqāʾiq Ḥawl al-Tajāwuzāt wal-intihakāt al-Musajallah Khilāl al-Fatrah al-Mumtaddah min 17 December 2010 ilā Ḥīn zawāl Mūjabihā], National Fact-Finding Commission on Abuses and Violations, *Report* (Tunis: 2012), p. 69, accessed on 11 March 2020, at: https://bit.ly/3kTB77t.

> activists were present from the early hours of the morning, and a number of angry youth joined in to protest the conditions that had driven a man to set himself on fire. The security forces attempted to disperse us using tear gas and grenades. Despite the fact that these young people were not politicized, their presence in the streets revealed their aptness in dealing with security forces. Whenever the security forces threw grenades toward them, they would pick them up and hurl them back.[16]

Following clashes between the municipal police and a large gathering of citizens who were marching in a protest led by activists and the family of Mohamed Bouazizi, Tunisian security forces and police used clubs and tear gas to disperse the demonstration. After protesters broke through the back door of the local police headquarters, a partial state of emergency was declared in the city, with over eighty people arrested. Security forces also increased their presence in a number of neighbouring provinces, especially Gafsa, where security outposts had been based since the beginning of the Mining Basin Uprising. Meanwhile, all entrances into Sidi Bouzid were closed, and the town was placed under siege.

> According to the report released by a fact-finding commission after the revolution, thousands of demonstrators filled the streets in front of the governorate headquarters to protest their socioeconomic conditions. Security officials present at the event insisted that the protestors had tried to break into the building and other government offices and to block the road. The law enforcement director of the south came to Sidi Bouzid with 100 officers and started guarding government buildings; he was then joined by the commander of the intervention units accompanied by approximately 500 troopers. Another 500 forces arrived at around midnight, in addition to around 400 soldiers from the National Guard.[17] The first statements by banned political parties were then issued in support of Bouazizi's cause. The statement issued by Al Nahda, which described the Bouazizi incident in detail and expressed sympathy for his family, spoke of the beginnings of a social uprising against unemployment, corruption, and inter-regional discrimination, and called for a national dialogue to prevent a crisis in the country.[18]

The Communist Workers' Party began its statement with a description of the protests that were continuing for the second day in Sidi Bouzid. Further, the party

16. Ibid.

17. Ibid., pp. 68–9.

18. See Azmi Bishara, *Tunisia's Glorious Revolution: The Structure of a Revolution and its Evolution through Its Daily Chronicles [al-thawrah at-tūnisiyah al-majīdah: bunyat al-thawrah wa ṣayrūratuhā min khilāl yawmiyātihā]*, (Beirut: ACRPS, 2012), pp. 390–1.

gave its statement a title taken from one of the protesters' slogans: 'Employment is a right, you band of thieves (*al-tashghīl istiḥqāq yā ʿiṣābat al-surrāq*)!'[19]

Day 3: 19 December 2010

The third day of the protests, 19 December 2010, represented a critical juncture. During the day, social and economic issues were addressed in the demonstrations held in front of the governorate headquarters, while at night the young protesters would burn tyres and clash with security forces. Dozens were arrested. According to Ali Bouazizi:

> In the Samarqand Café, a meeting place for all different hues of civil society with a garden and a large courtyard that allow for free discussion, two committees were formed. The first was the Committee for Citizenship and the Defense of Victims of Marginalization, which included all radical political parties, both legal and illegal, but without the buffoonish pro-Ben Ali parties. The committee also included a representative from the victim's family, the unemployed, the doctors' and lawyers' unions, and the Labor Union. The Islamists were not directly present due to the ban on Al Nahda, but some of the activists present were sympathetic to them. Nevertheless, ideological affiliations were not important because the demands were social in nature.
>
> The second committee was the Sidi Bouzid Committee, which was comprised of unionists and (legal) radical parties. After the committee was formed, we staged a protest march from the café to the governorate headquarters. Demanding the release of the detainees, we shouted: 'Defiance, defiance, till the prisoners are free!' and, 'Employment is a right, you band of thieves!' I participated in that protest, which was met with violence. We also focused on filming and documenting the event. Protests were typically followed by debates over the events of the day and the next day's program. Then we would upload the photos with Wael al-Aifi and put them on Facebook. My friend Noureddine al-Ouaidaidi, a producer for Al Jazeera, took these images directly from my Facebook account and broadcast them.
>
> As pressures mounted, the regime sent important figures originally from Sidi Bouzid, including Lamin Hafsaoui, General Director of the Tadamun Bank, and Mohamed Saad, a senior official in the UGTT. Tasked with pressuring me, Khalid al-Owayni, and several other influential activists, they approached my uncle hoping he would persuade me either to back down or to negotiate, but I didn't budge. My webpage was blocked at this point, so another page with a different name was set up. We were then able to disseminate images and video clips of events in Sidi Bouzid.[20]

19. *Tunisian Communist Workers' Party – al-Badil*, 18 December 2010, accessed on 14 December 2020, at: https://bit.ly/349xqnO.

20. Ibid.

These protests added to the controversy that dominated the Tunisian legal scene following the Tunisian Parliament's approval of a bill that would add a new clause to Article 61 of the Penal Code criminalizing acts that could be seen as harming the Tunisian economy abroad. The International Association for Human Rights, the International Organization against Torture, the Euro-Med Human Rights Network, Reporters without Borders, Amnesty International, and Human Rights Watch all agreed that this parliamentary action was intended to suppress media activities led by human rights defenders in Tunisia. Specifically, the objective of this legislation was to criminalize human rights advocacy on the pretext that such advocacy was harmful to negotiations between Tunisian authorities and the European Union over whether to grant Tunisia advanced status partnership.[21]

Due to the ongoing debates gripping Tunisia at the time, human rights groups dealt with Bouazizi's suicide from a legal angle, stressing that economic policies, criticism of which was prohibited by law at home and abroad, had triggered his decision to take his own life. Hence, the controversy stirred up by human rights organizations over the 'economic security law' shed important light on the protests in Sidi Bouzid.

On the third day, the Democratic Progressive Party issued a second statement in which it demanded formulation of a plan for democratic change to be implemented by 2014. Neither the activists on the ground, nor the parties, whether legal or banned, had begun thinking in terms of a revolution yet. Instead, the Democratic Progressive Party called for political life to be opened up and for the abolition of restrictions on the activities of parties and civil associations (especially in the media and the public spaces). Additionally, it called for a national convention on political and social reform with the participation of all party organizations and civil society associations in order to provide a path for transition to democracy by the year 2014.[22]

The Congress for the Republic Party also issued a statement signed by Moncef Marzouki calling for an end to the siege in Sidi Bouzid and demanding the declaration of a general strike. Marzouki stated,

> The events of Sidi Bouzid confirm anew that the country is in danger; therefore, it is the duty of all Tunisians and friends of freedom around the world to mobilize in order to save our country from the violence of an isolated clique that sees no option but further repression in order to continue on its path of looting and theft.[23]

21. *Turess*, 18 June 2010, accessed on 14 December 2020, at: http://bit.ly/2IYA0Wh.
22. See Bishara, *Tunisia's Glorious Revolution*, pp. 392–3.
23. See Ibid., pp. 394–6.

Day 4: 20 December 2010

Alternative communication tools played an important role in covering the spread of the protests and forming support committees in and outside of Sidi Bouzid. Initial footage of the events appeared on Al Jazeera brokered by digital activists, who also helped attract the attention of Tunisia's youth. Surprisingly, however, the protest movement that overtook Sidi Bouzid did not receive much union support above the provincial level; no unionist protest activities were organized. This state of affairs reflected a widely held belief in the regime's ability to contain this type of uprising with the tools of repression it had employed in previous uprisings.

> On the fourth day, they sent the Minister of Development to deliver a propaganda speech and promise major projects for Sidi Bouzid. The regime's supporters belonging to the décor parties were also mobilized in an attempt to contain the protest movement. However, the protests not only maintained their momentum, but escalated, now calling for the prosecution of the Trabelsi family (the family of Ben Ali's wife), chanting, 'Down with the 7 November regime!' ... We were aware of the authority's weakness and its empty promises. The problem lay in the ability to persist when faced with its repressive machinery. Since all institutions and establishments were under the control of the regime, the State could easily imprison you for life, kill you, or otherwise harm you. The highly trained security squads were employed to enter the neighborhoods on their motorcycles. Young people would string cables across the streets and provoke the security officers; once they tripped over them, the youth would attack them, kick them, and hurl stones at them. These ideas were completely the work of young protesters: during the day demonstrations were peaceful; and at night, hooded young men fought and clashed with the security forces.[24]

The expansion of the scope of the protests in the governorate of Sidi Bouzid was a turning point, with the districts of al-Meknes and Manzil Bouzian being the first areas to join the popular movement outside Sidi Bouzid. At the same time, there were early signs of coordination among the populations of the rebelling districts. In al-Meknes, confrontations between citizens and security forces continued until late in the evening. The security forces completely blocked the entrances to the city, and injuries were reported among the protesters, a number of whom attacked the Municipality and the National Guard headquarters. In Manzil Bouzian youth blocked the city's main thoroughfare with barricades.[25]

24. From the testimony of Ali al-Bouazizi.

25. *Turess*, 20 December 2010, accessed on 14 December 2020, at: https://bit.ly/3494P1Q.

Day 5: 21 December 2010

The regime tried to curb the popular uprising with promises that it would address the population's needs and resolve certain issues that had been sparking discontent among Tunisians for years. Steps such as these are usually accompanied by a propaganda campaign claiming that the population is satisfied with the steps taken by the regime. In a revolutionary situation, such manoeuvres can only contain some individuals, or at best some of the families of those harmed by official policies. One of the distinguishing features of the rise of a revolutionary mood is that the public begins to see such manoeuvres for what they are: mere attempts at containment, or partial concessions resulting from the weakness of the state which actually spur further protests.

> Despite young people's unresponsiveness to these ploys, they were received positively by older citizens, tens of thousands of whom began heading to provincial and social security administrations to receive the aid being offered by the government despite its demeaning nature. The aid offered by the State consisted of nothing but food packages: couscous, flour, and so forth, which was seen by many citizens, especially the youth, of Sidi Bouzid as an insult, as though their hometown were being treated as a disaster area. If anything, these tactics escalated events and further inflamed people's sentiments.[26]

Violence broke out at night and a police station was set on fire, an act that would be repeated during the Tunisian Revolution and on a much larger scale during the Egyptian Revolution. The uprising remained peaceful and non-violent for the most part but not entirely.[27] Peasant revolutions are usually armed, since they have no urban centres for civil rallies and no experience with non-violent protest. Besides, decision-makers are far away in the capital, and there is no way to affect them by political or popular pressure. An uprising of the periphery is not a peasant revolution; however, it is also remote from the centre and therefore, cannot influence the capital through civic pressure. People will, understandably, have meagre experience in civil political action, and many might wonder what good it will do them to stage quiet, peaceful demonstration in some remote, forgotten province.

The union's first reaction to the crisis began after a meeting between Sidi Bouzid's regional labour union and the governor, who agreed to the immediate release of thirty-four of the detainees, with the rest to be released within a month to two months at the most.[28] This did not help contain the crisis, and protests continued despite the security measures imposed by the Tunisian police, who

26. From the testimony of Lamine Al-Bouazizi.

27. The distinction we make is between peaceful and armed revolutions, and not between violent and non-violent.

28. *The Tunisian Observatory for Rights and Unionist Liberties – Tunis News*, 21 December 2010, accessed at: https://bit.ly/3qQql5r.

went so far as to assault journalists covering the events. When Tunisian security forces intensified their efforts in Sidi Bouzid, with relative success due to the help of ruling party supporters who assaulted the demonstrators, the protests escalated in the peripheral districts. One of these was the district of Jilmah, 26 kilometres from the centre of the governorate. Sources also reported clashes between security forces and protesters in the district of Sidi Ali Ben Aoun, where tear gas was used extensively.[29]

News agencies reported the use of slogans calling for employment, equal opportunities and development. The protests led to confrontations between police and demonstrators after protesters targeted police stations and the premises of the ruling party.[30] In this way, the protest movement moved beyond the centre of the Sidi Bouzid province on days 4 and 5. These events contributed to re-energizing the provincial centre in a feedback loop that was replicated in many regional centres and their environs. In addition to the spread of the protests, the response of the regional labour union in Sidi Bouzid impacted the course of the Tunisian Revolution as the movement evolved from localized protests to an uprising of an entire province.

Day 6: 22 December 2010

On day 6 of the protests, Hussain Naji, an unemployed 24-year-old, took his own life in front of the regional labour union in Sidi Bouzid by climbing atop an electric pole and hurling himself to the ground. Protests then renewed with even greater momentum in and around the district of Sidi Bouzid.[31] On this day, Sidi Bouzid saw the first concessions on the part of the security authorities; the Tunisian General Union reported that all those detained throughout the protests had been released.[32]

This scene was to be repeated many times during the Arab revolutions; protesters would interpret each concession by the authorities as a retreat, prompting them to raise the ceiling of their demands. As the protest movement gained momentum in the rebellious districts, people became bolder in challenging the security authority and its symbols, such as police stations, the premises of the ruling party, and governorate administrative buildings, which were now seen

29. *Facebook – Radio Kelma*, 21 December 2010, accessed on 14 December 2020, at: http://bit.ly/2LMwfo3.

Also see *Tunisian Communist Workers' Party – al-Badil*, 22 December 2010, accessed on 14 December 2020, at: https://bit.ly/37eE4Lq

30. *France 24*, 13 January 2011, accessed on 14 December 2020, at: https://bit.ly/2KwgiBS.

31. *France24*, 23 December 2010, accessed on 14 December 2020, at: http://bit.ly/3mt1YqX.

32. *Tunisian Communist Workers' Party – al-Badil*, 23 December 2010, accessed on 14 December 2020, at: https://bit.ly/34dphyF.

as icons of corruption, injustice, and inequitable development. Various news agencies reported confrontations between the people of al-Meknes and police forces during which a police vehicle was torched. Protesters threw stones and Molotov cocktails at the coordination committees affiliated with the ruling party, as well as the district and municipality administrative headquarters. In the Manzil Bouzian district 70 kilometres from Sidi Bouzid, protesters torched the district administration building and besieged the police station, leading security forces to escalate their use of tear gas grenades.[33]

On the same day, events spun out of control in Jilmah, where many participated in a demonstration calling for the right to work. The slogans used in protests were being unified across the governorate, headed by the slogan: 'Employment is a right, you band of thieves!' The following day numerous news agencies headlined their news reports with slogans that reflected the growing uniformity of the popular political mood across districts.

The most telling indication of progress in governorate-level coordination was the dissemination, by hundreds of Tunisian youth, of a list citing the names of the followers of the ruling party who had participated, on the evening of the sixth day, in the repression and persecution of the protesters.[34] This list can be found on early Facebook pages of the Tunisian Revolution. The same mechanism was also used in other Arab revolutions to such an extent that these lists, now coined 'lists of shame', included the names of the politicians, intellectuals, and artists who had shunned the revolution. The use of such lists was introduced by the Tunisian Revolution as a means of holding to account those who had participated in repression. In the age of social media, however, this tactic can deteriorate into a tool of incitement against anyone who holds different views.

On the sixth day, it became apparent that the protest movement had begun to spring up in neighbouring provinces, including the governorates of Gafsa and Kasserine, through union protests seeking to express solidarity with the people of Sidi Bouzid. These initial demonstrations were often led by white collar workers, among them lawyers who made an important contribution. In Kasserine, a group of fifteen lawyers dressed in their official courtroom attire conducted a sit-in, then marched to the headquarters of the local labour union in an expression of solidarity and support. The regional union in Kasserine also organized an assembly. By the end of day 6, peaceful demonstrations were being organized daily to protest the regime's actions and the socioeconomic conditions of the city's habitants.[35]

In parallel, unionists in the district of Bizerte organized a union assembly, while a committee was formed in the district of Jebiniana to support the people of Sidi Bouzid. Given the proximity of local labour union branches to their constituencies, they had no need to await directions from their headquarters in

33. *Kalimat Tunis*, 22 December 2010, accessed at: https://bit.ly/3gSKIdp.

34. Ibid.

35. 'Report by the National Fact-Finding Commission on Abuses and Violations Committed from 17 December 2010 to the End of its Mandate', p. 81.

the capital. In some cases, they also provided sanctuary for political activists from banned political parties.

Day 7: 23 December 2010

On the morning of day 7, the district of Sidi Bouzid witnessed the arrival of large security reinforcements from all over the country, and the roads leading to the governorate administration building were closed. Mohamed Nouri Jouini, Minister of Development and International Cooperation, tried to regain the initiative by making promises of local development and employment opportunities, while a union-led march in al-Meknes called for the right to work and the equitable distribution of development projects.

An analysis of the events of day 7 allows us to observe the mindset of the security establishment on how it was to deal with the nascent protest movement in the Sidi Bouzid governorate. A number of senior officials (district directors and governors) sent administrative memoranda to the imams of mosques requesting that they lower the volume of the *adhān* (the call to prayer) and refrain from broadcasting verses of the Quran,[36] and political security forces in the al-Monastir governorate launched an arrest campaign against 'religious youth', raiding a number of homes in the districts of Banbala, Khniss and al-Madyuni. A number of lawyers reported that the arrests were 'due to suspicions of their belonging to a Salafi group'.[37]

A state of confusion was clearly emerging in Tunisia's security establishment. The central government paid little attention to these events, leaving it to its security services to deal with the protest movement. On day 7, Tunisia signed new security agreements for 'Arab security cooperation',[38] while the day before, the state media had reported that Ben Ali welcomed the Tunisian Olympic swimmer Oussama Mellouli at the airport.[39] In short, the regime was acting as if everything was business as usual, and that the protest movement was a peripheral issue which, like earlier ones, could be easily managed.

The security forces focused their efforts, albeit fruitlessly, on quelling protesters who coordinated among each other using online social networks. Meanwhile, the uprising spread to all the districts of Sidi Bouzid and engaged the unionist movement throughout the governorate. At the same time, other governorates began to flare, starting with their urban centres. This movement took off once the unions in the regions decided to support their neighbouring province, Sidi Bouzid, and to raise the common demands and slogans.

36. *Turess*, 24 December 2010, accessed at: http://bit.ly/2LFuetz.

37. *Turess*, 24 December 2010, accessed on 14 December 2020, at: http://bit.ly/3r6eZKv.

38. *Kalimat Tunis Radio*, 23 December 2010, accessed on 14 December 2020, at: https://bit.ly/37ixOSM.

39. *Tunisian Ministry of Youth and Sports*, 22 December 2010, accessed at: https://bit.ly/37dz0a5.

In the village of Zannouch in the Gafsa governorate, two college-educated young men attempted to hold a symbolic protest in front of the municipal council, while a third young man set himself on fire.[40] Security reinforcements arrived in the village, resulting in clashes during which the protesters chanted: 'Employment is a right, you band of thieves!' and 'People's wealth is being stolen, and they languish behind bars (*filūs al-sha ͑b masru'īn, abnā' al-sha ͑b masjūnīn*)!'[41]

In summing up this first stage of the uprisings, we would do well to note the example of a young man by the name of Rushdi Harshani, who was fully involved in Tunisia's revolution even though, at that time, he was not affiliated with any political movement or party. Since his account is not dotted with politicized ideological language, his testimony offers a perspective on the interaction of communal, political, and unionist factors. Activists' boldness against security forces, and the role played in disseminating this sentiment through the media, helped to break down the barrier of fear and its debilitating effects. Under regimes that rely on people's fear of security forces and the negative repercussions of protest, breaking the barrier of fear can become a decisive factor in the struggle as it spreads and provides a model to be emulated by others. In describing the events of the first days in Sidi Bouzid, Harshani says:

> My role in the events was colored by a spirit of struggle due to both my family ties to Ali Bouazizi, who was involved in the Progressive Democratic Party, and the opposition environment in which I was brought up. After the flaring of protests in Sidi Bouzid, I joined the protest movement. In the beginning, matters were unclear to me. On the first day, I went to Ali and asked him who Mohamed Bouazizi was. He told me that the young man worked as a vegetable seller and that he was a friend. As far as I was concerned, this individual incident was the reason I entered into the fray of protest against injustice. I headed to the site of Bouazizi's suicide opposite the labor union office. His suicide inspired great sympathy and released the anger that was raging in the hearts of the locals. The news of Bouazizi's self-immolation spread and it was clear that the region was in shock. Sidi Bouzid is much longer than it is wide, so our houses extend along a single line, with my home facing the Samarkand Café, which served as the center of political debates in the city. The stores belonging to Ali, Wael and a cousin of mine are located close together along the same street as our house, which meant that we could communicate quickly without the use of telephones. We got busy filming and broadcasting events on the first day; we focused on the security forces, but they didn't notice because we were standing in front of our homes. . . . We were even able to seize the rifle of a soldier that was used to launch tear gas grenades. We also forced security forces to take off their uniforms and flee. The spread of these images increased confidence in the confrontations and helped to

40. *Tunisian Community Workers' Party – al-Badil*, 23 December 2010, accessed on 14 December 2020, at: https://bit.ly/3mlDfVo

41. Ibid.

> debunk the myth of the invincible security official; this was a symbolic victory, and we engaged in no acts of sabotage.

Rushdi is an example of an angry, aware young man who, being completely unknown to the security forces in the beginning, spontaneously joins political action:

> The events of Bouzian, where martyrs and injured fell, prompted us to head there immediately to film the victims inside the hospital and upload them on Facebook. In securing my movements, I took advantage of the fact that I had no record with the political security. Since our house was across from the governorate building, I did not participate in any violent acts, such as hurling stones and Molotov cocktails. Each of the neighborhoods in Sidi Bouzid, however, participated in its own way. These neighborhoods enjoyed a local specificity since their residents knew each other and were related. The family component in Sidi Bouzid played a prominent role along with that of the politicians, unionists, and parties.
>
> A neighborhood that won some renown during the Sidi Bouzid uprising was Barraqa. All its residents belonged to the Barquqi clan, and many were butchers. The Barraqa locals were thus experienced in fighting with knives and metal rods, and brave in challenging the security officers, giving little heed to tear gas. The same was true of the neighborhoods of Farjiya, al-Ibrahimiya, and al-Awasi (overcrowded neighborhoods in Tunisia known as 'the Smurfs' that were avoided by security even before the events), Wlad Belhadi, al-Khadra, al-Nur al-Gharbi, and al-Imarat. All these neighborhoods had committees organizing the protests, as well as correspondents who documented and disseminated news and images that could be re-broadcast.
>
> The protests evolved in Regueb, and I moved there myself; we could hear shots being fired, but stores were open and the city was divided into two halves: one confronting the security forces and the anti-riot police [Brigades de l'Ordre Public], and another that did not participate. In entering the city, we claimed to be strangers passing through.[42]

The Fact-Finding Commission reported that on 23 December, a high school teacher in al-Meknasi who had been a human rights activist and active in the opposition was abducted, abused and tortured by seven police officers from a different region. He was found the next day, unconscious, having been thrown out in the open by his abusers.

Nevertheless, the Tunisian Minister of the Interior issued an official statement claiming that the situation in Tunisia was normal and that the events in Sidi Bouzid were isolated incidents.

42. Rushdi Harshani, interview conducted in Doha for this book by two ACRPS researchers, Hamzeh al-Moustafa and Rami Salameh, 22 April 2011 in Doha.

Stage two: A popular uprising and the participation of unions and parties

In its second stage, the uprising expanded into several governorates. Each district was raising its demands and expressing its grievances. The political forces joining the condemnation campaign were also on the rise, with many of them calling for national investigation committees. It is not easy to determine when protests ceased to be mere acts of solidarity with Sidi Bouzid and turned into independent uprisings. What is certain is that there was a point of no return when the demonstrations ceased to be acts of protests against a specific practice of the regime, and became self-sustaining acts of protest against the regime as a whole. Determining the specific moment at which this shift took place is challenging because of the subtle dynamic between elements of solidarity and protest; at a certain point, however, specific factors gradually came to outweigh others. This is apparent not only in the nature of the protest activities but also in the political statements issued by the various political forces. Thus, for example, on 27 December, day 10 of the uprising, the Tunisian Communist Workers' Party called for escalation, saying,

> The Tunisian Communist Workers' Party reaffirms its support for growing movements that signal the possibility of an overwhelming popular uprising against exploitation, theft, corruption, and political tyranny. (The Party) considers it the responsibility of all the struggling forces today to unify the protest movement around a single central slogan: 'work, freedom, and national dignity,' and around clear social and political demands, so that sacrifices are not made in vain.[43]

Still, even the radical banned party which called upon people to unite around clear demands made no mention of a revolution that would have to be sustained until the regime was overthrown.

Day 8: 24 December 2010

Events in Sidi Bouzid escalated when unrest permeated all the cities in the province and security forces began using live ammunition. A group of seventy leftist and Arab nationalist lawyers,[44] who had been active in the protests since the first day, staged a demonstration in front of the local court. That same day, one protester was killed in Manzil Bouzian and others (one of whom died on 31 December) wounded. Police cars were torched, as was a train car. Other cities, such as Sfax, considered to be the largest labour city in Tunisia, witnessed union-organized

43. See Bishara, *Tunisia's Glorious Revolution*, pp. 405–6.

44. Fathi Lyasir mentioned them by name: Khaled Oweyna, Hatem Husni, Issam Hamduni, Moez as-Salhi, and Muhamad Munsiri. See Fathi Lyasir, *Lexicon of the Tunisian Revolution: 17 December 2010-23 October 2011 [Mu'jam al-Thawrah at-Tūnisiyah: 17 Dīsambir 2010-23 Uktūbar 2011]* (Tunisia: Muhammad Ali Publications, 2012), pp. 248–9.

solidarity vigils. In Manzil Bouzian, the protests had become so intense that the Ministry of Interior publicly admitted to the use of live ammunition, saying, 'Some officers were forced to use their weapons in legitimate self-defence, killing one of the assailants and injuring two others. A number of officers suffered burns, including two in a coma.'[45]

Kalimat Tunis radio (which wasn't aired in Tunisia and few people listened to it online especially those from the opposition parties and the well-educated Tunisians) reported on a massive demonstration that had gathered thousands of protesters in the streets of Manzil Bouzian only to be fired upon with live bullets, killing one protester. Demonstrators threw stones at security forces and torched three National Guard vehicles as security forces shot tear gas grenades and live ammunition at the demonstrators. Simultaneously, fire was set to the National Guard headquarters and one of the ruling party branches. Aided by a number of supporters from the ruling party, security forces raided homes using police dogs and arrested scores of young Tunisians accused of participating in the protests.[46] According to an Amnesty International report, the events in Manzil Bouzian were the turning point at which the regime decided to employ deadly force against the protesters, thus resulting in casualties,[47] which in turn catalysed the spread of the protests.

The spread of the protests to neighbouring provinces, Sfax in particular, happened in part because of Sidi Bouzid's inadequate health care infrastructure, which forced the locals to take their injured to nearby provinces.[48] The security services did not pursue the injured, nor did they prevent their transfer to neighbouring governorates for treatment, which broke the media blackout on the demonstrations. The people of Bouzian transported dozens of injured to Habib Bourguiba Hospital in Sfax, which later joined its fellow cities in the uprising, and as will be made clear below, had a decisive effect on the course of the revolution. Security forces attempted to besiege the entrances to the hospital in order to prevent visits to the wounded, but it was already too late for such measures.

45. *Turess*, 24 December 2010, accessed on 14 December 2020, at: https://bit.ly/3gPE5sz. The official pro-regime news agency appears to have erased its news archive from the time of the revolution. At any rate, an internet search is sufficient to retrieve the statement of the Ministry of Interior, which was presented by media outlets as the State's perspective on the events.

46. *Turess*, 24 December 2010, accessed on 14 December 2020, at: https://bit.ly/37idMrA.

47. 'Tunisia in Revolt: State Violence during Anti-Government Protests', *Amnesty International*, 1 March 2011, accessed on 14 December 2020, at: https://bit.ly/2JVISg2.

48. According to the National Institute of Statistics, Sidi Bouzid had only 441 hospital beds per 1,000 people in 2010 compared to 531 beds in Kasserine, 680 beds in Kairouan, and 1,679 beds in Sfax. See 'Statistical Yearbook – Tunisia 2006-2010', [al-Nashriyah al-Iḥṣā'iyah al-Sanawiyah li-Tunis 2006-2010], National Institute of Statistics NSI, p. 91, accessed at: https://bit.ly/3rkJNGX.

According to Najat Ben Mansour, a unionist who worked in Habib Bourguiba Hospital and reported events there to the media and legal organizations, the act of transferring the wounded and their families into Sfax was the trigger for the protest movement in the city.[49] Unionists at the hospital secretly transmitted information to the local unionist movement in Sfax, thereby breaking the media blackout that the political police had attempted to impose by besieging the hospital and banning visits.[50] No wonder, then, that protests broke out the next day in the northern town of Jebiniana led by hundreds of unionists who were in regular communication with the unionists of Sfax.[51]

At this juncture, parties which had a history of opposition but which had become part of the regime-sponsored 'democratic façade' also began to voice criticism against the state and express solidarity with Sidi Bouzid. The Movement of the Socialist Democrats issued a statement signed by the movement's leader, Ahmed Khaskhoussi, blaming the state for the violence and unemployment in Tunisia, even going so far as to cite the suppression of liberties as one of the main reasons for the popular uprising. A discrepancy here emerged in the stances of these political parties. For instance, the Green Party statement issued by its leader Munji al-Khamasi on 27 December spoke of 'mutual violence' between the protesters and the security forces. Hence, despite claiming to understand the hardships facing citizens, the Green Party did not identify the political regime as the culprit, preferring instead to blame the bureaucracy.

Day 9: 25 December 2010

By day 9, the protests had finally reached the capital city Tunis, where hundreds of unionists and activists gathered in Mohamed Ali Square, the central headquarters of the Tunisian Labour Union, to express their solidarity with the people of Sidi Bouzid and to protest security forces' use of live ammunition against the protesters. Starting in Mohamed Ali Square, demonstrators marched down al-Munji Salem Street. Union leaders made speeches in which they called for educated youth to be guaranteed decent-paying employment.[52] Security forces set up a cordon around the protest in order to prevent the demonstrators from taking their march to Habib Bourguiba Street; they also prevented a number of national figures – including Ali Larayedh, the official spokesperson and one of the main leaders of the banned Al Nahda Movement,[53] and Abdelkrim Harouni, secretary-general of the 'Freedom

49. Najat Ben Mansour, part of an interview conducted by ACRPS, 13 October 2011.

50. Ibid.

51. Ibid.

52. Al-Ḥiwār al-Mutamaddin, 25 December 2010, accessed on 14 December 2020, at: https://bit.ly/3mnjRaq.

53. He served as interior minister, and as prime minister, for a short time in the first post-revolution government.

and Justice Movement' (as well as a leading figure in Al Nahda) – from reaching Mohamed Ali Square.[54]

The protests' arrival in the capital was a pivotal moment in the course of events. The unionists' activity in the capital put the UGTT in a position which forced it either to respond to the unionists' demands or remain in alliance with the regime, especially after the opposition parties began to participate. Moreover, the spread of protests into Tunis, even on a limited scale, contributed to the increase of protests throughout Tunisia's provinces.

The early chapters of this book stressed how one of the main development imbalances in Third World countries relates to inequality: unequal distribution of income, unequal distribution of the fruits of development, and unequal growth among different regions. The widening developmental gap between centres and peripheries replicates the global split between North and South. In other words, centre–periphery polarization has become a national dilemma in post-colonial states. Furthermore, the growth of parasitic classes within these countries' ruling regimes, with their family monopolies and extensive cliental networks, causes them to look increasingly like systems of 'internal occupation'.

International organizations in the meantime have lauded Tunisia and its growth rates, as well as the government's adherence to instructions from the IMF and the World Bank with regard to lowering the budget deficit, balancing the budget, controlling inflation, and spurring growth. However, the broadening gap between regions, and the poverty and marginalization of vulnerable groups, have doomed a large portion of the populace to psychological, economic, and social insecurity. The agendas of international institutions have led to the formation of nominally patriotic local elites that quickly turn into 'bridgeheads' for these institutions into local societies, or a modernized form of quasi-colonial instruments as part of the process of globalization.

As the protest movement spread into Tunis, a curfew was imposed on Sidi Bouzid while most of the governorate's districts were besieged by security forces. Given the governorates' weak infrastructure, the regime used the city of Sfax as a base from which to transport hundreds of detainees from the province of Sidi Bouzid into state prisons. The locals also continued to transport their wounded to the Habib Bourguiba Hospital in Sfax.[55] However, the regime's plan to use the city as a security base to contain the province of Sidi Bouzid backfired when Sfax itself rose up in protest.

Tunisia then witnessed a spate of unionist strikes,[56] each of which championed its own demands. It was as if the general uproar provided an opportunity for every

54. *Reuters*, 25 December 2010, accessed on 14 December 2020, at: http://bit.ly/3nGNZiR.

55. *Turess*, 25 December 2010, accessed on 14 December 2020, at: http://bit.ly/37uL5bf

56. See the archives of the pro-opposition Tunisian news agencies such as Kalimat Tunis, and the international news agencies, such as Reuters.

sector to express its own grievances. The barrier of fear was steadily crumbling throughout the republic.

In dealing with the revolution, the Tunisian government resorted to what it deemed most effective: a crackdown with the use of massive security reinforcements to quell the protests while carrying out an aggressive campaign of home raids and arrests against those deemed the leaders of the protests. The government also hunted down union leaders who, once put on trial, were often charged with 'forming a gang', 'joining a criminal organization', 'sabotaging property' and other crimes that carried long prison sentences.

The 'security solution' also came with a complete media blackout, with authorities preventing all Tunisian and foreign journalists from reaching the sites of the unrest. In parallel with the security solution, the Tunisian government tried to address some of the protesters' demands, admitting that the youth's demands for employment were legitimate and declaring a comprehensive, nation-wide development project. In the second official reaction, the Minister of Development and International Cooperation Mohamed Mohamed Nouri Jouini stated that although protesters' demands were legitimate, they did not justify 'the use of violence in the protests'. The minister reiterated the usual clichés calling for dialogue to formulate solutions to the existing problems.[57] However, his statement reflected the absence of a clear or unified strategy for addressing the root causes of the upheaval. Indeed, it was a hollow proposal, as it neither identified the stakeholders nor did it set out a specific agenda for the dialogue being suggested.

Day 10: 26 December 2010

In Sfax, hundreds of unionists and activists gathered in support of the people of Sidi Bouzid, and the union's headquarters was surrounded by security forces that forcefully prevented demonstrators from taking to the street.[58] In the centre of Kairouan governorate, a protest march called for the siege on Sidi Bouzid to be lifted. Meanwhile, the regional union in the centres of the provinces of Nabeul and Medinine organized protest gatherings at the union headquarters, condemning the state's social policies and corruption.[59]

In the centre of the Siliana governorate, *al-Badil* reported that over 200 unionists and political activists had gathered to support the people of Sidi Bouzid. Demonstrators attempted to take to the street but were prevented by security forces, prompting them to end their gathering with a singing of the national anthem.[60] However, as the coming days would show, the protests of Siliana in the

57. *Al-Jazeera Net*, 26 December 2010, accessed at: https://bit.ly/3mmcWOI.

58. *Kalimat Tunis Radio,* 26 December 2010, accessed at: https://bit.ly/37iFp3K.

59. Ibid.

60. *Facebook Page – al-Badil*, 27 December 2010, accessed on 14 December 2020, at: http://bit.ly/2KhlZUa.

northwest multiplied and took place outside of the unionist cadres.[61] In parallel, the centre of the Sousse governorate witnessed a massive gathering in front of the regional labour union headquarters, demanding an end to the siege of Sidi Bouzid and the release of all detainees.

Day 11: 27 December 2010

Protests moved to the centre of Kasserine raising the slogans: 'Down with the Destour Party; down with the butcher of the people!' and, 'No to the Trabelsis, who pillaged the budget!' Soon thereafter, the other districts in the governorate also rose up, led by Firyanah, Thala and Sbeitla.[62]

Mohamed Ali Square in the capital city Tunis witnessed a sit-in in which hundreds of union activists participated. It was organized by the General Union for Social Funds, the General Association for Post and Communications, the General Union for Secondary Education, the General Union for Youth and Childhood, the General Union for General Practitioners, Pharmacists, and Dentists, and the General Union for Primary Education.[63] Hundreds of security officers surrounded the UGTT headquarters, blocking all the paths leading to the neighbourhood.[64]

At this stage the capital witnessed only gatherings and demonstrations of political and union activists. Demonstrators chanted slogans holding the government responsible for the social and economic situation; they had also begun challenging the extension of the presidential term, and sang the national anthem at several intervals, with protesters inviting security forces to join them rather than obey orders to quell the protests.[65]

Day 12: 28 December 2010

Before Ben Ali's first speech, specialized security forces, utilizing relatives of Mohamed Bouazizi who belonged to the ruling party, tried to negotiate with Bouazizi's mother and brothers. Leaders from the UGTT also participated in the negotiations in the hope of settling the matter financially. Bouazizi's mother was contacted by people linked to the ruling party, and told that if she agreed to meet the president, her son would be spared prosecution after recovery, and be granted

61. See notes on the section regarding day 22.

62. *al-Badil*, 17 December 2010, accessed on 15 December 2020, at: https://bit.ly/3oVtCyt.

63. Ibid.

64. Ibid.

65. Ibid. For a video of the sit-in in Mohammad Ali Square, see 'Manifestation-Place-Tunis – Mohamed-Ali-solidarity-avec – SidiBouzid-Lundi-27-12-2010', *YouTube video by the Tunisitunisia*, 27 December 2010, accessed on 15 December 2020, at: https://bit.ly/37ixC6a.

a decent post in the regional union.[66] After Ben Ali's overthrow, she said that she initially refused but eventually gave in to pressure from Tunisian security. Ben Ali promised to transport her son to a hospital in France and take care of the family financially.[67] The Tunisian president then visited Mohamed Bouazizi in the hospital.[68] This was a badly timed and mistaken move, however, as the issue was no longer merely a matter of a suicide attempt but had been overshadowed by far larger concerns.

In an attempt to employ what he may have considered political capital garnered through his choreographed visit to Bouazizi, Ben Ali made his first speech, broadcast on state television. In the speech he warned against violent protests, which he judged to be unacceptable and harmful to the country's image, and threatened the 'troublemakers' with harsh punishment. To this he added promises to create new job opportunities in the country. The speech was prefaced by images of the president's visit to Mohamed Bouazizi in a hospital in Ben Arous. Bouazizi's family was called to Tunis, along with the mother of Hussain Naji, who had also taken his own life during the events, and the father of al-Amari, who had been killed in Bouzian. In short, it was a propagandistic counterattack intended to promote the image of the regime and to address what the regime thought to be the origin of the problem, namely, an individual young man's self-immolation. However, the incident could neither be handled as an isolated event, nor was it the reason for the uprising. It had been merely a trigger that was now a symbol: a symbol of the public's rejection of social and economic deprivation, and of a yearning for human dignity that could not be defused by nominal gestures.

In retrospect, official media coverage of the visit was a tactical error, since it revealed both the significance of the upheaval taking place in the country, and the degree of concern felt by the regime,[69] which stood in stark contrast to the disregard for events that had been displayed in the official media up to that time. Offers of money were made to the martyrs' families, some of whom declined the payoff. From the perspective of the regime, the crisis had arisen entirely from the fact that a human tragedy had been exploited by vicious extremists for political gain. Hence, the regime deemed itself to have resolved the problem amicably with the victim's family, while those supposedly using this tragedy in order to stir up unrest for political purposes were trespassers to be dealt with harshly. This version

66. *Turess*, 29 December 2010, accessed on 15 December 2020, at: http://bit.ly/34n4skr.

67. *al-Sharq al-Awsat Newspaper*, 8 February 2011, accessed at: https://bit.ly/386wGAT.

68. The visit of deposed President Ben Ali to the young Bouazizi can be seen here: 'Tunisie: chomage et emeutes. Idem a la France!' *YouTube video by La Verite N'est Plus Ailleurs*, 30 December 2010, accessed on 15 December 2020, at: https://bit.ly/2Wl4uoB.

69. Edward Webb, for example, believes that Ben Ali's media apparatus made a huge mistake by broadcasting images of Ben Ali's visit to Bouazizi, as Tunisians were now aware of how fearful the regime had become, which in turn intensified the protests. See Edward Webb, *Media in Egypt and Tunisia: From Control to Transition?* (New York: Palgrave Macmillan, 2014), pp. 67–8.

of events reveals both the simplistic mentality underlying the regime's approaches and actions, and the naivety of those who believed that such a narrative would be credible to the public.

Ben Ali's defiant speech did nothing but fan the flames of protest and increase the coordination among the protesters across the various provinces. Demonstrators took to launching protests in desolate regions that were far from the provincial centres in order to weaken and disperse the efforts of the security forces. Video footage broadcast on social media websites showed serious violations being committed by the security forces besieging the rebellious areas, with police brutally raiding homes, stealing money, vandalizing property, and using indiscriminate violence. The videos also provided evidence of torture and violence against protesters and damage to private property.

The speech having failed to achieve its objective, the regime then attempted to distract from the crisis by focusing on the media. The Tunisian Parliament criticized Al Jazeera's coverage of the protests, claiming that the coverage was an attempt to 'besmirch the country's reputation and misguide the public in order to sow chaos and sedition . . . for questionable aims, promote false claims, and provide a platform for enemies to damage Tunisia by playing on emotions and spreading rumours aimed at spreading anarchy and destabilizing the country'.[70]

A note is in order here to clarify this matter. Al Jazeera, and to a lesser degree, the Arabic-speaking 'France24' channel, certainly played a prominent role in disseminating the news of the Tunisian Revolution. Media reports were, of course, not neutral but expressed clear sympathy with the protesters, particularly given the fact that the media relied on images and footage shot by the protesters and sent directly to media outlets and their websites. These channels also broadcast testimonies by eyewitnesses. Al Jazeera had been banned from reporting directly from Tunisia since 1996, and was thus free from the restrictions imposed on media correspondents functioning under the watchful eye of the regime, while on the other hand, it was forced to rely on reports of activists that were not always accurate. Furthermore, because of the strict censorship of their local media, Tunisians were forced to rely on reports from a foreign TV channel to find out what was happening in their own country. Whatever one's view of the 'professionalism' of this new style of reporting, it undeniably contributed to making the Revolution a major news item for Arab audiences throughout the Middle East and, indeed, the entire world. In addition, it highlighted the historic success of the Tunisian grassroots in removing a tyrant, thereby implying that other peoples of the Arab world might be able to do the same for themselves.[71]

70. *Al Jazeera Net*, 28 December 2010, accessed on 15 December 2020, at: https://bit.ly/3ntjpco.

71. This explains why a number of rulers and politicians, even academics, in other Arab countries quickly and repeatedly distanced themselves from the popular uprisings in Tunisia and Egypt.

It had long been clear that due to a common language and the media's desire to expand, Arab countries and media companies had created a pan-Arab media market in the region that went far beyond narrow political motives and specific nationalities, be they Egyptian, Saudi Arabian, Lebanese or Qatari. It was also clear that the ruling Arab regimes did not fear foreign (non-Arabic) media reporting on the Arab revolutions as much as they feared Arabic-speaking channels, which functioned as effective alternatives to censored media in their respective countries. While the coverage of other Arab satellite channels remained reserved due to the fear that unrest might spread into their own countries, Al Jazeera offered itself as a platform that had situated itself closer to public opinion than to ruling regimes. Eventually, the other channels were also forced to join the coverage, even if less extensively, in order to keep their audiences. This was also seen in the Egyptian Revolution, where Al Jazeera took the lead with its comprehensive live coverage while Arabic-speaking channels financed by other Gulf countries joined the coverage belatedly and, worse still, took the opposite stance, as each of them was influenced by the political agenda of the country that hosted or owned the channel in question.[72]

There is a central dimension to Arab revolutions which goes beyond similarities in the structures of ruling regimes, the suffering of the people, and comparable aspirations, namely: identification. That is to say, news from other Arab countries carries an emotional charge and motivating force that simply do not exist when an Arab audience follows news relating to non-Arab countries. Rather than viewing a protest as a distant event that would be impossible to imagine for themselves (as in the case of protests in Europe, Russia or some other distant location), Arab viewers may identify with protests in a neighbouring Arab country in such a way that they feel motivated and empowered to engage in similar protests themselves.

On the day of Ben Ali's speech, union-led protests in the city centre of the Kasserine governorate were accompanied by massive demonstrations in districts such as Firyanah and Foussana. In Firyanah, large demonstrations plied the city's streets, while the protesters began a sit-in in front of the district administration building, shouting slogans demanding their share of development and condemning corruption. That evening, the escalating protests were met with tear gas grenades and live ammunition.[73] Meanwhile, a video clip was posted on Facebook showing a demonstration in Foussana calling for democracy, freedom, and dignity.[74]

72. This is why things were different in the case of the Libyan and Syrian Revolutions, where Al Jazeera faced competition from other channels, such as the Saudi-financed al-Arabiya.

73. *Kalimat Tunis Radio*, 28 December 2010, accessed at: https://bit.ly/3mimlXD. See also: *Tunisia Communist Workers' Party – al-Badil*, 28 December 2010, accessed on 16 December 2020, at: https://bit.ly/34jDURc.

74. *Facebook*, 28 December 2010, accessed on 16 December 2020, at: https://bit.ly/37mgs7L.

Day 13: 29 December 2010

On day 13, Tunisian prime minister Mohamed Ghannouchi announced the president's decision to appoint new ministers of communication, commerce, youth and sports, and religious affairs. The same day, clashes in the city of Siliana were followed by the arrest of forty young men by security forces.

Curiously, although the al-Monastir governorate witnessed no protests worth mentioning, Saeed Yusuf, the union's secretary, declared on this day that he would not organize such protests, which, he claimed, 'disturb public order and cause riots'.[75] Al-Monastir's failure to participate in the uprising might be explained by the infiltration of the local unionist movement by pro-regime figures, particularly Saeed Yusuf, who was also an MP representing the ruling party. Later, Yusuf was physically assaulted by demonstrators, an event that was documented in a video clip,[76] though this assault should not detract from the fact that the Tunisian Revolution was a revolution of the periphery that was joined not only by the poor but by political and civil activists from the urban middle class. Al-Monastir is an economically developed urban centre from which many of the Bourguiba regime's elite hail. Not surprisingly, unemployment rates in the province – ranging between 5 and 9 per cent according to the National Institute of Statistics – are among the lowest in Tunisia, with little difference between the governorate's centre and periphery. It is also classified, according to ESCR standards, as having a lower than average rate of absolute deprivation, indicating that there is an inverse relationship between the readiness of parties and unions to lead protests and the economic and social well-being of their local bases; of this, al-Monastir is a clear case in point.

Day 14: 30 December 2010

As part of a reshuffle that included the appointment of three new governors, Ben Ali sacked the governor of Sidi Bouzid. A day before, Libya had announced the lifting of administrative restrictions on Tunisians wishing to travel and work in Libya, and Gaddafi had ordered that Tunisians be treated as Libyan citizens. This decision to support the Tunisian regime reflected Gaddafi's fear that the protests would spread into his own backyard, especially through Libya's east, where resentment against Gaddafi was already festering. This decision sharply contrasted with the actions of the Libyan authorities just two months prior to the uprisings, when Tunisia's Ben Gardane region had witnessed dissent by Tunisian workers at the Ras al-Jdir border crossing after the Libyan authorities issued a decree limiting commercial exchange between the two countries through the ports of Sfax and Benghazi.

In the meantime, the siege on Jebiniana, one of the largest districts of Sfax, continued for the second day. In those two days, the security forces had chased young protesters through residential neighbourhoods, forced café owners to close

75. *Turess*, 29 December 2010, accessed on 16 December 2020, at: http://bit.ly/38cIWzR.
76. 'Tunis First', *Facebook*, 29 April 2011, accessed at: https://bit.ly/2ISsU5L.

their shops, imposed a curfew on the residents and cut off the city's electricity supply.[77] Jebiniana represented the link between the centre of the Sfax governorate and the Mahdia governorate, which was also witnessing unionist movements and popular unrest. Once the protest movement strengthened in the central provinces and expanded eastward, the regime had begun employing Sfax as a base of action for the forces repressing the protest movement due to the city's security infrastructure, which included detention centres, prisons and security equipment. Meanwhile, the protest movement in Mahdia, Kairouan and Gabes was in the process of turning into a popular uprising as it had in Sidi Bouzid, which was completely outside of regime control. This would signify that the central seat of authority in the region – Sfax – had been surrounded by protesting regions and could soon fall into the hands of the revolution.[78]

Day 15: 31 December 2010

On this day, lawyers rose up as a united front throughout Tunisian provinces, as they themselves represented one of the segments of Tunisian society most affected by the practices of the former regime given the rampant corruption in Tunisian courts. In addition to lawyers' role in the uprisings of the periphery, they made a significant contribution by holding protest actions in cities that had not taken part in the revolution.

The Freedom and Justice Movement[79] announced that police had raided the lobby of the courthouse in the suburb of Sidi Ḥusayn and assaulted the lawyers who had assembled in solidarity with the protest movements. The courthouse was surrounded by a large force headed by figures from the political police, and the neighbourhood was sealed off from the rest of the city. In the capital city Tunis, lawyers were prevented from entering the Hall of Justice, and when they gathered in front of the Lawyers' Association, they were shoved, kicked, and beaten with batons by security forces, with many suffering serious injuries.[80] A video posted on a Tunisian Facebook page captured footage of the lawyers assembled in the Tunisian capital calling: 'Ben Ali, you coward. . . . A lawyer is not to be insulted (*Ben ʿAlī yā jubān, al-muḥāmī lā yuhān*)!'[81]

The organization's statement also noted that a number of attorneys in the north-western Jendouba district had been prevented from entering the courthouse,

77. *Kalimat Tunis Radio*, 30 December 2010, accessed at: https://bit.ly/3akgrmz

78. This scenario would materialize on the following 12 January.

79. An association founded as a human rights organization in 2009 by Muhammad al-Nuri, an Al Nahda activist, after his return from exile in France.

80. *Facebook Page – The Freedom and Justice Movement*, 31 December 2010, accessed on 16 December 2020, at: http://bit.ly/3r5woDc.

81. 'Violent Clashes Today in Tunis', [*muṣādamāt ʿanīfah al-yawm fī Tūnis al-ʿāṣimah*], *Facebook – The people of Tunisia Are Setting Themselves on Fire, Mr. President,* 28 December 2010, accessed on 16 December 2020, at: https://bit.ly/3gPKPql.

and that some had been abducted. One of these was Rabih el-Kharayfi, a lawyer and member of the political bureau of the Democratic Progressive Party who was kidnapped by individuals wearing plain clothes, then abandoned in a neighbourhood on the city's periphery. In Gafsa, lawyers were attacked and besieged inside the city's courthouse, while in Bizerte, the courthouse was surrounded, thus preventing its attorneys from holding their solidarity sit-in. Similarly, political opposition activists, human rights activists and unionists who gathered at the regional labour union were attacked, with some of those present reporting grave injuries. In Mahdia, attorney Hisham al-Qarfi was assaulted. Four young men from the city of Um al-Arais were prosecuted in Gafsa for setting fire to a government vehicle and attempting to damage street property. In Sfax, video footage was taken of a large demonstration of lawyers chanting the famous verse: 'If the people desire to live, fate must respond.'[82]

The Unionist Democratic Federation, a décor party headed by Ahmad al-Inubli, issued its second statement since the outbreak of the revolution, placing responsibility for the failure of the development plans not on the ruling regime but on the regional authorities. The Federation claimed that the authorities were not implementing the central development plans and that the failed Tunisian media was incapable of facing the challenges of the foreign media.[83]

Day 16: 1 January 2011

The ruling RCD issued a statement in response to the criticisms of the French Socialist Party, which it accused of interfering in Tunisia's domestic affairs and falling for 'media disinformation' after it criticized the violent repression of the protests in Sidi Bouzid. The RCD labelled these claims as untrue, adding that 'Tunisia is a sovereign state that takes lessons from nobody on matters of development and democracy'.[84]

The banned Al Nahda Movement, many of whose supporters and activists were arrested, issued a statement condemning the 'unjust political trial' and the subsequent six-month sentence handed down against the Al Nahda activist Saleh Abdullah. On the ground, security forces continued to surround the district of Jebiniana after clashes with protesters in the city, resulting in more arrests.[85] On that day, the nation-wide protest movement began to spread in the centres of the provinces of Siliana and al-Kef, where protests called for the right to work, a sign

82. 'The people of Tunisia Are Setting Themselves on Fire, Mr. President', *Facebook*, 28 December 2010, accessed at: https://bit.ly/3aaFkkG.

83. 'The Sidi Bouzid protests reveal the shortcomings of Tunisian parties', *DP Press*, 31 December 2010, accessed at: https://bit.ly/3ahFYgq.

84. *Kalimat Tunis Radio*, 1 January 2011, accessed at: https://bit.ly/34h4L0c.

85. *Turess*, 1 January 2011, accessed on 16 December 2020, at: http://bit.ly/2Ku23NL.

of the escalation of protests in the north-western region.[86] As students in schools and high schools began to take part in the protests, the RCD organized meetings in branches of the Ministry of Education in order to 'decisively confront those attempting to manipulate the students and increase the role of RCD members in exposing the names and characters of enemies and suspects'.[87]

Day 17: 2 January 2011

News of Mohamed Bouazizi's death spread, which intensified the protests in the provinces after a relative lull in previous days. On this day, Amer Ben Mohammed Fatteh also died in Gafsa from the burns he had inflicted on himself on 27 December after losing his job as a firefighter.

The regime tried frantically to prevent protests in downtown Sfax as security forces cracked down on a unionist solidarity gathering in front of the regional labour union.[88] A unionist from Sfax filmed the secretary-general of the regional labour union refusing to participate and 'threatening those present if they disobeyed his instructions', while relying on a number of regime supporters shouting pro-regime slogans. It should also be mentioned that many of the protesters were school students, six of whom were arrested on that day.[89] Security forces also detained the father and uncle of a young man who had been shot during the Manzil Bouzian clashes and taken to the Sfax hospital.[90]

Meanwhile, sieges and chases continued in Jebiniana, and political police began visiting students' homes and forcing them to sign pledges not to participate in protests.[91] A similar incident was also reported in one of the cities of the Mahdia governorate, where a number of RCD officials in the al-Shabba district forced a number of students, along with their parents, to go to the house of one of the officials. Once there, they were warned not to engage in any political activities; some of those present were forced to sign a pledge stating that they would not participate in protests in their schools but would instead call upon Ben Ali to run for another presidential term in 2014.[92]

By this time the regime was attuned to the possibility that students would rise up in Sfax and the surrounding provinces, particularly given the fact that the end

86. 'The people of Tunisia Are Setting Themselves on Fire, Mr. President', *Facebook*, 28 December 2010, accessed at: https://bit.ly/3r4aTCw.

87. During a meeting of the General Assembly on 29 December 2011, the RCD called for the mobilization of its supporters in order to confront the popular protests See *Al-Hiwar Net*, 1 January 2011, accessed on 16 December 2020, at: https://bit.ly/2K7ekbg.

88. *Kalimat Tunis Radio*, 2 January 2011, accessed at: https://bit.ly/3oUg0DC.

89. *The Nawat blog*, 2 January 2011, accessed at: https://bit.ly/3p9qPC3.

90. *Turess*, 2 January 2011, accessed on 16 December 2020, at: http://bit.ly/2KcXIic.

91. 'The people of Tunisia are setting themselves on fire, Mr. President', *Facebook*, 28 December 2010, accessed at: https://bit.ly/37oWdGq.

92. *Kalimat Tunis Radio*, 2 January 2011, accessed at: https://bit.ly/2Wix5L0.

of the vacation and the students' return to school was nearing. Extraordinary measures were thus taken to preserve the city, whose uprising would constitute a crushing blow to the regime in the country's central and southern regions.

Day 18: 3 January 2011

The Tunisian Communist Workers' Party issued a statement declaring a popular revolution to change the regime and establish a democratic system. The statement also lauded the 'steadfastness of the masses' who had refused to be fooled by Ben Ali's promises of reform. Nevertheless, the party stopped short of predicting specific developments. Well aware that this was a leaderless popular uprising, the statement called for the formation of a unified political leadership for the national opposition.[93]

When news of Bouazizi's death emerged, a wave of popular unrest broke out in various districts in Kasserine, most notably in Thala. On the day when students were scheduled to return to school after their winter break, clashes broke out when a peaceful demonstration staged by primary and secondary school students was met with tear gas bombs and batons.[94] Violent confrontations ensued, and official headquarters of the ruling RCD were torched.[95] By this time, protests were spreading into the centres of the Jendouba, Baja, al-Kef and Siliana provinces in northwest Tunisia, primarily in the form of sit-ins by unemployed college graduates. The authorities received some of the protesters and ordered some employers to accept their job applications 'in an attempt to contain the anger and postpone the repercussions of the country's social crisis'.[96]

Samir Kouka, a French language teacher who had participated in the first day of protests in the Siliana governorate, summed up the situation as follows:

> The protests began in the governorate of Siliana on 2 January when the locals learned that the authorities had appointed numerous people from Sidi Bouzid to educational positions in our province. This prompted dozens of unemployed young men to head toward City Hall and demand equity in employment, as well as the appointment of Siliana teachers in other regions. However, the Governor and the Mayor responded with violence, to which the protesters reacted by assaulting City Hall.[97]

Given the immaturity of the union movement in Siliana and Jendouba – a result of the scarcity of institutions in these agricultural regions – the regime was able

93. See Bishara, *Tunisia's Glorious Revolution*, pp. 415–17.

94. 'Report by the National Fact-Finding Commission', p. 97.

95. *Turess*, 3 January 2011, accessed on 16 December 2020, at: http://bit.ly/3nuxDJX.

96. *Turess*, 3 January 2011, accessed on 16 December 2020, at: http://bit.ly/2Khyqzn.

97. Samir Kouka, interview conducted through Skype by the researcher at ACRPS Hani Awwad, 20 October 2011.

to infiltrate it without difficulty. Later, on day 22 of the revolution, the protests turned violent given the lack of union organization or leadership in these two governorates.

On the same day, students returned to their schools and colleges, with several experiencing confrontations with the security forces. Various media outlets reported that primary and secondary school students in Kasserine, Gabes, Gafsa and Mahdia had vocally supported the people of Sidi Bouzid, condemning corruption and demanding freedom.[98] Protests by teenage students succeeded in embarrassing the security apparatus, since the regime could not suspend their classes, as that would contradict the regime's claim that state institutions, including educational institutes, were functioning as normal. The regime also realized, however, that the return of students would strengthen the protest movement, as predicted by Tunisian reports.[99]

Not yet being responsible for supporting families or having entered the job market, high school students would be unlikely to protest unemployment and poverty but would be more inclined to raise slogans calling for freedom and an end to corruption. Consequently, the regime found it difficult to contain their protests with promises of reform and resorted to violence instead.[100]

Day 19: 4 January 2011

Confrontations continued in the city of Thala. Events quickly spun out of control as protesters torched the premises of the RCD, the city hall, the police station and numerous police vehicles, prompting security forces to call for reinforcements from the governorates of Sousse and Mahdia. In Kasserine, a large protest marched through the city streets, with the security forces resigned simply to watch after having failed to disperse the demonstration.[101] Kasserine eventually witnessed a decline in security enforcements as the regime became aware that it could not afford to withdraw security personnel from Sfax, which was of greater strategic importance than Kasserine. Thus, instead of calling for reinforcements from the central and eastern governorates, the regime began confronting protesters with live ammunition.

Protests on this day were concentrated in the governorate of Sfax, where students staged strikes in some of the city's colleges and marched in demonstrations. Security forces proceeded to arrest those who participated in college protests and

98. *Kalimat Tunis Radio*, 3 January 2011, accessed at: https://bit.ly/3mmLNvm.

99. *Turess*, 31 December 2011, accessed on 16 December 2020, at: http://bit.ly/3r8z431.

100. The exception was in the student demonstrations in the poverty belts surrounding the Tunisian capital after 20 January 2011, where the slogans voiced by the students focused on the right to work and condemning poverty. The difference lies in the fact that most protesters were college students who had moved into Tunis's poor neighbourhoods while pursuing their educations and who needed to work to support themselves.

101. *Turess*, 4 January 2011, accessed on 16 December 2020, at: http://bit.ly/2WricGk.

summoned their parents. Strikes took place at the colleges in Jebiniana, al-Amira, al-Hinsha and al-Huzuq and spread to a lesser extent into some cities in the Baja governorate, which borders on Sfax.[102] With the escalation of student protests, most of which gripped the central and eastern regions, the Tunisian uprising began to spread among the middle classes, exposing the woes of an economic class whose needs were not being met by government policies.

On this day Mosbah ben Amara Johar died of self-inflicted burns after the commissioner of the city of Métlaoui refused to meet him and threatened to arrest him instead.

Day 20: 5 January 2011

The funeral procession for Muhammad Bouazizi in Sidi Bouzid took place under tight security. As massive protests began in the Kasserine governorate, particularly in the Thala district, and as student demonstrations intensified in Sfax and its environs, student protests continued in a number of provinces, including Sidi Bouzid, al-Kef, Sousse, Kebili and Gafsa.[103]

On the same day, the Renewal Movement (formerly the Tunisian Communist Party) issued a statement signed by its president, Ahmad Ibrahim, calling on the government to engage in dialogue and reform, thereby making clear that the party did not embrace the idea of overthrowing the regime.[104]

Day 21: 6 January 2011

The lawyers held a nation-wide strike. In Sfax, they went so far as to refuse to receive a delegation from the regional labour union headed by its secretary-general.[105] Unionists from Sfax's Justice Department expelled their secretary-general following his condemnations of the protest movements and his attempts to contain union demonstrations on day 17 of the revolution.[106] Similar positions were adopted by the various regional unions, reflecting the resentment among the regional unionist leaders towards the policies of the ruling party. Contrary to the acquiescence displayed during the Mining Basin and Ben Gardane uprisings, regional unions began to push for a separation between the UGTT and the ruling party in an effort to reclaim the role it had played in the 1978 crisis.

An emergency meeting was held by the executive bureau of the union's general leadership, after which they released statements expressing solidarity with the

102. *Turess*, 4 January 2011, accessed on 16 December 2020, at: http://bit.ly/3gVVz6t.

103. *Kalimat Tunis Radio*, 5 January 2011, accessed at: https://bit.ly/3gQyHW5.

104. See Bishara, *Tunisia's Glorious Revolution*, pp. 418–19.

105. *France 24*, 6 January 2011, accessed on 16 December 2020, at: https://bit.ly/2WhAhH0.

106. Facebook Page of *Kalimat Tunis Radio*, 6 January 2011, accessed on 12 December 2020, at: https://bit.ly/3oVSIgt.

protests in Sidi Bouzid, calling upon the government to resolve the grievances fuelling the protests and affirming the need for democratic reforms.[107] Five days later, succumbing to pressure from its branches, the Executive Committee of the UGTT allowed the relevant regional unions on 11 January to declare strikes.[108]

Two noticeable developments occurred on this day. First, student protests increased in the centre of the Sfax governorate, with many colleges holding strikes for the second day running. The strikes were accompanied by street protests and confrontations with security forces.[109] In al-Shabba district, one of the centres of the Mahdia governorate, students also went on strike and security forces waged a crackdown on students who attempted to march in protest.[110] Second, protests escalated in the north-western region, al-Kef, Siliana and, in particular, the central-western region of Kasserine. According to reports from news agencies and social networks, the majority of these demonstrators were unemployed youth. Protests thus took a clear demand-based approach in the marginalized provinces, focusing primarily on the need for employment opportunities, while protests in the urban centres, especially Sfax, had a unionist character and were led by lawyers and students who were able to raise the ceiling of demands to include freedom and democracy.

On this day, the army was deployed to protect government buildings in a number of regions on orders from the president, thus exposing the security forces' need for army support.[111] On this day, too, a young man tried to set himself on fire after police officers assaulted him repeatedly and accused him of encouraging the youth to demonstrate. He attempted suicide in the regional transport station in Kasserine and ended up with serious burns.[112]

Day 22: 7 January 2011

On the evening of 7 January demonstrations broke out in different areas of Siliana. Police lobbed tear gas grenades at protesters who had set fire to government institutions in the governorate capital. That morning, unemployed locals also assembled in front of the governor's hall demanding the right to work. In the district of Makthar, clashes took place between demonstrators and security forces, and the city hall was torched as were a number of government buildings. In the Bourweis

107. *Kalimat Tunis Radio*, 6 January 2011, accessed at: https://bit.ly/37manYY.

108. See day 26 of these diaries.

109. From the testimony of Najat Ben Mansour.

110. '*Kalimat Tunis Radio*, 6 January 2011, accessed at: http://bit.ly/3mjznUU.

111. This video, for example, shows the entry of the army vehicles into Thala on 6 January 2011: 'Sidi Bouzid Tunisia', *YouTube video by Freedom4Tunisias kanal*, 6 January 2011, accessed on 16 December 2020, at: https://bit.ly/3gSQgEH.

112. 'Report by the National Fact-Finding Commission', p. 101.

district, protesters torched the mayor's office, the ruling party's headquarters and the regional farmers' union; they also destroyed the 7 November monument.[113]

Events in Siliana included looting and sabotage against private businesses. Where organized unions and political parties were absent, protest turned to angry rioting and looting by un-politicized crowds. Pro-opposition news outlets either sidelined these incidents or failed to report them altogether so as to avoid serving the regime's propaganda machine, which described the entire protest movement as one of sabotage and terrorism. The website of the Kalimat Tunis Radio devoted just a few words to the burning down of a private company in the Makthar district,[114] while *al-Badil* only referred to these events in passing.[115]

In his testimony, Samir Kuka said:

> Beginning on 2 January, daily protests occurred demanding the right to work. The protests reached their height on 7 January, when the demonstrators torched the city hall for the second time. Undeniably, some have exploited this opportunity to loot private property and commercial buildings. The protestors, most of whom were unemployed, did not belong to any political entity or union. In keeping with the trend in the northwestern region, the General Labor Union did not rally the Siliana protests; on the contrary, its role was to contain public anger, as it had been heavily infiltrated by the Ben Ali regime.[116]

In regions where protesters lacked a unionist or political framework, vandalism reigned as angry citizens assaulted private establishments. The events of Siliana would constitute the model for the events of Jendouba on day 25, as well as later events in the Tunisian capital, where companies and stores were vandalized and looted. In parallel with the protests in the northwest, the student protests in Sfax and its environs were growing rapidly for the fifth day in a row. Jebiniana witnessed violent clashes between students and security forces, who besieged their colleges and prevented them from marching in the street.[117]

On this day a relatively sizeable demonstration marched in Regueb, which was already gripped by civil disobedience and paralysis. The police reaction to the demonstration was very violent, involving the use of live ammunition that left twenty injured.[118] A similar police response met the residents of Kasserine's al-Zouhour neighbourhood when they marched to the central square demanding their right to jobs and a dignified life.[119]

113. *Turess*, 7 January 2011, accessed on 16 December 2020, at: http://bit.ly/3gWxAUI.

114. Ibid.

115. *Tunisian Communist Workers' Party – al-Badil*, 7 January 2011, accessed on 16 December 2020, at: http://bit.ly/3oPNRh0.

116. From the testimony of Samir Kuka.

117. *Turess*, 7 January 2011, accessed on 16 December 2020, at: http://bit.ly/38drX0r.

118. 'Report by the National Fact-Finding Commission', p. 74.

119. Ibid., p. 81.

After remaining silent for twenty days, the US State Department summoned Tunisia's ambassador and handed him a letter expressing US concern over the manner in which the protests in Tunisia were being handled. The letter also called for the respect of individual freedoms and, more specifically, internet freedom.[120]

Stage three: A popular revolution calls for the fall of the regime

Day 23: 8 January 2011

The third stage of the revolution saw extensive use of live ammunition by security forces. As protests spread throughout the country with the participation of the UGTT local activists and school and college students, union leaders started joining protesters following calls from the regional unions in different provinces, with many gathering in Mohamed Ali Square in front of the union headquarters in Tunis. A meeting between Tunisian prime minister Ghannouchi and members of the union's executive bureau in which Ghannouchi sought their help to curb the protest movement in Tunisia provoked the unionists to intensify their participation.

The demands arising from the sit-in in the capital initially stopped at condemnation of the authorities for their use of live ammunition, pledges of solidarity with the protesters and calls for the government to engage in serious dialogue that would respond to the demands of the protest movement.[121] However, unionists who had gathered in the square overlooking the union headquarters then began chanting slogans attacking the regime and the Trabelsi family.[122]

Protests and confrontations further escalated in the cities of Thala and Kasserine. In Thala, dozens of wounded fell in various districts of the province,[123] and three were killed. In Kasserine two people were killed during the daytime demonstration after being shot by police officers.[124]

Some north-western cities witnessed limited student activity. In the Jendouba governorate, security forces used teargas and rubber bullets to disperse students, while in Firyanah and al-Jraisa (in al-Kef province), student protests and clashes with the security forces continued. In the Sfax governorate, al-Skhira joined the student protests, where students and their parents came out of their schools shouting slogans demanding equitable development and employment.[125] On

120. *BBC Arabic*, 7 January 2011, accessed on 16 December 2020, at: http://bbc.in/3oR02tQ

121. *Kalimat Tunis Radio*, 8 January 2011, accessed at: http://bit.ly/2KyggZT.

122. *Ramadan Ben Omar Facebook*, 8 January 2011, accessed on 16 December 2020, at: https://bit.ly/3nC3t7m.

123. Amnesty International, 'Tunisia in Revolt', 16.

124. 'Report by the National Fact-Finding Commission', pp. 83–4.

125. *Kalimat Tunis Radio*, 8 January 2011, accessed at: http://bit.ly/2LHpeot

the same day, army units were deployed in the governorates of Sidi Bouzid and Kasserine in an effort to protect government institutions.

With this phase of protest in the capital also came the slogan *degage* ('Get out!'), a cry that summed up all previous slogans and demands.

Day 24: 9 January 2011

By day 24, the regime was fully aware that the movement targeted its very existence and that the repressive measures taken had backfired. However, the authorities assumed that the demonstrations continued to spread due to their hesitation to deploy bold enough force against the demonstrators. Hence, rather than offering concessions, they resorted to violence, and in less than two days, over twenty-five demonstrators in Kasserine had been killed by police.

On this day, Rached Ghannouchi issued a statement on behalf of Al Nahda in which he compared the events in Kasserine to the 'actions of Zionists in Palestine' and called for the unification of efforts behind the uprising. Placing full responsibility for the massacres on the shoulders of the state, Ghannouchi called for the authorities to immediately cease firing at protesters, to lift the siege on Thala and Kasserine and other besieged towns and cities and to release detainees. The statement also expressed full support for the uprising and its legitimate demands for decent living conditions, respect for the dignity of the citizen and an end to despotism and venality.[126] It did not, however, call directly for the overthrow of the regime. Moncef Marzouki, by contrast, issued a statement in the name of the Congress for the Republic Party calling for the overthrow of the dictator and the end of the regime.

The UGTT issued a statement 'calling for the withdrawal of security forces and the lifting of the siege on Kasserine and Thala, releasing all those detained during the recent protests, enacting a mechanism instituting unemployment benefits and opening a comprehensive national dialogue on political reform in Tunisia'.[127] This was the first statement manifesting disengagement from the regime after years of domestication. Before issuing this statement, the General Labour Union, which had come under great popular and unionist pressure as a result of growing unemployment and economic deterioration, endeavoured to convince the Tunisian government to resolve these matters.[128]

The majority of the deaths among the protesters in Kasserine and Thala were due to gunshots; it appears, from a controversy that later emerged in Tunisian newspapers, that Tunisians confused security men using live bullets and wearing

126. See Bishara, *Tunisia's Glorious Revolution,* pp. 420–1.

127. *Kalimat Tunis* , 9 January 2011, accessed on 16 December 2020, (found in *Turess)* at: http://bit.ly/3aob066

128. Following a 8 January meeting with members of the Union's executive bureau, Prime Minister Ghannouchi told his interlocutors that economic issues were beyond his purview. Ibid.

black masks with 'snipers',[129] because they were not used to seeing this image. It is also possible that masks had been used to conceal the identity of the security agents who lived in the same area so as to protect them from retaliation by victims' families. At any rate, the imagery of the masked sniper became specifically linked to the governorate of Kasserine. The Fact-Finding Commission confirmed that security forces that used live ammunition were in some cases stationed on the tops of buildings.[130] The fact that the majority of the victims in the Kasserine governorate fell at the hands of alleged snipers suggests that, faced with the spread of protests in many regions, the regime chose to employ deadly force against internal provinces that were considered the hub of civil disobedience but which lacked the means to threaten the regime with severe repercussions even if it escalated its repressive measures. This can be also validated by the president's alleged orders to bombard Kasserine's Zuhour neighbourhood.[131] By contrast, authorities refrained from using brutality in regions that were capable of threatening the regime, such as Sfax, preferring to 'contain' them until the very last minute.[132]

The report issued by the Fact-Finding Commission indicates that after 5 people were killed in Thala on the night of 8 January, the intervention units' local commander contacted the units' general commander informing him that he could no longer maintain the situation in Thala and requesting backup, which arrived on 9 January. During Rached Ammar's hearing on 3 April 2011, Ammar confirmed that the army had been ordered to enter Thala on 8 January 2011. Troops had, in fact, left their position in Kasserine and headed to Thala. However, they were then recalled by the Minister of the Interior, either because the minister did not want

129. The Tunisian *al-Shuruq newspaper* conducted an interview with a Tunisian sniper who condemned the conflation of snipers with ordinary security forces, published 25 August 2011.

130. 'Report by the National Fact-Finding Commission', p. 90. In the aftermath of the revolution, being criticized for failing to deal with the issue of snipers, the interim prime minister, Beji Caid Essebsi, later exclaimed that 'the snipers of al-Kasserine and Thala were imprisoned some time ago'. See 'Exclusive: Prime Minister Beji Caid Essebsi in an interview with "Al-Sabah"', *Al-Sabah newspaper*, 3 April 2011, accessed on 16 December 2020, at: http://bit.ly/34MUwB9

131. There is some reason to believe that bloggers invented the story (quoted in Al Jazeera) that Ben Ali's order to bombard the neighbourhood in Kasserine was disobeyed by the army. They invented it in order to encourage the people to escalate the struggle. In the other hand, according to Taoufik Bouderbala, head of the National Fact-Finding Commission on the Abuses Committed during the Revolution, Ben Ali's regime did in fact order the army 'to bomb the area from the air', but the army did not obey the order. See Noureddine Jebnoun, 'In the Shadow of Power: Civil–Military Relations and the Tunisian Popular Uprising', *The Journal of North African Studies*, vol. 19, no. 3 (2014), p. 305.

132. It was later revealed that there were no more than two victims in the Sfax governorate protests.

to acknowledge the failure of his troops, or because he had been transmitting an order of his president, who did not trust the army.

It would be safe to assume that the army eventually began taking a more pragmatic approach towards events. In the case of Kasserine, the army probably did not carry out orders to attack given the neighbourhood's high population density, the uselessness of such an action and the conviction that the protests could be contained with minimal loss of life. An in fact, two days later, following a curfew, the wave of protests in the Kasserine governorate abated, though it erupted in other provinces.

To conclude, the army did not join the revolution in Kasserine but remained loyal to the regime. If an order was, in fact, issued to bombard the protesters, the army's failure to carry it out may be understood as meaning that it saw no justification for attacking a densely populated neighbourhood and that the demonstrations could be repressed with the use of security forces, which is what actually took place.

On this day Khaled ben Salih Khdimi set himself ablaze on the street in Sousse. He was transferred to Farhat Hachad Hospital, where he died on 7 April. Suicides through self-immolation became a veritable phenomenon in those weeks of the Tunisian Revolution. However, this was more than a mere sign of despair, as people were openly challenging the regime.

Day 25: 10 January 2011

Demands for employment, the end of corruption and other grievances were now replaced with the call for a new political era. In tandem, Tunisian opposition political parties began to raise the ceiling of their demands. This stage of the revolution witnessed increased participation by the middle classes, which involved the mobilization of journalists, lawyers and engineers, some of whom were arrested as a result of their engagement. The popular reaction was gutsier than that of the parties and the unions; for example, people began shouting slogans challenging the president personally, as in the demonstrations of the Gafsa governorate.[133]

Meanwhile, events continued to escalate in the governorate of Sfax. In central Sfax, the student protests appeared to be more determined. When security forces assaulted a student protest, prompting students to seek shelter in nearby poor neighbourhoods, local residents began to support the demonstrators.[134]

After students were forcibly prevented from taking to the street in the centre of the Gabes governorate (south of Sfax), protests were staged on most college campuses. The al-Hammah district in the same governorate saw a demonstration that began from the headquarters of the local labour union with the participation

133. *Kalimat Tunis Radio*, 10 January 2011, accessed at: http://bit.ly/3r2HBUX.

134. *Kalimat Tunis Radio*, 10 January 2011, accessed at: http://bit.ly/2WyqGvH.

of hundreds of students and citizens, and ended with their occupation of the ruling party headquarters in the city.[135]

In the centre of Kairouan, east of Sfax, student protests continued with unionist participation. In the Sidi Bouzid demonstrations, slogans vilified the Trabelsi family, and photos of the president were torn up[136] for the first time and even set on fire.

In Tunis, YouTube showed clips of student gatherings inside colleges and secondary schools, as well as the Faculty of Science in the university complex, at the Khazendar Institute, and in the Basaj Square in the centre of the capital.[137] In contrast to student demonstrations in the central-eastern provinces, those in the capital featured students that came mostly from the poverty belts surrounding Tunis. With the escalation of the student protests, the Tunisian Ministry of Education suspended classes in all Tunisian schools, institutes, and universities in a desperate attempt to deprive the students of spaces in which to assemble.[138]

Protests launched by unemployed locals erupted in the Jendouba governorate (in northwest Tunisia), which led to acts of vandalism. The National Railway Company had to suspend its activities and cancelled its trains to the governorate.[139]

The fact that the slogans had begun targeting the top echelons of the state, and that several headquarters of the ruling party had been assaulted in a number of districts and governorates, indicated that the Tunisian Revolution had reached a point of no return. Social, economic, and reformist political demands receded and were replaced by new slogans that presented the overthrow of the president as its main objective.

The president was thus forced to address the Tunisian people in a second televised speech in which he described the ongoing troubles as 'the work of a mercenary and terrorist minority being mobilized from abroad by parties that are unhappy with Tunisia's success'. Ben Ali threatened that 'whoever seeks to harm the interests of the country and misguide its children and youth will be prosecuted by the law'. At the same time, he announced plans to double the country's employment capacity, diversify sources of employment during 2011 and 2012, and create 300,000 new jobs. Ben Ali promised to hold a national conference in February, inviting all relevant constitutional bodies and civil society organizations to offer their respective visions on job creation in the coming years. He also thanked Libyan leader Gaddafi for 'the generous initiative facilitating the travel of Tunisians in Libya and decreeing that they be treated like Libyans, which

135. *Kalimat Tunis Radio*, 10 January 2011, accessed at: http://bit.ly/2KboZRZ .

136. *Kalimat Tunis Radio*, 10 January 2011, accessed at: http://bit.ly/2WnMolT.

137. 'Tunisie sidi bouzid 2011-01-10', *YouTube video by canada1981*, 10 January 2011, accessed on 16 December 2020, at: https://bit.ly/2Wl145d.

138. *BBC Arabic*, 10 January 2011, accessed on 16 December 2020, at: http://bbc.in/37lhSPQ.

139. *Kalimat Tunis Radio*, 10 January 2011, accessed at: http://bit.ly/3rapUmH.

demonstrates genuine brotherhood and support'.[140] The address was accompanied by a number of security measures, including: the deployment of the army in some Tunisian cities and the dismissal of Interior Minister Rafiq Belhaj Kacem.

Ben Ali's address, which revealed the crisis in which the regime found itself now that it realized that the protesters were seeking its overthrow, put forth the claim that the revolution was the creation of a foreign conspiracy. Similar claims would be repeated later by the regimes in Egypt and Syria, Libya and Yemen during their respective revolutions. The focus on protesters' economic demands while neglecting their political dimension and the justification of violence by a focus on 'terrorism' were likewise echoed during subsequent revolutions in other Arab countries. The Tunisian government attempted to curry favour with influential Western powers, simultaneously urging them to stand by the regime, and warning them that the Islamist alternative would directly harm their interests. This was consistent with the positions taken by Western establishments towards loyal despotic regimes in the Middle East, where the rules of the cold war concerning allies still prevailed (due to considerations such as Israel's 'security', oil and terrorism).

The last inference to be drawn from the speech pertains to the popular revolution's maturation in the peripheries and its readiness to move into the centres, beginning with Sfax and ending with the capital Tunis. The deployment of the army and the removal of the interior minister reflected the regime's admission of failure. In this case, it is unclear whether this failure was because the minister had used insufficient violence, or excessive violence, in quelling the protests. Be that as it may, the decree was presented to the masses as an instance of officials being held accountable, though the reason was his failure to suppress the revolution, and the purpose was to contain popular anger.

Another sign that the Tunisian army might not actually defend the regime emerged in Regueb (in the Sidi Bouzid governorate), where a certain army unit offered protection to a number of protesters who had taken refuge near the army vehicles. This was seen as an indication that the army could be neutralized in the ongoing struggle between the people and the government. Alternatively, it might have been merely the spontaneous, isolated action of a few soldiers. However, the protesters applauded the incident in hopes of encourage such an attitude.[141]

On this day five demonstrators were killed in Kasserine and eleven were badly injured, while the first demonstration in the city of Kairouan was organized.

140. See Bishara, *Tunisia's Glorious Revolution*, pp. 364--8.

141. 'Tunisie sidi bouzid – 10-01-2011', *YouTube video by canadacanada1981*, 10 January 2011, accessed on 16 December 2020, at: https://bit.ly/2Ka2YTM.

Stage four: Revolution at the centre and the fall of the regime

Day 26: 11 January 2011

Following Ben Ali's second speech, Tunis joined the ongoing confrontations between security forces and protesters. Political and human rights activists were the first to demonstrate in the capital but poor neighbourhoods would join them soon thereafter. YouTube showed videos of unprecedented demonstrations in the al-Tadhamoun neighbourhood, for example, where violent clashes flared between youth and police forces, who used tear gas grenades and live ammunition to disperse the crowds.[142] Many lawyers and unionists were violently assaulted on Habib Bourguiba Street, and the headquarters of the Democratic Progressive Party and the Journalists' Union were besieged by the secret police.[143] In the evening, demonstrations turned into riots, including assaults on businesses, stores and banks as had occurred in the neighbourhood of Sidi Ḥusayn.[144] The pro-regime media deliberately covered the acts of sabotage, stressing that this was the nature of the protests. In previous days of the revolution, there had already been an indication that demonstrations had the potential to turn chaotic in marginalized regions protesting against poverty and demanding the right to work. The acts that were used by the regime to distort the image of the revolution were, nonetheless, of critical importance, as they marked the revolution's entrance into the capital; they also debilitated the internal security forces, which lost control over the situation.

On day 26, the United States expressed 'concern' following reports that Tunisian security forces had used 'excessive force' to disperse demonstrators in Tunisia.[145] In an interview with Al-Arabiya satellite channel, US Secretary of State Hillary Clinton claimed that no communication was ongoing at the time between the United States and the Tunisian government, stressing that Washington was not a party to the escalating confrontations between protesters and Tunisian authorities, and that the United States would contact Tunisian officials once the situation had calmed down.[146] Until Ben Ali's actual fall, the US administration presumed that its ally would prevail.

Day 26 witnessed the first official reaction from French authorities when France's Foreign Minister Michele Alliot-Marie expressed her regret over the violence in Tunisia but failed to condemn the excessive use of force against the

142. See 'Tunisie sidi bouzid 2011-01-11', *YouTube video by canCEacanCEa1981*, 11 January 2011, accessed on 16 December 2020, at: https://bit.ly/34iImj0.

143. *Al-Hiwar*, 11 January 2011, accessed at: https://bit.ly/34iImj0

144. *Kalimat Tunis Radio,* 12 January 2011, accessed at: http://bit.ly/34iRt3o

145. *BBC Arabic*, 11 January 2011, accessed on 16 December 2020, at: http://bbc.in/384BGWQ.

146. *Al-Arabiya net*, 11 January 2011, accessed on 16 December 2020, at: http://bit.ly/3agL24t.

demonstrators. In fact, Alliot-Marie went further and offered French cooperation in security and maintenance of order.[147]

Day 27: 12 January 2011

As the Tunisian and international media began focusing on the capital, events in Sfax were increasingly ignored, and this despite the fact that a general strike was called by the UGTT and thousands of students and unionists were making their way to the public squares and streets. These protests were met with violent repression, but the authorities were careful not to cause deaths among the protesters due to the city's importance.[148]

Although newly appointed interior minister, Ahmed Friaâ, had released all those detained during the recent events, it made no difference,[149] and fifty thousand orderly protesters demonstrated in Sfax, calling for the fall of the regime. The next day, the country learned of the failure of Sfax's security forces to overcome the protests, while global media covered the massive protests but portrayed them as taking place in Tunis.

After the rally, protesters targeted and torched security branches, police cars, and the headquarters of the ruling RCD.[150] YouTube showed clips of massive, unprecedented demonstrations against the regime.[151] The strength with which Sfax entered the protest movement was the culmination of two weeks of unionist demonstrations in the city, which the security authorities had attempted to contain with every means at their disposal. Initially, they had banned peaceful gatherings, arrested and terrorized students, repressed unionist demonstrations, and besieged student assemblies in schools and colleges. According to the testimony of Najat Ben Mansour, the Kasserine massacre, west of Sfax, had galvanized the uprising in the city.

147. 'Michele Alliot-Marie is shocked at attempts to alter her statements', *France 24*, 7 February 2011, accessed at: https://bit.ly/3apblFw.

148. However, one protester was killed. This account is from the testimony of Najat Ben Mansour.

149. *Al Jazeera Net*, 12 January 2011, accessed on 16 December 2020, at: http://bit.ly/38du4Bp.

150. *Sky News Arabiya*, 11 January 2011, accessed on 16 December 2020, at: http://bit.ly/2KATEIg. For a scene showing the burning of security vehicles, see 'Tunisia Ben 'Ali Sfax 12/1/2011', *YouTube video by Med BMN*, 12 January 2011, accessed at: https://bit.ly/2WyGRcp. For a scene showing the torching of the ruling party headquarters, see 'Mohamed Ben Jemaa', *YouTube*, 6 June 2011, accessed on 16 December 2020, at: https://bit.ly/3adVA4p.

151. Tens of thousands chant, 'with our blood, with our souls, we defend the Union' in 'Tunisie sidi bouzid 12/01/2011', *YouTube* video by canadacanada1981, 12 January 2011, accessed on 16 December 2020, at: https://bit.ly/2K3TjhE.

Geographically, the revolution was clearly expanding around the centre of Sfax. The protests had begun in the east, in Sidi Bouzid. By day 10 they had moved to Kairouan (northwest of Sfax), and by day 13, they had reached the Mahdia governorate (to the north). By day 25 they had escalated into the centre of Gabes (south of Sfax), the final culmination being an unstoppable uprising in Sfax.

Unlike that in the capital, the revolution in Sfax enjoyed broad support from unions and students alike; as a result, the city did not suffer extensively from riots and sabotage against private property despite the fact that it came under the full control of the masses that flooded the streets and squares. It should be noted that from the beginning of the uprising, the Sfax province witnessed only two deaths, a lower toll than that of any other province or city that had taken part in the uprising. At the end of that day, the army was deployed in the city amid the cheers of the citizens.[152] Sfax was a powerful loss to the regime, as it represented a union stronghold and an 'economic hub whose middle-class had fared well over the past decade'.[153]

To compare the revolutionary situation in Sfax on this day with that in the capital, it should be remembered that the unrest moved from the outskirts to the heart of the capital. Dozens of street vendors protested on Sidi Boumendil Street, where cheap imitations of Tunisian goods and merchandise smuggled in from Libya were being sold. The vendors gathered at the Bab Bahar Arch towards the end of Bourguiba Street and in Barcelona Square but were dispersed by security forces.[154]

Commenting on these events, Tunisian researcher Mohamed Boutalib notes that the confrontations in the capital took place between groups originally coming from Jilmah in Sidi Bouzid, and youth groups from the neighbourhoods of Bab al-Jdid and Al-Jazeera Road. Those involved then called on relatives and others from the same regions for support.[155]

The protests in Tunis on this day reflected the simmering resentment in the poverty belt around the capital as portrayed in many news reports. One report shows a funeral procession for one of the victims in Ariana, which rapidly turned into a demonstration involving hundreds of protesters. When some of the protesters were asked to explain their reasons for coming out, they spoke of poverty and unemployment. One interviewee said, 'We are fighting for bread', while another

152. See 'Mohamed Ben Jemaa', *YouTube* video, 6 June 2011, accessed at: https://bit.ly/38a5IIL.

153. Ben Ali's Collapse and the Origins of the Jasmine Revolution', in Christopher Alexander, *Tunisia: From Stability to Revolution in the Maghreb* (Abingdon: Routledge, 2016), p. 80.

154. 'The escalation of protests and the deployment of the army.'

155. Mohammad Najib Boutalib, 'The Political Dimensions of the Tribal Phenomenon in Arab Societies: A Sociological Approach to the Tunisian and Libyan Revolutions', [al-ab'ād al-siyāsiyah lil-ẓāhirah al-qabaliyah fī al-mujtama'āt al-'arabiyah: muqārabah susyulūjiyah lil-thawratayn al-tūnisiyah wa al-lībiyah], *Research Papers*, ACRPS, October 2011.

said, 'We have no problem with the President or the State and its policy; we just want our daily bread.'[156] At this point, motives no longer mattered. Any protest, its motivations notwithstanding, flowed in the same revolutionary stream.

The importance of social demands should not be discounted, for they constituted the revolution's point of departure, nor should the protests in Tunis be overemphasized. As slogans calling for the overthrow of the regime and the rejection of corruption in all its forms abounded in Tunisia's inner provinces, the capital was witnessing disturbances born out of the weakening of the regime. This induced protesters in the poverty belt to take to the streets, voicing their social demands and engaging in vandalism. For a better illustration of the events of this day, we cite the testimony of Ramadan Ben Omar, a teacher in al-Tadhamoun neighbourhood, one of the first neighbourhoods to witness protests after 10 January 2011. Ben Omar recounts:

> The first gathering of protestors in Tunis took place on 25 December 2010 in Mohamed Ali Square, which faces the headquarters of the Tunisian Labor Union. Things developed on 10 January 2011 following small-scale confrontations that had occurred over the previous days. Those protesting were mostly marginalized and unemployed youth, the majority of whom were affiliated with the General Union of Tunisia's Students, which includes youth who come from the internal regions to study in the capital, and who can only afford to reside in poor neighborhoods such as al-Tadhamoun. They would come during the day to demonstrate at the university and in Mohamed Ali Square, and then return in the evening to the cafes and their dorms. Being mostly poor and marginalized, they attacked the places that they perceived as the cause of their poverty, such as banks, corporations and other commercial establishments. I am not trying to justify their actions. However, they had not been accustomed to expressing their opinions in a controlled manner, and most of the properties (which were assaulted) belonged to powerful figures in the ruling party whom the youth regarded as symbols of the regime.[157]

A curfew was officially declared in the region of Greater Tunis from eight in the evening until five-thirty in the morning. The area witnessed an intense security deployment evoking a state of emergency, and all commercial establishments were closed.[158]

On the national level, the army completed its deployment in the rebellious regions. Its soldiers, however, behaved differently than the police, avoiding any

156. To view the report of Al-Arabiya channel in full, see www.youtube.com/watch?v=de0uct1mouy (video discontinued – accessed in July 2010).

157. From the testimony of blogger Ramadan Ben Omar, part of an interview conducted by ACRPS via Skype, 15 October 2011.

158. *Al Jazeera Net*, 13 January 2011, accessed on 16 December 2020, at: http://bit.ly/34DP5o3.

clashes with protesters. In the meantime, in addition to replacing the interior minister, Ben Ali ordered the establishment of a special commission to investigate corruption and the practices of some officials. Even so, popular demands were always one step ahead of the regime, and grew even more radical every time the regime retreated.

The UGTT began calling for strikes, though they did not declare a general strike throughout the country. Instead, on 11 January 2011, their administrative committee allowed each region to declare strikes. The branches of the Tunisian Labor Union in and around Sfax, the centre of gravity for unionist activism, were the first regional branches to declare a general strike on the next day. The principal theme of the general strike was a rejection of the use of live ammunition against the protesters. Gradually, the branches in Tunis followed suit.

On this day, Gerard Larcher, president of the French Senate, made a statement criticizing the Tunisian regime and condemning the use of force against civilian protesters. Larcher said, 'It is unnatural for a country with an advanced partnership agreement with the EU to neglect the most basic principles of democracy and human rights adopted in Europe.'[159] Needless to say, Larcher had been fully aware of the state of human rights in Tunisia prior to the revolution, and human rights violations had never, until then, interfered hampered good relations with the EU.

Day 28: 13 January 2011

The Last Speech As clashes continued throughout Tunisia, security forces withdrew from the areas of confrontation. The protests on this day were particularly large in the capital, where dozens of unionists demonstrated in Mohamed Ali Square with slogans such as: 'Out with Ben Ali!'; 'Down with the butcher of the people; down with the Destour Party!', 'O martyr, rest in peace, we shall overthrow the killer!', 'Freedom is a right, you band of thieves!', 'Ben Ali, you Sharon, the blood of the people is not cheap!' The Tunisian national anthem was also sung. Video clips show security forces surrounding the protesters and preventing them from exiting the square.[160] In the meantime, protesters in the poverty belt surrounding the capital continued to assault security and government headquarters, as well as private property.[161] Violent clashes erupted in the neighbourhoods of al-Mallasin, al-Sijoumi, al-Jabal al-Ahmar, Mannouba, Wadi al-Leil, al-Intilaqa, Qasr Assaid, al-Tadhamoun, al-Umran al-Ala, Ibn Khaldoun, al-Kabbariyya, Bou Mahl, Hammam al-Anf, al-Madina al-Jadida, al-Wardiya, Lakania, al-Muruj, al-Oweina,

159. *France 24*, 14 January 2011, accessed at: https://bit.ly/3oXUu0F.

160. *Facebook – Ramadan Ben Omar*, 13 January 2011, accessed on 16 December 2020, at: http://bit.ly/3ntXD8b.

161. From the testimony of Ramadan Ben Omar. Days later, videos showed the acts of looting.

Sukkara, al-Bahr al-Azraq, Carthage and the Bou Silsila neighbourhood in al-Marsa.[162]

That evening, Ben Ali delivered his third address to the people. In passionate vernacular language that he probably thought would draw him closer to the people, he asserted, '*fhimtkum* (I understand you!)!' He claimed to have been misinformed, promising to hold those responsible accountable, to take measures supporting political and journalistic openness, and to improve social conditions. He publicly ordered the police not to fire on protesters and confirmed that he would not run in the coming presidential elections. He lifted the ban on internet censorship, and instructed his government to lower the prices of basic goods, including sugar, bread and milk. On the same day, he dissolved the Tunisian government and called for early legislative elections. In short, he actually began introducing democratic reforms.

Simultaneously, false rumours spread that the Ben Ali had fired Rachid Ammar, chief of the General Staff of the Tunisian Army, and placed him under house arrest, and replaced him with Ahmed Chabir, director of Intelligence. It was said that these measures had been prompted by Ammar's refusal to commit to a more active role in suppressing the uprising, including the use of live ammunition against protesters, and that he had called on the president to resign and leave the country.[163] However, these rumours were all groundless hearsay. Ridha Grira, former Minister of Defence, later refuted them, stating that 'rumors claiming that General Rachid Ammar was relieved of his duties due to his refusal to carry out orders to fire (on protests) are baseless; at no point was he suspended'.[164] Rachid Ammar had not disobeyed non-existent orders.[165] Rather, the army had withdrawn from the capital's centre, handing over its positions to special security forces, although it had continued to guard public institutions and government buildings.

In reality, the army's position was not as clear as is claimed. During the revolution, Ammar's stance was ambiguous because it contradicted media reports, all of which stated incorrectly that he had demanded Ben Ali's resignation. The army's position was not officially and publicly confirmed until Ammar's first

162. *Kalimat Tunis Radio*, 13 January 2011, accessed at: http://bit.ly/3p2hrzJ.

163. Hadi Yahmad, 'The role of General Rachid Ammar in the events in Tunisia', [Dawr al-jinirāl rashīd ʿammār fī aḥdāth tūnis] *al-Baida News*, accessed at: https://bit.ly/3r3RjGQ.

164. *Turess* (Tunisia), 9 March 2011 accessed on 16 December 2020, at: http://bit.ly/37uXBaJ

165. Long after such facts were revealed, Fadhel Kaboub wrote that in January 2011, Rachid Ammar refused orders from Ben Ali's interior minister, 'Ali Seriati, to fire on protesters and decided to side with them instead. In fact, however, Seriati was not interior minister at that time but, rather, Ben Ali's security chief, and there had been no such orders to begin with. Seriati had instructed Ammar to forcefully subdue a mutiny by an anti-terrorist security unit, but he had refused to use force. See Fadhel Kaboub, 'The Making of the Tunisian Revolution', *Middle East Development Journal*, vol. 5, no. 1 (March 2013), 1350003-5.

media appearance after the revolution on 24 January 2011, when he said that the army had protected the revolution and contributed to its success, and that it would continue to guard its achievements.[166]

On 13 January 2011, around thirty-five people were shot and killed, and more than hundred injured, in demonstrations in different regions of Tunisia. Also on this day, French prime minister Francois Fillon expressed his concern over 'the disproportionate use of violence' in Tunisia, calling 'on all parties to exercise restraint and to choose the path of dialogue'.[167] A day before Ben Ali's departure, the French prime minister called for calm and restraint, but there was still no official French condemnation of the regime.

A triumphant revolution and the departure of the dictator

14 January 2011

After Ben Ali disbanded his cabinet and announced his decision to hold early legislative elections, events began to escalate. On this day, Tunisia witnessed violent protests and confrontations in the heart of its capital, after which Ben Ali declared a state of emergency in all Tunisian cities. It was explained on state television that any gathering over three individuals would be prohibited, and that security forces would use weapons against those who broke the curfew between five in the evening and seven in the morning.

The statement was followed by the positioning of units in al-Marsa, a neighbourhood not far from the Presidential Palace, and in the capital's al-Nasr neighbourhood. Meanwhile, demonstrations were taking place throughout the republic. In a show of protest which, in this location in particular, would theretofore have been unimaginable, thousands of demonstrators marched towards the Ministry of Interior on Bourguiba Street in the capital. According to one of the demonstrators:

> The streets were completely empty, and the withdrawal of the security forces opened the way for the flow of protestors. Those who marched from Mohamed Ali Square numbered fewer than 2,000, but the number doubled on our way to the Ministry of Interior. In the beginning, only one side of Bourguiba Street was filled with the masses; however, bit by bit, the other side slowly filled with demonstrators. The security forces attempted unsuccessfully to stop us at the street's entrance (at the Rome Junction) and near the municipal theatre. When we managed to enter Bourguiba Street, we sensed that Ben Ali's fall was imminent. It was a Friday, and for the first time, people came out of the mosques and joined the masses. Around eleven o'clock in the morning, we reached the Ministry of

166. *Al-Sharq al-Awsat newspaper*, 6 January 2011, accessed at: https://bit.ly/3oY818G.
167. *France 24*, 13 January 2011, accessed at: https://bit.ly/3gU6ygT.

> Interior, and the protest was dispersed at around four in the afternoon. At six in the evening, we heard the news of the President's departure from Tunisia.[168]

After many years of banning the simple act of walking near the Ministry of Interior, tens of thousands of protesters joined the demonstration at the ministry itself, a major symbol of repression, subjugation and the arrogance of the dictatorship. It was an act so daring and symbolically significant that the authorities realized that the next target might well be the Presidential Palace. And this is precisely what some demonstrators declared after being dispersed that evening.[169]

It is difficult to determine the real reason for Ben Ali's departure; it is even doubtful that he, himself, knew the real reason for his exit. Was his fate really sealed by the time he left? Or was his departure itself the act that decided matters in favour of the revolution? Was he persuaded by the leader of his guard, Seriati, to leave the country in order to overthrow him after his departure, only to find that everything collapsed after that? Or was a coup arranged by Samir Tarhouni, a commander of an anti-terror brigade, who mutinied? The complete answer to the question regarding his departure and the roles of Tarhouni and Seriati is still unknown, although we know enough to sketch out realistic scenarios.

According to one version, Tarhouni, head of the Anti-terror Brigade (BAT) in the interior ministry, started a mutiny for reasons unknown (but he insisted in later investigations and interviews that it was his personal initiative because he didn't want to face demonstrators who may attack his barrack at any time), he decided to head to the airport to prevent the president's corrupt, ill-reputed in-laws from leaving the country. He arrested them and declared his readiness to hand them over to the army provided that the process be documented by the media. Two other units joined him from the National Brigade for Rapid Response (BNIR) and the Special Unit of the National Guard (USGN) headed by his friends. Overwhelmed by these events and by warnings (which turned out to be exaggerated) of demonstrations marching towards the Presidential Palace, Seriati persuaded the president to accompany his family to El Aouina Airport, where he could also protect him. Given his state of confusion and panic, Ben Ali was

168. From the testimony of Ramadan Ben Omar.

169. What interested some researchers even at this stage was the motivations of the participants, some of whom had social and even personal incentives, and some of whom came out of curiosity. Amin Allal, 'Trajectoires 'révolutionnaires' en Tunisie Processus de radicalisations politiques 2007-2011', *Revue française de science politique*, vol. 62, no. 5-6 (2012), p. 831. See also: Chaker Houki, 'Does the Generational Approach Provide an Explanation for the Tunisian Revolution?' [hal taṣluḥ al-muqārabah al-jīliyah asāsan li-qirā'at al-thawrah al-tūnisiyah?] *Siyasat Arabiya,* Issue 32 (May 2018), p. 27. Though interesting, such surveys miss the main issue, namely, that the revolution was a political phenomenon whose goal was to overthrow a twenty-three-year dictatorship, and once the revolution had gained such unstoppable momentum, personal motivations ceased to matter.

persuaded to board the plane with his family to Saudi Arabia, his intention being simply to escort them there and come back immediately.[170]

The major reason was the tension that built up at the airport due to a possible clash between the mutineers and the army units. Chief of Staff Rachid Ammar refused to attack the mutineers at the airport, preferring to reach a negotiated solution. Seriati, who overestimated the size of the mutiny, was also frustrated by the army's unwillingness to engage in combat against Tunisian security forces, and seems to have informed the president of his inability to protect him under these circumstances.[171]

After the aircraft departed, Sami Sik Salim (the officer in charge of the palace, and third in command after Seriati) called the prime minister to Carthage Palace and pressured him to take over the responsibilities of the president, who would no longer be able to perform his duties.[172]

Tunisian researcher Nourreddine Jebnoun presents another version of events in an article from 2014.[173] This alternative account holds that after martial law was declared across the country, Ben Ali instructed Grira, his Minister of Defence, to put Rachid Ammar in charge of security, as well as coordination of army and security force operations. On the day of Ben Ali's escape, Seriati ordered a helicopter from Grira for a 'reconnaissance mission' and appointed an officer from the National Guard to fly it. However, Lajimi decided to send an officer from Military Intelligence with the crew to ensure that Seriati did not give orders to fly over the Presidential Palace and assassinate Ben Ali.[174] Later that day, Grira asked Ammar if he had received any orders to close the Tunisian airspace. However, Ammar assumed that Ben Ali was misinformed. Grira called Ammar a few minutes later to inform him that 'Islamists' from an anti-terrorist unit within the

170. Some writers emphasize that the pilot was ordered to leave the President and his family in Saudi Arabia and come back, while Yadh Ben Achour in his important book on the revolution claims that it was a mere coincidence that the plane left without him. See Yadh Ben Achour, *A revolution in the Land of Islam [Tūnis: Thawrah fī bilād al-islām]*, Fathi ben al-Haj Yehia (trans.), (Tunis: Tunisia Institute for Translation and Cérès publisher, 2018), p. 90.

171. Jean-Baptiste Gallopin, 'Dilemma and Cascades in the Armed Forces – The Tunisian Revolution', *Democracy and Security*, vol. 15, no. 4 (2019), pp. 339–44.

172. According to one Tunisian writer who insists on a conspiracy involving foreign powers, Ghannouchi was summoned to the palace before the aircraft departed. See Salem Ben Hussein, *The Hidden Story of the Tunisian Revolution [al-qiṣṣah al-khafiyah lil-thawrah at-tūnisiyah]* (Sfax: N.P., 2016), pp. 108–12. An opposing narrative is presented by Tunisian writers involved in the revolution who emphasized the revolutionary dimension of the events of 14 January, and who consider the president's escape a direct outcome of popular pressure on the system. See, for example, Hamadi Ben Mim, *The Secrets of the Tunisian Revolution [asrār al-thawrah at-tūnisiyah]*, 2nd ed. (Tunis: Thakafia Print, 2019), pp. 118–21.

173. Jebnoun, pp. 307–9.

174. Later that day, Grira instructed Lajimi to capture Seriati. Ibid., p. 309.

interior ministry had detained Ben Ali's family at the airport, and he delivered Ben Ali's order for Ammar to neutralize these elements, using live ammunition if necessary. In fact, the combatants of the Anti-Terrorist Brigade of the National Police were not Islamists, and were joined later by defectors from four major security force units. Even though the officer who detained Ben Ali's family at the airport confirmed that he made this move on his own and had not been given any orders to do so, Ammar assumed that someone was behind this decision.

Ammar kept the Minister of Defence informed of the situation at the airport; however, he refused orders to use lethal force against the soldiers holding Ben Ali's family hostage on the grounds that they were armed, and that a confrontation with them might lead to a bloodbath since the airport was quite crowded. Instead, he had sent a senior security officer to negotiate the release of the hostages. Three hours later, they were freed.

Seriati decided that Ben Ali's family should depart from the military El Aouina Airport. However, this was against military protocol, as the civilian crew on board the presidential jet did not have permission to use the military airport; thus, the base had to report to the Army Chief of Staff. The crew also did not follow safety regulations, as the jet refuelled in a hangar that might have set off an explosion, according to the testimony of Air Force Chief of Staff Major-General Taieb Lajimi.

Embarrassed by his failure to prove to Ben Ali that he had the situation under control, Ridha Grira, the Minister of Defence, tried to deny any responsibility for the fact that he had allowed military air traffic (four helicopters) to fly overhead, causing Ben Ali to think mistakenly that they were trying to prevent him from escaping. But this misunderstanding convinced him of Seriati's claims that he could no longer protect Ben Ali. Grira did, in fact, give permission to those helicopters to transfer military forces to El Aouina to be ready to deal with the events at the civilian airport. He also decided unilaterally to reinforce Tunis the capital with more troops without informing Ammar.

Seriati claimed that the reason he had urged Ben Ali to leave the country was to save Tunisia from a deadly conflict, as he feared bloody clashes between loyalist security services and defectors. However, he denied having any ambition to seize power for himself.

Ghannouchi is said to have confirmed that Ben Ali's plan was initially just to leave the country until the situation settled down, not to step down permanently. In fact, Ben Ali called Ghannouchi several times on 14 and 15 January, blaming him for the constitutional measures taken at that time and expressing his desire to return to Tunisia.

The fact-finding report, which is devoted in part to the events of 14 January,[175] begins by recalling the testimony of Ali Seriati, who asserted that on 13 January, they had begun receiving reports of the houses of Leila Trabelsi's family members

175. The narration below summarizes the report's version of events. See 'Report by the National Fact-Finding Commission', pp. 229–71.

being torched one after the other.[176] Consequently, the report affirms, family members started preparing to leave the country the next day. Meanwhile, Ben Ali was worried on account of rumours that plain-clothes officers were giving out the addresses of Trabelsi households.

Early in the afternoon of 14 January, cars from presidential security escorted Leila's sister and other members of her family to the airport. Samir Tarhouni claimed that after he heard from his wife, who worked in the control tower, about events at the airport, he decided to go there. On his way, he informed the twelve officers who accompanied him that he wanted to prevent the Trabelsis from leaving the country.[177]

Tarhouni's action was baffling to both airport security and his commanders. He himself mentioned in a call with Jalel Boudriga, director-general of the Anti-Riot Police (Brigades de l'Ordre Public), that his orders had come from Seriati. However, he later denied this, saying that this had only been a way to justify his action. At the same time, he insisted that he did receive 'orders from above'[178] to prevent the family from leaving. He then requested backup from the commander of the national rapid intervention brigade, who rushed to the airport with forty officers around 4:10 p.m. Tarhouni also called the commander of the National Guard Special Unit, who joined him around 5:00 p.m. with sixty officers.

The disputes between Tarhouni on one side and Boudriga, Rachid Ammar, the army commander and the Minister of Justice on the other ended when Tarhouni asked for a TV crew to come and film the hostages' surrender to the army. Tarhouni then withdrew from the airport at 8:00 p.m.

The report asks the important question of who instructed Tarhouni to act, and the answer it deems most probable is that he acted of his own accord. However, the report remains sceptical about his timing and reasons, since he was 'following the movements of the family for three days through one of his security guards'.[179] According to the report, the same suspicion prompted the Minister of Defence to arrest Seriati that night on charges of treason. The report concludes that Tarhouni's mutiny and the cooperation of other units 'confused all and turned out to be a historic moment that profoundly affected the proceedings planned for that day'.[180]

Concerning Ben Ali's exit, the report begins in the morning of 14 January 2011, when Seriati received a message from Mohamed Ghariani, secretary-general of the RCD, conveying an item circulating on Facebook to the effect that nearly 5,000 people were heading towards the Presidential Palace (which was untrue). Seriati decided to surround the palace with three layers of security: first, the army, second, the police and lastly, presidential security officers, so that the latter would not have to confront a demonstration. In his testimony, Seriati mentioned that there

176. Ibid., p. 229.
177. Ibid, pp. 231–2.
178. Ibid., p. 237.
179. Ibid., p. 239.
180. Ibid., p. 242.

were many decisions taken and many events that occurred that day without his knowledge. The report asserts the probability of this claim. Seriati also admitted that he had insisted that Ben Ali travel abroad with his family, as he considered it his primary duty to preserve the president's safety.[181]

After comparing different story lines and narratives about the time and way Ben Ali left the country, the report concludes that his departure had been neither planned nor expected. He had decided to accompany his family to the airport given Seriati's insistence that he could be better protected at a military airport. Seriati had been concerned for the president's security due to news of demonstrators stealing arms from security barracks and burning down the homes of members of the Trabelsi family.

The presidential plane took off at around 6:00 p.m. and landed in Jeddah Airport shortly after midnight. When the pilot called the director of Tunisair from Jeddah asking what to do, the latter inquired of the Minister of Defence, who stated that 'according to military intelligence, a huge demonstration will take place on 15 January, and if the President returns, a blood bath might ensue'. Therefore, the pilot was advised to have his crew return to Tunis, and to leave Ben Ali in Saudi Arabia[182] with the understanding that if necessary, another aircraft would be sent to bring him home. This was a crucial decision, since it confirms, along with other sources, that Ben Ali had planned to come back but was essentially stranded outside the country. Persuaded by Seriati to depart, especially after being informed of the mutiny at the airport, and after misinterpreting the landing of army commando helicopters at the military base before the plane took off, he decided to join his family on board but was then left in Jeddah. Leaving him there does not appear to have been planned, as we know that the prime minister was summoned to the Presidential Palace and persuaded by Officer Selim Sik to take over the president's duties based on the constitutional mandate to do so because the president had left the country.

It is no easy task to make sense of this seemingly fortuitous chain of events – this peculiar mix of mutiny, conspiracy, confusion, lack of coordination, mistrust, and panic, and this in a regime that had appeared so well organized. Even the state's own security apparatuses had conflicting evaluations of the situation. Some of them certainly resented the corruption of the ruling family; others realized that the protests could only be stopped by lethal force on a scale they were disinclined to resort to; while others may have thought that the rule of this president was doomed.

There is no telling how things would have evolved had Ben Ali remained in the country. His exit undoubtedly hastened the collapse of the regime, but the state institutions initially remained intact. The combined collapse of the regime and the resiliency of state institutions opened the way for a democratic transition led by political elites from within both the regime and the opposition. Ben Ali's

181. Ibid., p. 252.
182. Ibid., p. 270.

departure led first to the collapse of his security apparatus which, once viewed as more powerful than the army itself, had been severely undermined by mutiny in its ranks; and this in turn emboldened even more segments of Tunisian society to take to the streets.

Following the president's departure, his prime minister, Mohammed Ghannouchi announced that he would be taking over the presidency based on Article 56 of the Constitution.[183] Constitutional jurists and politicians then began to cast doubts on the legitimacy of Ghannouchi's claim to be entitled to step in based on the fact that according to Article 57 of Tunisia's Constitution, presidential powers are to be transferred to the Speaker of Parliament. And this is what transpired the following day.

Two articles of the Tunisian Constitution are relevant to the question of the vacancy of the presidency. Ghannouchi had cited Article 56, which reads that:

> when incapable of fulfilling his duties in a temporary manner, the President can delegate his powers to the Prime Minister, except for the authority to dissolve the Parliament. . . . During this temporary incapacitation of the President of the Republic, the cabinet shall remain in place until the condition subsides, even if a vote of confidence has been advanced. The President of the Republic must inform the Speaker of Parliament of his temporary delegation of authority.

The reality, however, as most of the people wanted to see it, was that the people had overthrown the president. If so, then the top position in the state was now vacant, in which case the applicable text of the Constitution would be Article 57, which reads:

> Upon the vacancy of the position of the President of the Republic due to death, resignation, or a permanent incapacity, the authorities of the presidency are to be immediately transferred to the Speaker of Parliament in a temporary faculty for a term no less than 45 days and not exceeding 60 days. The acting President is to be temporarily sworn in by Parliament, and when necessary, at the office of the Parliament. The temporary acting President may not run for presidential election even if he resigns. The acting President is to carry out temporarily all presidential duties, but shall not be permitted to use referendums, dissolve the Cabinet, dissolve Parliament, or enact the exceptional measures listed in Article 46.

The Constitution was thus used to transfer power out of the president's hands, in which manner state institutions were preserved and a power vacuum was successfully avoided.

183. *BBC Arabic*, 14 January 2011, accessed on 16 December 2020, at: http://bbc.in/3nuf7RR

In response to Ben Ali's departure, White House spokesman Mike Hammer read a statement which said:

> We condemn the continuing violence against civilians in Tunisia, and we call upon the Tunisian authorities to fulfill the important commitments made by President Ben Ali in his address to Tunisians, including respect for basic human rights and the much-needed process of political reform . . . the Tunisian people have the right to select their leaders, and we shall closely watch the latest developments.[184]

Notably, even after the dictator's exit from Tunisia, the US government highly valued the promises he had made in his last speech, demanding that the elected government commit to these promises.

The United States thus moved, awkwardly, from openly supporting a dictatorial and despotic regime to giving advice on democratic transition, as if the US administration had always been in support of democracy in Tunisia. On 15 January, US president Barack Obama praised the 'courage and dignity' of the Tunisian people, calling for transparent and free elections and expressing his confidence that the future of Tunisia would be brighter if led by the votes of the Tunisian people.[185] US Secretary of State Hillary Clinton joined the chorus, expressing her hope to work along with Tunisians throughout the transition of power. Clinton stated, 'We are determined to help the people and the government to establish peace and stability in Tunisia; we hope they will work together to build a society that is stronger, more democratic, and respectful of human rights.' On 20 January, US State Department Spokesman Phillip Crowley said that 'the Tunisian government must manage the transitional phase toward democracy',[186] and on 26 January, Obama declared that his country supported 'the people of Tunisia and its democratic aspirations after being rid of dictatorship'.[187]

The Tunisian Revolution challenged the United States, for the first time in the Middle East, to choose between supporting a genuine popular revolution calling for democracy and standing by an allied regime. Initially having sided with the regime, the United States found itself in a quandary when faced with the intensity of anti-regime sentiment in the country.

In light of the United States' military venture In Iraq, the Obama Administration had recently abandoned the pretext of 'exporting democracy' by military intervention (as justified by neo-conservatives under George W. Bush in the context of the war against terrorism) in favour of frank support for friendly

184. *BBC Arabic*, 14 January 2011, accessed on 16 December 2020, at: http://bbc.in/3oZR8dK.

185. *Al-Jazeera Net*, 15 January 2011, accessed at: https://bit.ly/387s79K.

186. *BBC Arabic*, 20 January 2011, accessed on 16 December 2020, at: http://bbc.in/3r2BwYx.

187. *Al-Jazeera.net*, 26 January 2011, accessed at: https://bit.ly/3aldhiq.

dictatorial regimes in order to preserve stability and protect the interests of the United States and its allies. Ironically, the Tunisian people had come out with demands for democracy even as this shift in US policy was taking place. Openly confused, US policy makers hesitated to abandon the allied regime in Tunisia until after its fall. Meanwhile, their attention was focused on the Islamist movement, fearing that democracy could lead to Islamist movements winning the popular vote.[188]

The West's readiness to desert its local allies once they grew weak was also exhibited in Egypt, causing much distress to US-allied Arab regimes. It has long been clear that Western states operate according to calculated interests and that personal friendships between Third World leaders and officials in Western administrations do not run deep. Hence, this was not the first time the US government had found itself embarrassed by its friendships with a dictator, justifying such ties based on interests or an alliance against a common enemy only to backtrack on such justifications once the dictator in question lost his grip on power.

The very night of Ben Ali's departure, France announced that it had refused to receive its former ally on its territory.[189] In so doing, France abandoned a friend whom it had never criticized but whom, on the contrary, it had up to that time promoted as a model to be emulated. Moreover, all available sources point to the fact that Ben Ali never actually requested asylum in France and that France's vocal rejection of 'his request' was an attempt to save face. Those involved in the affairs of the region and who knew of the relationship between Ben Ali and Emir Nayif Bin Abdel Aziz al-Saud knew that Ben Ali's first call would be to the Emir.

France's official declaration of support for the revolution finally came on 15 January, the day marking the fall of Ben Ali. This declaration was soon followed by advice on the urgent need for free, fair elections in Tunisia. (How easily Western countries that have supported a dictator pivot to handing out advice on democracy once their erstwhile ally has been overthrown!) France also claimed that it had taken precautions to prevent any 'suspicious' movements of Tunisian accounts and assets in France[190] – transactions which, until shortly before this, had been welcomed. On 15 January, French government spokesman Francois Baron said that France did not expect the relatives of the former Tunisian president, who were

188. During subsequent Arab revolutions, America's stance on the Islamist current started to shift (albeit for a short period of time) based on debates that took place in Western think tanks and within the US Administration regarding the usefulness of boycotting Islamists in view of the moderate current emerging within Islamist movements.

189. *Al-Jazeera Net*, 15 January 2011, accessed at: https://bit.ly/3aity7R.

190. *France 24*, 15 January 2011, accessed on 16 December 2020, at: http://bit.ly/3r4kWYA.

at the time in France, to remain on French territory, and that they should leave France, thereby exhibiting a hypocrisy that by this time knew no bounds.[191]

An interim president, dismantlement of the private army and the return of those in exile

15 January 2011 and its aftermath

On this day, Tunisia's Constitutional Council declared the presidency officially vacant. This allowed for a transfer of presidential powers to Speaker of Parliament Fuad al-Mubazzaa, who then tasked Mohamed Ghannouchi with forming a new government.[192] Tunisian television also quoted the Constitutional Council as stating that, in keeping with the Constitution, new presidential elections would take place within sixty days.[193]

It was thereafter announced that General Ali Seriati, director of Presidential Security, and Slim Chiboub, brother-in-law of the deposed president, had been arrested in Ben Gardane on their way to Libya.[194] Meanwhile, special army units apprehended the defectors of the National Guard with the help of Tunisian army helicopters. The military institution in Tunisia maintained the characteristics of a national army, identifying itself with the sovereignty of the state regardless of the government's ideology.

At this stage, the licenced political parties began to issue statements affirming their support for the overthrow of the regime. This did little to restore their image, however, considering that they had not participated in the revolution and had even hesitated to join the protests. The Renewal Movement, for example, issued a statement describing the dictator's departure as a victory for the Tunisian people, even though it had not called for his departure in its previous statements.

Al Nahda specified a number of measures to be taken in order to preserve the revolution, most notably the creation of a Constituent Assembly tasked with rewriting the Constitution, the dissolution of Parliament and the Constitutional Council, and the holding of legislative elections within six months, which would result in the formation of an inclusive national salvation government.

191. *al-Yawm al-Sabi'*, 15 January 2011, accessed on 17 December 2020, at: https://bit.ly/3amAn8C.

192. *BBC Arabic*, 15 January 2011, accessed on 16 December 2020, at: http://bbc.in/3r4nJkw.

193. One author's emphasis on 'civil society organizations' led him to conclude that the UGTT was the one institution able to fill the power void left by Ben Ali. See Safwan M. Masri, *Tunisia: An Arab Anomaly* (New York: Columbia University Press, 2017), p. xxxii. This is of course not true, as the void was filled by figures from the regime itself in keeping with the Tunisian Constitution.

194. This in itself indicates that he was not involved in a coup attempt against Ben Ali.

From the struggle to oust Ben Ali to the struggle to oust the regime

The revolution had demanded the president's removal, and revolutionaries resisted intellectuals and activists who were satisfied with the reforms the interim president had promised under duress. Similarly, they resisted those who were content with what they considered the epic achievement of Ben Ali's departure, demanding the overthrow of the entire regime through the removal of its figures and the officials who belonged to the ruling party. Eventually, the demands of the revolution extended to include the removal of ministers, security officials and even judges. At this stage, however, the activists who had outbid each other in presenting such demands lacked a clear alternative agenda, nor did they constitute a leadership that could, or was willing to, implement such an agenda. Furthermore, the transition could not be carried out without the state institutions being run by figures of the old regime. However, leading figures from the regime, including the army, understood that this was a revolution and that the only way out of their dilemma was a pluralist democratic system. In short, they understood that regime change was inevitable; hence, they did not attempt to salvage the regime but only the state's institutions.

There comes a time, however, when sector-affiliated peaceful demonstrations raising just demands begin to lose support and become a burden on democratic transition, at least from the perspective of the general public, especially riots broke out in several governorates with no clear demands.

This pattern is not typical of revolutions that break the state apparatus through a coup, or produce a clear revolutionary command that takes the place of the existing regime. Instead, the Tunisian Revolution besieged the regime from without, as it were, prompting it to open its door to change following the dictator's removal. This, however, did not impress the rebellious masses, which rejected the regime's gradual reforms and began protesting anew, particularly when they sensed that the centres of power were still in place and that the regime might regain its authority if not forced into radical reforms. At this point, debates began on whether to return to normal life, or to persist in protest actions until all demands were met.

The revolutionary movement quickly transformed into an unending string of disparate demands-based struggles led by various sectors which seized upon this opportune moment for protest. Protest at this point became relatively easy, with little to lose, and could be employed by different segments of civil society to prevent their causes from being neglected amid the flurry of political issues in the country. Viewing its own cause as central and eminently worthy, each group drew public attention to its suffering, convinced that the time was right to protest all forms of injustice.

Influenced by the praise lavished upon it from all sides even for things it had not done, the Tunisian army accepted the role of protector of the revolution. It was able to do so by acting on three fronts: pursuing the small 'security' circle of the former regime while maintaining the continuity and functioning of state institutions, confronting attempts to wreak havoc in major cities and guaranteeing the security needed by the masses to pursue their struggle against and, eventually break with, the regime. On 16 January 2011, the army arrested around fifty 'private' soldiers belonging to Ben Ali's bodyguard in Tunisia's southern Tataouine province as they were attempting to escape into Libya in unmarked cars. Meanwhile, the army continued to pursue individuals whom it believed were attempting to create instability in the country. They arrested the former Tunisian interior minister, Rafiq Belhaj Kacem, in his hometown of Baja as he was preparing to escape to Algeria. An army unit also arrested Kais Ben Ali, nephew of the deposed president, following a shootout in the coastal town of Masakin east of the capital Tunis.

Despite their limited role in the revolution, the parties suggested programmes for the transition, being organized bodies that saw themselves as the actors best qualified to overthrow the regime and usher in a democratic era. Meanwhile, the executive bureau of the UGTT called for the immediate dissolution of the professional branches of the former ruling party and the formation of a national committee to review the Constitution and all laws relating to political reform. The union also demanded a legislative pardon, a clear separation between political parties and state structures, and a radical review of the concept, structures and functions of security in Tunisia.

In the midst of these calls, Mohammed Ghannouchi announced the formation of a transitional national unity government whose mission would be to achieve the transition to democracy by reforming the laws regulating public life and preparing for free and transparent elections under the supervision of an independent commission and international observers. Ghannouchi declared that all those detained and imprisoned because of their ideas or political activism would be released and that a general legislative pardon law was being drafted.[195]

Despite popular protests against retaining any elements of the former regime, the new cabinet included six ministers from the previous government, including the ministers of defence, interior, finance and foreign affairs. Three opposition leaders were also given ministerial positions: Ahmad Ibrahim, head of the Renewal Party, became Minister of Higher Education; Ahmad Najib al-Shabbi, founder of the Progressive Democratic Party, was appointed Minister of Regional Development; and Mostafa Ben Jaafar, secretary-general of the Democratic Forum for Labor and Freedoms, was made Minister of Health. Minister of Foreign Affairs Kamel Morjane, Minister of the Interior Ahmed Friaâ, Minister of Defence Ridha Grira and Minister of Finance Mohamed Ridha Chalghoum all kept their previous positions.[196] Under popular pressure and ongoing demonstrations against the government, three ministers affiliated with the Tunisian General Labor Union resigned from the cabinet on 18 January, their stated reason being that the cabinet's makeup was still dominated by the old ruling party.

On 18 January 2011, Tunisian prime minister Mohammed Ghannouchi defended the decision to retain ministers from the previous government, stressing

195. *BBC Arabic*, 18 January 2011, accessed on 16 December 2020 at: http://bbc.in/3r6hTPi.

196. Ibid.

that he had kept the ministers with 'clean hands' who had always worked to protect the interests of the country.[197] This approach which, in spite of militant protests, rejected the eradication mentality and at the same time accepted the transition to democracy as a goal shared by the country's central political forces, was the right beginning for Tunisian democracy.

At the same time, beginning on 18 January 2011, a form of social activism emerged with the formation of citizens committees in neighbourhoods and cities in order to defend them from instances of looting and sabotage. Individuals from the security apparatus loyal to the deposed president were accused of being behind these attacks. The army attempted to aid the population in preserving security, providing phone numbers for citizens to call when they encountered suspicious vehicles or armed individuals.[198]

Several parties called for the creation of a Constituent Assembly in which all political and unionist forces would participate in order to establish a Second Republic with a new constitution during the transitional phase, to be followed by parliamentary elections under international supervision. The Tunisian League for the Defence of Human Rights stressed the necessity of holding accountable those responsible for murdering and injuring innocent citizens during peaceful protests. The League stressed the importance of prosecuting all those who had fired at protesters, as well as those who had issued the commands to do so; they noted that those detained during the events, in addition to political prisoners, should be released, allowing the return of political exiles and promptly issuing a general legislative pardon.

On 20 January the new cabinet held its first meeting, in the course of which it made a number of decisions, most importantly: acknowledgement of all banned political parties and movements; proposal of a draft law that would pardon all political prisoners in the country;[199] and announcement of a 3-day mourning period for those killed during the popular protests.[200] On this same day, Acting President Fuad al-Mubazzi' and Prime Minister Mohamed Ghannouchi tendered their resignations from the former ruling party,[201] as did all members of the Tunisian interim cabinet who had belonged to the RCD.[202]

197. *al-Watan newspaper*, 19 January 2011 accessed on 16 December 2020, at: https://bit.ly/37nihRS.

198. *France 24*, 18 January 2011, accessed on 16 December 2020, at: http://bit.ly/3oYDCXQ.

199. *BBC Arabic*, 20 January 2011, accessed on 16 December 2020, at: http://bbc.in/2LJW0oX.

200. *BBC Arabic*, 20 January 2011, accessed on 16 December 2020, at: http://bbc.in/2IUENYO.

201. *Al-Jazeera.net*, 20 January 2011, accessed at: https://bit.ly/3h5SfpD .

202. *Doualia*, 20 January 2011, accessed on 16 December 2020, at: https://bit.ly/3gVxyfD.

In a televised broadcast, interim President Fuad al-Mubazzi' promised to make a complete break with the past, build an independent judiciary and allow freedom of the press.[203] In one of its first decisions after its formation, Ghannouchi's government approved a general legislative pardon draft law that included all political prisoners and prisoners of opinion. At the same time, a large number of Tunisian security forces held a protest in front of the interim government's headquarters in Kasbah, downtown Tunis. The protesting security officers denied responsibility for the murders that had taken place during the revolution, with a number of them wearing a red sign. In an event unprecedented in Tunisia's history, angry members of the police intercepted the car of interim President Fuad al-Mubazzi on 23 January 2011 and prevented it from reaching the government's headquarters in the Kasbah until security intervened and opened the way for the motorcade.

On 24 January 2011, in the army's first public statement following Ben Ali's deposition, General Rachid Ammar called upon demonstrators to empty the square facing the government headquarters (during the so-called Kasbah 1 protests and sit-ins). Some viewed Ammar's statements as an attempt to reassure the people that the army retained authority over the interim government, while others understood his statement to mean that the army leadership might benefit from the state of instability as a means of strengthening its position within the state. However, neither of these interpretations was correct. Unlike its Egyptian counterpart, the Tunisian army had no political ambitions, not even for a role in the interim period.[204]

Despite the army's attempt to assert its role as protector of the revolution, the revolutionary activists preferred to rely on themselves. The youth movement and its protests in the Kasbah, or what became known as Kasbah 1 (23–27 January 2011) and Kasbah 2 (25 February 2011), expedited the decision to hold elections for a Constituent Assembly to be tasked with drafting a new constitution. Tunisians took to the streets to protect their revolution, and these movements, some of which were dispersed by force, represented an important development that did not receive sufficient media attention since, by this time, Arab and international media were too busy following the events of the Egyptian Revolution. Protest demonstrations continued calling for the overthrow of the interim government, removal of the figures from the previous era and the dissolution of the RCD. In

203. France *24*, 20 January 2011, accessed on 16 December 2020, at: http://bit.ly/37rGd6K.

204. It should be noted that the Tunisian Army was founded on 24 June 1956, and was composed of around 50,000 soldiers, 37,000 of whom belonged to the land force. The Army was used mainly to help execute civilian projects and to combat natural disasters. It also participated heavily in peacekeeping missions under the mandate of the United Nations. Since 1960, Tunisia has contributed to the UN-sponsored peacekeeping forces, with 1,000 Tunisian soldiers taking part in the peacekeeping mission in the Democratic Republic of Congo.

the midst of the popular pressure to eliminate the figures of the former regime, Abdullah Kallel, head of the advisors' council in the second chamber of Parliament and former interior minister, resigned from his post two days after being placed under house arrest.

Minister of Foreign Affairs Kamel Morjane resigned from the cabinet on 27 January 2011, following several days of protests calling for the departure of the ministers associated with the RCD.[205] Mohammed Ghannouchi then announced a new interim government in which Ben Ali's ministers would be forbidden to occupy any major position in relation to foreign or domestic affairs, defence or finance. He appointed Ahmed Ounaies as Minister of Foreign Affairs and publicly listed the members of government who would be tasked with organizing democratic elections.[206]

The Tunisian government tried to manage the situation by taking several steps, including the announcement of Ahmad Najib al-Shabbi's succession as Minister of Regional Development, the agreement to pay DT 500 million (USD 354 million) in compensation to the families of those killed during the revolution and to accept licencing requests for banned political parties. On 26 January, the interim Tunisian government issued an international arrest warrant for Ben Ali and his wife Leila, as well as other members of his family, and the next day, a claim was filed with the Swiss federal government to recover the money and properties that had been smuggled out of Tunisia by the deposed president, his family and his close associates. On 28 January, the Interpol issued arrest warrants for the deposed Tunisian president and six of his relatives on 27 January.

In the meantime, Sheikh Rached Ghannouchi declared his intention to return to his homeland after being granted a passport by the Tunisian Embassy in London, stressing that his movement should not be excluded from the political process. He stated, 'Al Nahda . . . responds to the people's need for their identity, and for Islam to be the framework for the demands of justice and freedom.'[207] Ghannouchi asserted his intention to engage in political, cultural and social activism among the people rather than seeking political posts, noting that the younger members of his movement would take part in managing the country towards a just and acceptable form of rule.

The National Progressive Party issued a statement from Gabes University accusing the army of conspiring with the security forces of the previous regime and of aiding the RCD militia in attacking the protesters in the Kasbah Square. The statement claimed that the military establishment was not neutral and that the army's claim of standing on the side of the people was not supported by the

205. *BBC Arabic*, 27 January 2011, accessed on 16 December 2020, at: http://bbc.in/37mrEkF.

206. *France 24*, 27 January 2011, accessed on 16 December 2020, at: http://bit.ly/3oUVm6e.

207. *Al Jazeera.net*, 29 January 2011, accessed on 16 December 2020, at: https://bit.ly/3eDzWZj.

facts. Furthermore, on 30 January, a similar statement was issued by the National Committee for the Preservation of the Achievements of the Revolution, which was founded by young Tunisians who had protested in front of the government hall in the Kasbah.

On 31 January, Rached Ghannouchi announced that Al Nahda would mobilize in favour of the popular revolution. To this he added that his party would likely participate in fair parliamentary elections, although no final decision on the matter had been made yet.

Many cities, especially on the coast, witnessed chaos and vandalism in the days following the revolution, including the torching of a synagogue in the Gabes governorate south of Tunis. This may have happened in reaction to Ben Ali's ties with Israel and might have simultaneously served as a signal to Israel. Either way, these sentiments manifested themselves as an unjustifiable attack on a Jewish place of worship. Such incidents in the Tunisian Revolution were exceptional, however, and were met with public condemnation. It was rumoured that forces loyal to the former regime may actually have been behind this attack, the purpose being to sow chaos and division and to sour international public opinion on the revolution.

With the victory of the revolution and the media's tendency to glorify Mohamed Bouazizi as a hero, media reports and debates abounded regarding the use of suicide and self-immolation as a form of political protest. As mentioned earlier, news spread that a man by the name of Abdel Salam Traimish had preceded Mohamed Bouazizi in resorting to self-immolation in al-Monastir in protest against the confiscation of his cart. Traimish's family declared that their son, who had set himself on fire after being deprived of work, had been the first martyr of the revolution, and the inspiration for what Mohamed Bouazizi had done. The father of the young Traimish said in an interview. 'My son . . . started the revolutionary process that flared at the hands of Bouazizi.' The young Abdel Salam Traimish, thirty years of age, had indeed committed suicide through self-immolation inside city hall on the morning of 3 March 2010. The suicide had followed a city official's decision to prevent Traimish from setting up his cart, from which he sold light snacks, in the centre of the city. The news of Traimish's self-immolation had been broadcast at the time by several media channels. However, the incident had not sparked an uprising as did Mohamed Bouazizi's self-immolation only months later.[208] But now that an act of self-immolation had triggered the revolution, Traimish's family wanted a share in the glory.

After a wave of violence that included an attack on the Ministry of the Interior, Tunisian interior minister Farhat Rajhi declared on 2 February that former members of the security services were carrying out a conspiracy to undermine the state. Meanwhile, in the capital, roaming gangs attacked several schools.

On the level of civic action, journalists working in different media outlets launched a national campaign to 'purge' media institutions of journalists who

208. al-*Quds al-Arabi*, 31 January 2011, accessed on 16 December 2020, at: http://bit.ly/3h0mAWy.

were affiliated with the former regime. The campaign called for removing all those employed by media institutions who did not hold a college degree in journalism or some other specialization and replacing them with graduates from the College of Journalism.

On 3 February 2011, the interior minister announced that the interim president would be appointing new governors throughout the republic in keeping with the aim of purging members of the former regime. In this way, the Tunisian Revolution strove to usher in an era of democratic transformation, complete with new symbols and new faces that had not been implicated in the service of despotism. On 4 February 2011, the entire staff of the former president's office were terminated and the ruling party's activities were suspended in anticipation of its dissolution on 6 February.[209] The revolutionary demands, however, did not stop here. Protests were renewed in a number of governorates in rejection of the appointment of new governors who had held senior positions under the former regime and the failure to dismiss cabinet members loyal to Ben Ali.

On 7 February, Al Nahda held a press conference in which it presented its agenda for the next phase, including an explanation of its positions on questions of democracy, human rights and the Personal Status Code. The speakers emphasized the political and civic character of their movement, stressing that the rights of women were not up for debate. They also noted that Tunisia's civil code had been formulated by the clerics of Zaituna Mosque and that it constituted a part of Islamic jurisprudence.[210]

Up until the revolution, media outlets in Tunisia had been restricted primarily to the two state television channels and private (though not independent) radio and television channels, such as the pro-regime 'Nesma' and 'Hannibal' television stations. After the revolution, these channels were transformed into forums for the discussion of events in the country and its future. And new private channels were founded. Political figures and intellectuals were hosted to discuss the former and current regimes in an unprecedented atmosphere of freedom of speech and civic dialogue. Democracy had opened the door to populism even when it worked against democracy itself and the practice of exaggerating the flaws of the transition phase became a means of arousing nostalgia for the old regime.

209. *BBC Arabic*, 6 February 2011, accessed on 16 December 2020, at: http://bbc.in/2WsHvYx.

210. 'Ennahda Movement returns to the Tunisian political scene', [ʿawdat ḥarakat al-nahḍah at-tūnisiyah lil-sāhah al-siyāsiyah al-tūnisiyah], *Maghrebia*, 9 February 2011, accessed at: https://bit.ly/3nrwJOi.

From the regime in abstract to institutions: regime officials as civil servants of the transition and the HIROR

After Ben Ali's departure and the beginning of the regime's collapse, creative societal forces emerged: civic discourse, debate over the future and advancing the question of whether, or how, to purge state institutions of figures from the former regime.[211] The names of the corrupt and those implicated in crimes against the people were listed in detail, with many calling for them to be held accountable. Simultaneously, particular demands were voiced with the hope that they could be achieved right away. Whether sparked by revolutionary zeal or by instrumentalist calculation, such hope was consistent with the knowledge that the post-revolution state was weak and malleable and that it would be easy to make it concede to people's demands. All these manifestations were to be expected alongside the chaos that erupted for a short period of time and had to be overcome by the state and the popular committees that emerged locally to protect the revolution. However, the phenomenon that was qualitatively new was the appearance of an expanding public domain for dialogue among citizens which heralded a better future.

Given the temporary weakness of the state's structures, however, worrisome developments ensued, such as outbreaks of old tribal tensions in the periphery, the spread of crime, attacks on public properties, unlicenced construction and so forth. Similar events were also witnessed in Egypt after its revolution. Such incidents pose no threat as long they remain exceptional and do not evolve into a generalized panic. The principal guarantee that a regime can be reformed in accordance with the principles of the revolution is the existence of a lively public space occupied by the forces of change. Needless to say, it is crucial that the revolutionary forces have a clear say in the state's legitimacy and an agreed-upon understanding that the desired alternative to despotism is democracy. Despite the importance of political pluralism, this unified vision must rise above particular demands and the ensuing chaos must be reined in by the state apparatus as it regains its vitality and confidence.

Given the chain of successes achieved by the Tunisian uprising, including daily resignations and expulsions of former regime figures, the protesters' collective consciousness began shifting towards a complete rupture with the former regime. In this context, the National Council for Freedoms organized a protest gathering on 8 February 2011 in front of the parliament building, calling for its dissolution and the creation of a Constituent Assembly. Hundreds gathered in protest after a session of Parliament that had approved granting interim President Fuad al-Mubazzi the power to issue laws in the form of decrees in several domains – electoral law, media law, international agreements, general pardons and terrorism. This law, which was passed under Article 28 of the Constitution, granted the interim president absolute legislative power. This was necessary in order for the

211. The Higher Authority for Realization of the Objectives of the Revolution, Political Reform and Democratic Transition (HIROR).

state to launch the transition. However, the power granted was only nominally absolute; substantially it was bounded by the goals of the transition.

On 7 February 2011, the Tunisian political scene was brimming with questions regarding the army's recent decision to call up the reserve, including ground troops, the Air Force and the Navy.[212] Under the pressure of popular queries, the Tunisian Ministry of Defence issued a statement on 10 February in which it clarified that the decision to call up the reserve had been 'a legal measure taken in accordance with the General Basic Law for Military Personnel and the National Service Law'. The ministry added that the aim of the measure was 'to protect citizens, public and private properties, and high risk institutions, so as to reassure citizens and enable them to return to their work without fear'.[213]

The explanation offered by the military establishment came after manifestations of lawlessness had been observed in the Tunisian capital. The decision to call up the reserve was a response to a real need for security and came about to dispel genuine fears aroused by the unrest that had followed the collapse of the state's interior security apparatus. Never before had the Ministry of Defence been obliged to explain any step it had taken to the citizenry. Regardless of how well-founded citizens' concerns may have been, and whatever the clarifications issued, this incident illustrated the emergence of a culture in which new mores and protocols would thenceforth govern the relationship between government ministries and the people.

When civil officials of the old regime continued as servants during the transition process, they were attacked and accused of being counter-revolutionary. In response, they formed and legalized an institution that incorporated representatives of the major political and civil forces to prepare for the democratic election of a Constituent Assembly that would include no one from the ruling party. In so doing, it merged a nominated institution that was supposed to draft the needed political reforms with civil movements which were formed to guard the 'spirit' of the revolution and to guarantee that its goals were achieved. The National Council for the Protection of the Revolution, established on 11 February 2011, was comprised of twenty-eight different political parties and associations, including: the Tunisian Human Rights League (LTDH), the National Council for Liberties in Tunisia (CNLT), The National Syndicate of Tunisian Journalists (SNJT) and the Tunisian Association of Democratic Women (ATFD). All these associations were brought together by the UGTT and the Tunisian Order of Lawyers (ONAT), with some political parties, to form the Council for the Protection of the Revolution to oversee the government's implementation of the revolution's demands.

The UGTT then approached Ghannouchi's government and requested official recognition of the Council for the Protection of the Revolution. After a lengthy dialogue and internal debate within the government, then-prime minister

212. *BBC Arabic*, 8 February 2011, accessed on 16 December 2020, at: http://bbc.in/3ahrm0h.

213. *The Arab Information Center*, 12 February 2011 accessed at: https://bit.ly/34kbqXq.

Mohammed Ghannouchi suggested a compromise, that is, that the Higher Political Reform Commission be integrated with the UGTT's National Council for the Protection of the Revolution. Eventually, the Political Reform Commission was merged with the National Council for the Protection of the Revolution to form the Higher Authority for Realization of the Objectives of the Revolution, Political Reform and Democratic Transition (HIROR), thus officially institutionalizing the transition.

HIROR functioned as a forum for different political parties which also issued election regulations. The HIROR drafted a set of principles which became the preamble for the Tunisian Constitution. The rule governing decision-making in the HIROR was consensus after dialogue. There was to be no voting in an unelected forum. The general mood in the HIROR was modernist and secularist. The Islamists were a minority, and when the majority insisted on breaking the rule and voting when it was a matter of preserving the modern achievements of the republic, Al Nahda accused the HIROR of appropriating the will of the Tunisian people and preventing elections, or anticipating election results, by imposing a set of pre-determined facts on a future elected legislative council. Al Nahda left the HIROR in June 2011 after the majority insisted on enacting the 'Republican Covenant', most of whose elements were incorporated into the Preamble and Article 2 of the Constitution, which laid out the civil character of the state.

Over time, the protests and demonstrations evolved from demanding the dissolution of Parliament to demanding the dissolution of Ghannouchi's cabinet, which had begun isolating the former ruling party and dismissing its leading figures. Ghannouchi's government had also decided to jail Belhaj Kacem, former Minister of the Interior, on charges of first-degree murder. On 11 February, the Ministry of Interior's media and communications unit started an official Facebook page that featured the ministry's news and activities, job announcements, and audiovisual recordings. The page also contained a section where visitors could freely discuss matters of interest.[214] Yet despite all these measures, nothing could slow the momentum of the protests, which in the month of February resumed on an almost daily basis in a call for the government's overthrow. The suppression of the demonstrations of 25 February resulted in damage to the business district as well as several fatalities. Hence, succumbing to pressure, Ghannouchi resigned on 27 February, and the interim president appointed 84-year-old Beji Caid Essebsi in his place. Essebsi, as previously mentioned, was a major figure of the Bourguiba era who held various ministerial posts between 1963 and 1991, including the ministries of the interior, defence and foreign affairs. Essebsi also served as Speaker of Parliament until 1990.

Essebsi's cabinet included twenty-two ministers and eleven deputy ministers, with the majority of the ministers of the previous cabinet maintaining their positions, and the appointment of four new ministers to replace those who had resigned after Ghannouchi's departure. The four new cabinet members included

214. The Ministry of Interior's Facebook page can be found at: http://bit.ly/3r3520i.

Ahmad Ibrahim (secretary-general of the Renewal Movement) and Abderrazak Zouari, who became Minister of Regional Development in place of Ahmad Najib al-Shabbi (former secretary-general of the Democratic Progressive Party).

Responding to relentless grassroots pressure, interim president Fu'ad al-Mubazzi announced that a new Constituent National Assembly would be elected on 24 July 2011 and that it would be charged with managing the country and drafting a new constitution. This development followed al-Mubazzi's announcement on 4 March that the 1959 Constitution would be suspended on the grounds that it no longer fulfilled the aspirations of the people and that it presented an obstacle to the organization of transparent elections. Eventually, the election of the National Constituent Assembly was postponed until 23 October 2011

The HIROR prepared six important edicts for the democratic transition: Decree-law 27 (April 2011) for the formation of the Higher Independent Authority for Elections, Decree-law 35 (May 2011) concerning the elections of the Constituent Assembly, Decree-law 87 (September 2011) concerning the establishment of political parties, Decree-law 87 (September 2011) concerning the establishment of associations, Decree-law 115 (November 2011) concerning the freedom of audiovisual media and the establishment of a Higher Independent Authority of Audiovisual. It also offered a platform for dialogue among Tunisia's political forces, civil associations and social movements on the coming political system. The Constitution was to be drafted by an elected institution. However, the dialogue and the attempt to reach agreement among the various political forces took place in an unelected forum, which actually set the tone before the elections.

No acts of retaliation were taken by the Tunisian Revolution except for the trial in absentia of the ousted Ben Ali, the confiscation of his properties, the exclusion of RCD leaders and members from the Constituent Assembly elections by a decree enacted on 10 May 2011 and the dismissal of some commanders of the security apparatus.

The revolutionary forces were not alone, of course, in post-revolutionary Tunisia, as even in this early phase, some elements of society objected to the ongoing protests. There were two types of demonstrations that broke out in the aftermath of the revolution. In the impoverished Kasbah, protesters called for banning of the RCD, the dismissal of its ministers and the election of a Constituent Assembly, while in the capital's well-to-do Al Menzah suburbs, demonstrators presenting themselves as the so-called 'silent majority' protested against the continuation of the protests and called for 'social peace and security',[215] although they were neither silent, nor a majority.

After the elections, the interim president and the prime minister attended the first session of the Constituent Assembly. The prime minister resigned on 23 November 2011, followed by the president, both of whom transferred power peacefully to the president and prime minister chosen by the Constituent Assembly.

215. Sami Zemni, 'From Revolution to Tunisianité: Who Are the Tunisian People?' *Middle East Law and Governance*, vol. 8, nos 2–3 (2016), p. 137.

CONCLUDING REMARKS

One: In the foregoing chapters, we have analysed the background, triggers and dynamics of the Tunisian Revolution, a classic example of a reformist revolution that forced a ruling regime to accede to popular demands by handing political power to an elected institution. The theme has not been revolutions in general but a specific kind of revolution, that is, one which ultimately results in democratic transformation, however undemocratically it may have been managed along the way.

The acts of protest that lead to a revolution are not unique to themselves. That is to say, they are no different from other protest actions which the regime and the people may have experienced before, the exceptions being that: (1) they are sustained for a relatively long time due to their ability to flesh out the grievances and frustrations of various sectors of society, (2) they encompass relatively large segments of the population and (3) the regime exhibits confusion in the face of the protests' unexpected and rapid spread, and the enormous scale of popular participation.

This protest evolves from an uprising to a revolution as it: (1) escalates its demands to that of the dictator's departure or regime change; (2) spreads and intensifies to a point where it can only be quelled by the use of violently repressive measures that may present the army and security forces with a dilemma; and (3) produces a situation in which any concession by the regime short of the departure of the dictator and any use of power short of total repression by the combined force of the military, security apparatus and political leadership simply result in further escalation.

The Tunisian Revolution began as an outburst of public discontent maintained by community solidarity and organized local activism. It became a regional uprising as it spread across inland governorates whose urban centres led the protest in forms that ranged from peaceful to violent and from spontaneous to highly organized. This interchange confused the authorities, who were unable to isolate flashpoints of protest. This relatively protracted mass protest movement was triggered by social and economic deprivation, humiliation and a powerful drive to restore dignity through the act of protest. It was then nurtured, spread and intensified by these same sources of indignation to the point of no return – the point at which nothing would suffice but the abolition of the current regime in its entirety.

There is a certain point in the development of popular uprisings when protests continue to expand no matter what tools are used by the regime to confront them. Threats, as in the first speech of the ex-president, generated more protests, while concessions, as in his third speech, simply convinced the protesters that the regime was being weakened and that they could continue to press for its fall. This is the point where the security response becomes crucial. If the army and the security forces are united with the regime and face the civil protests, whether peaceful or violent, with unlimited force, it becomes very difficult to continue an unarmed protest. Conversely, if the uprising continues to expand and begins to demand regime change and if the security forces are unwilling to exploit the violent means necessary to quell the revolution, the regime is doomed.

There came a point in the short history of the Tunisian Revolution where, being worn down by the adamant protests, whether violent or peaceful, some elements of the security forces began chafing at the burden of protecting the regime, especially the corrupt circles surrounding it. The army did not rebel outright, of course, but neither did it actively suppress the revolution. As a consequence, the decisions being made by the regime reflected doubt and uncertainty regarding the loyalty of the security forces and whether the army would continue standing with it unconditionally. This state of mistrust, confusion and lack of coordination within the regime was central to what drove the president out of the country. The fall of the dictator was inevitable now; however, what happened next would depend on whether the high-ranking elements of the regime and the opposition would come together to implement the revolution's demands.

The president's departure from the country could have led to a power grab by the military or other branches of the regime. In this case, however, the army had no ambition to seize power, and the spirit of the revolution was so prevalent that the individuals in the regime with a civic conscience were convinced that the only way out of the crisis was a democratic solution to be negotiated with the opposition. However, the issue of democracy was not raised for the first time during the revolution; rather, it had become a topic of discussion before then, in the context of opposition to the authoritarian regime. Islamists and secular opposition movements had begun communicating with each other since 2003, producing programmes for regime change that would guarantee human rights on multiple levels within a democratic framework. In other words, democracy was not a mere afterthought of the revolution; rather, it had been a conscious, agreed-upon objective among the various forces opposed to the regime since before the revolution began. State institutions that remained stable after the departure of the president stood ready to lead the country through a democratic transition and to negotiate the nature of the transition period with the opposition. In this unique constellation, revolution would open the way to democracy.

The revolution was not steered by a national leadership; nor was the uprising manipulated by particular organized forces to become a revolution. Not having a single head, the revolution could not, and would not, seize power to change the regime itself. Rather, it demanded that it be changed, and in this way, it served as a vivid illustration of a reformist revolution. Unlike revolutions that are planned from above or, even if unplanned, are taken advantage of by an 'avant-garde' in order to seize power and enforce a regime change according to its world view, this is the kind of revolution that can pave the way for democracy.

The possibility that a revolution might pave the way for a transition to democracy is not envisaged by the field of 'transitology' (which concerns itself with the transition from authoritarian rule). According to transitology literature, a transition from authoritarian rule to democracy must begin with a reform from above that causes a split in the regime itself. Once this split has occurred, all that is required in order for the transition to democracy to take place (apart from a prevailing consensus on the state as a stable national institution) is the presence of moderate leaders within both the regime and the opposition who can negotiate a democratic outcome. However, there is no expectation that such negotiations might be set in motion by a revolution from below rather than by reforms from above.

The top-down reforms that took place in the late 1970s and 1980s in Tunisia and other Arab countries did not lead to a democratic transition. On the contrary, they led to regime consolidation by allowing the opposition to run only in elections to non-decision-making bodies. The regime used the reforms to contain protests and/or to improve its international image when it was subjected to pressure or due to changes in the regional and international scene (a drop in oil prices, the fall of the Socialist Bloc, the Gulf War, etc.). However, the reforms were revoked at will after each crisis had passed.

As stated earlier, revolutions led by an ideological avante garde in order to seize power could most likely lead to another authoritarian regime. On the other hand, revolutions without explicit leadership may lead not to democracy but to anarchy, the dismantling of state institutions and even civil war. Democratic revolutions are more likely to lead to democracy, but not as a historical necessity. Such a revolution led to a democratic transition in Tunisia but failed to do so in Egypt.[1]

The modern history of both countries is distinguished by relatively early national institution-building and adoption of state nationalism, which became the official ideology of Tunisia's ruling party following independence. In both countries there is basic agreement on the legitimacy of the state itself augmented by ethnic and religious homogeneity and the absence of separatist movements or deep cleavages concerning the identity of the state or its territorial borders. Although in Egypt, the unresolved Coptic question remained an obstacle in the transition to democracy, it did not pose a problem during the revolution itself. The major difference lay in the political awareness and political culture of the elites of both the regime and the opposition and the role of the army. Another critical

1. For further discussion of the different potential outcomes of this transition, see my recent, *Problems of Democratization: A Comparative Theoretical and Applied Study [al-intiqāl al-dīmuqrāṭī wa ishkāliyatuh: dirāsah naẓariyah wa taṭbīqiyah muqāranah]* (Beirut: Arab Center for Research and Policy Studies, 2020), esp. Ch. 16, pp. 529–50.

factor was an external one, that is, the intervention of regional anti-democracy forces in the transition process in Egypt versus its absence in Tunisia.

The consensus on the state as a stable national institution and the absence of deep cleavages are important not only in the transition to democracy but in the revolutionary phase as well. The deep cleavages in other Arab countries (Syria, Yemen, and Libya, for example) manifested themselves in tribal, regional or sectarian identification with the regime so that revolutions led to a vertical split in the society, with broad sectors of society identifying with the struggle against the regime and others clinging to the regime as though their very lives depended on it.

Two: In Tunisia, there were no ethnic or sectarian cleavages as such. However, there were severe discrepancies among regions in terms of development indices, unemployment rates, quality of life, the degree of secularization and the internalization of the regime's ideology. These gaps continued to be reproduced and aggravated, while poverty (even in absolute numbers) remained a problem despite overall economic growth, an increase in average income and living standards, the spread of education and special trade relations with Europe. Such disparities did not threaten the unity of the nation or the state; they threatened only the authoritarian regime, which was intent on persecuting the political opposition, especially Islamists, confident that subversive political activism could always be controlled through surveillance, containment or repression. Consequently, it failed to anticipate the threat coming from the socio-economic domain – the very domain the regime had been praised for.

Since allowing political pluralism in 1981 at the end of Bourguiba's term, the ruling regime in Tunisia had concentrated its efforts on taming, containing or repressing the political opposition. The regime had viewed its containment of 'moderate' political opposition within legal political parties and 'innocuous' NGOs as a feather in its cap alongside the successes of the so-called Tunisian Miracle. As for the already existing legal opposition parties, they had in fact offered bold critiques of certain government policies; however, they dared not to question the regime itself. The illegal parties, the radical left and Islamists were persecuted by the regime to varying degrees, with radical political parties often relegated to prison and exile.

Despite its success in containing political parties, however, the Tunisian regime remained vulnerable to the threat posed by a popular uprising that might turn into a revolution. Unlike the actions of political parties, the source of such an uprising could not be tracked or controlled. How could the regime measure the build-up of rage due to feelings of deprivation and injustice in scattered swathes of society when the numbers told a different story: a story of higher growth rates, reduced illiteracy and falling poverty rates? Protests had, in fact, taken place in Tunisia before December 2010, most of them presenting demands for social and economic justice. However, popular revolts could easily be isolated and repressed, as were those that erupted in 2008 and 2010. Bourguiba's regime had even faced protests on a national scale, as in 1978 and 1984. However, it had been able to rely on its security forces, including the army, to contain the labour unions' leader within the ruling party and on Bourguiba's ability to blame others for the country's woes while holding himself aloof from critique as the 'father of the nation.'

We should not overlook the fact that the severity with which acts of protest were quelled had decreased compared with the brutal repression of the 1987 and 1984 uprisings. This does not mean that protests during Ben Ali's rule were not brutally repressed, of course but simply that fewer people were being killed in protests now that there was a heightened social awareness of political and human rights.

The modernization process in Tunisia seemed to be working. Indeed, praise had been lavished on the regime and its leader for the country's economic growth, stability, openness to foreign investment, increased life expectancy and better education. However, Tunisia's economy remained a peripheral one in a Europe-centred development model, and the economic reforms it had implemented according to IMF dictates had widened the gaps among social sectors and between coastal regions and the interior while exacerbating unemployment, especially among the educated. Ben Ali's regime had achieved greater economic development and higher living standards than Bourguiba's regime had. However, the latter had at least given the impression of being a meritocracy that enabled social mobility based on personal effort and qualification. It had also presented itself as a welfare state that took care of its subjects' needs and which could rely on an imagined unity between government and society as if the regime were an extension of the national liberation period.

What both regimes failed to take into account is that the welfare of the citizenry cannot be measured by changes in absolute numbers, which are often side effects of a modernization and growth process that does nothing to address the socio-economic inequalities that fuel feelings of deprivation and accumulated rage. It should be remembered in this connection that higher living standards and educational levels result in rising expectations and a keener awareness of existing socio-economic gaps; they awaken people to the absence of civil liberties and political rights and intensify their aversion to corruption (a phenomenon that was severely aggravated during Ben Ali's rule); similarly, they reinforce an awareness of the need for personal dignity and a sensitivity to humiliation, none of which can be separated from feelings of deprivation, resentment and anger, especially when unemployment rates continue to rise in the midst of overall economic growth.

The drop in economic growth that took place during the world economic crisis of 2008–9 played an important role in igniting the fury. However, the primary source of the ongoing rage was the deprivation produced by the aforementioned socio-economic gap; add to this the demoralization and cynicism that had resulted from Ben Ali's hypocritical introduction of political openness and reforms, only to revoke them thereafter, along with the spread of corruption and clientele networks.

The uprising in Tunisia's poorer regions was not sustained spontaneously but, rather, by dint of organization on the local level. Such organization could guide the protests but not control them. The core of the protesters consisted of youth and the unemployed who, though unarmed, were not necessarily peaceful. The protests took the form of everything from peaceful marches and sit-ins to riots, confrontations with security forces, attacks on ruling party premises and the torching of police departments. A similar phenomenon was witnessed in Egypt. Peaceful protests and sit-ins drew the attention of local, regional and global public opinion, while the confrontations exhausted security forces in both countries.

Nevertheless, all this would have been aborted like any other local uprising had it not spread to major cities like Sfax and the capital city of Tunis through unionists and other activists in urban areas. These activists served as the bridge between the working and middle classes.

Three: The seriousness with which its political leadership approached the matter of institution-building was crucial in the process of post -colonial nation building. Obstacles like ethnic or confessional cleavages did not exist in Tunisia. Moreover, the secularization process, which was not only institutional but ideological as well, infiltrated even the stronghold of traditional family relationships and affairs as impacted by the Personal Status Code and customs pertaining to women's rights. Following their independence from colonial rule, secular regimes emerged in numerous Arab countries. Secularization was imposed from above and religion was subordinated to the state, usually by a despotic regime; this was the case in Tunisia as well. However, in Tunisia, the secularization process so permeated the consciousness of large segments of society that it took on a social and intellectual life of its own and thus no longer needed to be imposed top-down.

At the same time, the political struggle and economic modernization that had taken place since colonialism (and possibly even before) created a gap between coastal and inland areas. Splits in the nationalist movement then modified this gap as people in the south seemed to be more exposed to the Arab nationalist and Islamist political culture,[2] while the coastal regions, although their population was also Arab and Muslim, were more open to secularization and Western culture. They were all still Tunisians, but of different social strata and cultural persuasions.

Unlike secularism, the ethnicization and essentialization of the Tunisian identity à la Bourguiba as a replacement for an affiliation with Arab and Muslim culture never really took root among the people. The secularization not only produced a leftist and nationalist opposition but targeted the poor, deprived segments of the middle class and intellectuals who rejected the prevailing ideology of the ruling party (on account of its foreign policy, its repressive domestic policies, or both) and who, as a consequence, were susceptible to a counter-ideology and culture which were closer to their understanding of their identity. In short, no society is absolutely homogenous, and even in Tunisia, 'other' identities were being produced.

Moreover, since trade unions, political parties and civic associations had acquired a wider margin for political action despite the authoritarian regime, they began accumulating experience and engaging in mutual dialogue. Until the turn of

2. The Arab nationalist and Islamist mindset, which took different forms within the ruling party itself, had been repressed long before the so-called Islamic awakening of the 1970s.

the twenty-first century, the Tunisian regime had succeeded in keeping the secular nationalist, leftist and liberal opposition separate from the Islamist opposition. This was due both to the hegemonic secular culture and to the aspiration to preserve the social achievements of the modern state in light of Islamist movements' increasing strength since the Iranian revolution, especially in view of the developments in Algeria in the 1990s.

However, elements of the opposition that the regime had failed to contain succeeded in overcoming these fears and thus entered into dialogue and cooperation with the Islamist movement against authoritarianism. This dialogue also helped the Islamist movement to appreciate the particularities of Tunisian society and state, thereby enabling it to take a more pragmatic approach to dealing with secular parties, and to engage in the process of drafting a democratic alternative to the regime. The Tunisian opposition is one of the few oppositions in the region that have actually drawn up a scheme of how the country should be ruled after authoritarianism. As a result, and as noted in the introduction, democracy was not merely a chance outcome of contentious politics after the revolution but a goal shared by numerous opposition factions. The political parties that crafted the 'Call of Tunis' agreement in 2003,[3] the parties and associations that formed the October 18 Collective, the general labour union, other societies and movements, and some leading figures of the old regime who had become genuine servants of the transition from authoritarian rule constituted the 'human agency' that guided the revolution towards a democratic alternative to the authoritarian regime against which it had arisen.

As noted earlier, the Tunisian Revolution was not led by any political party that could or wanted to seize power. Rather, it was a reformist revolution that willingly left it to state institutions and opposition parties to interpret and implement the revolution's demands in cooperation with the popular movement once the old structures of power had been turned on their heads. In fact, there would have been no way to implement the necessary reforms or make a safe transition to democracy without the help of state institutions.

A revolution is a break with the past: a new constitution, a new legitimacy. If a revolution does not lead to an attempt to build a more just system of rule based on the values that prompted people to reject the injustice of deprivation, authoritarianism and inequality, it will revert to being a mere revolt. However, until the new system emerges and takes root, the country will pass through a sensitive interim period (the first phase of the transition process) which, if not handled carefully, may either turn chaotic or allow a powerful organized force to take over and reproduce the old despotism.

3. The 'Call of Tunis' agreement, signed in Aix-en-Provence in 2003 by Al Nahda, the Congress for the Republic (CPR) and the Democratic Forum for Labour and Liberties (FDTL). The agreement called for a new constitution that guarantees the principles of democratic system and the sovereignty of people as the only source of authority and that guarantees rights and liberties according to the international declaration of human rights.

The revolution was not spearheaded by political parties, nor did these parties meet immediately after 14 January to lead the country. When they met later, the contest for power was ever-present, and instead of taming the chaos, they could have become part of this chaos if state institutions had not been properly managed and prepared for a transition period.

Hence, there is a phase in which, first, state affairs should be kept running and state services performed; second, unjust laws must be repealed and interim regulations enacted, while leaving all major legislation to the democratically elected legislature; and third, a dialogue with the opposition that struggled against the old regime must be commenced and institutional venues for dialogue and for launching the transition to democracy must be produced.

EPILOGUE

THE TRANSITIONARY PERIOD: DEMOCRACY AGAINST ALL ODDS

I

One of the most interesting debates ever witnessed by comparative politics has to do with the issue of transition to democracy as viewed by advocates of the modernization approach and proponents of the so-called transitology (the study of transition from authoritarian rule). Denying the necessity of the structural preconditions stipulated by modernization theorists (such as a certain level of economic growth, education, urbanization, and the size of the middle class), transitologists emphasize human agency and political factors such as the attitudes of political elites. However, many modernization theorists view democracy as the offspring of a specific culture. In so doing, modernization theorists perpetuate the false dichotomy of 'Islam versus democracy'. Some of them reduce this cultural prerequisite to the availability of a supportive political culture. However, it remains a nebulous concept if not limited to a society's influential elites, their experience and political skills, a position with which this book concurs. As for Modernists, they treat the outcomes of the long evolution of first democracies as preconditions for a successful contemporary transition in the present.

Different theories outline different variables as decisive for the success of a transition to democracy. All, however, rightly agree on a fundamental condition such as a social-political consensus on the state and the absence of deep cleavages that would threaten the unity of society in the event that the authoritarian regime loses its grip on the state. None of the sides in the controversy emphasizes the role of the army in politics, the role of the so-called deep state, the geostrategic importance of the country, or the role of external factors, including the regional environment. However, factors such as these are indispensable for the understanding of the Tunisian experience.

Although Tunisia is ethnically and religiously more homogeneous than Arab countries in which revolutions have led to sectarian, ethnic or regional splits and even civil war, this is not to say that civil wars or other divisions were inevitable in these other countries. Rather, developments of this nature were, in large part, the ruling regime's reactions to popular uprisings, its readiness (or lack thereof) to carry out reforms, the political culture of the opposition leadership and its ability to create partners in dialogue and reform if the protesters could not generate appropriate leadership. Nevertheless, it would be fair to say that revolution in such countries was a risky enterprise and that reform would have been more secure. A problem emerges when regimes in such countries prove impervious to reform yet prevent the emergence of an organized political opposition; however, historical processes do not wait, and spontaneous popular protests may still erupt.

Unlike the Egyptian army, the Tunisian army had no ambition to seize political power. It could have done so, in fact, on two occasions: after the departure of Ben Ali and during the 2013 crisis when some political forces urged the commanders of the Tunisian army to put an end to the rule of the Troika government. Tunisian military's lack of political ambition is part of its doctrine; it cannot be explained by its small size, poor equipment and the fact that it was neglected by the authoritarian regime, which invested more resources in other security agencies. This is not valid reasoning, however, as the same argument pertaining to the marginalization of the army has been used elsewhere to explain the very opposite phenomenon, that is, political ambition so excessive as to lead to a military overthrow.

In Tunisia, 'enlightened' and/or pragmatic figures from the old regime were prepared to provide leadership in the transition phase, while in Egypt, the 'deep state'[1] resisted change and was even ready to cooperate, once the time was 'right', with a military coup against the first elected president in Egyptian history. Unlike Syria and Libya, there were organized opposition parties in Egypt and Tunisia with both experience and some degree of leeway for action. This fact notwithstanding, in neither country did the opposition parties lead the revolution, though they came to play significant roles in it once it had begun. The Tunisian opposition was more capable of negotiating, bargaining and making compromises given its political background. Powerful trade unions and civilian organizations with real constituencies at the national level were available to facilitate dialogue and prevent partisan polarization from monopolizing the public sphere. In neither Egypt nor Tunisia did the size of the middle class or the overall level of education play a significant role in the transition, though such factors may certainly have played a vital part in the consolidation of democracy. Far more decisive in both cases was the disposition of the political elites (both secular and religious) and the stance taken by the military.

Tunisia's interim government, in cooperation with the HIROR – which was a civil institution, a guiding forum and a platform for dialogue encompassing all major pro-democracy political and social forces – led the country from the end of the revolution to the election of a Constituent Assembly. In Egypt, the interim period, or the first part of the transition phase, was managed by the army, and

1. By 'deep state', we mean the security apparatus, leading bureaucrats and the judiciary in the event that they develop an agenda independent of the political leadership. Granted, this is not the original definition of 'deep state' (derived from Turkish experience), which has more to do with ideologized secularist nationalist security networks inside the state bureaucracy. Here, however, the term has been adapted to the Egyptian experience after the revolution.

no such forum was founded. So, unlike in Tunisia, no real political and societal dialogue concerning the major themes of democracy and its constitution was conducted before the elections. The mobilization for elections and the contest for power (who will rule?) preceded the agreement on the major issues of the constitution (how will the country be ruled?). This was a fatal blow to consensus-building on democracy among the major political forces in Egypt.

Contests and political rivalries in a transition to democracy are not harmful as long as they are handled within the framework of a commitment to democratic procedures. This was the case in Tunisia, but not in Egypt, where the army, supported by a conservative judiciary and an intransigent political opposition, exploited the deep divisions among the political actors involved in the January 2011 revolution in order to undermine the first experience of an elected president and parliament. The major political forces in Egypt did not trust one another, nor did they recognize their joint responsibility for the success of the transition from authoritarian rule to democracy. Despite their ineffectual policy making, the Islamists who had been elected to office were made to shoulder full responsibility for the social and political situation during the time of transition. The Islamists insisted on a form of rule that relied on a slim majority, while the secular opposition worked to undermine the government's policies, as the state apparatus and the army retained effective rule.

Conscious resistance to democratic transition may develop into full-scale counter-revolution, that is, organized action intended to sabotage the democratic transition by turning the transition period into an extended state of chaos that repels large portions of the population from the notion of democracy, thereby preparing the way for the rehabilitation of authoritarian rule.

It is practically impossible to rule a country with an absolute electoral majority if the state bureaucracy is not yet committed to democracy and when most of the economic, political and cultural elites oppose the political force that has won this majority. Realizing this fact, Al Nahda could have formed an absolute majority with the Popular Appeal list (26 seats) directly after the October 2011 election; however, it preferred to align with two secular parties. Indeed, even this appeared insufficient to Al Nahda leader Rached Ghannouchi, who, in retrospect, reckoned that they should have done more to expand the coalition (as they were obliged to do after the 2013 crisis).[2] Democratic countries are ruled not only by democratic majorities but also by bureaucracy; moreover, a country's economic and cultural elites may be supportive or obstructive. And if this is important in an established democracy, it is all the more important during a transition to democracy. There is no way to face all this if nearly half of the population has been pushed towards the opposition. The first phases of transition (before democracy is consolidated) require large coalitions committed to democracy.

2. Rached Ghannouchi, 'Tunisia: From the Revolution to the Constitution' [Tūnis: min al-thawrah ilā al-dustūr] *Siyasat Arabiyya,* no. 18 (2016), pp. 108–9.

Attempts were indeed made to sabotage the transition in Tunisia. Fortunately, however, there were enough political forces interested in a successful transition to make it possible to bargain and compromise.[3] Additionally, the army kept its commitment to the goals of the revolution. Reactionary regional forces were too busy frustrating democracy in Egypt – a far more significant and regionally influential player – to be bothered with obstructing the transition in Tunisia. (However, the UAE promised substantial economic aid to the Tunisian government after 2014 if, unlike Egypt, it agreed to exclude the moderate Islamists from future elections.[4])

Numerous wealthy authoritarian regimes in the Middle East were understandably keen to avoid being harmed by the spate of Arab uprisings in 2011. Such regimes were aware, of course, that it was not the revolutions in Eastern Europe or in Indonesia, the world's largest Muslim state, that were most likely to impact the Arab countries but, rather, the revolution in the small Arab state of Tunisia, and this due to a shared language, culture, history and common aspirations. Arab regimes were initially taken off guard by the Arab uprisings of 2011; but since 2012, they have been determined to resist. This has resulted in their lending financial support to counter-revolutionary media and political forces in countries such as Tunisia, Egypt, Libya and Yemen. (Given the particular fragility of the state in Libya and Yemen, foreign interference has been all the more destructive there.)

The role of reactionary Arab regimes whose rulers not only feel threatened by the transition to democracy in the Arab world but also have the financial means to fight it has been a significant hindrance to democracy. The fact that Tunisia does

3. As Monica Marks rightly notes, academic researchers tend to portray Islamists as the parties most prone to intransigence in situations calling for dialogue and compromise with other parties. However, both secularist and religious political movements in Egypt and in Tunisia included purist elements that resisted compromise with the other side. Monica Marks, 'Purists and Pluralists: Cross-Ideological Coalition Building in Tunisia's Democratic Transition', in Alfred Stepan (ed.), *Democratic Transition in the Muslim World: A Global Perspective* (New York: Columbia University Press, 2018), pp. 92, 98.

4. Masmoudi accuses the UAE of direct involvement in supporting pro-Ben Ali journalists and opposition groups against the Troika and later the coalition of 2014, and of linking any financial support for the government during Essebsi's presidential term with their attempt to repeat the Egyptian experience. According to Masmoudi, 'Nidaa Tounes movement repeated publicly that they had received promises of economic support from the UAE of at least $125 billion over five years if Nidaa Tounes won the elections.' Nidaa Tounes won the elections and the promise of financial support was never fulfilled, because Nidaa Tounes included Al Nahda in its coalition. Beji Caid Essebsi actually 'told journalists . . . that the UAE conditioned its economic support on 'repeating the Egyptian scenario,' which Essebsi is said to have rejected because it was not in Tunisia's interests.' Radwan Masmoudi, 'The Failure of the International Community to Support Tunisia,' in Alfred Stepan (ed.), *Democratic Transition in the Muslim World*, pp. 152–4.

not enjoy geostrategic significance by sharing borders with Israel, for example, or by virtue of being situated atop a sea of oil has spared it intensive foreign intervention but didn't prevent protracted efforts for influence. By the same token, however, it has failed to attract much support for its democratic experiment. Given its difficult economic situation and the serious challenge this poses to a young democracy, Tunisia's efforts should, by all rights, have been rewarded with support from established democracies the world over. However, little, if any, support has been forthcoming from democracies in the West, and this despite the fact that the European Union played an indispensable role in encouraging democratic transition in Spain and Portugal in the 1970s and in Eastern European countries in the 1990s. Meanwhile, the United States still extends billions of dollars' worth of financial and military aid to authoritarian regimes in the region.[5] In short, it may be said that Tunisia's heroic experiment in democracy has succeeded in the face of formidable obstacles and in spite of a dauntingly unfriendly milieu.

There was initially some enthusiasm expressed at the G8 Summit, held in June 2011, to support countries of the Arab Spring with $80 billion, including $25 billion for Tunisia. However, the promises made were not kept. In 2016, despite the fact that Freedom House had granted Tunisia the highest possible score for political rights in 2016, it only received USD 166 million, barely one-tenth of the foreign aid allocated to Jordan or to Egypt under Sisi.[6]

The following figures show the drop in direct foreign investments measured by GDP after the revolution and the contraction of capital investments estimated by the same measure. The negative impact of this drop on growth, employment and the capability of the state to meet the expectations of the Tunisian public after the revolution is obvious (Figures E.1 and E.2).

Against this background, the spread of protests and strikes was understandable; however, it inevitably aggravated instability and fear of investors. After all, capital is a coward! This vicious cycle threatens the Tunisian economy, the plans of the government for human development and probably democracy itself (Table E.1).

5. In her book on democracy assistance, Sarah Sunn Bush considers the NGOs in themselves as the civil society and holds that assistance to these organizations was in fact assisting democracy in Tunisia prior to the 2011 revolution. Applying this same criterion after the revolution, she blames the lack of democracy assistance funding given to Tunisian NGOs on the latter's alleged combativeness and lack of professionalism. However, true democracy assistance in Tunisia would mean providing economic support to the democratic state itself through the difficult transition period, a fact which Sunn Bush totally overlooks. See Sarah Sunn Bush, *The Taming of Democracy Assistance: Why Democracy Promotion Does Not Confront Dictators* (Cambridge: Cambridge University Press, 2015), esp. Ch. 8, pp. 187–208.

6. Masmoudi, 'The Failure of the International Community to Support Tunisia,' pp. 149–50.

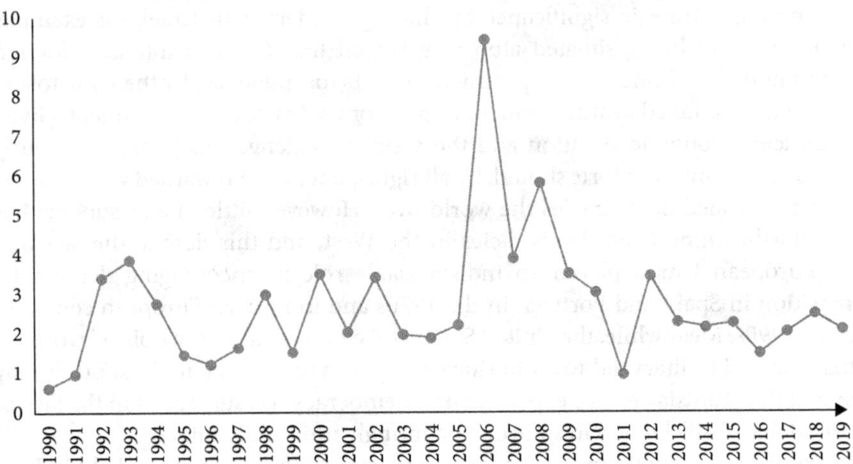

Figure E.1 Tunisia's FDI per cent of GDP (1990–2019). Foreign Direct Investment (FDI) are the net inflows of investment to acquire a lasting management interest (10 per cent or more of voting stock) in an enterprise operating in an economy other than that of the investor. It is the sum of equity capital, reinvestment of earnings, other long-term capital and short-term capital as shown in the balance of payments. This series shows net inflows (new investment inflows less disinvestment) in the reporting economy from foreign investors, and is divided by GDP. *Source*: 'Foreign direct investment, net inflows (% of GDP) – Tunisia', *The World Bank Data*, accessed on 11 February 2021, at: http://bit.ly/3q57x1n.

Tunisia is the only successful transition to democracy in the Arab region, and unlike the Eastern and Southern European democracies,[7] the Tunisian democracy has been established against all odds in a hostile environment. Consequently, it needs, and deserves, all the support it can get, whether in grants or investments, in order to overcome the social and economic hardships that pose an ever-present threat to democracy. This is crucial for the consolidation not only of Tunisian democracy but of any nascent democracy in the Arab world. Additionally, unions, associations and responsible opposition parties must evince some restraint in order to have a successful democratic transition process.

II

Now we come to the issue of what I refer to as the political culture of influential elites. I have referred repeatedly, since the start of the post-revolutionary period, to the danger of replacing the divide between authoritarianism and its opponents with a schism between secular and religious ideologies and their followers.

7. Suffice it to mention one factor which is the incentive of joining the European Market (Spain and Portugal) and the European Union (Eastern Europe) was supportive of the democratization process.

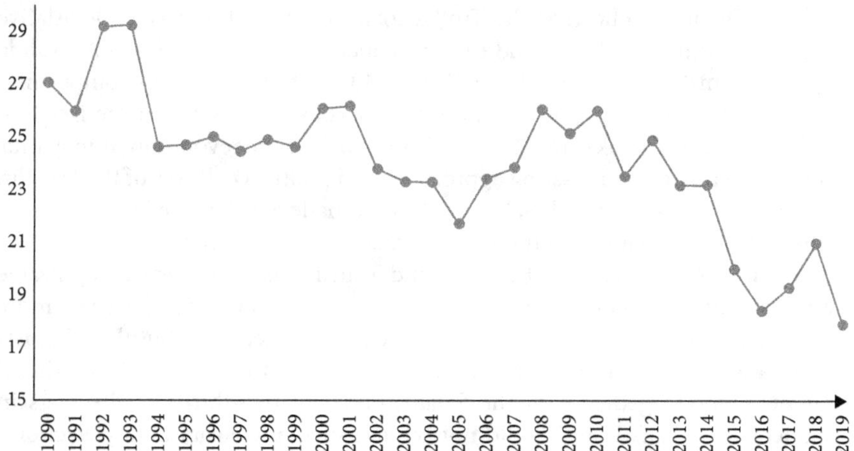

Figure E.2 Tunisia's capital investment per cent of GDP (1990–2019). Gross capital formation (formerly gross domestic investment) consists of outlays on additions to the fixed assets of the economy plus net changes in the level of inventories. Fixed assets include land improvements (fences, ditches, drains and so on); plant, machinery and equipment purchases; and the construction of roads, railways and the like, including schools, offices, hospitals, private residential dwellings and commercial and industrial buildings. Inventories are stocks of goods held by firms to meet temporary or unexpected fluctuations in production or sales and 'work in progress'. According to the 1993 SNA, net acquisitions of valuables are also considered capital formation. *Source*: 'Gross capital formation (% of GDP) – Tunisia', *The World Bank Data*, accessed on 11 February 2021, at: http://bit.ly/3q5pH33.

Table E.1 Social Movements and Protests in Tunisia

Year	Total Number of Social Movements and Protests in Tunisia
2015	4,965
2016	8,713
2017	10,452
2018	9,365
2019	9,091
2020	8,759

Source: 'Annual Report on Social Protests 2015', *Forum Tunisien pour les Droits Economiques et Sociaux (FTDES)*, 3 August 2016, p. 60, accessed on 11 February 2021, at: https://bit.ly/3aW9uH2; 'December 2020 Report on Social Protests, Suicides, Violence, and Immigration', *Forum Tunisien pour les Droits Economiques et Sociaux (FTDES)*, vol 87, p. 3, accessed on 11 February 2021, at: https://bit.ly/3pcn1ze.

This division, between religiosity and secularism, blurs the distinction between democracy and authoritarianism, whereby the rivalry could lead either side to legitimize alignments with the old regime as an act against the other party.

Major Tunisian political elites succeeded in overcoming this polarization by subordinating it to the important mission of successful democratic transition. The legacy of bargaining and compromise was demonstrated in the 2003 'Call of

Tunis', the 'October Collective', the Troika coalition in the first elected legislative institution in Tunisian history and the subsequent agreement between Al Nahda and Nidaa Tunis[8] to overcome the crisis in 2013. Such dialogue and compromise never took place in Egypt, although political parties actually had more freedom in Egypt during Mubarak's time than in Tunisia before the revolution. It may thus be concluded that the contrasting approaches and political cultures of the Muslim Brotherhood in Egypt and Al Nahda in Tunisia made a difference in this case, as did the contrasting features of the secular parties in both countries.

The difference between the Egyptian and Tunisian Islamists was recognizable when the Islamists made up the political opposition but became even more apparent after they had come to power. Some might object: yes, but the Islamists in Tunisia were forced to compromise because, unlike the Muslim Brotherhood in Egypt – who, together with the Salafis, obtained two-thirds of the seats in parliament – Tunisia's Islamists did not achieve such a majority in any elections. The Muslim Brotherhood in Egypt made up a majority in parliament together with a competing fundamentalist organization which actually sought to outbid them in Islamist rhetoric. This competition limited the Brotherhood's ability to bargain and negotiate with Egypt's secular parties. However, this did not concern them at the time, as they felt themselves to be in such a position of strength that they welcomed secularists to join them on their own terms only. As for Egypt's secular parties, they were unwilling to cede ground to the Muslim Brotherhood; instead, they were prepared to cooperate with forces from the old regime and the army to overthrow the newly elected government under Mohamed Morsi.

Al Nahda supported an election law that called for proportional representation, consciously avoiding a 'first past the post' system,[9] which would have granted Al Nahda an absolute majority in the Constituent Council. They avoided having to rule by majority for fear of repeating the Algerian scenario or a backlash from the state apparatus, the business community and regional players. A similar fear underlay the Egyptian Muslim Brotherhood's initial declaration that they would not nominate a presidential candidate and their pledge to limit the number of candidates they nominated for parliament. However, the Brotherhood later shed this prudence and broke its promises.

In Tunisia, an attempt was made to escalate the polarization throughout 2011–14. However, it failed to split the Tunisian democracy itself. Al Nahda, which did not enjoy an absolute majority and itself went through ideological reforms, was far more open to bargaining and concessions than the Muslim Brotherhood in Egypt and not only established a coalition with secular democratic forces from the onset but was ready to cede its premier position in the government to avoid a national split at a time of crisis. Al Nahda understood that it would not be able to govern

8. Also known as Nidaa Tounes.

9. The first-past-the-post (FPTP) system is also known as the simple majority system. In this voting method, the candidate with the highest number of votes in a constituency is declared the winner.

under the regional or even local balance of power which prevailed at that time and which was not determined by vote counts. Conversely, the hard-core secular, albeit pragmatic, forces understood that excluding Tunisia's moderate Islamists would set them on a perilous track back to authoritarianism while simultaneously strengthening radical Salafi Islamists.

Disguised as new political parties, forces from the ousted regime made unrelenting attempts to provoke a secular-religious polarization among Tunisians in a bid to marginalize both the moderate Islamists and the pragmatic secular forces, which by this time had formed a democratic coalition. In so doing, the *ancien régime* found an unlikely partner in the opposition's radical leftists and nationalists. This secular-religious division could easily be turned into a polarization between two cultural identities, and rather than fostering a discussion regarding government programmes and organization, identity politics would promote a division of 'us' and 'them', thus replacing pluralism with exclusion.

The confessional and ethnic cleavages that have obstructed revolution in other countries, not to speak of democratic transition, are not present in a homogeneous society like Tunisia, where the only possible vertical division would be between the coastal and marginalized regions of the inland. Moreover, this division can be addressed through a conscious development policy, as socio-economic disparities between coastal and inland regions nurture some of the divisions between the religious and the secular. Thousands of young Tunisians, enticed by extremist Salafi-Jihadi trends (including Ansar al-Sharia, which has been outlawed by the Tunisian democracy) to leave their country to fight in Syria, for example, and those who choose to attempt illegal emigration to Europe are two faces of the same phenomenon, namely the socio-economic and cultural alienation of young people in their own country. Not surprisingly, such youths hail primarily from Tunisia's poorest regions. Hence, a crucial challenge facing Tunisian democracy is to develop these impoverished regions and implement solutions to the issue of unemployment, both of which may go a long way towards easing the combined socio-economic and cultural tensions that generated the protests which led to the revolution, and which could yet destabilize Tunisia's fledgling democracy.

III

Emerging as the leading party in the Constituent Assembly elections, Al Nahda formed a coalition with CPR and FDTL. However, it failed to persuade the Progressive Democratic Party to join the coalition. Radical leftist and Arab nationalist parties preferred to remain in the opposition, as they viewed the Constituent Council as a regular parliament in an old democracy with a government that warranted a militant opposition.

The inflated numbers of electoral lists (1,519) and candidates (11,686) might have turned out to be simply an exaggerated response to the excitement of holding the country's first democratic elections. Instead, however, it turned to be an early sign of a problematic political culture in which too many people, thinking they

Table E.2 Results of the October 2011 Constituent Assembly Elections

Party	Votes	% of Votes	Seats	% of Seats
Al Nahda Movement	1,501,320	37.04	89	41.01
Congress for the Republic (CPR)	353,041	8.71	29	13.36
Popular Petition	273,362	6.74	26	11.98
Democratic Forum for Labor and Liberties (FDTL)	284,989	7.03	20	9.22
Progressive Democratic Party	159,826	3.94	16	7.37
The Initiative	129,120	3.19	5	2.31
Democratic Modernist Pole	113,005	2.79	5	2.31
Afaq Tunis (Afek Tounes)	76,488	1.89	4	1.84
Tunisian Workers' Communist Party	63,652	1.57	3	1.38
People's Movement	30,500	0.75	2	0.92
Movement of Socialist Democrats	22,830	0.56	2	0.92
Free Patriotic Union	51,665	1.26	1	0.46
Democratic Patriots Movement	33,419	0.83	1	0.46
Maghrebin Liberal Party	19,201	0.47	1	0.46
Democratic Social Nation Party	15,534	0.38	1	0.46
New Destour Party	15,448	0.38	1	0.46
Progressive Struggle Party	9,978	0.25	1	0.46
Equity and Equality Party	7,621	0.19	1	0.46
Cultural Unionist Nation Party	5,581	0.14	1	0.46
Independent Lists	62,293	1.54	8	3.67
Total votes of parties and lists represented in the Assembly	**3,228,873**	**79.65**	**217**	**100**
Total votes for the rest of the parties and lists	**824,335**	**20.34**	**0**	**0**
Total	**4,053,208**	**100**	–	–

'National Constituent Assembly Elections in Tunisia', *The Carter Center*, 23 October 2011, pp. 32–3, 53–4, accessed at: http://bit.ly/2MkoUd6; and, 'Final Report on the Tunisian National Constituent Assembly Elections', *National Democratic Institute*, 23 October 2011, p. 19, accessed at: https://bit.ly/3nTSq9R.

The 2011 National Constituent Assembly elections involved 11,686 candidates spread over 1,519 lists: 54.6 per cent represented political parties, 43.3 per cent were independent and 2.4 per cent were from within party coalitions. The total number of parties competing in these elections came to approximately 100, only 27 of which won seats in the National Constituent Assembly.

deserve to be leaders themselves, are unwilling to join an organization that they do not lead (Table E.2).

According to the decrees detailing its structure and functions, the Constituent Assembly was to serve one year only and draft a democratic constitution during this period of time. However, it ended up serving for three years. This issue became yet another source of tension, as the secular opposition and Premier Essebsi himself began claiming that the Assembly had lost its legitimacy once the initial year had elapsed. This was not a fair claim, given that rarely has a democratic constitution been drawn up by an elected body in only one year. The task of drafting a constitution and presenting it to the nation was far more important than the time span required. But this was not the real dispute.

Determined to change the results of the next elections, secularist parties and forces from the old regime set out to mobilize their constituencies against the ruling coalition. Concerned about Islamist dominance, they had no difficulty playing on their constituencies' existing fears of Al Nahda. Their task was further facilitated by the fact that it is all too easy to catch one's government in error during times of instability, unrest and high expectations, particularly if said government is made up of inexperienced,[10] once-persecuted opposition parties.

As noted earlier, Tunisia's opposition had a tradition of dialogue between political and civil forces which dated back to the pre-revolution era and which had continued after the revolution during the HIROR mandate. For example, the symposium of political parties, hosted by the head of HIROR in August and September 2011, had issued a declaration which laid out a road map for the institutions established during the transition period. This roadmap emphasized the importance of concord (*tawāfuq*) in transition institutions and of voting only after exhausting all efforts to reach it. The word 'concord' appeared in the decree which founded HIROR, which stipulates that the decisions of these institutions are to be made by concord and by a majority if concord cannot be reached.[11] There was an aversion to and even fear of decisions by a majority that would split the society into two camps such that one pole could dictate its will to the entire society, especially on basic constitutional issues. Indeed, this fear had proved to be justified after the Egyptian Revolution and its aftermath. Moreover, societies and minority political forces need time to learn to accept being governed by representatives of the majority, to wait for a change of state leadership in subsequent elections and to have confidence that they will have fair chances.

The Islamists in Egypt insisted on governing with a slim majority of less than 52 per cent after the election of 2012 and with a president who had not won the majority of the votes in any of Egypt's major cities. The distrust among political forces led to a polarization between two camps; the commitment of the state apparatus to democracy was more than questionable; and the secularist pole was ready to undermine the elected president and to legitimize the re-involvement of the army. One of the most important conclusions to be drawn from the comparison between the cases of Tunisia and Egypt is the unfeasibility of ruling a country in a transition phase when those supporting the fall of the dictatorship merely

10. Indeed, some writers maintain that the main problem lay in the fact that the ruling political elite was now composed of people who had never governed before. See Fathi Lyasir, *Dawlat al-Huwāt: Sanatān min Ḥukm al-Troika fī Tūnis* [The Amateur State: Two Years of Troika Rule in Tunisia] (Tunis: Muhammad Ali Publications, 2016).

11. 'Decree-law No. 2011-6 dated 18 February 2011, creating the Higher Authority for the Achievement of the Revolution's Objectives, Political Reform and Democratic Transition', *Official Gazette of the Republic of Tunisia,* No. 13, 1 March 2011, pp. 96–7, accessed on 18 February 2021, at: https://bit.ly/37q5aPs. In the official English translation, *tawāfuq* is rendered 'consensus' (*Ijmaa'* in Arabic) rather than 'concord': 'The authority decisions are [to be] made by consensus and failing this the majority [vote]. The president vote is casting in the event of a tied vote.' It is clear that this is not the only mistake in the official translation.

represent a majority of the total population but without support from the economic and cultural elites or a majority of the votes in major cities. This is especially the case when elements of the old regime are still diffused within the state's apparatus. The only way to maintain control in such a situation would be to suppress the opposition, and even then, the ruling political force would need the cooperation of the security forces, the army and the opposition to the old regime, the latter of which is imperative if the new regime is to enjoy revolutionary legitimacy.

It was this pragmatic logic which led Al Nahda to give up its demand that political figures from the old regime be prevented from running for election, which was a prevalent position in the Troika coalition. Elements of the old regime were excluded from the 2011 National Constituent Assembly but not from the parliament elected in 2014. (A lustration law presented in the Constituent Council could have passed if Al Nahda had allowed only one of its members to vote for it.) Moreover, unlike Interim President Moncef Marzouki, Al Nahda did not concern itself with transitional justice. The revolution was followed by a debate over transitional justice; commissions were formed, and investigations were conducted, but transitional justice was not served, which means that society was denied the opportunity to engage in a dialogue that would make reconciliation possible and consolidate the position of no return to dictatorship. This is one of the reasons that files remained open and that suspicions towards old political elites who had been allowed to participate in the political process continued to linger. A crucial figure preventing transitional justice was Essebsi, who opposed the legal procedures and insisted that Tunisia needed reconciliation more than it needed transitional justice in order for Tunisian investors to return safely to the country. He apparently did not want to see that transitional justice is the only path to genuine, solid reconciliation.

Some Al Nahda members, like Sadok Chourou and Habib Ellouze, spoke openly of Islamizing the Constitution. Their suggestion was to reference the Shari'a as a source of legislation as many other Arab countries have done. However, the Constituent Assembly and Al Nahda itself rejected this suggestion, as well as the proposal to consider Islam the official religion of the state. Instead, it was decided to keep the definition of the state as worded in the 1957 Constitution, which reads: 'Tunisia is a free, independent and sovereign state. Its religion is Islam, its language is Arabic, and its form of government is the Republic.'[12] An article criminalizing blasphemy, though supported by some Al Nahda members, was removed from the draft of the Constitution, as was an item in the Preamble that defined women and men's role as complementary rather than as equal.

Al Nahda leaders sought to justify such concessions to their constituency by addressing them in Islamic terms, which prompted secularists to accuse Al Nahda of double talk and hidden agendas. At least at the beginning, the opposition to the Troika government fished for damning evidence in Al Nahda's policies, especially

12. See 'Constitution of the Republic of Tunisia,' *Publications of the Official Printing Office of the Republic of Tunisia, 2010*, accessed on 12 October 2020, at: https://bit.ly/3jVaKO0; especially Chapter 1, Article 1.

its tolerance towards Islamist extremists and its failure to take action against them. There were even conspiracy theories claiming that Al Nahda had been behind attacks committed by Islamist extremists.

Islamists at certain universities interfered in issues of dress code, especially for women. Angry young people, suddenly free to express their inclinations in public, at times failed to appreciate the boundaries between the public and private spheres. However, citizens should be discouraged from violating others' civil liberties even – or, perhaps, especially – if they do so in the name of religion. Moreover, in the atmosphere of freedom that prevailed after the revolution, Salafi and other extremist religious voices emerged in the public sphere, including preachers from Egypt and Saudi Arabia. Tunisians were not used to these public manifestations of Islamic fundamentalism.

Islamist radicalism actually flourished most not under democracy, but under secularist despotism, despite the fact that democracy granted it more freedom of expression. Some young people who had been culturally alienated and/or economically marginalized under the old regime felt betrayed by the politicians. They felt that Al Nahda had turned its back on them by making deals with elements of the old regime, especially with the aggravation of the economic situation after the revolution. No wonder, then, that extremist Salafis found fertile soil among the youth to propagate their teachings and even recruit fighters for ISIS and other extremist groups to be sent to Syria and elsewhere. This was not the fault of democracy. It was, nevertheless, a warning sign for future governments (most of which were not controlled by Al Nahda). Social calamities that bred uprisings and a revolution in Tunisia might not engender another revolution in the future. However, they might produce various strains of populism and violent extremism, both of which can burden democracy.

The first violent collisions between Islamists and secularists took place on 18 October 2012, when Mohamed Lotfi Nagdh, a coordinator for the newly established Nidaa Tunis in the governorate of Tataouine, was killed after clashes with the local League for the Protection of the Revolution (LPR). Not long before this, the LPR had taken part in the Kasbah 1 and Kasbah 2 sit-ins, which involved Islamist Arab nationalists, human rights activists, leftists and others. After the elections held in October 2011, the leftist parties had withdrawn from the LPR, which had been formed to replace local councils and municipalities, and which contained an active religious element. According to Ben Achour, the LPR even formed militias in the service of the religious political movement.[13] Members of its leadership were also involved in founding the al-Karama Coalition (Coalition de la dignité), which ran against Al Nahda in the 2019 elections. There was a fear among the secularists that LPR would turn into a violent armed militia of Al Nahda Movement. Hence, it was accused of murdering Nagdh and attacking the headquarters of the UGTT on 4 December 2012. The LPR was also unjustifiably

13. Ben Achour, *Tūnis: thawrah fī bilād al-islām*, pp. 182–3.

suspected of involvement in the assassination of leftist politicians and was dissolved by the court in 2014.

The situation deteriorated with the assassination of two leftist political leaders: Chokri Belaid, leader of the leftist secular Democratic Patriots' Movement, on 6 February 2013, and Mohamed Brahmi, founder and former leader of the People's Movement, on 25 July of the same year. The Troika government not only condemned the killing but declared the Ansar Al-Shari'a movement, the prime suspect in the assassinations, a terrorist organization. Ansar Al-Shari'a, as well as other Salafi movements such as al-Islah Party (The Reform Front Party/*Jabhat al-Islah*), were rivals of Al Nahda and had often accused it of collaborating with the CIA[14] and betraying Islamist principles.

The opposition's escalation of protests after the assassinations marked the beginning of a crisis that might well have derailed the entire transition. The new Nidaa Tunis Party (founded in April 2012) established a 'Union for Tunisia' along with members of other parties, including the RCD, leftist and secularist activists, members of the UGTT and the National Employers' Union. The more radical leftist political formations such as the Popular Front did not join the movement until Brahmi's assassination. This was followed by the formation of a Tunisian branch of the National Salvation Front after the model of the one formed in Egypt. The National Salvation Front consisted of the 'Union for Tunisia' and the 'Popular Front', which launched a 'departure' (*raḥīl*) campaign, like Egypt's 'rebellion' (*tamarrud*) campaign against the elected President Morsi.

Eventually, a compromise was reached between the Islamists, represented by Rached Ghannouchi, and the radical secular pole (excluding the leftists and nationalists of the Popular Front) which was both more secular and less revolutionary than the two secular parties of the Troika. This compromise saved Tunisia from a veritable split between Islamists and secularists.[15]

The opposition's demonstrations against terrorism were unprecedented in both size and scope. They were encouraged by the mass movement in Egypt (especially the mass demonstrations of 30 June 2013), followed by the 3 July military coups d'état. The split culminated on 26 July 2013 in the resignation of sixty members of the Constituent Assembly, who challenged its legality on the pretext that it had exceeded its time frame of one year; hence, the assembly was actually reduced to representing one camp rather than two. The President of the Assembly, Mustapha Ben Jaafar, a pragmatic and experienced politician, chose wisely to suspend parliament until a compromise was reached. He also invited the different sides

14. Emmanuel Karagiannis, 'The Rise of Electoral Salafism in Egypt and Tunisia: The Use of Democracy as a Master Frame,' *The Journal of North African Studies*, vol. 24, no. 2 (2019), p. 216.

15. According to propaganda being promoted by the opposition, the secularists in the Troika coalition had been infiltrated by Islamists and, therefore, did not represent the secular camp, the result being a widespread fear of an Islamist takeover of sorts.

to continue work on the Constitution in what was termed the Consent Forum, in which each party, had a single vote.

The compromise that was needed in order to overcome the crisis demanded painful concessions from Al Nahda, and could not have been reached without the pragmatic leadership of Ghannouchi (Al Nahda) and Essebsi (Nidaa Tunis). Both of them elderly and astute politicians, the two men held a series of secret meetings in Paris, the most important of which took place on 14 August 2014.

The 2013 National Dialogue Convention was hosted by the Tunisian National Dialogue Quartet, which was comprised of the Tunisian General Labor Union (UGTT), the Tunisian Confederation of Industry, Trade and Handicrafts (UTICA), the Tunisian Human Rights League (LTDH) and the Tunisian Order of Lawyers (ONAT). The compromise mediated by the Quartet entailed: (1) formation of a government of technocrats who would not be eligible to run in the subsequent elections and (2) agreement on a date for the next presidential and parliamentary elections. Twenty-two parties, including Al Nahda and the Democratic Forum, signed a road map to the next elections and agreed on both the resignation of the current government (following promulgation of the Constitution, which was Al Nahda's condition for this concession) and the formation of an interim, non-partisan government that would serve until the elections were held.

IV

The slogan raised by Essebsi (for Nidaa Tunis) in the 2014 elections was 'a civil state for Muslim people'. This slogan was essentially an interpretation of Article 1 of the Constitution, which states that Tunisia is an Arab state whose religion is Islam, as meaning that Islam is the religion not of the state (which is civil in nature), but of the people.[16]

The outcome of the 2014 election was a defeat for the Troika, as the two secular parties that entered the coalition with Al Nahda were now marginalized by the polarization that had taken place during the previous two years. Their social and political constituency would become a militant opposition to the "opportunist" coalitions of Al Nahda. Al Nahda itself lost twenty seats and 10 per cent of the vote. Nidaa Tunis came in first, although it fell twenty-nine seats short of a majority. Essebsi was elected president only in the second round of the presidential elections against Moncef Marzouki. However, the compromise that was achieved withstood the polarizing tension of the runoff election. Although Nidaa Tunis could have formed a secular coalition without Al Nahda, the latter was nevertheless invited to join it.

Viewing the 2014 election as a contest between two cultures and mindsets – those of 'modernism' and 'backwardness' to use Nidaa's terms – the party had vowed initially not to serve with Al Nahda in a single cabinet. In general the only

16. The Tunisian Constitution describes the state several times as 'a civil state'.

thing that united leftists, rightists, Destouris, unionists and liberals in Nidaa Tunis was their shared animosity towards the Islamists, while Al Nahda considered Nidaa Tunis a mere extension of the old regime. Consequently, the coalition they formed after the elections shocked many people in both camps. It had no partisan or political logic, but only a national logic of saving the transition period, and perhaps the country itself. For populists from both extremes, the coalition was only a manifestation of unscrupulousness of politicians who wanted to rule at all costs. (Table E.3).

Table E.3 Results of the October 2014 Parliamentary Elections

Party	Votes	% of Votes	Seats	% of Seats	Change Compared to Previous Elections
Nidaa Tunis	1,279,941	37.56	86	39.1	New Party
Al Nahda Movement	947,034	27.79	69	31.7	−20 seats
Free Patriotic Union	137,110	4.02	16	7.3	+15 seats
Popular Front[a]	124,654	3.66	15	6.9	+11 seats
Afaq Tunis	102,916	3.02	8	3.7	+4 seats
Congress for the Republic (CPR)	72,942	2.14	4	1.8	−25 seats
Democratic Current	65,792	1.93	3	1.3	New
People's Movement	45,799	1.34	3	1.3	+ 1 seat
The Initiative	45,086	1.32	3	1.3	−2 seats
Current of Love[b]	40,924	1.20	2	0.9	−24 seats
Republican Party[c]	49,965	1.47	1	0.4	−15 seats
Democratic Alliance Party	43,371	1.27	1	0.4	New
National Salvation Front	5,977	0.18	1	0.4	New
Movement of Socialist Democrats	5,792	0.17	1	0.4	−1 seat
Independent List 'Rehabilitation'	5,236	0.15	1	0.4	New
Independent List 'Majd Aljareed'	5,111	0.14	1	0.4	New
The Farmers' Voice Party	3,515	0.10	1	0.4	New
Independent List 'Call of Tunisians Abroad'	1,814	0.05	1	0.4	New
Total votes of parties and lists represented in the Assembly	**2,982,979**	**87.51**	**217**	**100**	–
Total votes for all other parties and lists	**425,191**	**11.88**	**0**	**0**	–
Total	**3,408,170**	**100**	–	–	–

'Final Report on the 2014 Legislative and Presidential Elections in Tunisia', *National Democratic Institute*, p. 28, 53–6, accessed at: https://bit.ly/3aJUIoh.

The 2014 Parliamentary Elections included 1,327 lists: 1,230 inside Tunisia and 79 abroad. The lists in Tunisia included 737 party lists, 159 coalition lists and 334 independent lists.

[a] A coalition that was formed in October 2012 from numerous left-wing political parties and independents, including the Tunisian Workers' Communist Party and the Democratic Patriots' Unified Party.

[b] Known previously as the Popular Petition for Freedom.

[c] It was formed on 9 April 2012 after a merger between secularist and liberal parties, including the Progressive Democratic Party (PDP) and the Tunisian Republican Party.

Tunisia could not have weathered the crisis without this compromise; nor could the compromise itself have endured had the two leaders not convinced their constituencies of its value. Nidaa Tunis included not only figures and loyalists from the old regime, especially from Bourguiba's era, but trade unionists and leftist activists as well. The pragmatic elements of Nidaa Tunis were actually affiliates of the RCD and the Destour Party, while its radical secularist and leftist elements opposed adding Al Nahda to the coalition after the elections of 2014. Indeed, they viewed such a move as treasonous. The repercussions of the rapprochement with the Islamists within Nidaa Tunis and Essebsi's desire to bequeath the party leadership to his son led to several splits in the movement, which never regained its former cohesion.[17]

Al Nahda, on the other hand, lost votes to the more radical al-Karama in the following elections (2019) and probably also to the pool of abstainers, while the secular camp continued to fracture in the absence of a unified leadership. Radical and leftist nationalist parties that had been part of the 2013 polarization continued in existence, but they grew weaker with every election cycle. Before the revolution, some of these parties had joined forces with Al Nahda in opposition to the ousted regime. Following the revolution, by contrast, the ruling coalitions required a pragmatic leadership that wanted to be part of the government running the country and which would be willing to bear responsibility together with other, previously rival forces composed of people who hailed from the old regime. However, this was incompatible with the radical mindset.

After Nidaa Tunis was virtually fragmented following Essebso's accession to power, but it was practically dissolved with the death of its founder, remnants of the old regime who were already working hard against him and Al Nahda became more vocal and active on the political scene. These included declared opponents of the revolution, corrupt figures who combined business with politics and who were financed by Gulf states that had actively worked against democratic transformation. Such figures employed populist tactics, exploiting people's socio-economic hardships not in order to reform government policy but as a means of undermining democracy itself. Their entrance into political life provoked another pro-revolutionary populist reaction not only against them but against Al Nahda itself, which was prepared after the 2019 elections to enter into a coalition with figures whom it had accused of corruption during the election and pledged never to cooperate with.

The 2019 elections signalled a crisis surrounding political parties in general. The splintering of parties, the flitting of politicians from one party to another, the

17. Based on the author's personal acquaintance and long conversations with Ghannouchi, it is clear that what most worried Ghannouchi during this period was the deterioration in Nidaa Tunis, and the question of who might be qualified to succeed Essebsi. Ghannouchi was right to be thus concerned after the death of Essebsi, Al Nahda found it very difficult to reach agreement with Nidaa Tunis, which no longer possessed a leader who was accepted by the majority of currents in the secular camp.

establishment of small splinter parties encouraged by the absence of an electoral threshold, the irresponsible exchanges of slanderous statements and the prolonged negotiations required to form coalitions (which were presented by the media as a fight over war booty while the burning issues of unemployment and uneven development remained unaddressed) led to a dangerous political fatigue which did not bode well for the young democracy. Situations of this nature are fertile soil for incitement against 'political elites' in general – a classic mark of populism and a preface to campaigns against parliamentary democracy.

This, in fact, is precisely what happened in 2019 with the election of Kais Saied, who boasted openly of never having voted in any election, nor even in the very election he won; who offered neither a concrete programme nor experience but just one slogan "the people wants…"; and who had played no role in the revolution. Rather, his only redeeming features were a puritan outlook, and the fact that he was not a politician. Saied is a president who is opposed to the system that he is supposed to preside over and who tries to expand his presidential authorities in a modified parliamentarian system by turning routine procedures such as the swearing in of ministers into issues of central importance. By rejecting major-party candidates for the position of prime minister and refusing to swear in certain ministers, he sought to impose his own appointees on the prime minister, benefitting from the fact that the parliament had failed to appoint a constitutional court which, according to the Constitution, is authorized to decide in disputes concerning the powers of the different authorities and to determine the constitutionality of controversial laws and to settle disputes between the various state authorities.

Despite losing an additional seventeen seats in 2019, Al Nahda came in first given the lack of any sizeable secular party to challenge it. The fragmentation of parties and declining public participation in elections are simply different facets of the same phenomenon. The electoral system in Tunisia is based on proportional regional electoral method with no threshold. This fact, coupled with the low voting turn out, as the case of the 2019 parliamentary elections, made it possible for a party to become the third biggest bloc in the parliament (with 22 seats) by receiving only 184,000 votes out of the 8,500,000 eligible voters. This applies to the fourth biggest bloc in the parliament (won 21 seats with only 168,732 seats). In other words, the third biggest bloc won 10 per cent of the seats with receiving only 2 per cent of the eligible voters (6.4 per cent of the actual votes).

Be that as it may, this early political fatigue, manifested in declining voter turnout and a state of disarray and disintegration, has been exploited by organized powers of the old ruling party which, in the guise of the Free Destourian Party, work systematically to disrupt and fragment parliament in order to render it ineffective and alienate the public from the concept of democracy while stirring up nostalgia for the Ben Ali era. Meanwhile, as mentioned earlier, the populist Kais Saied undermines the parliament in his own way using the angry mood of the people and their vulnerability to populist discourse, especially during the spread of the Covid-19 pandemic (Tables E.4 and E.5).

Table E.4 Results of the 6 October 2019 Parliamentary Elections

Party	**Votes**	**% of Votes**	**Seats**	**% of Seats**	**Change Compared to Previous Elections**
Al Nahda Movement	561,132	27.79	52	23.96	- 17 seats
Heart of Tunisia[a]	415,913	14.55	38	17.51	New
Democratic Current	183,464	6.42	22	10.14	+ 19 seats
Dignity Coalition	169,651	5.94	21	9.68	New
Free Destourian Party[b]	189,356	6.63	17	7.83	+ 17 seats
People's Movement	129,604	4.53	16	7.37	+ 13 seats
Tahya Tounes	116,582	4.08	14	6.45	New
Machrouu Tounes	40,869	1.43	4	1.84	New
Republican People's Union	59,924	2.10	3	1.38	+ 3 seats
Nidaa Tunis	43,213	1.51	3	1.38	−83 seats
Errahma Party	27,944	0.98	3	1.38	+ 3 seats
Tunisian Alternative	46,046	1.61	3	1.38	New
Afaq Tunis	43,892	1.54	2	0.92	−6 seats
Hope and work independent list	45,196	1.58	2	0.92	+ 2 seats
Social Democratic Union	29,828	1.04	1	0.46	New
Popular Front	32,365	1.13	1	0.46	−14 seats
Socialist Destourian Party	16,235	0.57	1	0.46	New
Green League List	5,667	0.20	1	0.46	+ 1 seat
Current of Love	17,749	0.62	1	0.46	−1 seat
The Farmers' Voice Party	9,366	0.33	1	0.46	No change
Esh Tounsi list	46,401	1.62	1	0.46	New
Independent lists[c]	37,188	1.28	10	4.61	–
Total votes of parties and lists represented in the Assembly	**2,267,585**	**87.48**	**217**	**100**	–
Total votes for the remaining parties and lists	**590,602**	**12.52**	**0**	**0**	–
Total	**2,858,187**	**100**	---	–	–

'Final Accepted list of Candidates for the 2019 Legislative Elections', [al-Qā'imah al-Mutarashshiḥah al-Maqbūlah Niha'iyan lil-Intikhābāt al-Tashrī'iyah 2019] *The Independent High Authority for Elections (ISIE) [al-Hay'ah al-'Ulyā al-Mustaqillah lil-Intikhābāt]*, accessed at: http://bit.ly/2WKjTOD; 'Preliminary Results of the 2019 Legislative Elections', [al-Natā'ij al-Awwaliyah lil-Intikhābāt al-Tashrī'iyah 2019] *The Independent High Authority for Elections (ISIE) [al-Hay'ah al-'Ulyā al-Mustaqilla lil-Intikhābāt]*, accessed at: http://bit.ly/2NfhxUP; 'Decision by the Independent High Authority for Elections dated 9 October 2019 regarding the announcement of the preliminary results for the 2019 legislative elections', [Qarār al-Hay'ah al-'Ulyā al-Mustaqillah lil-Intikhābāt Mu'arrakh fī 9 'Uktūbar 2019 Yata'allaq bi at-Taṣrih bil Natā'ij al-Awwaliyah lil-Intikhābāt al-Tashrī'iyah 2019] *The Independent High Authority for Elections (ISIE) [al-Hay'ah al-'Ulyā al-Mustaqillah lil-Intikhābāt]*, 9 October 2019, p. 2, accessed at: http://bit.ly/2ISQgEX; 'Distribution of Seats in the Assembly of the Representatives of the People', [Tawzī' al-Maqā'id Dākhil Majlis Nuwwāb al-Sha'b], *Official Twitter Account of the Independent High Authority for Elections (ISIE)*, 10 October 2019, accessed at: http://bit.ly/2r9JaWB.

[a] Heart of Tunisia led by businessman Nabil Qaraui (jailed on corruption charges), Tayha Tunis led by ex-Prime Minister Yousef al-Shared and Mashrou Tounes, all of them considered heirs to Nidaa Tunis, together won sixty seats.

[b] Founded in 2013 by Hamid Karoui, a former minister in Ben Ali's cabinet, and many former members of the Constitutional Democratic Rally Party (RCD) under the name 'the Destourian Movement', it was renamed the Free Destourian Party in 2016. Its leader, Abir Musi, an MP who obtained 4.2% of the vote in the presidential elections, does not acknowledge the democratic constitution and calls publicly for a return to the old regime.

[c] These include the 'Back to the Origin' list, the 'Goodness' list, the 'Excellence' list, the 'Independent Youth' list, the 'Citizenship and Development' list, the 'Faithfulness to the Covenant' list, the 'Giving and Liberality' list', the 'We are all Tunisians' list, the 'Silyanah in our Eyes' list, and the 'We Are Here' list.

The Independent Higher Electoral Commission accepted 1,506 lists in the 2019 parliamentary elections: 1,341 were inside Tunisia and 165 outside. Of those inside Tunisia, 668 were party lists, 324 were coalition lists, and 514 were independent.

Table E.5 Tunisian participation in post-revolution elections

Elections		Voter Turnout (%)
2011 Constituent Assembly Elections 23 October 2011		86 per cent of registered voters (52 per cent of eligible voters)
2014 Parliamentary Elections 26 October 2014		67.7 per cent of registered voters (47.7 per cent of eligible voters)
2014 Presidential Elections	First Round 23 November 2014	62.9 per cent of registered voters (44.5 per cent of eligible voters)
	Second Round 21 December 2014	60.1 per cent of registered voters (42.5 per cent of eligible voters)
2018 Municipal Elections 6 May 2018		35.6 per cent of registered voters
2019 Parliamentary Elections 6 October 2019		41.7 per cent of registered voters (34.1 per cent of eligible voters)[a]
2019 Presidential Elections	First Round 15 September 2019	48.98 per cent of registered voters
	Second Round 13 October 2019	57.8 per cent of registered voters

'Final Report on the Tunisian National Constituent Assembly Elections', p. 15; 'National Constituent Assembly Elections in Tunisia', p. 45; 'Final Report on the 2014 Legislative and Presidential Elections in Tunisia', p. 45; 'The Preliminary Results of the Second Round of the Presidential Elections', [al-Natāʾij al-Awwaliyah lil-Dawr al-Thānī lil-Intikhābāt al-Riʾāsiyah] *The Independent Higher Authority for Elections (ISIE)* [al-Hay'ah al-'Ulyā al-Mustaqillah lil-Intikhābāt] 22 December 2014, accessed at: http://bit.ly/31izDZP; Haifa Mzalouat, 'A Step Forward for Independents', *Carnegie Endowment for International Peace,* May 10, 2018, accessed at: http://bit.ly/2pqNobr; 'The Independent Higher Authority for Elections 9 October 2019 decision regarding the announcement of the preliminary results for the 2019 legislative elections', p. 2; 'Carter Center Preliminary Statement on Tunisia's Parliamentary Elections', *The Carter Center,* 8 October 2019, accessed at: http://bit.ly/32httuo; 'The Independent Higher Authority for Elections decision regarding the announcement of the preliminary results for the first round of the presidential elections 2019', ['Qarār al-Hay'ah al-'Ulyā al-Mustaqillah lil-Intikhābāt al-Muta'alliq bi at-Taṣrīḥ bil-Natāʾij al-Awwaliyah lil-Dawrah al-Ūlā lil-Intikhābāt al-Riʾāsiyah 2019] *The Independent Higher Authority for Elections (ISIE) [al-Hay'ah al-'Ulyā al-Mustaqillah lil-Intikhābāt]*, 17 September 2019, p. 1, accessed at: http://bit.ly/2Mmx2tP; 'Preliminary Statement of the IRI-NDI Election Observation Mission to Tunisia's 13 October 2019 Presidential Runoff Election', *IRI-NDI Tunisia International Election Observation Mission*, 14 October 2019, p. 2, accessed at: https://bit.ly/3hmkd0d.

[a] This means that out of 8,500,000 citizens with the right to vote, only 2,946,682 exercised this right.

V

The economic and social conditions that led to the revolution have remained unaltered. Democracy contains the protests, preventing them from erupting into a full-scale revolution. However, their continuation threatens to corrode a system already besieged by populist and nationalist right-wing trends that openly propagandize in favour of the ousted regime and against the revolution.

Despite Tunisia's grim short-term economic prospects immediately after the revolution, not only due to the repercussions of the revolution itself but also because of the ongoing crisis in Libya,[18] its economic future appeared bright from the perspective of international financial institutions, which predicted that

18. Libya had been a major employer of Tunisians, and Libyans, major consumers of services in Tunisia.

Table E.6 GDP Growth (Annual %) (2008–20)

Year	GDP Growth (Annual %)
2008	4.24
2009	3.04
2010	3.51
2011	−1.92
2012	4.00
2013	2.88
2014	2.97
2015	1.19
2016	1.16
2017	1.92
2018	2.66
2019	1.04
2020 – Q1	−2.1
2020 – Q2	−21.7
2020 – Q3	−6.0

'GDP growth (annual %) - Tunisia', *The World Bank Data*, accessed at: https://bit.ly/33HdkRu; 'Tunisia GDP Annual Growth Rate', *Trading Economics*, accessed at: http://bit.ly/32Tc0bV

growth would rebound during the two subsequent years. Factors that promised to contribute to achieving growth included the resumption of exports, large government investments, the package of reforms proposed by the transitional government and an annual GDP growth rate of nearly 5 per cent in 2011–12.[19] The interregional income gap is gradually narrowing. However, international investments have not been quick to enter the country, nor has international aid. Tourism was badly impacted by terrorism, and no sooner had it recovered from this setback than it was hit again by Covid-19. Meanwhile, the Libyan crisis has persisted, IMF's hopeful predictions have not been fulfilled and the problems of slow economic growth, unfair distribution of income and regional development and widespread unemployment remain significant threats to democratic consolidation in Tunisia (Table E.6) (Figure E.3).

In order to overcome regional disparities, state involvement was needed to lay the infrastructure for transport, energy and other services, encourage investments and support agriculture in these regions. However, the economic policies implemented under Al Nahda and Nidaa Tunis became more liberal. Social injustice and relative deprivation nevertheless remained a source of anger among Tunisians, which have remained a major challenge for democracy in Tunisia. Such issues have also been a source of unrest as evidenced by the protests of 2015, 2016, 2017 and 2021. On 17 January 2016 protests which had begun in Kasserine spread to Kebili, Gafsa, Kairouan and Sidi Bouzid, eventually reaching the al-Tadhamoun

19. 'Tunisia: Preliminary Conclusions of the 2010 Article IV Mission'. *International Monetary Fund IMF*, 15 June 2010, accessed at: http://www.imf.org/external/np/ms/2010/061510a.htm.

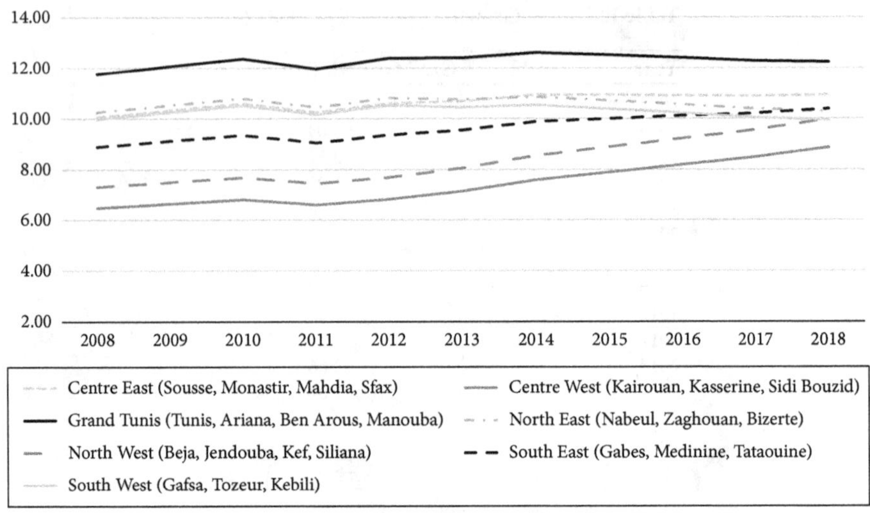

Figure E.3 Subnational GNI per capita in thousands of USD (2011 PPP) (2008–18). 'GNI per capita in thousands of US$ (2011 PPP)', *Global Data Lab*, accessed at: https://bit.ly/37qOp5P.

neighbourhood in the capital, where a curfew was imposed. The 2017 protests started in Ben Gardane and Tataouine. It was similar protests that had initially sparked the Tunisian Revolution. However, democracy did make a difference, as nobody was killed in these demonstrations,[20] and the same was true for the much larger protests of January 2021.

Human dignity was a pivotal driver of the Tunisian Revolution (as it was of the Arab revolutions in general). Article 37 of the 2014 Constitution guarantees the right to assembly and peaceful demonstration, while according to Article 23 the state is required to protect human dignity and physical integrity. The same Article prohibits mental and physical torture and stipulates that crimes of torture shall not be subject to any statute of limitations.[21] Furthermore, the Constitution is being enforced in practice, a fact which distinguishes democracy from other systems. In no other system of rule is the text of the Constitution so binding for those in power. A possible threat to the constitution is the serving populist president who declaratively opposed it, albeit, in the meanwhile, and in the absence of a constitutional court, is content with interpreting it as if it were a constitution of a presidential system.

20. In one of them, in fact, a policeman was injured. See Ben Achour, *Tūnis: thawrah fī bilād al-islām*, pp. 267–8.

21. 'Tunisia's Constitution of 2014', *Constitute Project*, accessed at: https://bit.ly/33RaFFi.

When the Tunisian Revolution broke out, it was initially motivated by social injustice and unemployment, especially among educated youth. Once the dictator had been overthrown, however, the revolution's main achievements were: (1) reforms within the regime which led to a phase of democratic transition, (2) the introduction of political freedoms (though the socio-economic structures remained unaltered) and (3) the drafting and institution of a democratic constitution.

The new Constitution did not emerge ex nihilo, of course. Rather, it was derived from the goals of the revolution, the dialogical tradition of the Tunisian opposition and principles embedded in the founding decree of 23 March 2013 and the 10 May 2011 decree regarding the National Constituent Assembly elections.[22] The Tunisian Constitution was the outcome of a dialogue among the major political forces in Tunisia that had committed themselves to democratic procedures.[23]

The major achievement of the first phase of the transition period, the Tunisian Constitution of 2014, is a liberal democratic charter similar to that of any long-established democracy, and the fact that it contains some compromises does not stain it or diminish its democratic character. Liberal democratic constitutions are neither theories nor theoretical generalizations; indeed, embedding democratic principles within a specific socio-historical context is one of the most important challenges faced by those drafting such a document, and this in two senses: (1) the expression of national culture in the constitution itself and (2) the readiness simultaneously to bridge gaps and preserve liberal democratic principles. Compromises do not always resolve disputes; sometimes, they simply suppress contradictions. Thus, for example, the Tunisian Constitution identifies the religion of the state (meaning, the religion adhered to by the majority of Tunisians), while at the same time pledging to protect freedom of conscience and the sanctities of the Tunisian people. A contradiction is admittedly present here, but its solution was left to a constitutional court (as yet to be formed at the time) in the event that disputes emerged in the nitty-gritty of daily life. The same applies of the mixed parliamentarian-presidential character of the system as couched in the constitution although the spirit is that of a parliamentarian system.

The Tunisian Constitution was not only unanimously agreed upon, but implemented as well. Although the socio-economic injustices that had caused the revolution to erupt had not changed, a democracy had nevertheless emerged, which was itself a great achievement. However, democracy is not a path that necessarily leads to social justice. Growth and social justice can be achieved in Tunisia, but this will depend on the economic and social policies of its successive governments and unions' cooperation with them. Partisan politics are not facilitating this process, to say the least, which is the major weak point exploited by populist politicians.

Now that it has passed two peaceful transfers of power, Tunisia is a democracy, but it is as yet an unconsolidated one. The challenge of Tunisian democracy is to

22. Ben Achour, *Tūnis: thawrah fī bilād al-islām*, p. 362.

23. The Salafis remained aloof from the idea of a democratized Tunisian Identity (Tunisianité).

turn the national consensus on the Constitution into a constitutional patriotism such that democracy becomes a component of the Tunisian identity and to set out and implement a plan for economic growth and regional and human development. Then, and only then, will Tunisia rise above the economic and political hardships that still pose a danger to its democracy. These are the tasks of elected state organs, but they will only succeed if they become the shared responsibility of state and civil society.

POSTSCRIPT

DEMOCRACY IMPERILLED BY POPULISM

Within a relatively short period of time, the dangers of populism noted in the Epilogue have materialized. Given the importance of the events now taking place in Tunisia, especially since I had previously warned of the dangers facing Tunisian democracy, the publishing house has kindly accepted this Postscript even though it had finished editing the book and commenced the design process.

On the evening of Sunday, 25 July 2021, Tunisian president Kais Saied announced the dismissal of Prime Minister Hisham Al-Mashishi, his assumption of executive power with the help of a government headed by a prime minister appointed by himself and the presidency of the Public Prosecution Office. In addition, he announced the freezing of Parliament for a period of thirty days, legislation by presidential decree and the lifting of immunity from Members of Parliament.

Although Saied based his declaration on Article 80 of the Tunisian Constitution, he actually violated the Constitution, and Article 80 in particular. The president published this presidential order in writing on 30th July in the *Tunisian Official Gazette*. The written decision included the provision that the suspension of Parliament could be extended beyond the thirty-day period.

Article 80, which pertains to exceptional measures, states,

> In the event of imminent danger threatening the nation's institutions or the security or independence of the country and hampering the normal functioning of the state, the President of the Republic may take any measures necessitated by the exceptional circumstances, after consultation with the Head of Government and the Speaker of the Assembly of the Representatives of the People and informing the President of the Constitutional Court. The measures shall be announced in a statement to the people.

However, Saied consulted with neither the Head of the Government nor the Speaker of Parliament steps that are intended to unite the various state institutions in facing the presumed danger. Saied failed to specify what this danger was (though he mentioned corruption and the government's paralysis in dealing with the pandemic). Hence, his aim was not to face a danger but to seize all state powers and subject them to his own authority.

According to the second paragraph of Article 80,

> The measures shall aim to guarantee, as soon as possible, a return to the normal functioning of state institutions and services. The Assembly of the Representatives of the People shall be deemed to be in a state of continuous session throughout such a period. In this situation, the President of the Republic may not dissolve the Assembly of the Representatives of the People, nor may a motion of censure against the government be submitted.

The third paragraph of Article 80 states that 'thirty days after these measures enter into force, and at any time thereafter, the Speaker of the Assembly of the Representatives of the People or thirty of its members may apply to the Constitutional Court to rule on whether or not the exceptional circumstance still obtains'.

The last paragraph of Article 80 indicates that 'the court shall issue its decision publicly within a maximum of 15 days, and the implementation of these measures shall cease when the reasons therefor cease to exist. The President of the Republic shall address a statement to this effect to the people'.

The Tunisian president has violated every paragraph and clause in the article on which he has based his actions, and which expressly forbids him to freeze Parliament and dissolve the government. It also necessitates the existence of a constitutional court, which does not currently exist in Tunisia. Parliament failed to form such a court due to partisan disagreements, even though it is an absolute necessity, especially within a mixed parliamentary-presidential system that may need a judicial authority to decide on issues pertaining to the different powers and their limits . When the elected parliament in 2019 succeeded in enacting a law that regulates the nomination of the court, Kais Saied blocked it, turning a formal procedure into an essential veto power, just as he obstructed the government's work by refusing to allow some ministers to be sworn in before him.

Tunisians elected a president who never uttered the word 'democracy' in any of his public appearances and who even boasted that he had no declared political program. Furthermore, he has openly declared several times that he is against the Constitution and the existing political system. The amorphous system of elected councils from bottom to top, and from the periphery to the centre, of which he spoke in his numerous television appearances before his election, is reminiscent of the revolutionary committees that formed an arm of the Gaddafi regime in Libya. The president, who is affiliated with no political party, has repeatedly expressed contempt for parties and Parliament and has not voted in any elections since the beginning of the democratic transition, including the one in which he himself was elected.

Some ascribed to him an eccentric character. Be that as it may, his presidency has proven to be a threat to this fledgling democracy. He ascended to power by virtue of his populist rhetoric against parties, politicians and Parliament; vague accusations of conspiracies and plots taking place in Parliament; random charges accusations of corruption against unnamed individuals during his many television interviews; and support from initiatives that brought together angry young people disaffected by conditions in the country. The majority of Tunisians elected a person with a populist rhetoric who prided himself on being 'untainted' by politics and money. Luckily for him, his opponent in the second round was a businessman accused of corruption and considered close to the previous regime. Hence, voting for Saied appeared to be a vote in support of the revolution's program and objectives, to which he paid lip-service but in which he played no part. In fact, he was not known to have taken any stance in opposition to the Ben Ali regime.

Since his election, Saied has acted as if the Tunisian system were a presidential one. As such, he has sought to make the government answerable to him and not to Parliament. He refused to consult with parliamentary blocs in regard to choosing candidates to form the government and only asked them to send written suggestions of names. In recordings of his meetings with the government and the Speaker of Parliament—which the presidency has been keen on distributing to the media—the president is always heard reproaching politicians. And in a move unprecedented in Tunisia's history, he has delivered a series of political speeches in military barracks.

The president took these steps on the pretext that the crisis brought about by the Covid-19 pandemic was an 'imminent danger' after the country witnessed demonstrations that included an attack on the headquarters of the Al Nahda Movement. Al Nahda has the largest bloc in Parliament, but not the majority. Hence, it does not rule the country but only heads the Parliament. It has entered into many coalition deals and worked on political appointments while perpetuating the image of a ruling party even when it should have been in the opposition. Its need for close alignments and coalitions with secular parties was used by opportunists of all kinds, including corrupt politicians like the party whose candidate lost against Saied and whom Al Nahda accused of corruption. These expedient partners were not committed to this 'cooperation'. Moreover, given the long-standing hostility toward the movement in quarters of the old regime, as well as the old allies it has abandoned, it was in the president's interest to make his campaign against the Parliament look like a struggle with Al Nahda.

Al Nahda did not rule Tunisia. Rather, thanks to a coalition with the second list in Parliament, it supported a government of technocrats which the president rejected because the prime minister did not agree to nominate some of his adherents as ministers. And the fact that its leader presided over Parliament made it easy to equate him with the Parliament as a whole.

Political opportunism, manoeuvrings and partisan intrigues are widespread in established democracies, but the Tunisian political parties did not take into consideration the fact that the Tunisian democracy is not consolidated yet and that the Tunisian public may be easily alienated by such phenomena and vulnerable to the influence of populist anti-party propaganda. Kais Saied took advantage of the Tunisian people's resentment against the parties and Parliament over their contentiousness, constant skirmishes and mutual defamation, as well as the continuous crises between the Parliament and the presidency. However, he himself had contributed to and helped to prolong these very crises, all the while allowing the country's many economic problems to worsen under the pandemic. Therefore, despite opposition from the majority of parties and legal organizations, the steps taken by the president have been supported by the Tunisian public, which is suffering from the deterioration of the economy and early 'political fatigue', while major civil institutions' positions on his actions have fluctuated between opposition, fear and reservation.

In the few statements he has made to dispel widespread domestic and international concerns over the future of democracy in Tunisia, Saied has chosen his words carefully, emphasizing that he will respect the freedom of expression and the rule of law, but without committing himself to preserving democracy in Tunisia.

What is worrisome here is the combination of the president's ambitions with the society's proneness to being swayed by angry populist rhetoric against elites and the readiness of state agencies to unhesitatingly accept and carry out the president's orders simply because they are accustomed to the authoritarian presidential system. Such agencies view the position of the president as being closer to their definition of the state than are the competing and squabbling parties in Parliament.

Some political elites, hesitating under pressure from the street, are waiting to see what the president will do, 'because no one knows what he has in mind', which reflects a mood akin to that of a dictatorial regime with no checks and balances. The truth is that the president acts on what he has in mind. However, he does so gradually, while not revealing his true aims. As of this writing, he has dismissed the Ministers of Defence and the Interior, the Director of the Interior Ministry's Internal Intelligence and the Director of State Television. So, what does this have to do with the economic and social crisis (not to speak of Covid-19)?

It is clear that Saied has objectives in mind and that he will not stop unless he is stopped: internally by a coalition of democratic forces, and externally by international pressure from democratic countries which hesitate in the face of the enthusiastic support Saied enjoys from anti-democratic regional forces.

On the other hand, the majority of Tunisian political and civil elites are still committed to democracy. The Tunisian people experienced a full decade of freedom in the sense of respect for their civil rights and liberties, and it would be difficult for them to give that up now. This is all that Tunisian democracy can bet on in the face of such dangers.

Democracy is not a solution to economic and social issues but, rather, the alternative to despotism and tyranny. Nevertheless, ruling elites' policies may prompt people to prioritize social-economic issues over democracy by associating economic deterioration with the democratization process. Economic and social issues need to be addressed by the programs and policies of the ruling political forces in cooperation with the institutions of society. This may require a change in the ruling forces, which is possible under a democratic system. As for changing the system itself, it serves goals other than the declared ones. The democratic system is not responsible for the worsening of economic and social issues, and abandoning democracy will not solve them. On the contrary, it will simply add the burden of despotism, whose bitterness the Tunisian people know all too well.

BIBLIOGRAPHY

Arabic Books

al-Kawwari, Ali Khalifa (ed.). *Tyranny in Modern Arab Regimes [al-Istibdād fi Nudhum al-Ḥukm al-ʿArabiyah al-Muʿāṣirah]*. 2nd ed. Beirut: Center for Arab Unity Studies, 2006.

al-Kawwari, Ali Khalifa et al. (eds.). *Naḥwa Kutlah Tārikhiyah Dīmuqrāṭiyah fi al-Buldān al-ʿArabiyah [Towards a Historical Democratic Front in the Arab Countries]*. Beirut: Center for Arab Unity Studies, 2010.

Al-Sghayyar, Umayra Aliyya. *al-Yūsifiyūn wa-Taḥarrur al-Maghrib al- ʿArabī [The Youssefis and the Liberation of the Arab Maghreb]*. Tunis: al-Maghāribiyah lil-Ṭibāʿah wal-Nashr wal-ishhār, 2007.

al-Shatir, Khalifa (ed.). *The National Movement and the Independent State*. Tunis: Center for Economic and Social Studies and Research, 2005.

Ben Achour, Yadh. *Tūnis: thawrah fī bilād al-islām [Tunisia: A Revolution in the Land of Islam]*. Fathi Ben al-Haj Yahya (trans.). Tunis: Tunisian Institute for Translation/Cérès for Publications, 2018.

Ben Ashour, Mohamed al-Fadil. *al-Ḥarakah al-adabiyah wal-fikriyah fī tūnis [The Literary and Intellectual Movement in Tunisia]*. 3rd ed. Tunis: al-Dār at-Tūnisiyah lil-Nashr, 1972.

Ben Hussein, Salem. *al-qiṣṣah al-khafiyah lil-thawrah at-tūnisiyah [The Hidden Story of the Tunisian Revolution]*. Sfax: np., 2016.

Ben Mim, Hamadi. *asrār al-thawrah at-tūnisiyah [The Secrets of the Tunisian Revolution]*. 2nd ed. Tunis: Thakafia Print, 2019.

Belkhodja, Tahar. *al-Ḥabīb Būrqība: Sīrat Zaʿīm [Habib Bourguiba: The Story of a Leader]*. Cairo: al-Dār al-Thaqāfiyah lil-Nashr, 1999.

bin Ḥamīdah, ʿAbd as-Salām. *Tārīkh al-Ḥarakah al-Niqābiyah al-Waṭaniyah lil-Shaghghīlah bi Tūnis (1924–1956) [The History of the Unionist Labor Movement in Tunisia (1924–1956)]*. vol. 2. Sfax: Dār Muhammad ʿAlī, 1984.

Bishara, Azmi. *al-intiqāl al-dīmuqrāṭī wa ishkāliyatuh: dirāsah naẓariyah wa taṭbīqiyah muqāranah [Problems of Democratization: A Comparative Theoretical and Applied Study]*. Beirut: Arab Center for Research and Policy Studies, 2020.

Bishara, Azmi. *al-Mujtamaʿ al-Madanī: Dirāsah Naqdiyyah [Civil Society: A Critical Study]*. Beirut: Center for Arab Unity Studies, 1998.

Bishara, Azmi. *al-thawrah at-tūnisiyah al-majīdah: bunyat al-thawrah wa ṣayrūratuhā min khilāl yawmiyātihā [Tunisia's Glorious Revolution: The Structure of a Revolution and its Evolution through its Daily Chronicles]*. Beirut: ACRPS, 2012.

Bishara, Azmi. *Fī al-Masʾalah al-ʿArabiyah: Muqaddimah li-Bayān Dīmuqrāṭī ʿArabī [On the Arab Question: A Preamble to a Democratic Arab Manifesto]*. 4th ed. Doha and Beirut: ACRPS, 2018 [2007].

Bishara, Azmi. *Thawrat Misr: Mina al-Thawrah ilā al-Inqilab [Egypt's Revolution. vol. II: From Revolution to Coup]*. Doha/Beirut: ACRPS, 2016.

Bouazizi, Mohsen. *al-Ta'birāt al-Iḥtijājiyah wal-Majāl al-Ijtimā'ī [Expressions of Protest and the Social Sphere]*. Tunis: ad-Dār al-'Arabia lil-Kitāb, 2009.

Bouqarra, Abd al-Jaleel. *Ḥarakat Āfāq: min Tārīkh al-Yasār at-Tūnisī, 1963–1975 [The Afaq Movement: From the History of the Tunisian Left, 1963–1975]*. Tunis: Dār Sras lil-Nashr, 1993.

Essebsi, Beji Caid. *al-Ḥabīb Būrqība .. al-Muhimm wal-Ahamm [al-Habib Bourguiba: The Important and the Most Important]*. Muḥammad Ma'ālī (trans.). Tunis: Dār aj-Janūb lil-Nashr, 2011.

Fayez, Sara. *al-Aḥzāb wal-Ḥarakāt al-Siyāsiyah fī Tūnis [Parties and Political Movements in Tunisia 1932–1984]*. Damascus: Maktab Khadamāt al-Ṭibā'ah, 1986.

Hanafi, Sari (ed.). *Ḥalat al-Istithnā' wal-Muqāwamah fī al-Waṭan al-'Arabī [The State of Exception and Resistance in the Arab World]*. Beirut: Center for Arab Unity Studies, 2010.

Labyaḍ, Salim. *al-Hawiyah: al-Islam, al-'Urūbah, at-Tawnasah [Identity: Islam, Arabism, Tunisization]*. Beirut: Center for Arab Unity Studies, 2009.

Lahmar, Mouldi (ed.). *Al-Thawrah at-Tūnisiyah: al-Qādiḥ al-Maḥallī Taḥt Mijhar al-'Ulūm al-'Insāniyah [The Tunisian Revolution: Examining the Triggers through the Prism of the Humanities]*. Doha and Beirut: ACRPS, 2014.

Laroui, Abdellah. *Mujmal Tārīkh al-Maghrib [The History of the Maghreb]*. vol. 3. Casa Blanca and Beirut: Arabic Cultural Centre, 2007.

Lyasir, Fathi. *Dawlat al-Huwāt: Sanatān min Ḥukm al-Troika fī Tūnis [The Amateur State: Two Years of Troika Rule in Tunisia]*. Tunis: Muhammad Ali Publications, 2016.

Lyasir, Fathi. *Mu'jam al-Thawrah at-Tūnisiyah: 17 Dīsambir 2010-23 Uktūbar 2011 [Lexicon of the Tunisian Revolution: 17 December 2010–23 October 2011]*. Tunisia: Muhammad Ali Publications, 2012.

Tunisia's Revolution [Thawrat Tunis.] Doha and Beirut: ACRPS, 2012.

Vilali, Muhamad Mukhtar and at-Taher ben Yousef. *Al-Qiwā al-Muḍāddah lil-Thawrah fī Tūnis [Counter Revolutionary Forces in Tunisia]*. Tunis: Fann at-Ṭibā'ah, 2013.

Foreign Languages Books

Alexander, Christopher. *Tunisia: From Stability to Revolution in the Maghreb*. Abingdon: Routledge, 2016.

Aminzade, Ronald A. et al. (eds.). *Silence and Voice in the Study of Contentious Politics*. Cambridge: Cambridge University Press, 2001.

Bayat, Asef. *Life as Politics: How Ordinary People Change the Middle East*. 2nd ed. Stanford, CA: Stanford University Press, 2013 [2010].

Beau, Nicolas and Jean-Pierre Tuquoi. *Notre ami Ben Ali: L'envers du "miracle tunisien" [Our Friend Ben Ali: The Other Face of the "Tunisian Miracle"]*. Paris: La Découverte, 1999.

Beinin, Joel and Frédéric Vairel (eds.). *Social Movements, Mobilization, and Contestation in the Middle East and North Africa*. Redwood City, CA: Stanford University Press, 2011.

Bush, Sarah Sunn. *The Taming of Democracy Assistance: Why Democracy Promotion Does Not Confront Dictators*. Cambridge: Cambridge University Press, 2015.

Chalmers, Douglas A. et al. *The New Politics of Inequality in Latin America: Rethinking Participation and Representation*. Oxford: Oxford University Press, 1997.

Clancy-Smith, Julia. *Tunisian Revolutions: Reflections on Seas, Coasts, and Interiors*. Washington D.C.: Georgetown University Press, 2014.

Collected Works. vol. 21. Moscow: Progress Publishers, 1965.

Cox, Robert W. *Production Power and World Order*. New York: Columbia University Press, 1987.

Dabashi, Hamid. *The Arab Spring: The End of Postcolonialism*. London and New York: Zed Books, 2012.

Davis, Mike. *Planet of Slums*. Brooklyn: VERSO, 2006.

de Tocqueville, Alexis. *The Ancien Régime and the French Revolution*. Jon Elster (ed.). Arthur Goldhammer (trans.). Cambridge: Cambridge University Press, 2011 [1856].

Di Palma, Giuseppe. *To Craft Democracies: An Essay on Democratic Transitions*. Berkeley: University of California Press, 1990.

El-Said, Hamed and Jane Harrigan (eds.). *Aid and Power in the Arab World: IMF and World Bank Policy-Based Lending in the Middle East and North Africa*. New York: Palgrave MacMillan, 2009.

Elster, Jon and Rune Slagstad (eds.). *Constitutionalism and Democracy*. Cambridge: Cambridge University Press, 1988.

Gana, Nouri (ed.). *The Making of the Tunisian Revolution: Contexts, Architects, Prospects*. Edinburgh: Edinburgh University Press, 2013.

Hamid, Shadi. *Temptations of Power: Islamists and Illiberal Democracy in a New Middle East*. New York: Oxford University Press, 2014.

Hampsher-Monk, Iain (ed.). *Revolutionary Writings*. Cambridge: Cambridge University Press, 2014.

Hannah Arendt, *On Revolution*. New York: Penguin, 1990 [1963].

Harrod, Jeffrey. *Power, Production, and the Unprotected Worker*. New York: Columbia University Press, 1987.

Hibbou, Beatrice. *The Force of Obedience: the Political Economy of Repression in Tunisia*. Cambridge UK and Malden Mass: Polity Press, 2011.

Hobsbawm, Eric. *The Age of Revolution 1789-1848*. New York: Vintage Books, 1996 [1962].

King, Stephen J. *Liberalization against Democracy: The Local Politics of Economic Reform in Tunisia*. Bloomington: Indiana University Press, 2003.

Kuhn, Thomas S. *The Structure of Scientific Revolutions*. 3rd ed. Chicago and London: University of Chicago Press, 1996.

La Transition démocratique en Tunisie: Etat des lieux [Democratic Transition in Tunisia]. Tunis: Diwan Éditions, 2012.

Linz, Juan and Alfred Stepan (eds.). *The Breakdown of Democratic Regimes*. Baltimore and London: Johns Hopkins University Press, 1978.

Lenin, Vladimir. *«Left Wing» Communism: An Infantile Disorder*. Moscow: Progress Publishers, 1950.

Masri, Safwan M. *Tunisia: An Arab Anomaly*. Lisa Anderson (Foreword). New York: Columbia University Press, 2017.

McCarthy, Rory. *Inside Tunisia's al-Nahda: Between Politics and Preaching*. Cambridge: Cambridge University Press, 2018.

McCarthy, Rory. *Inside Tunisia's al-Nahda: Between Politics and Preaching*. Cambridge: Cambridge University Press, 2018.

Moore Jr, Barrington. *Social Origins of Dictatorship and Democracy: Lord and Peasant in the Making of the Modern World*. Boston: Beacon Press, 1966.

Moore, Barrington. *Injustice: the Social Bases of Obedience and Revolt*. New York: Palgrave Macmillan, 1978.

O'Donnell, Guillermo and Philippe C. Schmitter (eds.). *Transitions from Authoritarian Rule: Tentative Conclusions about Uncertain Democracies*. vol. 4. Baltimore: Johns Hopkins University Press, 1986.

Perkins, Kenneth. *A History of Modern Tunisia*. 2nd ed. Cambridge: Cambridge University Press, 2014.

Roberts, Adam et al. (eds.). *Civil Resistance in the Arab Spring: Triumphs and Disasters*. Oxford: Oxford University Press, 2016.

Sadiki, Larbi. *Rethinking Arab Democratization: Elections without Democracy*. 1st ed. Oxford: Oxford University Press, 2009.

Salame, Ghassan (ed.). *Democracy without Democrats?: Renewal of Politics in the Muslim World*. Beirut: Center for Arab Unity Studies, 2000.

Serra, Narcís and Joseph E. Stiglitz (eds.). *The Washington Consensus Reconsidered: Towards a New Global Governance*. Oxford: Oxford University Press, 2008.

Skocpol, Theda. *States and Social Revolutions: A Comparative Analysis of France, Russia, & China*. New York: Cambridge University Press, 1979.

Solimano, Andrés, Eduardo Aninat and Nancy Birdsall (eds.). *Distributive Justice and Economic Development*. Ann Arbor: University of Michigan Press, 1999.

Stepan, Alfred (ed.). *Democratic Transition in the Muslim World: A Global Perspective, Religion, Culture, and Public Life*. New York: Columbia University Press, 2018.

Tilly, Charles. *European Revolutions: 1492–1992*. London: Blackwell, 1993.

Tunisia in Revolt: State Violence during Anti-Government Protests. London: Amnesty International, 2011.

Vandewalle, Dirk (ed.). *North Africa: Development and Reform in a Changing Global Economy*. London: Palgrave Macmillan, 1996.

Vasconselos, Álvaro and George Joffé (eds.). *The Barcelona Process*. London: Frank Cass Publishers, 2000.

Webb, Edward. *Media in Egypt and Tunisia: From Control to Transition?*. New York: Palgrave Macmillan, 2014.

Zartman, Ira William (ed.). *Tunisia: The Political Economy of Reform*. Boulder and London: Lynne Rienner, 1991.

Zayani, Mohamed. *Networked Publics and Digital Contention: The Politics of Everyday Life in Tunisia*. Oxford: Oxford University Press, 2015.

Arabic Journal Articles

al-Shabbi, Najib. "al-ʿAlaqa bayn al-ʾIslāmiyīn wa al-ʿIlmāniyīn: Tajribat 18 Uktūbar fī Tūnis [The Relationship between the Islamists and the Secularists: 18 October's Experience in Tunisia]." *al-Adab*. vol. 58. nos. 11–12 (2010).

Ghannouchi, Rached. "Tūnis: min al-thawrah ilā al-dustūr [Tunisia: From the Revolution to the Constitution]." *Siyasat Arabiyya*. no. 18 (2016).

Houki, Chaker. "hal taṣluḥ al-muqārabah al-jīliyah asāsan li-qirāʾat al-thawrah al-tūnisiyah? [Does the Generational Approach Provide an Explanation for the Tunisian Revolution?]." *Siyasat Arabiya*. no. 32 (May 2018).

Labyaḍ, Salim. "al-Azamāt al-Ijtimāʿiyah wal-Siyāsiyah wa-Idāratuhā: Tunis 1957-1987 [Socio-Political Crises and Their Management: Tunisia 1957–1987]." *Majālāt ʿUlūm Insāniyah (Tunis)*. vol. 18. no. 2 (2005).

Foreign Languages Journal Articles

Allal, Amin. "Trajectoires 'révolutionnaires' en Tunisie Processus de radicalisations politiques 2007–2011." *Revue française de science politique*. vol. 62. no. 5–6 (2012).

Anderson, Lisa. "Political Pacts, Liberalism, and Democracy: The Tunisian National Pact of 1988." *Government and Opposition*. vol. 26. no. 2 (1991).

Ash, Timothy Garton. "Revolution: The Springtime of Two Nations." *The New York Review* (1989).

Bayat, Asef. "Revolution in Bad Times." *New Left Review*. vol. 80 (March/April 2013).

Bellin, Eva. "Civil Society: Effective Toll of Analysis for Middle East Politics?." *Political Science and Politics*. vol. 27. no. 3 (1994).

Bellin, Eva. "The Politics of Profit in Tunisia: Utility of the rentier paradigm?." *World Development*. vol. 22. no. 3 (March 1994).

Breuer, Anita, Todd Landman and Dorothea Farquhar. "Social Media and Protest Mobilization: Evidence from the Tunisian Revolution." *Democratization*. vol. 22. no. 4 (June 2015).

Brownlee, Jason. "Hereditary Succession in Modern Autocracies." *World Politics*. vol. 59. no. 4 (2007).

Davies, James C. "Toward a Theory of Revolution." *American Sociological Review*. vol. 27. no. 1 (1962).

Gallopin, Jean-Baptiste. "Dilemma and Cascades in the Armed Forces: The Tunisian Revolution." *Democracy and Security*. vol. 15. no. 4 (2019).

Gallopin, Jean-Baptiste. "Dilemma and Cascades in the Armed Forces: The Tunisian Revolution." *Democracy and Security*. vol. 15. no. 4 (2019).

Geyer, Georgie Anne. "Tunisia: A Country that Works." *The Washington Quarterly*. vol. 21. no. 4 (1998).

Gill, Stephen. "Globalization, Democratization and Politics of Indifference." *Globalization: Critical Reflections* (1996).

Hachana, Mohamed Nejib. "Twenty Years of Change: Tunisia's Journey of Progress Continues." *Mediterranean Quarterly*. vol. 19. no. 2 (2008).

Haggard, Stephan and Robert R. Kaufman. "The Political Economy of Democratic Transition." *Comparative Politics*. vol. 29. no. 3 (1997).

Hibou, Béatrice. "Domination and Control in Tunisia: Economic Levers for the Exercise of Authoritarian Power." *Review of African Political Economy*. vol. 33. no. 108 (2006).

Hurt, Stephen, Karim Knio and Magnus Ryner. "Social Forces and the Effects of (Post) Washington Consensus Policy in Africa: Comparing Tunisia and South Africa." *The Round Table*. vol. 98. no. 403 (June 2009).

Jebnoun, Noureddine. "In the Shadow of Power: Civil–Military Relations and the Tunisian Popular Uprising." *The Journal of North African Studies*. vol. 19. no. 3 (2014).

Jebnoun, Noureddine. "In the Shadow of Power: Civil–Military Relations and the Tunisian Popular Uprising." *The Journal of North African Studies*. vol. 19. no. 3 (2014).

Jerad, Nabiha. "The Tunisian Revolution: From Universal Slogans for Democracy to the Power of Language." *Middle East Journal of Culture and Communication*. vol. 6. no. 2 (2013).

Kaboub, Fadhel. "The Making of the Tunisian Revolution." *Middle East Development Journal*. vol. 5. no. 1 (March 2013).
Karagiannis, Emmanuel. "The Rise of Electoral Salafism in Egypt and Tunisia: The Use of Democracy as a Master Frame." *The Journal of North African Studies*. vol. 24. no. 2 (2019).
Kavanaugh, Andrea et al. "Media Use by Young Tunisians during the 2011 Revolution vs. 2014 Elections." *Information Polity*. vol. 22. no. 2–3 (2017).
Keane, John. "Refolution in the Arab world." *Open Democracy*, 28/4/2011.
Ketchley, Neil and Christopher Barrie. "Fridays of Revolution: Focal Days and Mass Protest in Egypt and Tunisia." *Political Research Quarterly*. vol. 73. no. 2 (2020).
Lawrence, Sherry. "Was the Revolution Tweeted? Social Media and Jasmin Revolution in Tunisia." *Digest of Middle East Studies*. vol. 25. no. 1 (2016).
Lipset, Seymour Martin, Kyoung-Ryung Seong and John Charles Torres. "A Comparative Analysis of the Social Requisites of Democracy." *International Social Science Journal*. vol. 45. no. 2 (1993).
Mahjoub, Azzam. "Economic, Social and Cultural Rights in Tunisia: An Assessment." *Mediterranean Politics*. vol. 9. no. 3 (2004).
O'Brien, Thomas. "The Primacy of Political Security: Contentious Politics and Insecurity in the Tunisian Revolution." *Democratization*. vol. 22. no. 7 (December 2015).
Pevná, Katarína. "Revolutions in Tunisia and Egypt and Political Participation of Islamists." *International Issues & Slovak Foreign Policy Affairs*. vol. 20. no. 2 (2011).
Pilati, Katia et al. "Between Organization and Spontaneity of Protests: the 2010–2011 Tunisian and Egyptian Uprisings." *Social Movement Studies*. vol. 18. no. 4 (2019).
Plaetzer, Niklas. "Civil Society as Domestication: Egyptian and Tunisian Uprisings Beyond Liberal Transitology." *Journal of International Affairs*. vol. 68. no. 1 (Fall/Winter 2014).
Rousselin, Mathieu. "Modern Communication Technologies and the Extension of the Territory of Struggle: Conceptualizing Tunisia's Jasmine Revolution." *New Media and Society*. vol. 18. no. 7 (August 2016).
Rustow, Dankwart A. "Transitions to Democracy: Toward a Dynamic Model." *Comparative Politics*. vol. 2. no. 3 (1970).
Rustow, Dankwart A. "Transitions to Democracy: Toward a Dynamic Model." *Comparative Politics*. vol. 2. no. 3 (1970).
Sadiki, Larbi. "Political Liberalization in Ben Ali's Tunisia: Façade Democracy." *Democratization*. vol. 9. no. 4 (September 2010).
Sanchez, Alejandro. "Tunisia: Trading Freedom for Stability May Not Last – An International Security Perspective." *Defense Studies*. vol. 9. no. 1 (2009).
Stafford, Eoghan. "Stop the Presses! Media Freedom in Authoritarian Regimes: A Case Study of Ben Ali's Tunisia." *The Journal of the Middle East and Africa*. vol. 8. no. 4 (October-December 2017).
Warf, Barney and Peter Vincent. "Multiple Geographies of the Arab Internet." *Area*. vol. 39. no. 1 (2007).
Wood, Pia Christina. "French Foreign Policy and Tunisia: Do Human Rights Matter?." *Middle East Policy*. vol. 4. no. 2 (June 2002).
Zemni, Sami. "From Revolution to Tunisianité: Who Are the Tunisian People?." *Middle East Law and Governance*. vol. 8. no. 2–3 (2016).

Zemni, Sami. "The Tunisian Revolution: Neoliberalism, Urban Contentious Politics and the Right to the City." *International Journal of Urban and Regional Research*. vol. 41. no. 1 (January 2017).

Interviews Interviews

Lamine Al-Bouazizi. Personal Interview conducted by ACRPS researchers Hamzeh al-Moustafa and Rami Salameh in Doha. April 19, 2011.

Ramadan ben Umar. Personal Interview conducted via Skype. October 15, 2011.

Ali Bouazizi. Personal interview conducted by ACRPS researchers Hamzeh al-Moustafa and Rami Salameh in Doha. April 22, 2011.

Rushdi Harshani. Personal interview conducted by two ACRPS researchers Hamzeh al-Moustafa and Rami Salameh in Doha. April 22, 2011.

Najat Ben Mansour, Personal Interview conducted by ACRPS. October 13, 2011.

Samir Kouka. Personal interview conducted via Skype by ACRPS researcher Hani Awwad. October 20, 2011.

Online Articles, Working Papers, and Seminars

Aeschimann, Eric. "La Tunisie a rejoint le modèle historique general." *Libération*. 17/1/2011. Accessed on 6/11/2020, at: https://bit.ly/35sQPky

al-Aswad, al-Tahir. "The Pillars of Tunisian-American Relations." *The Africa Center for Studies and Political Research*. December 8, 2007, accessed at: https://bit.ly/2Lraxpj

al-Hamidi, Bachir. "Two years after the repression of the Mining Basin Uprising." *al-Hiwar al-Mutamaddin* (*Civilized Debate*). June 7, 2010.

Al-Ḥiwār al-Mutamaddin. December 25, 2010, accessed on December 14, 2020, at: https://bit.ly/3mnjRaq

Ayadi, Mohamed and Wided Mattoussi. "Scoping of the Tunisian Economy." Working Paper no. 17. *Brookings Institution* (2016).

Bishara, Azmi. "The Great Popular Tunisian Revolution." *Commentary*. ACRPS. January 26, 2011, accessed at: https://bit.ly/2K2Rl0J

Boutalib, Mohamed Najib. "The Political Dimensions of the Tribal Phenomenon in Arab Societies: A Sociological Approach to the Tunisian and Libyan Revolutions" [al-ab'ād al-siyāsiyah lil-ẓāhirah al-qabaliyah fī al-mujtama'āt al-'arabiyah: muqārabah susyulūjiyah lil-thawratayn al-tūnisiyah wa al-lībiyah]. *Research Papers*. ACRPS. October 2011.

Dasūqī, 'Āṣim (ed.), *Al-Thawrah wal-Taghyīr fī al-Waṭan al-'Arabī 'Abr al-'Uṣūr [Revolution and Change in the Arab Homeland Throughout History]*. Proceedings of the Symposium Held by the Egyptian Society for Historical Studies. Cairo: Center for Social Studies and Research at the Cairo University College of Arts, 2005.

El-Mahdi, Rabab. "Orientalising the Egyptian Uprising." *Jadaliyya*. 11/4/2011. Accessed on 7/2/2021, at: http://bit.ly/3aHoLeF

Hardt, Michael and Antonio Negri. "Arabs are democracy's new pioneers." *Guardian*. 24/2/2011. Accessed on 25/1/2021, at: http://bit.ly/36HvxQB

Hermassi, Abdelbaki. "al-Islām al-Iḥtijājī fī Tūnis [Islamic Protest in Tunisia]." *A paper presented at a seminar entitled al-Ḥarakāt al- Islāmiyah al-Mu ʿāṣirah fī al-Waṭan al- ʿArabī (Nadwa) [Modern Islamic Movements in the Arab World].* Maktabat al-Mustaqbalāt al- ʿArabiyah al-Badīlah, al-Ittijahāt al-Ijtimā ʿiyah wal-Siyāsiyah wal-Thaqāfiyah. 5th ed. Beirut: Center for Arab Unity Studies, 2004.

Mzalouat, Haifa. "A Step Forward for Independents." *Carnegie Endowment for International Peace*. May 10, 2018. Accessed at: http://bit.ly/2pqNobr

National Constituent Assembly Elections in Tunisia." The Carter Center. October 23, 2011. Accessed at: http://bit.ly/2MkoUd6

Žižek, Slavoj. "For Egypt, this is the miracle of Tahrir Square." *Guardian*. 10/2/2011. Accessed on 25/1/2021, at: http://bit.ly/3oJBfYo

Documents and Reports

"Annual Report on Social Protests 2015." *Forum Tunisien pour les Droits Economiques et Sociaux (FTDES)*. 3/8/2016. Accessed on 11/2/2021, at: https://bit.ly/3aW9uH2

"Carter Center Preliminary Statement on Tunisia's Parliamentary Elections." *The Carter Center*. October 8, 2019. Accessed at: http://bit.ly/32httuo

"Census results by topics: Presentation." *Institut National de la Statistique. Statistiques Tunisie*. Accessed at: https://bit.ly/3mIgZ9p

"Constitution of the Republic of Tunisia." *Publications of the Official Printing Office of the Republic of Tunisia, 2010*. Accessed on 12/10/2020, at: https://bit.ly/3jVaKO0

"December 2020 Report on Social Protests, Suicides, Violence, and Immigration." *Forum Tunisien pour les Droits Economiques et Sociaux (FTDES)*. vol 87. Accessed on 11/2/2021, at: https://bit.ly/3pcn1ze

"Decision by the Independent High Authority for Elections dated October 9, 2019 regarding the announcement of the preliminary results for the 2019 legislative elections" [Qarār al-Hay'ah al-'Ulyā al-Mustaqillah lil-Intikhābāt Mu'arrakh fī 9 'Uktūbar 2019 Yata'allaq bi at-Taṣrih bil Natā ʾij al-Awwaliyah lil-Intikhābāt al-Tashrī'iyah 2019]. *The Independent High Authority for Elections (ISIE) [al-Hay'ah al-'Ulyā al-Mustaqillah lil-Intikhābāt]*. October 9, 2019. Accessed at: http://bit.ly/2ISQgEX

"Decree-law No. 2011-6 dated February 18, 2011, creating the Higher Authority for the Achievement of the Revolution's Objectives, Political Reform and Democratic Transition." *Official Gazette of the Republic of Tunisia*. no. 13, 1/3/2011. Accessed on 18/2/2021, at: https://bit.ly/37q5aPs

"Final Accepted list of Candidates for the 2019 Legislative Elections" [al-Qā'imah al-Mutarashshiḥah al-Maqbūlah Niha'iyan lil-Intikhābāt al-Tashrī'iyah 2019]. *The Independent High Authority for Elections (ISIE) [al-Hay'ah al-'Ulyā al-Mustaqillah lil-Intikhābāt]*. Accessed at: http://bit.ly/2WKjTOD

"Final Report on the 2014 Legislative and Presidential Elections in Tunisia." *National Democratic Institute*. Accessed at: https://bit.ly/3aJUIoh

"Final Report on the Tunisian National Constituent Assembly Elections." *National Democratic Institute*. October 23, 2011. Accessed at: https://bit.ly/3nTSq9R

"Measuring Poverty, Inequalities and Polarization in Tunisia: 2000–2010." *Statistiques Tunisie* (November 2012). Accessed at: https://bit.ly/2KbRnDg

"Preliminary Statement of the IRI-NDI Election Observation Mission to Tunisia's October 13, 2019 Presidential Runoff Election." *IRI-NDI Tunisia International Election Observation Mission*. October 14, 2019. Accessed at: https://bit.ly/3hmkd0d

"Report by the National Fact-Finding Commission on Abuses and Violations Committed from December 17, 2010 to the End of its Mandate" [Taqrīr al-Lajnah al-Waṭaniyah li istiqṣāʾ al-Ḥaqāʾiq Ḥawl al-Tajāwuzāt wal-intihakāt al-Musajallah Khilāl al-Fatrah al-Mumtaddah min 17 December 2010 ilā Ḥīn zawāl Mūjabihā]. National Fact-Finding Commission on Abuses and Violations. *Report* Tunis: 2012. Accessed on March 11, 2020, at: https://bit.ly/3kTB77t

"Statistical Yearbook - Tunisia 2006–2010" [al-Nashriyah al-Iḥṣā'iyah al-Sanawiyah li-Tunis 2006–2010]. National Institute of Statistics NSI. Accessed at: https://bit.ly/3rkJNGX

"The 2019–20 Arab Opinion Index Main Results in Brief." Arab Center for Research and Policy Studies. Accessed on 6/11/2020, at: https://bit.ly/3f6IIgY

"The National Survey of Population and Employment for the year 2008." [al-Masḥ al-Waṭanī ḥawl al-Sukkān wa-al-Tashghīl li-sanat 2008]. Republic of Tunisia: The Ministry of Development, Investment and International Cooperation (National Institute of Statistics NSI – 2008). Accessed at: https://bit.ly/37cOuv9

"The National Survey of Population and Employment for the year 2010." *Republic of Tunisia: The Ministry of Development, Investment and International Cooperation*, (National Institute of Statistics NSI - June 2011). Accessed at: https://bit.ly/37xN2lY

"Tunisia: Preliminary Conclusions of the 2010 Article IV Mission." *International Monetary Fund IMF*. June 15, 2010. Accessed at: http://www.imf.org/external/np/ms/2010/061510a.htm.

"Tunisia's National Institute of Statistics, 2010." Accessed at: https://bit.ly/3oMs89y

"Tunisia's Constitution of 1959 with Amendments through 2008." *Constitute Project*. Accessed at: https://bit.ly/2KSPhZU

"Tunisie en Chiffres 2018." *Institut National de la Statistique. Statistiques Tunisie*. Accessed at: https://bit.ly/36Iyp05

al-Alani, Aliya. "The Movement of Socialist Democrats: From Foundation to the First Conference")Faculty of Social Sciences, Department of History. Tunis University, Tunisia 1986.

ILO. *Economically Active Population Estimates and Projections*. 5th Edition. Revision: 2009.

Republic of Tunisia: Ministry of Development and International Cooperation. "General Census of Population and Housing for the Year 2004 - First Issue: First Results." (National Institute of Statistics, March 2005). Accessed at: https://bit.ly/3mRmWRj

The National Fact-Finding Commission on Abuses Committed from December 17, 2010 to the End of its Mandate. *Report by the National Fact-Finding Commission on the Abuses Committed*. Tunis: 2012. Accessed on 11/3/2020, at: https://bit.ly/3kTB77t

Tunisia's National Institute of Statistics. "Population Census 2004: Economic Characteristics of the Population." Accessed at: https://bit.ly/3nbWYIk

Official Data Reports and Portals

"External debt stocks (% of GNI) – Tunisia." *The World Bank Data*. Accessed at: https://bit.ly/3mY2MFt

"Foreign direct investment, net inflows (% of GDP) – Tunisia." *The World Bank Data*. Accessed on 11/2/2021, at: http://bit.ly/3q57x1n

"GDP (current US$) – Tunisia." *The World Bank Data*. Accessed at: https://bit.ly/3dCeDFf

"GDP growth (annual %) – Tunisia." *The World Bank Data*. Accessed at: https://bit.ly/33HdkRu

"GDP per capita (current US$) – Tunisia." *The World Bank Data*. Accessed at: https://bit.ly/3nomuuh

"GNI per capita in thousands of US$ (2011 PPP)." *Global Data Lab*. Accessed at: https://bit.ly/37qOp5P

"Gross capital formation (% of GDP) – Tunisia." *The World Bank Data*. Accessed on 11/2/2021, at: http://bit.ly/3q5pH33

"Households and living conditions: Poverty." *Statistiques Tunisie*. Accessed at: https://bit.ly/33X5Gmp

"IMF: World Economic Outlook (WEO) Database, October 2020." *Knoema*. Accessed at: https://bit.ly/3gq6jKf

"Inflation, consumer prices (annual %) – Tunisia." *The World Bank Data*. Accessed at: https://bit.ly/37xtuhA

"Internet Users Statistics for Africa." *Internet World Stats*. Accessed on November 17, 2020, at: https://bit.ly/3pyxKpc

"Sub-national HDI." *Global Data Lab.* Accessed at: https://bit.ly/2LnCPBc

"Suicide mortality rate (per 100,000 population) – Tunisia." *The World Bank Data*. Accessed on 16/2/2021, at: https://bit.ly/37kMEYB

"Suicide mortality rate, female (per 100,000 female population) – Tunisia." *The World Bank Data*. Accessed on 16/2/2021, at: https://bit.ly/3aqSYQu

"Suicide mortality rate, male (per 100,000 male population) – Tunisia." *The World Bank Data*. Accessed on 16/2/2021, at: http://bit.ly/3u2K9nE

"Tunisia GDP Annual Growth Rate." *Trading Economics*. Accessed at: http://bit.ly/32Tc0bV

"Tunisia Government Debt to GDP." *Trading Economics*. Accessed at: https://bit.ly/33CDWTR

"Tunisia Internet Users." *Internet Live Stats*. Accessed on November 2, 2020, at: https://bit.ly/3jIAwEg\

"Tunisia Unemployment Rate2005-2020 Data." *Trading Economics*. Accessed at: https://bit.ly/37MZBtx

"Tunisia." *Internet World Stats*. Accessed on November 2, 2020, at: https://bit.ly/34MYRUZ

"Tunisia: Government spending, percent of GDP." *The Global Economy*. Accessed at: https://bit.ly/33TSoH4

"Tunisia: Human Development Indicators." *United Nations Development Programme: Human Development Reports*. Accessed at: https://bit.ly/373Bfg3

"Unemployment, total (% of total labor force) (national estimate) – Tunisia." *The World Bank Data*. Accessed at: https://bit.ly/3gcAzrU

"Unemployment, youth total (% of total labor force ages 15–24) (modeled ILO estimate) – Tunisia." *The World Bank Data*. Accessed at: https://bit.ly/3oCKutE

Miniwatts Marketing Group. "Arabic Speaking Internet Users' Statistics: Internet user statistics in population stats for the countries and regions with Arab speaking internet users." *Internet World Stats*. March 23, 2012. Accessed on December 12, 2020, at: https://bit.ly/2JWnFT3

News Websites

Al-Arabiya net: Online Website of the Pan Arabi TV news channel Al-Arabiya based in Dubai.

Al-Badil: Official website of the Workers' Party, a Marxist–Leninist political party in Tunisia.

al-Baida News: Website used to give the latest information and news to people from all over the world.
Al-Hiwar Net: Online website of the Arabic language Al-Hiwar satellite TV channel broadcasting from London.
AlJazeera.net: Online Website for the Pan Arabi TV channels of Al Jazeera Media Network based in Doha.
al-Sharq al-Awsat Newspaper Online website of an Arabic international newspaper headquartered in London.
al-Watan newspaper: Online website of the daily morning Arabic language political newspaper that is based in Doha, Qatar.
al-Yawm al-Sabi': Daily electronic newspaper issued by the Egyptian Company for Press, Publication, and Advertising.
Amnesty International: Online Website of Amnesty International, an international non-governmental organization with its headquarters in the United Kingdom focused on human rights.
BBC Arabic: the Arabic language website for the BBC TV and radio broadcasts.
Constitute Project: Online Website of Constitute, a creation of the Comparative Constitutions Project in partnership with Google Ideas, with financial support from Indigo Trust and IC2.
Democratic Unionist Website: Online website of The Unionist Democratic Union, a political party in Tunisia with pan-Arabist ideology.
Doualia: The first Arab electronic newspaper issued from Paris.
Facebook: online social media and social networking service.
France 24: French state-owned international news television network based in Paris.
Human Rights Watch: Online Website of Human Rights Watch, an international non-governmental organization, headquartered in New York City, that conducts research and advocacy on human rights.
Kalimat Tunis Radio: Online website owned and operated by Sihem Bensedrine, a Tunisian human rights activist.
Maghrebia: Online website of a Moroccan public television channel. It is a part of the state-owned SNRT Group.
Reuters: Online website of an international news organization owned by Thomson Reuters.
Sky News Arabiya: Online website of an Arabic 24-hour rolling news channel broadcast mainly in the Middle East and North Africa. It is a joint venture between UK-based Sky Group and Abu Dhabi Media Investment Corporation.
The Independent High Authority for Elections (ISIE): Official website of The Independent Higher Authority for Elections, an independent public body endowed with legal personality and financial and administrative autonomy, headquartered in Tunis and whose main mission is to ensure free, pluralist, honest democratic elections and referendums. and transparent.
The Nawat blog: Independent collective platform founded in April 2004 and blocked in Tunisia until January 13, 2011.
The Tunisian Observatory for Rights and Unionist Liberties – Tunis News: Online Website of The Tunisian Observatory for Rights and Liberties.
Tunisia Africa News Agency: Wesbite of Tunis Afrique Presse (TAP), a Tunisian press agency founded in 1961.
Tunisian Ministry of Youth and Sports: Online website of The Ministry of Youth and Sports of Tunisian, charged with overseeing the field of sports in Tunisia.

Turess: Tunisian website that collects news and articles from 45 Tunisian newspapers, classifies them, and then arranges them according to their importance. All of this is done in an automated way that has been developed by a team of Arab engineers.
Twitter: American microblogging and social networking service on which users post and interact with messages known as "tweets".
UNDP-POGAR: Official website of The United Nations Development Programme (UNDP), Regional Bureau for Arab States (RBAS), which launched the Programme on Governance in the Arab Region (POGAR) in early 2000.
Youtube: Online video platform owned by Google.

INDEX

www.ingramcontent.com/pod-product-compliance
Lightning Source LLC
Chambersburg PA
CBHW060145280326
41932CB00012B/1643